*Cambridge studies in medieval life and thought*

*Edited by* WALTER ULLMANN, LITT.D., F.B.A.
*Professor of Medieval History in the*
*University of Cambridge*

*Third series, vol. 18*

# COMMUNITY, CLASS AND CAREERISM

Cheshire and Lancashire Society in the Age of
*Sir Gawain and the Green Knight*

D0931705

# CAMBRIDGE STUDIES IN
# MEDIEVAL LIFE AND THOUGHT

### THIRD SERIES

# COMMUNITY, CLASS AND CAREERISM

## CHESHIRE AND LANCASHIRE SOCIETY IN THE AGE OF *SIR GAWAIN AND THE GREEN KNIGHT*

### MICHAEL J. BENNETT
*Lecturer in History, University of Tasmania*

CAMBRIDGE UNIVERSITY PRESS

CAMBRIDGE

LONDON   NEW YORK   NEW ROCHELLE
MELBOURNE   SYDNEY

Published by the Press Syndicate of the University of Cambridge
The Pitt Building, Trumpington Street, Cambridge CB2 1RP
32 East 57th Street, New York, NY 10022, USA
296 Beaconsfield Parade, Middle Park, Melbourne 3206, Australia

First published 1983

Printed in Great Britain at the University Press, Cambridge

Library of Congress catalogue card number: 82–43 54

*British Library Cataloguing in Publication Data*
Bennett, Michael J.
Community, class and careerism: Cheshire and
Lancashire society in the Age of *Sir Gawain and
the Green Knight*. – (Cambridge studies in medieval
life and thought. 3rd series; v. 18)
1. England – Social life and customs – History
I. Title
942.03′8   DA110
ISBN 0 521 24744 6

TO MY MOTHER
IN HONOUR OF MY FATHER

# CONTENTS

# MAPS

# TABLES

# ACKNOWLEDGEMENTS

This study has been a major preoccupation for over ten years, and it is a pleasure to express formally my gratitude to some of the many people who have served to lighten my load and restore my flagging spirit. Due acknowledgement must be made first of all to the scholars, past and present, whose collective labours have made this sort of enquiry conceivable; then to the archivists and librarians who have rendered assistance beyond the call of duty, most particularly to Mr B. Redwood, Miss G. Mathieson and Mr D. Reid and their staffs at the Cheshire Record Office, the John Rylands University Library, Manchester, and the Stockport Central Library; next to my teachers, colleagues and friends on both sides of the globe for their inspiration and fellowship, especially to the late Professor A. R. Myers, Dr J. A. Tuck, Mr P. H. W. Booth and Dr P. Hosker; to Professor W. Ullmann, the general editor of this series, Mrs E. Wetton, Mr R. Bourke and other members of the Cambridge University Press staff, for their meticulous attention to my text; to Mrs E. Underwood for her assistance with the proofs, and to my mother Mrs V. A. Daniels for her work on the index; and finally to my wife Fatimah for far more than I can adequately express.

HOBART, TASMANIA
*21 June 1982*

## NOTE

The interests of clarity and consistency have dictated some compromises with modernity. Thus the spelling of names of persons and places has been standardised in conformity with current style. A line has been drawn, however, at accepting all the bureaucratic innovations of recent times. In particular, the county boundaries which served so well for five centuries before and after the period of this study have been preserved in their pristine form.

# ABBREVIATIONS

| | |
|---|---|
| *B.I.H.R.* | *Bulletin of the Institute of Historical Research* |
| *B.J.R.L.* | *Bulletin of the John Rylands Library* |
| B.L. | British Library, London |
| *B.P.R.* | *Register of Edward the Black Prince* (4 vols., H.M.S.O., 1930–3) |
| *B.R.U.C.* | A. B. Emden, *A Biographical Register of the University of Cambridge to 1500* (Cambridge, 1963) |
| *B.R.U.O.* | A. B. Emden, *A Biographical Register of the University of Oxford to A.D. 1500* (3 vols., Oxford, 1957–9) |
| *C.Ch.R.* | *Calendar of Charter Rolls* (6 vols., H.M.S.O., 1903–27) |
| *C.C.R.* | *Calendar of Close Rolls*, Edward III to Henry VI (33 vols., H.M.S.O., 1896–1947) |
| *C.F.R.* | *Calendar of Fine Rolls* (H.M.S.O., in progress) |
| *C.Fr.R.* | 'Calendar of French Rolls', part I in *44th D.K.R.* (H.M.S.O., 1883), and part II in *48th D.K.R.* (H.M.S.O., 1887) |
| *C.N.R.* | 'Calendar of Norman Rolls', part I in *41st D.K.R.* (H.M.S.O., 1881) |
| C.S. | Chetham Society |
| *C.Pap.L.* | *Calendar of Papal Registers. Papal Letters* (H.M.S.O., in progress) |
| *C.P.R.* | *Calendar of Patent Rolls*, Edward III to Henry VI (34 vols., H.M.S.O., 1891–1910) |
| *Ches. Pleas* | 'Calendar of Deeds, Inquisitions and Writs of Dower, enrolled on the Plea Rolls of the Palatinate of Chester', part I in *28th D.K.R.* (H.M.S.O., 1867), and part II in *29th D.K.R.* (H.M.S.O., 1868) |
| *Ches. R.R.* | 'Calendar of Recognizance Rolls of the Palatinate of Chester', part I in *36th D.K.R.* (H.M.S.O., 1875), and part II in *37th D.K.R.* (H.M.S.O., 1876) |
| *Cheshire Sheaf* | *The Cheshire Sheaf* (Chester, in progress) |
| *D.K.R.* | *Reports of the Deputy Keeper of Public Records* (H.M.S.O., in progress) |

| | |
|---|---|
| *Ec.H.R.* | *Economic History Review* |
| *E.H.R.* | *English Historical Review* |
| *H.M.C.* | *Reports of the Royal Commission on Historical Manuscripts* (H.M.S.O., in progress) |
| H.M.S.O. | Her Majesty's Stationery Office |
| J.R.U.L. | John Rylands University Library, Manchester |
| *J.C.A.S.* | *Journal of the Chester Archaeological Society*, formerly *Journal of the Chester and North Wales Archaeological, Architectural and Historical Society*, new series |
| *L.C.A.S.* | *Transactions of the Lancashire and Cheshire Antiquarian Society* |
| *L.C.H.S.* | *Transactions of the Historic Society of Lancashire and Cheshire* |
| *La.P.R.* | 'Calendar of the Chancery Rolls of the County Palatine of Lancaster', part I in *32nd D.K.R.* (H.M.S.O., 1871), and part II in *33rd D.K.R.* (H.M.S.O., 1872) |
| L.C.R.S. | Lancashire and Cheshire Record Society |
| P.R.O. | Public Record Office |
| R.O. | Record Office |
| R.S. | Rolls Series |
| *T.R.H.S.* | *Transactions of the Royal Historical Society* |
| *V.C.H.* | *Victoria History of the Counties of England* (London, in progress) |

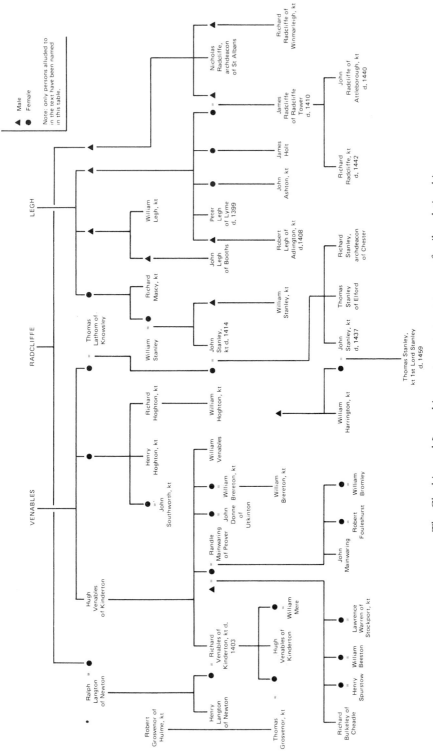

The Cheshire and Lancashire gentry, 1375–1425: some family relationships

x

Land over 500 ft

0                    20 km

0           10 miles

LONSDALE
HUNDRED

R. Lune

Lancaster

Clitheroe

AMOUNDERNESS
HUNDRED

R. Ribble

Preston

BLACKBURN
HUNDRED

LEYLAND
HUNDRED

Chorley

Wigan

WEST
DERBY
HUNDRED

SALFORD
HUNDRED

R. Irwell    Manchester

Stockport

Liverpool

WIRRAL
HUNDRED

Warrington

R. Mersey

BUCKLOW
HUNDRED

R. Bollin

MACCLESFIELD
HUNDRED

R. Weaver

Knutsford

EDISBURY
HUNDRED     Northwich

Macclesfield

R. Dee

Chester

NORTHWICH
HUNDRED

R. Dane

Middlewich

Congleton

BROXTON
HUNDRED

NANTWICH
HUNDRED

Nantwich

Map 1. Outline map: Cheshire and Lancashire

xi

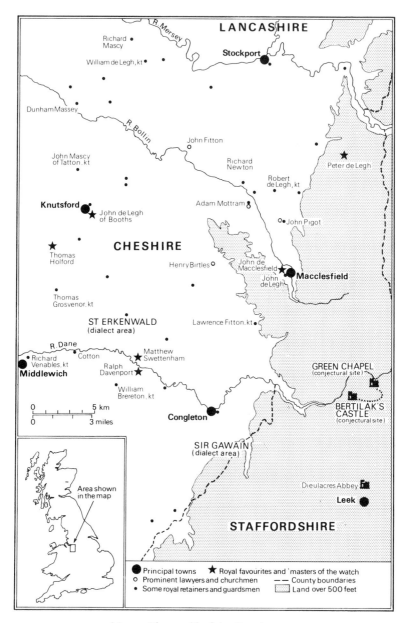

Map 2. The world of the *Gawain*-poet

# INTRODUCTION

There are few studies of English society in the later middle ages to match the impressive array of scholarship for the period between the Reformation and the Civil War. Of course historians working on the age of Chaucer and *Sir Gawain and the Green Knight* are far more constrained by their sources than colleagues writing on Shakespearian England. Yet, while the dearth of personal and unofficial sorts of evidence is to be lamented, relevant documentation is by no means lacking. In fact, even in the study of a relatively small region the copiousness of the source material is often formidable. In addition to the magnificent series of records produced by the chancery, the exchequer and the law courts at Westminster, there are classes of record specific to particular localities. With regard to the Northwest there are the archives of the palatinates of Chester and Lancaster, the diocesan material at Lichfield, and the muniment collections of local gentry. Demonstrably, to work unaided through more than a fraction of this evidence would take a life-time. Fortunately in the past hundred years or so much learned effort has been expended in cataloguing, sorting and abstracting the more important material. The achievement of the Public Record Office and numerous record societies in calendaring and publishing material from the later middle ages has been impressive. At the same time the labours of several generations of antiquarians and historians, at both a national and local level, in combing through the records to compile lists of office-holders, manorial histories, biographical registers and so on, have provided the necessary groundwork for the systematic study of English society in this period.[1] If the sources are less plentiful and varied than the materials surviving from later epochs, it must be conceded that a far higher proportion of the extant material is available to the historian in accessible and digestible form. To emulate the

---

[1] For historians of Cheshire and Lancashire society, the work of G. Ormerod, J. P. Earwaker and W. Farrer is of inestimable importance: G. Ormerod, *The History of the County Palatine and City of Chester*, ed. T. Helsby, 2nd edn (3 vols., London, 1882); J. P. Earwaker, *East Cheshire* (2 vols., London, 1877–80); *V.C.H. Lancaster*, 6 vols. See also Chester R. O., Earwaker MSS., and Manchester Central Reference Library, Farrer MSS.

achievements of colleagues in later centuries, the historian of late medieval English society must build on this advantage.

In attempting a study of English society in the later middle ages there are few clear models to follow. For the most part, scholarship in this field has been disarmingly modest and unassuming in its approach to social phenomena. Deference to the sources has been its great virtue, and the institutions which produced the records, and the activities which they documented, have been studied in considerable detail. Through the researches of successive generations of scholars, all the more important institutions of national life – crown and parliament, the royal administration and the courts of law, the church and universities, military organisation and local government – have been meticulously dissected and rendered comprehensible. Indeed what can perhaps be regarded as the 'great tradition' in late medieval English social history – the analysis of the manorial records of the large ecclesiastical estates – has proved enormously successful in providing quantifiable data in serial form on many aspects of social life.[2] Yet there are problems in approaching late medieval society exclusively through the institutions which kept and preserved records. Obviously all classes of evidence provide only limited, and potentially distorted perspectives on the past. It needs little stressing that governmental, fiscal, judicial, military and other sorts of administrative record present only an official version of relationships, and offer only fragmentary visions of a wider society. For all their richness of detail and depth of coverage, the manorial records of ecclesiastical corporations likewise have their hidden biases, and tell little about the lives of the vast majority of English villagers who did not live on large estates. Indeed the main limitation of this approach is its inability to provide a framework around which a more complete and balanced model of late medieval English society can be constructed. It is instructive that, in their attempts to present a wider view of social life, historians tend to turn from the formal records to the one category of evidence which seems to offer a fairly generalised vision of the social past – contemporary literature. To read F. R. H. du Boulay's *Lordship of Canterbury* and his *An Age of Ambition* in close succession, however, is to become aware of the wide gap between careful research and inspired synthesis which seems to characterise even the best work in the field.[3] The one is a fine piece of scholarship based on the archiepiscopal

---

[2] See the magnificent work of B. Harvey on the Westminster estates and the detailed studies on individual manors by the pupils of J. A. Raftis: B. Harvey, *Westminster Abbey and its Estates in the Middle Ages* (Oxford, 1977); E. B. Dewindt, *Land and People in Holywell-cum-Needingworth, Structures of Tenure and Patterns of Social Organisation in an East Midlands Village, 1272–1457* (Toronto, 1972).

[3] F. R. H. du Boulay, *The Lordship of Canterbury. An Essay on Medieval Society* (London, 1966), *An Age of Ambition. English Society in the Late Middle Ages* (London, 1970).

archives at Lambeth: the other is a stimulating overview of English society in the later middle ages, with a felicitous use of literary sources. It must be confessed, nonetheless, that somehow the two studies seem to depict totally different worlds. It is almost as if Chaucer's pilgrims never met up with the archbishop's bailiffs on the long road to Canterbury.

This study is committed to the attempt, albeit vain in absolute terms, to present a more 'rounded' picture of English society in the later middle ages. Drawing inspiration from R. H. Hilton's work on the West Midlands in the late thirteenth century,[4] recent scholarship on Tudor and Stuart England, and the approach of modern social anthropologists, it is founded on the conviction that this goal can best be approached through a conspectus of regional studies, in which individuals, groups and communities can be observed interacting in the widest possible range of capacities. Needless to say, in defining a field of investigation, it was felt more appropriate to be guided by reference to geographical factors and observable patterns of social life than by archival convenience. At the same time it was considered important that the region under discussion should be sufficiently large to have maintained a reasonably wide complement of institutions and activities, but at the same time sufficiently small to make possible a consideration of most of the available documentation and a more than passing acquaintance with all the main *dramatis personae*. Similarly, with regard to the chronological scale of the study, it was felt appropriate to steer a middle course between a detailed examination of social life at a particular cross-section in time and an exploration of social change over a much longer time-span. In the event, the region selected for study was the northwestern corner of England, though it soon became apparent that the Ribble represented a major divide in social terms, and that Cheshire and south Lancashire would make a more coherent field of investigation. Finally, the period chosen for study was the last quarter of the fourteenth century and the first quarter of the fifteenth century. Enclosing the reigns of Richard II and the first two Lancastrian kings, and witnessing the flowering and decay of a vigorous literary culture whose finest product was *Sir Gawain and the Green Knight*, the fifty years between 1375 and 1425 are not without their special significance in Cheshire and Lancashire history.[5]

The following study of Cheshire and Lancashire society is organised in eleven chapters grouped into three sections. Naturally enough, the first

---

[4] R. H. Hilton, *A Medieval Society. The West Midlands at the End of the Thirteenth Century* (London, 1966).

[5] See in general M. J. Bennett, '*Sir Gawain and the Green Knight* and the literary achievement of the North-West Midlands: the historical background', *Journal of Medieval History*, 5 (1979), 63–88.

main section is concerned with the social geography of the Northwest, and after a preliminary survey demonstrating the physical and historical identity of the lands between the Dee and the Ribble, there are chapters discussing the importance of solidarities based on the region, counties and lesser administrative units in the functioning of English society. In the second main group of chapters the social structure of the Northwest is viewed from a rather more conventional perspective. After an initial chapter on the Cheshire and Lancashire population at this time, there follow chapters on the two main 'classes' in the region: the 'lords' and the 'peasants'. Moving outside the restricted world of rural society, the third main section considers the local men involved in trades and professions, and discusses their experience of careerism both inside and outside their native region. Accordingly there are separate chapters on manufacturing and commerce, the church, and military service, while the first half of the tenth chapter is concerned with the legal profession and government service. In the second half of this chapter there is a survey of the relations between the Northwest and the centres of power and influence in the kingdom, and an assessment is made of the impact of royal patronage and local careerism on the political, social and cultural life of the region. Finally, an attempt is made in the concluding chapter to assess the 'typicality' of the Cheshire and Lancashire experience, and to discuss in general terms the nature of social change in the period under consideration.

## Chapter 1

# THE REGIONAL SOCIETY

Englishmen in the later middle ages had a well developed sense of their national identity. Their common experience of statehood already stretched back at least half a millennium, and the widespread belief in the Trojan foundation of the realm of England gave them a shared mythical past. By the fourteenth century, traditions regarding the nation's history were regularly drawing strength from provincial sources. In 1352 Edward III summoned Ranulf Higden from the very margins of his kingdom to bring his chronicles to Westminster to consult with the royal council.[1] Presumably the aged monk of Chester was expected to dredge up historical precedents to support some new claim of the English crown. It is not known how he had come to the attention of the king and councillors, but a number of connections can be surmised. In fact there existed innumerable institutional and personal channels through which talent and resources from all corners of the realm could be drawn into national projects. In addition to his being a native of the earldom of Chester, the appanage of the king's eldest son, and a member of a monastic order with houses all across the kingdom, Higden was doubtless known to some of the many men from his own district who had established themselves in the capital.[2] Even if he were not personally acquainted with John Winwick, keeper of the privy seal, or the numerous other clerks and soldiers from the Northwest attaining distinction in the realm at large, the chronicler was certainly aware of the general phenomenon of social mobility. In a memorable passage in *Polychronicon*, he characterised his own countrymen as restless and ambitious, ever discontented with their lots and responsive to the lure of better prospects elsewhere, ever inclined to emulate their social superiors and to take the whole world as their province.[3]

It is important to bear in mind this picture of a bustling, highly

---

[1] J. Taylor, *The 'Universal Chronicle' of Ranulf Higden* (Oxford, 1966), p. 1.

[2] M. J. Bennett, 'Sources and problems in the study of social mobility: Cheshire in the later Middle Ages', *L.C.H.S.*, 128 (1978), 59–95.

[3] R. Higden, *Polychronicon*, ed. C. Babington and J. R. Lumby (9 vols., R.S., 1865–86), II, pp. 168–70.

mobile nation, but for the moment it is appropriate to stress again the well-attested localism of English life. Throughout the middle ages, and indeed well into modern times, patterns of social organisation necessarily remained extremely localised in character. From the earliest Anglo-Saxon migrations, geographical factors had served to diversify patterns of settlement. Even among settlers of similar racial origins, the immense contrasts in the English landscape ensured wide variation in the economic and social institutions it sustained. The process of political unification between the tenth and fourteenth centuries did little to eliminate regional differences at this level, and in some respects even accentuated them by encouraging centralisation and specialisation within a national framework. Naturally enough, at a time when travel across the realm remained arduous, even if far from uncommon, provincial identities were nourished by the comparative ease and frequency of short-distance communication, and the inevitable parochialism of village life. Even at the close of the middle ages there was still no standard vernacular language which was fully comprehensible to all Englishmen, and it is significant that the major dialect boundaries of the age of Chaucer and *Sir Gawain and the Green Knight* corresponded so well with the territorial divisions of Anglo-Saxon times.[4]

Since the pioneering work of F. W. Maitland, scholars have shown a keen appreciation of the importance of studying early English society within firm geographical parameters.[5] Over the past few decades there have appeared a succession of studies of the rural economy and society of medieval England which have admirably substantiated the value of the localised approach. Based largely on the records of large ecclesiastical estates, detailed analyses have been provided of economic and social conditions in areas of the Fenlands, Devon, Leicestershire, Kent and elsewhere, and major contributions have been made to the tasks of charting and making comprehensible the complex patterns of development in provincial England.[6] Yet none of these works aimed at an analysis of

[4] S. Moore, S. B. Meech and H. Whitehall, *Middle English Dialect Characteristics and Dialect Boundaries* (Ann Arbor, 1935). For a more sophisticated and complex picture of dialectal variation, the historian awaits the publication of the atlas being prepared in the Middle English Dialect Project, University of Edinburgh. The author would like to thank Professor A. McIntosh and Mr M. Benskin for allowing him a preview of some of their findings.

[5] F. W. Maitland, *Domesday Book and Beyond* (Cambridge, 1897).

[6] H. C. Darby, *The Medieval Fenland* (Cambridge, 1940); R. H. Hilton, *The Economic Development of Some Leicestershire Estates* (Oxford, 1947); H. P. R. Finberg, *Tavistock Abbey. A Study in the Social and Economic History of Devon* (Cambridge, 1951); E. Miller, *The Abbey and Bishopric of Ely. The Social History of an Ecclesiastical Estate from the Tenth to the Early Fourteenth Century* (Cambridge, 1951); W. G. Hoskins, *The Midland Peasant. The Economic and Social History of a Leicestershire Village* (London, 1957); J. A. Raftis, *The Estates of Ramsey Abbey. A Study in Economic Growth and Organisation* (Toronto, 1957); J. A. Raftis, *Tenure*

6

the social structure of an entire region, most being solely concerned with tenurial relations on a single estate. Indeed the only full-length study of a regional society in late medieval England to have appeared in print so far is R. H. Hilton's monograph on the West Midlands. In his introduction he identified his theme as 'the society of peasants, townsmen, knights, barons and clergy' living in his chosen district at the end of the thirteenth century.[7] This perspective obviously allowed a far more comprehensive assessment of social life than that afforded to the historian of one major lordship. If a full appreciation of the complexity of late medieval English society is to be obtained, it must be built on a conspectus of such studies.

This contribution to the grand project takes for its province the little world from which Ranulf Higden was drawn in 1352, and in which the author of *Sir Gawain and the Green Knight* and his patrons were rooted. It is a study of Cheshire and Lancashire society in the late fourteenth and early fifteenth centuries, the period in which the *Polychronicon* was being copied and continued in monasteries right across the realm, and when alliterative poetry experienced a brief but glorious 'revival' in the Northwest. It is felt that the two counties represented a fairly distinct region in the later middle ages, and accordingly make a reasonably coherent field of enquiry. Obviously it cannot be pretended that this regional society was entirely self-contained, and indeed considerable attention is later paid to those sections of the local population pursuing careers in other parts of the kingdom. At the same time it must be stressed that no hard-and-fast social boundaries can be drawn around the two counties, and that the region could plausibly be extended to embrace neighbouring areas of Flintshire and the Welsh Borderlands, the sub-Pennine portions of Staffordshire and Derbyshire, and even the more remote Lake District. In this regard it is perhaps most useful to think in terms of a 'core' region set within larger, and ultimately overlapping social networks. In the following section it is claimed that Cheshire and south Lancashire, in particular, constituted just such a 'core' region.

I

Bounded on the west by the Irish Sea and flanked to the east by the Pennine uplands, Cheshire and Lancashire form a comparatively well-defined geographical area.[8] To the north, around Lancaster, the mountains

*and Mobility. Studies in the Social History of the Medieval English Village* (Toronto, 1964); du Boulay, *Lordship of Canterbury*; Harvey, *Westminster Abbey and its Estates.*

[7] Hilton, *West Midlands*, p. 1.

[8] The two counties are often treated as a distinctive region by modern geographers: e.g. T. W. Freeman, H. B. Rodgers and R. H. Kinvig, *Lancashire, Cheshire and the Isle of Man* (London, 1966).

and the sea cut across to leave only the narrowest corridor of lowland along the Lune Valley and around Morecambe Bay. Even in the south, where the region appears more open-ended, the Ellesmere moraine presented a sizeable barrier to communications with the Midlands and the rest of the kingdom. Hemmed in by a series of uplands which stretch from North Wales right around to the Lake District, the Northwest had a clear physical identity. Indeed the surrounding highlands actually form a complete watershed, leaving local streams to wend their westward course independently of the major drainage systems of the Midlands, the Welsh Borderlands and Yorkshire. Although the Mersey and Ribble rivers, with their wide estuaries and marshy banks, have served to divide the region socially, their distinctive orientation graphically attests to its geographical integrity.

Though physically separate from other parts of the kingdom, the Cheshire and Lancashire landscape was far from homogeneous. The sharp contrast between the flat, dank peatlands of southwest Lancashire, the lush, undulating countryside of the Cheshire Plain, and the bleak moorlands of the Pennine fringe, are as remarkable as any region can offer. Yet this scenic diversity does not necessarily detract from the overall identity of the region. Since the character of the landscape tended to change with the rising contours from west to east, such variation served to unite rather than to divide the two counties. Other physical factors determined analogous patterns of land utilisation on both sides of the Mersey. The entire Northwest was characterised by a poor climate and difficult soils; the wet, badly drained coastal region, the heavy clay soils of the central belt, and the cold infertile uplands all presented major problems for the agriculturalist. Few villages in either shire seem to have supported the strict arable regimes which characterised the Midlands. There were open-fields in the better farming areas, but they seem to have been far less significant in terms of total land utilisation than elsewhere in the country. More detailed research needs to be completed on the rural economy of the region, but it is clear that neither county can be satisfactorily ascribed to either the *champion* or highland zones into which historical geographers have tended to divide medieval England.[9]

The general remoteness of the Northwest and its relatively inhospitable climate and terrain ensured that throughout the region settlement was both late and unintensive. In comparison with most other parts of England, Anglian colonisation in the seventh and eighth centuries was extremely

[9] For a recent synthesis of research on Cheshire and Lancashire field systems see G. Elliott's contribution in A. R. H. Baker and R. A. Butlin (eds.), *Studies of Field Systems in the British Isles* (Cambridge, 1973), pp. 41–92.

half-hearted. Indigenous Celtic communities survived longer than in most regions, and in the ninth and tenth centuries Norse settlers could still find room for their own colonising activities along the western seaboard. Even at the time of the Domesday Book the penetration of the dense oak forests which covered vast tracts of Cheshire and Lancashire had scarcely been commenced. Only small areas of lowland – around Chester, in Wirral and southwest Lancashire, and along the more fertile valleys – were settled at all thickly in this period, and throughout the middle ages new land was continually being brought under the plough. Until the Industrial Revolution the region remained one of the most sparsely populated regions of England. Apart from the ancient city of Chester, there were few substantial towns or large nucleated villages in the region. Habitation tended to be dispersed in loosely structured villages and hamlets, and local parishes were typically very extensive. Indeed, in terms of the number of dependent townships, the region could boast the three largest parishes in the kingdom.[10]

The distinctive geography of the Northwest not only served to characterise patterns of settlement in the region, but also influenced its entire historical development. Its remoteness and intractability made it a poor and underdeveloped corner of the kingdom, and such conditions left a marked impression on the evolution of regional society. Few parts of Cheshire or Lancashire were sufficiently fertile to produce a large marketable surplus of grain, and the region was too poor to maintain a truly opulent landed élite or a flourishing commercial sector. Its distance from the main centres of power and population also discouraged the establishment of aristocratic households in the area and inhibited the economic development of the region. Nevertheless the torpidity of the rural economy was not entirely detrimental to the living conditions of the population. In a region where manorialism and villeinage never took deep root, and where there were always opportunities for internal colonisation, the peasantry were freer and perhaps more prosperous than their fellows in other parts of the kingdom. Indeed the absence of both an opulent aristocratic élite and a down-trodden servile peasantry adds to the distinctiveness of the region in the later middle ages. In Tudor times, interestingly enough, the region was renowned both for the number and

---

[10] The parishes of Whalley, Great Budworth and Prestbury: D. Sylvester, *The Rural Landscape of the Welsh Borderland. A Study in Historical Geography* (London, 1969), p. 180. See also Freeman, Rodgers and Kinvig, *Lancashire, Cheshire and the Isle of Man*, pp. 27–54; I. B. Terrett in H. C. Darby and I. S. Maxwell (eds.), *The Domesday Geography of Northern England* (Cambridge, 1962), pp. 330–418; G. H. Tupling, *The Economic History of Rossendale* (C.S., n.s. 86, 1927); F. Walker, *The Historical Geography of South-West Lancashire* (C.S., n.s. 103, 1939).

quality of its gentry families and for the modest affluence and sturdy independence of its yeoman stock.[11]

Cultural influences also contributed to the distinctive character of Cheshire and Lancashire society. By the time of the Domesday Book the region had already shared a long and confused history of colonisation, conquest and cultural assimilation. The indigenous Celtic peoples, Anglian settlers from both Northumbria and Mercia, Danes from east of the Pennines and Norsemen moving inland from the Irish Sea had all left their imprint on the palimpsest of local society. Indeed the racial character and social institutions of the two counties were arguably the most hybrid in the realm. If early English society can be divided into three main cultural zones — the Celtic fringe, the Anglo-Saxon heartland and the Danelaw — the Northwest stands out as the only region where all three spheres overlapped. Indigenous Celtic place names and settlement patterns seem to have survived on a scale unmatched in most parts of England, while diverse Teutonic customs appear to have been implanted by successive waves of conquerors and colonisers emanating alternately from the Northeast and the Midlands. On the whole Cheshire and Lancashire reveal stronger northern influences, most notably in their parochial topography and their lack of the frankpledge system, which can perhaps be associated with the early penetration of the region by Northumbrians or the Scandinavian domination of the late ninth and early tenth centuries. On the other hand, the systematic colonisation of most of the region does seem to have been the achievement of settlers moving up from the Midlands. In fact, from the mid-seventh century onwards, with only a short interlude of Scandinavian rule, Cheshire and south Lancashire were subject to Mercian control, and the Ribble river came to constitute a major political, ecclesiastical and linguistic divide. Even at the time of the Norman Conquest and Domesday Book the area later known as Lancashire was divided into two parts, the northern half being in the earldom of Northumbria and the archbishopric of York, and attached to Yorkshire, and the southern half being in the earldom of Mercia and the bishopric of Lichfield, and attached to Cheshire. Manifestly the lands between the Dee and the Ribble shared a common historical background, and for many centuries the two sides of the Mersey maintained a common culture in fields as diverse as vernacular literature and land measurement. The old association between Cheshire and south Lancashire lived on not only in the ecclesiastical sphere with the archdeaconry, and later the bishopric of

---

[11] E.g. see M. Drayton, *Polyolbion* (London, 1612), pp. 171–2, and W. Camden, *Britannia*, transl. E. Gibson (London, 1695), p. 555.

Chester, but also in a common cultural heritage which was as distinctive as its roots were diverse.[12]

After the tenurial revolution and the administrative changes set in train by the Norman Conquest, Cheshire and Lancashire continued to develop along parallel lines. The earldom of Chester and the honour of Lancaster were both constituted as strong territorial units, and granted out by the Norman kings to trusted lieutenants. This policy of creating sizeable concentrations of power in the Northwest seems to have been dictated by strategic considerations, and from the earliest times the two counties were charged with the defence of the kingdom's frontiers. Through extensive military service on the Welsh border and on the western approaches from Scotland the Northwest naturally developed strong martial traditions, and in the later middle ages the region was highly valued as a recruiting-ground.[13] Meanwhile the earls of Chester and the lords of Lancaster added to their territorial powers in the Northwest through the acquisition of franchisal rights, and after the devolution of the lordships to the crown, the process by which the shires achieved separate administrative and juridical status was officially encouraged. In 1375 the palatinates of Chester and Lancaster were the appanages of Edward III's sons, the Black Prince and John of Gaunt, and in the following decades the two counties likewise proved valuable to Richard II and the Lancastrian kings as independent sources of royal power.[14] Indeed, largely through their close connections with members of the royal family, Cheshire and Lancashire acquired a significance in national affairs totally out of keeping with their remoteness and indigence. Their most important resource in this period seems to have been man-power, and large numbers of local clergymen, soldiers and administrators achieved distinction in the royal service.[15] While the operations of royal patronage undoubtedly broadened the horizons of local careerists, contact with people from other parts of the kingdom often served merely to reinforce provincial loyalties. Certainly the Cheshire and Lancashire population was more than usually inbred. Between 1374 and 1427 a quarter of all the papal dispensations

---

[12] F. T. Wainwright, 'The Anglian settlement of Lancashire', *L.C.H.S.*, 93 (1941), 1–44, 'North-West Mercia, 871–924', *L.C.H.S.*, 94 (1942), 3–55, 'The Scandinavians in Lancashire', *L.C.A.S.*, 58 (1946), 71–116; J. McN. Dodgson, 'The English arrival in Cheshire', *L.C.H.S.*, 119 (1968), 1–37.

[13] H. J. Hewitt, *Medieval Cheshire. An Economic and Social History* (C.S., n.s. 88, 1929), pp. 157–60.

[14] G. Barraclough, 'The earldom and county palatine of Chester', *L.C.H.S.*, 103 (1951), 23–57; R. Somerville, 'The duchy and county palatine of Lancaster', *ibid.*, 59–67.

[15] Bennett, 'Social mobility'.

granted to English couples for consanguineous marriages were issued to residents of the archdeaconry of Chester.[16]

II

Cheshire and Lancashire, and more especially the area between the Dee and the Ribble, not only shared similar patterns of social organisation but also represented in some measure a real regional community. Of course, the social horizons of the vast majority of the population were severely restricted. Even the local gentry families tended to regard their county as their *patria*, and such sentiments were strengthened by the palatine liberties of the two shires. Yet there is definite evidence of inter-communication between Cheshire and Lancashire men, and of its importance in the functioning of local society. In this section it is intended to consider both the social groups whose interests ranged across the Mersey boundary and the collective enterprises which helped to forge a sense of regional identity in the Northwest.

Given that Cheshire and Lancashire shared a rather remote and inaccessible corner of the country, whatever geographical mobility there was in the region served to bind the two counties together. Clearly Lancashire, and more particularly the portion south of the Ribble, depended on routes through Cheshire for access to the more central parts of the kingdom. From Roman times the main thoroughfare through Lancashire was the highway which passed southwards through Lancaster, Preston and Wigan. After crossing the Mersey at Warrington the traveller could then choose to take the road to Chester and North Wales, to head for Nantwich and the Welsh Borderlands, or to take the Middlewich road en route for Newcastle under Lyme, Coventry and London. In all three cases, at least one staging-post in Cheshire would have been required. For Cheshire men travelling northwards similar conditions obtained. The northern and northeasterly roads which radiated outwards from the Cheshire salt-towns of Nantwich, Middlewich and Northwich crossed through Lancashire before traversing the Pennines. The Gough Map reveals a highway linking Chester with Liverpool, presumably by means of the ferry at Birkenhead, while a contemporary itinerary noted a route

<hr>

[16] Twenty-seven of the 107 dispensations enrolled in the papal chancery for English couples in this period were for local men and women: *C. Pap. L.*, IV, pp. 412–13, 432; V, pp. 209, 282, 307, 374, 383, 396, 461, 507, 527–8, 540, 542, 578; VI, pp. 62, 70, 106, 444, 459, 462; VII, pp. 219, 227, 259, 363, 365, 379. Note also the dispensations secured for local couples by Bishop Langley: *The Register of Thomas Langley, Bishop of Durham 1406–1437*, ed. R. L. Storey (6 vols., Surtees Soc., 164, 166, 169, 170, 177, 182, 1956–70), I, pp. 165, 173–5.

traversing the eastern fringe of Cheshire to cross the Mersey boundary at Stockport. Closed around by a series of uplands which included the Welsh Borderlands and the Pennine Chain, the two counties necessarily shared the same meagre network of overland communications.[17]

These thoroughfares served as arteries of commerce, and the most mobile sections of the local population were the tradesmen, whether the well-established merchant families or the itinerant peddlers, carriers and craftsmen who hawked their wares from market to market. For the commercial classes, administrative divisions would have taken second place to the more natural boundaries of a geographical region, and indeed the connections of many trading families ramified throughout the Northwest. The overriding size and significance of Chester was of fundamental importance in this process of integration. The city was the nodal point in a commercial network which embraced not only Cheshire and Lancashire but also North Wales and the Welsh Borderlands. A major seaport for trade with Ireland and Gascony, it was the most important market-centre in the region for luxury goods and specialised services. Not unnaturally, the city attracted merchants and craftsmen from all parts of the Northwest, and a large proportion of its population originated in Lancashire, the Welsh Borderlands and elsewhere outside Cheshire. Its leading mercantile houses had connections in other towns in the region. Richard Strangeways and Roger Ditton, aldermen of Chester in the 1390s, were the scions of Manchester and Liverpool tradesmen. After Ditton's death his estate in Chester and Middlewich passed to his son-in-law, Roger Derby, another Liverpool merchant.[18] Almost all the more notable families of the Northwest had representatives in two or more local towns. Branches of the Bretherton family were established at Wigan and Preston, while the Crosse family was prominent in both Wigan and Liverpool.[19] The Wettenhalls, who proliferated around Nantwich and Chester, and the Oulegreves, who were operating in Manchester as well as their native Knutsford, were two of the many families that established sons in business in London.[20]

Doubtless commercial operations in other parts of the kingdom

[17] W. B. Crump, 'Saltways from the Cheshire Wiches', *L.C.A.S.*, 54 (1940), 84–142; B. Dickins, 'Premonstratensian itineraries from a Titchfield Abbey MS. at Welbeck', *Proceedings of the Leeds Philosophical and Literary Society. Literary and Historical Section*, 4 (1936), 349–61; *Facsimile of the Ancient Map of Great Britain in the Bodleian Library, Oxford, A.D. 1325–1350* (Ordnance Survey, 1935).

[18] *A Middlewich Chartulary*, part II, ed. J. Varley and J. Tait (C.S., n.s. 108, 1944), pp. xxxi–xxxii.

[19] Lancashire R.O., DDF/578, DDF/1461, DDHe/50, DDHe/60/7, DDK/B/1542.

[20] P.R.O., CHES 17/5, m.9d; S. L. Thrupp, *The Merchant Class of Medieval London* (Chicago, 1948), pp. 373, 359.

occasioned a great deal of collaboration among the trading families of the two counties. Local merchants travelled together along the arduous road to London, and were fellow members of the Trinity Guild at Coventry.[21] Business-minded gentlemen and tradespeople from both counties shared in the commercial exploitation of Wales and Ireland. Thus the Bolds from Lancashire and the Bulkeleys from Cheshire acquired prominence in the boroughs of North Wales, and together accumulated a massive estate in Caernarfon and Anglesey.[22] Indeed the reinvestment of commercial riches in local property further contributed to the integration of town and countryside across the region. Early in the fourteenth century the Erneys family, a wealthy mercantile house of Chester, obtained half the manor of Speke in southwest Lancashire.[23] The admission of William Laghok, late of Speke, as a freeman of Chester in 1393 was perhaps a product of this manorial connection.[24] This latter tradesman later transferred his business to St Neots in Huntingdonshire, whence his son went on to become a citizen and tallow-chandler of London. Yet even at the end of the fifteenth century, the family retained its connections with southwest Lancashire and other parts of the region.[25] Information of this sort testifies both to the vital role of the trading classes in the integration of regional society, and to the importance of provincial connections in the organisation of national commerce.

In the ecclesiastical sphere the Northwest also functioned as a relatively cohesive social unit. Cheshire and Lancashire south of the Ribble were united as the archdeaconry of Chester, and the region enjoyed considerable independence from the bishop at Lichfield.[26] The evidence suggests that the local church was extremely provincial in character. Over three-quarters of the parishes in the archdeaconry were in the gift of local patrons, and the resident body of clergymen was overwhelmingly local in complexion.[27] Between the seven Cheshire and four Lancashire deaneries of the archdeaconry of Chester, however, there was a considerable degree of intercommunication. The pivotal importance of the city of Chester with its numerous shrines, churches and religious houses must again be stressed, and throughout the period it acted as a magnet for ambitious clerks and

---

[21] *The Register of the Trinity Guild, Coventry*, ed. M. D. Harris (Dugdale Soc., XIII, 1935), *passim*.

[22] T. Jones-Pierce, 'Some tendencies in the agricultural history of Caernarvonshire in the later Middle Ages', *Transactions of the Caernarvonshire Historical Society*, 1 (1939), 18–36.

[23] *V.C.H. Lancaster*, III, pp. 132–3.

[24] *Chester Freeman Rolls*, part I, ed. J. H. E. Bennett (L.C.R.S., 51, 1906), p. 1.

[25] *Norris Deeds*, ed. J. H. Lumby (L.C.R.S., 93, 1939), no. 564.

[26] P. Heath, 'The medieval archdeaconry and the Tudor bishopric of Chester', *Journal of Ecclesiastical History*, 20 (1969), 243–52.

[27] M. J. Bennett, 'The Lancashire and Cheshire clergy, 1379', *L.C.H.S.*, 124 (1973), 11.

devout laymen from all corners of the Northwest.[28] On the other hand, the city was not always the administrative centre of the archdeaconry. The archdeacons of Chester often chose Warrington as their base.[29] The latter town was both conveniently placed at the boundary of the two shires and suitably remote from the competition of other ecclesiastical jurisdictions. Furthermore, with its parish church, its rural deanery, and its much revered house of Austin friars, it was an important religious centre in its own right. In local wills bequests were commonly made to the Augustinians at Warrington as well as to the Franciscans, Dominicans and Carmelites at Chester.[30] Indeed the religious houses of the region complemented each other in the provision of spiritual services. Each maintaining a single convent in the archdeaconry, the four mendicant orders inevitably attracted recruits and endowments from both counties. An analogous complementarity existed in the monastic sphere. The abbey of St Werburgh and the nunnery of St Mary at Chester, the earliest and wealthiest Benedictine foundations, remained of central importance. The two largest Cistercian houses — Vale Royal and Whalley — held properties in both counties, while the priories of Birkenhead, Norton and Holland were all situated close to the county boundary, and received novices from both sides of the Mersey. In ecclesiastical matters the two counties were clearly interdependent. Even among unbeneficed clerks there was a great deal of mobility in and between the various deaneries,[31] and among their more privileged brethren there was a continuous traffic in local benefices. While the archdeaconry of Chester was merely one of the many administrative units which ultimately linked the parish with the papal court, its significance in the organisation of social life must not be underestimated. In their dealings with the church, layman and clerk alike found themselves operating in a regional context, and local churchmen promoted elsewhere in the kingdom often retained strong provincial loyalties.[32]

The physical identity of the region and the interdependence of the two counties in the commercial and ecclesiastical spheres ensured a considerable degree of social intercourse between the Cheshire and Lancashire gentry. Obviously the local gentry had interests, duties and connections which

---

[28] See D. Jones, *The Church in Chester 1300–1540* (C.S., third series 7, 1957).

[29] Chetham Library, Manchester, Raines MSS., vol. XI, p. 33.

[30] E.g. see wills of Sir Thomas Dutton and John Butler of Warrington: *The Register of Henry Chichele, Archbishop of Canterbury 1414–1443*, ed. E. F. Jacob (4 vols., Canterbury and York Soc., 1937–47), II, pp. 88, 221. See also Jones, *Church in Chester*, pp. 96–7.

[31] Bennett, 'Lancashire and Cheshire clergy', 15–16.

[32] E.g. Thomas Langley of Middleton: R. L. Storey, *Thomas Langley and the Bishopric of Durham* (London, 1961), pp. 2–8.

could lead them far from their own demesnes. While the community of the shire was the most significant grouping in the lives of most of their class, the leading gentry families at least associated regularly with their peers in neighbouring counties. The more eminent knightly houses, in particular, aspired to more distinguished company than could typically be found within a single shire. Whether tournaments and other such extravagances were a regular feature of local life cannot be ascertained, but it is perhaps significant that when the Cheshire knight, Sir John Danyers, called a tournament in Edward III's reign he chose Warrington as its venue, doubtless on account of its accessibility to the chivalry of both counties.[33] Indeed the regional solidarity of the knightly class was most strikingly demonstrated in 1386–7 when Sir Robert Grosvenor was struggling to defend his heraldic rights in the Court of Chivalry. During the trial over two hundred depositions were collected on his behalf, the vast majority of which were from his Cheshire neighbours. Unlike Sir Richard Scrope, his rival, he was unable to mobilise support for his cause among peers of the realm, and his credit extended no further than the Warwickshire knight Sir William Bagot and the Welsh squire Owain Glyndŵr, both of whom in any case had Cheshire interests. Still, in marked contrast to the pitifully small number of deponents from outside the region, over fifty Lancashire knights and gentlemen turned out to testify on his behalf at specially convened sessions at Warrington and Lancaster.[34]

Quite a number of the Lancashire deponents admitted kinship with the house of Grosvenor, and indeed intermarriage between gentry families from the two counties was by no means uncommon in the early fourteenth century. Naturally enough, bonds of affinity were strongest in the neighbourhood of Warrington, where the Butlers, Bolds and Haydocks from Lancashire and the Duttons and Danyers's from Cheshire had long been closely associated. In the late fourteenth and early fifteenth centuries a number of prominent families acquired the marriages of heiresses from across the border. The Gerards, Athertons and Radcliffes all gained estates in Cheshire, while the Leghs, Stanleys and Mascys obtained properties in Lancashire. Sir John Stanley and Peter Legh of Lyme, two favourites of Richard II, amassed lands on both sides of the Mersey. A younger son of the Stanleys of Storeton in Cheshire, the former acquired by marriage to Isabella Lathom the manors of Lathom and Knowsley in Lancashire, but retained extensive interests in his native shire. A cadet of the Leghs

[33] *B.P.R.*, III, p. 59.
[34] N. H. Nicolas, *The Scrope and Grosvenor Controversy* (2 vols., London, 1832), I, *passim*; R. Stewart-Brown, 'The Scrope and Grosvenor controversy, 1385–1391', *L.C.H.S.*, 89 (1937), 1–22.

of Adlington in Cheshire, the latter obtained the neighbouring estate of Lyme through marriage to the daughter of Sir Thomas Danyers. Meanwhile he inherited Lancashire properties from his grandfather, Thurstan Norley, and shortly before his execution by Bolingbroke in 1399 he began to consolidate his interests in the Warrington and Wigan areas by arranging an alliance between his son and the heiress of Sir Gilbert Haydock.[35]

At the same time the administrative duties undertaken by the Cheshire and Lancashire gentry served to extend their horizons beyond their native shires. The local men holding office in the two palatinates clearly shared common attitudes and interests. Interestingly enough, there is evidence of collaboration between the two sheriffs, Sir Robert Legh and Sir Ralph Radcliffe, in the troubled months of 1399.[36] A certain number of knights and gentlemen even held positions of responsibility in both counties, and successful administrative careers were nurtured in a regional context. Administrative talent and legal training secured the fortunes of men like William Troutbeck, James Holt, William Chauntrell and James Strangeways on both sides of the Mersey. Similarly careerists who achieved distinction at a national level retained their local connections, and co-operated in furthering the interests of kinsmen and compatriots.[37] Prominent local commanders, like Sir Hugh Calveley, Sir John Stanley and Sir John Radcliffe, recruited extensively from both counties, and common military experiences in lands as far afield as Castile and Prussia inevitably forged strong bonds between the two county communities. In a similar fashion, influential courtiers and government officials from the Northwest, like Sir David Cradock, Sir Hugh Holes, John Macclesfield and Thomas Langley, formed the nuclei of social groupings which effectively linked court and country. Cheshire and Lancashire men in London and elsewhere seem to have maintained close contact, and their collective involvement in property transactions provides striking evidence of regional solidarity.[38]

The close bonds between Cheshire and Lancashire careerists were not

---

[35] W. F. Irvine, 'The early Stanleys', *L.C.H.S.*, 105 (1953), 45–68; J.R.U.L., Legh of Lyme Muniments, N/1/55, M/4/67.

[36] *C.C.R. 1396–1399*, p. 505; *C.P.R. 1396–1399*, p. 585.

[37] See also Bennett, 'Social mobility', 80–2.

[38] E.g. the witnesses to a notarial instrument involving the Savage family, which was drawn up in London on 16 March 1406 included Sir John Stanley, Robert Lawrence and Roger Poghden from Lancashire as well as Sir William Stanley, John Macclesfield, Matthew Mere, Richard Fitton and Geoffrey Mascy from Cheshire: *Cheshire Sheaf*, third series, item 6820. See also the settlement made by Ralph Standish, with witnesses from both counties, at Cognac in Guyenne in 1368: *Calendar of Standish Deeds*, ed. T. C. Porteus (Wigan, 1933), no. 258.

solely the product of geographical proximity. Such associations were also functions of the way in which the two counties were bound together in similar networks of patronage.[39] Although there was occasional conflict at a national level between the earls of Chester and the lords of Lancaster, there was never a clear-cut division of interest, even in times of crisis, between the two palatinates. From the thirteenth century the earldom of Chester had been held either by the king or his heir, and naturally there were always Lancashire men in the royal service. Conversely, the lords of Lancaster held important estates in Cheshire, and had an extensive following south of the Mersey. From 1399 the earldom of Chester and the duchy of Lancaster were often united in royal hands – for short periods under Richard II and Henry IV and for longer stretches under Henry V and Henry VI – and, although the two palatinates remained administratively distinct, in practice the two counties were increasingly assimilated into a single patronage system. Local families with influence at court were in a strong position to consolidate their power on a regional basis. By the second quarter of the fifteenth century the Stanleys of Lathom had amassed not only great territorial wealth but also high office in both counties. In the changing social conditions of the Lancastrian period this remarkable lineage virtually usurped the crown as the effective source of patronage in the region. The growing hegemony of the house of Stanley was a powerful factor in the further integration of the two county societies in the later fifteenth century.[40]

While a consciousness of a common identity might be fairly inferred from the shared experiences of men from the Northwest, the evidence is lacking to document convincingly such sentiments for the period under discussion. Rather surprisingly, the fine local school of alliterative poetry which flourished in the late fourteenth century is completely devoid of regional patriotism. While the attachment by men of the two counties to a provincial dialect and metre is instructive, it must be remembered that the authors of *Wynnere and Wastoure*, *Sir Gawain and the Green Knight* and *St Erkenwald* had interests and tastes which were in many respects metropolitan.[41] Of course, since a sense of regional identity could not have developed fully in isolation, but needed to be nourished through involvement in wider social settings, it might well be that this consciousness was still only latent in the fourteenth century, a time when after all local men were only just beginning to make their mark on the national stage.

[39] See below, Chapter 10.
[40] M. J. Bennett, '"Good Lords" and "King-Makers": the Stanleys of Lathom in English politics, 1385–1485', *History Today*, 31 (1981), 12–17.
[41] *Wynnere and Wastoure*, ed. I. Gollancz (London, 1920); *Sir Gawain and the Green Knight*, ed. J. R. R. Tolkien and E. V. Gordon, 2nd edn (Oxford, 1967); *St Erkenwald*, ed. R. Morse (Cambridge, 1975).

With the increasingly close association between the crown and the two royal palatinates from the end of Richard II's reign onwards, the two county communities seem to have become more aware of their common destiny. Under the adroit leadership of the house of Stanley, the men of the Northwest were uniquely successful in articulating and advancing a regional interest in the civil strife of the later fifteenth century.[42] In 1450 Cheshire and Lancashire men were associated together in the mind of a London chronicler as providing the military muscle for the unpopular Lancastrian regime, while in 1485 the two counties virtually arbitrated the fortunes of the realm at the battle of Bosworth.[43] In fact by the early Tudor era warm provincial pride had been fanned into the white heat of regional chauvinism. According to the ballads and poems extant in the Percy Folio manuscript, Henry VII and his son not only owed their throne to the gallantry and prowess of men from the Northwest, but were also prepared to acknowledge their debt of gratitude with lavish patronage. In one splendid flight of fancy Henry VIII is alleged to have proclaimed that 'whosoever rebuketh Lancashire or Cheshire shortly shall be deemed to die'.[44]

For certain sections of the population, Cheshire and Lancashire, and particularly the lands between the Dee and the Ribble, were coming to represent a distinctive and increasingly self-conscious regional society. Although the connections of most individuals were narrowly circumscribed, there were at least a number of social groups which actively maintained networks of personal relations embracing the entire region during the period under discussion. For the most part attention has been focused on the commercial classes, the clergymen and the leading gentry families, and it is from an investigation of their associations and interests that the existence of a provincial community has been inferred. It is probable, however, that regional loyalties permeated society even more deeply than might be supposed. Although there were disputes between men of the two counties and even open violence on the borders, such quarrels were as nothing compared with the differences which set the region apart from the rest of the kingdom. The common people of Cheshire and Lancashire shared not only a remote corner of the country with its own patterns of settlement and social organisation, but also a

---

[42] Bennett, 'The Stanleys in English politics'.

[43] *Six Town Chronicles of England*, ed. R. Flenley (Oxford, 1911); Bennett, 'The Stanleys in English politics'.

[44] E.g. see 'Lady Bessy', 'Bosworth Field', 'Scottish Field' and 'Flodden Field' in *Bishop Percy's Folio Manuscript. Ballads and Romances*, ed. J. W. Hales and F. J. Furnivall (3 vols., London, 1868), III, pp. 319–63, 233–59, 205–14, I, pp. 313–40. Quotation from *ibid.*, I, p. 333.

distinctive regional dialect and literary culture. The mobility of the labouring classes both in and between the two counties should not be underestimated, and even the humblest families were drawn into regional networks of relations through commerce, the church or military service. Even if the lower orders were rarely conscious of solidarities larger than their own village communities, the region remained a unit of considerable significance in the organisation of social life. Neither shire in the Northwest on its own was sufficiently populous or prosperous to sustain a vigorous commercial life, a respectable ecclesiastical establishment or an opulent governing élite. The two counties together allowed a higher degree of social differentiation and occupational specialisation than was possible within the ambit of either one alone. At the same time the regional community linked backwood parishes with the court and the capital, and established avenues of social mobility well-trodden by local careerists. It served as an informal framework through which the more dynamic elements of Cheshire and Lancashire society found expression, and accordingly represents a vital component in the social geography of late medieval England.

*Chapter 2*

# THE COUNTY COMMUNITIES

While regional associations remained completely informal, the county community early assumed institutional form.[1] The concept itself was fundamental to many important political developments in the thirteenth century, and H. Cam could describe the county even at this stage 'as an organism – a unit held together by proximity, by local feeling and above all by common living traditions and common responsibilities'.[2] At the same time none can doubt the vital role played by communities of the shire in the evolution and the progressive integration of English society until comparatively recent times.[3] Yet surprisingly little work has been done on their composition and activities in the later middle ages. Perhaps the main deterrent has been a lack of the right sort of sources, particularly material of a personal nature. Still, the Namierian researches of J. S. Roskell testify to the existence of much relevant data, and have often made it available in convenient form.[4] The copious documentation provided by the palatinate administrators, coupled with the rich muniment collections of local gentry families, in fact, offer an embarrassing wealth of evidence regarding the county communities of the Northwest.

The following discussion of the Cheshire and Lancashire communities centres on an analysis of the social relations of the gentry. Although the interests and connections of the more illustrious lineages transcended their own shire, the social world of most gentlemen was rooted in the network of personal connections and collective responsibilities which constituted the county community. While there were other social groups which interacted at a county level, it was the gentry which above all imbued the concept of community with real social meaning. In the following sections

---

[1] Parts of this chapter have been published: M. J. Bennett, 'A county community: social cohesion amongst the Cheshire gentry, 1400–1425', *Northern History*, 8 (1973), 24–44.

[2] H. M. Cam, *Liberties and Communities in Medieval England* (Cambridge, 1944), p. 247.

[3] J. R. Maddicott, 'The county community and the making of public opinion in fourteenth-century England', *T.R.H.S.*, fifth series 28 (1978), pp. 27–43; A. Everitt, 'The county community' in E. W. Ives (ed.), *The English Revolution 1600–1660* (London, 1968), pp. 62–3.

[4] See especially J. S. Roskell, *The Knights of the Shire for the County Palatine of Lancaster 1377–1460* (C.S., n.s. 96, 1937), a mine of information for the Lancashire county community.

it is proposed to gather evidence for the existence of two county communities in the region, and to evaluate these associations in terms of their functions both in the county administration and in the lives of individual members. To avoid needless repetition, the analysis is arranged according to the various categories of social involvement evidenced among the local gentry. Their relationships are discussed in terms of their involvement as members of kinship networks, a landowning class and a governing élite. Initially groups of Cheshire and Lancashire gentlemen are introduced through descriptions of two specific social occasions. These two events are then treated as case-studies, and the participants as sample groupings, whose social activities, both before and afterwards, provide the illustrative detail.

I

Towards the end of Henry IV's reign and the beginning of Henry V's reign there were two well-documented gatherings in the Northwest which can be usefully regarded as expressions of solidarity among the gentry of the two counties. An investigation of the Cheshire community most conveniently commences with a ceremony performed in Macclesfield church on 24 April 1412. More than sixty knights and gentlemen from all over Cheshire had assembled to take part in the settlement of property disputes between Sir Thomas Grosvenor and Robert Legh. A mass having been celebrated, the former professed the truth of the charters by which he claimed the disputed land. His oath was then affirmed by fifty-eight gentlemen each 'raising his hand at the same time towards the Host as a sign of the veracity of the oath'. Robert Legh accordingly relaxed his claims and an instrument to that effect containing the names of the numerous witnesses was drawn up by the public notary.[5] A rather more

---

[5] Cheshire R.O., DLT, Liber C, ff. 116–18. The Cheshire knights and gentlemen whose presence was recorded were Sir Lawrence Merbury, Thomas Danyers, John Legh of Booths, John Legh of High Legh, William Leicester, John Mainwaring, Randle Mainwaring, Matthew Mere, William Mere, Roger Mullington, Robert Toft, Richard Warburton (Bucklow hundred); Sir Lawrence Fitton, Richard Bulkeley, Hugh Davenport, Nicholas Davenport, Robert Davenport, Robert Legh, Lawrence Warren (Macclesfield hundred); Sir William Brereton, Sir Thomas Grosvenor, Adam Bostock, Ralph Bostock, John Brereton, William Brereton junior, Hugh Cotton, Thomas Cotton, Ralph Davenport, Thomas Haslington, Robert Needham, Hugh Venables, William Venables, John Winnington (Northwich hundred); John Brescy, John Cholmondeley, David Crewe, Robert Hassall, John Kingsley, Hugh Malpas, Thomas Starkey, John Woodhouse (Nantwich hundred); Hugh Dutton, Hugh Egerton, Philip Egerton, Urian Egerton, William Egerton, David St Pierre (Broxton hundred); William Beeston, John Donne, William Frodsham, John Manley, Richard Manley, Robert Overton, Henry Spurstow, Peter Starkey, Robert Winnington (Edisbury hundred); Sir John Poole, Sir William Stanley and John Whitmore (Wirral hundred): Ormerod, *History of Cheshire*, *passim*. Also in attendance were Sir John

formal occasion, the election of knights of the shire at Lancaster on 15 October 1414, provides a similarly useful focus for a consideration of the Lancashire community. At this particularly well-attended session of the county court John Stanley and Robert Lawrence were elected to represent Lancashire in parliament, and the thirty-eight suitors who appended their seals to the indenture of election provide a second convenient sample grouping.[6]

The gentlemen at Macclesfield in 1412 included members of most of the notable Cheshire lineages. The two protagonists, Sir Thomas Grosvenor of Hulme and Robert Legh of Adlington, were both persons of note in county affairs. The list of witnesses was headed by Sir Lawrence Merbury, sheriff of Cheshire, and included such prominent knights and squires as Sir William Brereton, Sir Lawrence Fitton of Gawsworth, Sir William Stanley, Sir John Poole, Adam Bostock, John Donne of Utkinton, John Legh of Booths, Hugh Venables of Kinderton, and Lawrence Warren of Stockport. Judging from the names of men witnessing final concords at the county court between 1410 and 1414, this group included around two-thirds of the active county notables.[7] In all likelihood the Lancashire gathering was even better attended, though only the names of the more illustrious electors were recorded. In addition to Sir Nicholas Longford, sheriff of Lancashire, there were no less than sixteen knights present, namely Richard Hoghton, William Harrington, Thomas Tunstall, William Butler, William Atherton, Nicholas Atherton, John Bold, Thomas Gerard, Robert Urswick, William Hoghton, Henry Hoghton, Richard Radcliffe of Winmarleigh, John Southworth, Gilbert Haydock, Richard Keighley and John Pilkington. Among the more notable squires named were Henry Langton, baron of Newton in Makerfield, and no less than six men who were to be knighted later in

Delves and Sir John Ashton, who normally resided in Staffordshire and Lancashire respectively; Henry Birtles and James Holt, the lawyers; and various clerks.

6  Roskell, *Lancashire Knights*, p. 210. The Lancashire knights and gentlemen who witnessed the election were Sir William Harrington, Sir Thomas Tunstall, Sir Robert Urswick, John Harrington, Robert Lawrence (Lonsdale hundred); Sir Richard Radcliffe of Winmarleigh, Nicholas Butler, Thomas Clifton (Amounderness hundred); Sir Henry Hoghton, Sir Richard Hoghton, Sir William Hoghton, Hugh Standish, Ralph Standish (Leyland hundred); Sir Nicholas Atherton, Sir William Atherton, Sir John Bold, Sir William Butler, Sir Thomas Gerard, Sir Gilbert Haydock, Sir John Southworth, Thomas Bradshaw, William Bradshaw, Robert Halsall, Henry Langton, Hamo Mascy, Henry Scarisbrick, John Stanley (West Derby hundred); Sir Richard Keighley, Sir Nicholas Longford, Sir John Pilkington, Gilbert Barton, Richard Barton, Thurstan Holland, Robert Holt, Ralph Radcliffe, Richard Radcliffe of Radcliffe (Salford hundred); Nicholas Hesketh and Richard Shirebourne (Blackburn hundred): *V.C.H. Lancaster*, passim.

7  P.R.O., CHES 31/26-7. Sir William Stanley attended ten of the eleven documented sessions.

their careers. Needless to say, the group hailed from all corners of the shire. From the far north came Sir Thomas Tunstall and John Harrington of Cartmel; from the south of Manchester came Sir Nicholas Longford and Thurstan Holland; from the Fylde came Thomas Clifton and Nicholas Butler; and from high Ribblesdale came Richard Shirebourne of Stonyhurst. While most of the sample were actually domiciled along the central lowland corridor running down from Lancaster to Warrington, this in no way impugns its representative character, since gentry seats were naturally thin on the ground in the outlying, hilly districts.[8]

The two meetings of local gentry have obvious relevance in a study of county communities in action. Before making too many assumptions from what might prove wholly untypical occurrences, however, it is necessary to place both occasions in their contexts. Obviously the gathering of so many Cheshire gentlemen at Macclesfield cannot have been fortuitous, since it had previously been agreed that the dispute between Grosvenor and Legh would be settled by a public oath by Grosvenor and twenty-five other gentlemen.[9] Though some of the group perhaps had business of their own in the town, it appears that the co-ordination of social activity held a high place in their scale of priorities. Piecing together evidence from a variety of sources it is possible to trace other meetings between gentlemen in this sample in the weeks previous to their gathering at Macclesfield on 24 April 1412. In Chester on Friday 15 April, John Manley settled all his property in the city on a group of trustees who included Sir William Stanley and five others from the Macclesfield group.[10] Many had been in Chester for the county court on the Tuesday. Richard Manley and Matthew Mere, the escheator and attorney-general, were present as also were Sir Lawrence Merbury and his under-sheriff, Thomas Haslington. David Crewe and John Brescy, coroners of Nantwich hundred, made presentments at these sessions, while cases involving Robert Legh, Robert Davenport, David St Pierre and William Venables were also heard.[11] The presence in Chester of other gentlemen from the sample in the same week is recorded in the recognizance rolls: Sir John Poole and others entered a bond concerning his daughter's marriage, while Sir Lawrence Fitton, Robert Legh, Hugh Davenport and Robert Davenport were bound over to keep the peace.[12] Manifestly Cheshire gentlemen were well accustomed to acting together in a variety of capacities, and their collective activities confirm the existence of a close, if completely informal, network of relations which embraced the entire county.

---

[8] See below, Chapter 5.

[9] Cheshire R.O., DLT, Liber C, f. 117.

[10] B.L., Harleian MS. 2077, f. 218.

[11] P.R.O., CHES 29/115, m. 14.

[12] P.R.O., CHES 2/84, m. 2d.

The meeting of the thirty-eight gentlemen at Lancaster cannot be construed entirely as a social occasion. Arguably the group had nothing more in common than their interest in the parliamentary election. While this might account for the attendance of certain individuals, however, it cannot explain the peculiar size and composition of the assembly of 1414. The indentures from other fifteenth-century elections in Lancashire indicate that the presence of so many county notables was exceptional.[13] However great their interest in the election, it is likely that the electors had other concerns. Fortunately it is possible to trace some of the immediate antecedents to this meeting. The problem uppermost in the minds of Sir Thomas Gerard, Henry Langton and Ralph Standish, for example, was a longstanding dispute between them over the valuable advowson of Wigan church. Conflict had become so acrimonious that both the king and the bishop of Durham had been involved in helping to find a settlement.[14] Earlier in the month Gerard and Langton had bound themselves in 1,000 marks to abide certain agreements made between them and Standish.[15] On the day after the election the gentlemen met in Wigan to make further arrangements regarding the settlement of their disputes.[16] According to the new terms the three protagonists and their kinsmen were required to release all actions pending between them in the presence of Sir Richard Hoghton, Sir Thomas Tunstall, Sir William Harrington and another knight. Gerard and Langton were also obliged to pay Standish 400 marks, and the quarrel over Wigan church was to be put to the arbitration of Sir Richard Hoghton, Sir Richard Radcliffe, Sir Richard Keighley, William Bradshaw and four others. Doubtless there had been consultations in Lancaster on this topic the previous day, and that the parties had ridden down to Wigan together. The new agreement also made provision for several more meetings. Further bonds were entered into by Gerard, Langton and Standish on 17 and 20 October.[17] It is unlikely, however, that the dispute was amicably settled before the summer when most of the parties left for service in the French wars. The betrothal of Standish's grandson to Gerard's grand-daughter some years later perhaps paved the way for a more lasting settlement.

The assemblies at Macclesfield in 1412 and at Lancaster in 1414 can therefore be regarded as examples of county communities in action. It is not pretended that such large gatherings were particularly regular features of local life, but the fact that they were possible at all is indicative of a high degree of cohesion among the county families. While some of the

[13] Roskell, *Lancashire Knights*, pp. 206–26 and 23.     [14] *Standish Deeds*, no. 129.

[15] *Ibid.*, no. 128.     [16] *Ibid.*, no. 129.

[17] *Ibid.*, nos. 130–2.

lesser gentry probably owed their involvement in such meetings to their association with more powerful neighbours, it is evident that it was the county, and not a particular local magnate, which provided the fundamental source of cohesion. After all the members of both samples can be found acting together in a variety of permutations and contexts. In the following sections three of the more important categories of social involvement are illustrated in greater detail. At the same time there is attempted an analysis of the functions, whether personal, social or institutional in origin, of social cohesion at the county level. In order to give more substance to the discussion, all the examples are derived from the activities of the gentlemen present in Macclesfield and Lancaster on the above mentioned occasions.

II

Most basically, the two groups of gentlemen were closely associated through ties of kinship and marriage. Even with the limited genealogical data available, the degree of interrelatedness is remarkable.[18] Many of the participants bore the same surnames. At Macclesfield, Sir William Brereton, Richard Manley, Randle Mainwaring and Adam Bostock were accompanied by their sons, William and Hugh Venables, and Matthew and William Mere were uncles and nephews, and the various Leghs, Davenports and Egertons were all related in the not too distant past. At Lancaster, Sir Richard Hoghton was attended by his son and brother, Sir William and Sir Nicholas Atherton were brothers, and the Harringtons, Radcliffes, Bradshaws and Standishs were all cousins. Of course, relationship in the male line represented only the most obvious of blood ties, but the illicitness of consanguineous marriage kept the gentry aware of even the remotest connections. Two sets of genealogical notes survive from the fifteenth century to record the affinities of two prominent local lineages.[19] From an account of the progeny of an earlier baron of Kinderton, it is apparent that Hugh Venables, Hugh Davenport, Richard Bulkeley, John Mainwaring and the wives of five other members of the Cheshire sample were first cousins. Similarly a table of descendants of the steward of Blackburn around 1300 included not only three members of the Radcliffe clan but also Sir John Pilkington, Sir Robert Urswick, Henry Langton, Ralph Standish, Nicholas Butler, Richard Barton, Nicholas Hesketh, and John Harrington. Indeed, if it were possible to trace the ancestries of all

---

[18] Almost all the genealogical information is derived from Ormerod, *History of Cheshire* and *V.C.H. Lancaster*. See genealogical table above.

[19] Cheshire R.O., DLT, Liber C, f. 132; Manchester Central Reference Library, Farrer MSS., 36/1.

their families over several generations, all the members of the two samples could doubtless be accommodated within the confines of two reasonably compact, if exceedingly involved, genealogical tables.[20]

The blood relations existing between local gentry families stemmed from the matrimonial arrangements of earlier generations. In the same way the marriage alliances of members of the two groups served to integrate the county communities ever more completely. At Macclesfield, John Donne, William Brereton, Adam Bostock and John Poole were all accompanied by sons-in-law, while at Lancaster Richard Hoghton was attended by his daughter's husband, John Southworth. Even larger numbers were related as brothers-in-law. Among the Lancashire group, Thomas Tunstall, John Stanley and Richard Shirebourne were all brothers-in-law of William Harrington, while Robert Halsall and Gilbert Barton stood in the same relation to Henry Scarisbrick. Then there were the numerous pairs of gentlemen united by the marriages of their children. In Cheshire, William Stanley was linked in this way to John Poole, Robert Legh and William Venables, while north of the Mersey the sons of William Atherton and Henry Scarisbrick were married to daughters of John Pilkington, and the son of Nicholas Butler and the daughter of William Harrington were wedded to children of William Butler.

Intermarriage among the gentry class represented far more than the union of individuals. It established a whole new network of relations between the families involved, and parents usually began the delicate task of arranging suitable matches long before their children reached adulthood. Ralph Standish was betrothed as a child to a member of the Bradshaw family, and the agreement of 1359 bears witness to the hardheaded practicality of the parties concerned. William Bradshaw's grandfather had bound himself 'to plough, sow and successfully harvest' the lands settled on the young couple, to supply them with eight oxen, ten cows and other livestock, and to furnish them with household goods and utensils worth £10.[21] Ralph Standish was one of the oldest men in the Lancashire group, but the arrangements of his younger colleagues were equally lacking in sentiment. Inevitably the connections of the father, rather than the inclinations of the child, determined the course of matrimony. Thus in 1413 Hugh Davenport betrothed his daughter to a Davenport of Calveley, but the girl's name was left blank in the contract, presumably to be filled in when it was decided which daughter would have the marriage.[22] Nor

---

[20] Dispensations were frequently obtained for consanguineous marriages. E.g. in 1398 William Leicester received a licence to marry his fourth cousin, the sister of Hugh Dutton: Cheshire R.O., DLT, deed A5.   [21] *Standish Deeds*, no. 74.

[22] J.R.U.L., Bromley-Davenport Muniments, Calveley deed 'e'.

could the feelings of the couple have been consulted in a covenant of 1407 in which John Cholmondeley betrothed his grandson to 'one of the daughters' of John Legh of Booths.[23] The business of finding suitable matches for a house full of daughters was irksome, and the local gentry depended on each other to alleviate an onerous parental chore.

Marriage without disparagement was the basic principle of match-making and, if there were variation in status and wealth, imbalances could be remedied in the contract. Accordingly marriages among the gentry took the form of complex business transactions. The right to arrange the marriage of an heir or heiress was a valuable feudal perquisite, and had long since become a marketable commodity. In 1394 Randle Mainwaring purchased the marriage and wardship of Richard Bulkeley for £230, while in 1417 Robert Lawrence paid £100 for the marriage of the orphaned heir of Nicholas Hesketh.[24] Nor were the mercenary concerns of the speculator in wardships so markedly different from the attitudes of the parent. The wording of the marriage covenants is significant in this respect. It was common for the father to 'grant' the marriage of his son in return for a financial consideration. Often the grantee was the father of the intended bride and the payment constituted her dowry, but the tone of the transaction remains significant. The amounts varied con-siderably. In Cheshire Sir Thomas Grosvenor gained 400 marks for the marriage of his heir, while Thomas Danyers received only 20 marks for the marriage of his first-born.[25] In south Lancashire Henry Scarisbrick's father was willing to pay 100 marks for the marriage of Gilbert Barton in 1397, and 200·marks for the marriage of Robert Halsall in 1405.[26]

Intermarriage necessarily involved commitments from both households. Whereas the family of the bride had to raise a dowry, the family of the groom had to provide landed income to maintain the new household. Marriage covenants usually stipulated that a certain amount of property should be settled on the couple in joint tenure. Thus in the agreements of 1397 and 1405 the Barton and Halsall families offered jointures worth 10 marks and £10 respectively in their alliances with the Scarisbricks. More spectacularly, in his alliance with the Standish family Sir William Butler settled a third of his valuable Warrington estate on himself and his new wife jointly.[27] The wife's claims on her husband's lands did not

[23] Keele University Library, Legh of Booths Charters, no. 54.
[24] *C.P.R. 1391–1396*, p. 507; Manchester Central Reference Library, Farrer MSS., 47/1/5, Hesketh deed H434.
[25] Cheshire R.O., DLT, deed A8; J.R.U.L., Rylands Charters, R62414/904–5.
[26] Lancashire R.O., DDSc/43a/132 and 141.
[27] Warrington Municipal Library, Bold Deeds, no. 544.

end with the jointure, however, and if she were left a widow a third of the estate was automatically assigned as dower. In 1413 the mother of Nicholas Hesketh was still in possession of a third of his patrimony, for in that year she leased her dower lands to him for £22.[28] The widowed mother of Henry Scarisbrick similarly occupied a third part of the inheritance until well after the son's own death.[29] A subsequent marriage by the dowager could further confuse the situation. When William Bradshaw's mother remarried, she brought not only her own dower lands, but effective control of the entire estate into the hands of Sir John Pilkington. Manifestly, when such property interests were at stake, the connubial connections of the local gentry could easily become too close for material comfort.

Marriage alliances inevitably occasioned a great deal of interaction within the two county communities. At the betrothal, arrangements were commonly made for the domicile of the couple until they came of age. In 1403 Randle Mainwaring agreed to maintain the son of Ralph Davenport as well as his own daughter until they reached twenty years of age.[30] Sir John Poole agreed 'for to fynde the same John of Legh and his wif and a man and two horses mete and drynke two yer next suwyng when the forsaide John of Legh wol come to the hous of the same John of Pulle after the spoucesaile'.[31] Since alliances were often contracted at a tender age, there was always the chance that one of the parties might die or repudiate the betrothal before the actual marriage. In most covenants provision was made for such eventualities, and bonds were entered into to abide the terms of the agreement. In 1411 Randle Mainwaring, with the help of five others of the Cheshire sample, bound himself in £200 to keep faith with Ralph Davenport.[32] Similarly in the agreement between Sir John Pilkington and Henry Scarisbrick in 1406, William Bradshaw, Gilbert Barton and Robert Halsall stood as guarantors.[33] In such a situation it was advantageous to make alliances with families of solid repute and, preferably, with whom regular relations were already established.

The county community thus formed the natural framework for the matrimonial arrangements of the local gentry, and it is hardly surprising to find that the vast majority of alliances were concluded within a single shire. In its turn, the development of an extended network of kinship was

[28] Manchester Central Reference Library, Farrer MSS., 51/10/1, Hesketh deed (additional) 8.

[29] Lancashire R.O., DDSc/43a/153.     [30] J.R.U.L., Mainwaring MSS., deed 203.

[31] J.R.U.L., Cornwall Legh MSS., deed 75.

[32] J.R.U.L., Bromley-Davenport Muniments, Davenport deed 6.

[33] Lancashire R.O., DDSc/28/5–7.

a major factor in the integration of county society. After all, the bonds of affinity established by marriage often outlasted the lives of the couple originally concerned. The descent of property kept men keenly aware of their genealogical connections, and family relationships could breed fierce antagonisms as often as brotherly love. The disputes between Grosvenor and Legh in 1412, and between Gerard, Langton and Standish in 1414, had their origins in such wrangles. Then there were problems of conjugal compatibility and family honour. The experience of William Butler's first marriage cannot have been wholly unusual. In the 1390s he 'toke to wife and weddyt' a daughter of Henry Hoghton, but after living together for a season the couple 'cowthen kyndely accorde in so muche that [William] avoydet the sayd gentillwoman from hym, and after that as hit was supposit with awten any lawfull particion hade betywene thaym' he took another wife.[34] It is a measure of the resilience of the county community that such potentially divisive incidents could be satisfactorily resolved, but it is noteworthy that in his subsequent marriage Butler had to make over a third of his estate as jointure, and that the grant was witnessed by a whole array of local notables including Thomas Gerard, William Atherton, Nicholas Atherton, John Bold and John Southworth.[35]

Given these sorts of problems, it would be naive to regard kinship and affinity among the Cheshire and Lancashire gentry as sure indicators of factional allegiance. The role of family relationships in such close communities must be conceived in more general terms. To many local gentlemen association with kinsmen and affines was a source of profit and strength; to many others it was a source of enmity and waste. For better and for worse, however, it brought into close personal contact lineages of similar standing from all corners of the shire. The family ties of the local gentry, probably more than any other single factor, made the two counties of the Northwest face-to-face communities.

### III

Though most also bore the title of knight or squire, all the men taking part in the ceremonies at Macclesfield and Lancaster were acknowledged to be gentlemen. Despite gradations of rank and differences of wealth, it is fitting as well as convenient to group them together as 'gentry'. The remarkable reordering of the upper strata of English society which brought forth this celebrated social grouping was indeed well advanced by the early fifteenth century. Lacking the power and prestige of the

---

[34] W. Beamont, *Annals of Warrington* (2 vols., C.S., o.s. 86, 87, 1872–3), II, pp. 250–1.
[35] Warrington Municipal Library, Bold Deeds, no. 544.

magnates of the realm, and increasingly diffident about their own status as nobles, knights in the provinces had clung to the concept of gentility. At the same time the ranks of the gentry had been swollen by many lesser men who had the means to bear arms and hold office in the shire. By the period under discussion the gentle-born were set apart as a small and readily identifiable governing élite, and the distinction between 'gentle' and 'common' was the crucial divide in county society. Though the term has some connotations inappropriate to this age, the gentry of late medieval England can be usefully regarded as a distinctive social class.[36] Obviously the possession of landed estate was the material basis of their class identity, and in this section it is intended to discuss the role of property in engendering interaction and reciprocity among the gentry of the Northwest.

The proprietorship of large estates inevitably involved whole networks of social relations. Many of the gentlemen in the two samples were neighbours, who regularly interacted on matters of mutual concern. Sir Thomas Gerard and Sir William Atherton held moieties of the manor of Ashton in Makerfield, and must have acted in concert in matters regarding the administration of the vill. Henry Scarisbrick and Robert Halsall held the adjacent manors of Scarisbrick and Halsall, and in 1397 the two families collaborated in the consolidation of their separate demesnes.[37] Unfortunately the practical, working arrangements made by landlords were seldom recorded. Only when customary practices failed were formal settlements found necessary, as in 1411 when David Crewe secured permission from his neighbours to control the stream feeding his mill.[38] Other local gentlemen stood in social relation as lords and tenants. Among the Lancashire men who owed suit to Sir William Butler's honorial court at Warrington were Sir William Atherton, Sir John Bold, Sir Richard Keighley, Sir Thomas Gerard, Robert Halsall, Hamo Mascy, William Bradshaw, Henry Scarisbrick and Richard Radcliffe of Radcliffe. Even if the significance of feudal relationships had declined considerably by this time, homage had still to be performed, services personally rendered, rents paid, and wardship occasionally exacted, all providing additional occasions for social intercourse.

The disposition of landed estate, in particular, demanded close co-operation between local gentry families. It has been noted how a purely private property settlement drew over sixty gentlemen to Macclesfield in

---

[36] P. Laslett, *The World We Have Lost* (London, 1965), pp. 22–3. For a thorough assessment of the origins of the gentry class see N. Saul, *Knights and Esquires. The Gloucestershire Gentry in the Fourteenth Century* (Oxford, 1981), pp. 6–29.

[37] Lancashire R.O., DDSc/43a/130.      [38] Cheshire R.O., DMW/105.

1412, and it would be possible to document innumerable other similar, if more modest gatherings from local muniment collections. A property arrangement of some consequence, like the release by William Venables to his nephew, Hugh Venables of all rights in the Kinderton estate in 1407, was witnessed by a whole array of Cheshire notables.[39] Meanwhile a lease by Henry Langton in 1412 was attested by Sir William Butler, Sir Gilbert Haydock and Ralph Standish.[40] Likewise local gentlemen exchanged services as trustees in property settlements. Thus Sir Thomas Grosvenor was granted the lands of a member of the Venables family around 1410, to be held in trust after the grantor's death for specific purposes: for the first ten years the profits of the estate were to be used to make bequests and to pay for masses, and then the lands were to be bestowed on younger sons of Thomas Grosvenor or Hugh Venables.[41] In Lancashire, Sir Richard Keighley similarly granted his patrimony in trust to Thomas Bradshaw of Haigh at the end of Richard II's reign.[42]

It might seem strange that the gentry of the Northwest should continually have to involve themselves in the affairs of their neighbours, attesting the authenticity of deeds and conniving in legal fictions. In the later middle ages it was a necessary feature of life. Facilities for the official registration of property transactions were inordinately expensive, while the rigidities of the land law made grants in trust virtually indispensable. In such circumstances it was natural to call on the services of neighbouring gentlemen, and to reciprocate these services in turn. If disputes arose, these were the men whose testimony would in any case be called. In a Lancashire suit involving Richard Radcliffe of Radcliffe, Robert Holt and others in 1410, the assize included William Butler, William Atherton, Nicholas Atherton, Hamo Mascy, Henry Scarisbrick, Thurstan Holland and Gilbert Barton.[43] In addition local gentlemen could normally be relied upon to act faithfully as witnesses and trustees. If their mere word seemed insufficient, bonds might be entered as additional security.

The network of trust and co-operation among the various lineages was inevitably fragile. Friction was endemic in communities in which property interests were so completely entangled. Yet even conflict could serve as an agent of social cohesion. In an extremely litigious age the good offices of neighbours were in constant demand, not only as jurors but also as guarantors. Arraigned on a murder charge in 1400, Nicholas Atherton had

---

[39] Cheshire R.O., DVE/K/28.

[40] J.R.U.L., Legh of Lyme Muniments, M/2/31.

[41] Eaton Hall, Chester, Eaton Charters, no. 380.

[42] *Lancashire Inquisitions*, ed. W. Langton (2 vols., C.S., o.s. 95, 99, 1875–6), I, p. 116.

[43] Lancashire R.O., DDIb (unclassified).

to call on Thomas Gerard and Ralph Standish to stand bail.[44] In quarrels likely to generate violence large sums had to be pledged that the contending parties would keep the peace. In the feud between John Donne and the son of Sir William Stanley which raged from 1414 to 1416 a whole succession of Cheshire gentlemen stood as guarantors of their peaceable behaviour, including Sir Lawrence Fitton, Sir John Poole, John Whitmore, Roger Mullington, Richard Warburton, John Kingsley, Ralph Bostock, Hugh Dutton and six other members of the sample.[45]

While local gentlemen were clearly no strangers to the law courts, it was more convenient and far less expensive to settle disputes informally. To this end the services of other landowners were often called on for out-of-court settlements. Thus the disputes between Langton, Gerard and Standish in 1414 occasioned the involvement of several local arbiters. Similarly late in Richard II's reign a boundary dispute between the prior of Burscough and the Scarisbricks was put to the arbitration of John Bold, Hugh Standish and others, while the final settlement was attested by Sir Richard Hoghton, Sir Thomas Gerard and Nicholas Atherton.[46] Meanwhile in 1408 panels of local gentlemen were established to adjudicate 'all actions pending between' William Venables and Sir William Stanley.[47] Significantly at this stage the region had no great aristocratic lineage to take the lead in the informal resolution of discord. The manner in which the local gentry responded to the insecurities of life and the inadequacies of the legal system is therefore of particular interest. For most of this period at least they do not seem to have sought protection in the retinue of a powerful patron. Rather their system was one of mutual credit and collective security in which no single lineage predominated. Leadership in Cheshire and Lancashire society was vested in two tightly-knit oligarchies and this system of social control was perhaps as typical a feature of English society at this time as the more notorious system of 'bastard feudalism'.[48]

IV

The involvement of the Cheshire and Lancashire gentry in local politics is also well-evidenced. Until comparatively recent times English governments were almost entirely dependent on the unpaid services of the landed gentry. Their qualifications for the tasks of local administration were

[44] *Lancashire Palatine Plea Rolls*, ed. J. Parker (C.S., n.s. 87, 1928), p. 59.
[45] *Ches. R.R.* II, p. 209.
[46] Lancashire R.O., DDSc/43a/133.
[47] P.R.O., CHES 2/80, mm. 8, 3d.
[48] Of course, the Stanleys of Lathom were laying the foundations of their future regional hegemony during this period: see below, Chapter 10.

obvious. They alone combined a detailed knowledge of conditions in the provinces with the wealth and leisure to perform governmental chores with a modicum of efficiency and impartiality. In this section it is intended to show some of the ways in which the government drew on the services of members of the county communities, and in the process occasioned further collaboration among local gentlemen.

The gentry never completely monopolised the office of the county administration. In the upper echelons there were always a few persons of national consequence involved in local government. The justiciar of Chester, the earl's personal representative in the palatinate, was usually a nobleman, though local knights and lawyers like Henry Birtles and James Holt commonly served as deputies and justices *una vice*.[49] The chief justice at Lancaster and the chancellor of the county palatine were likewise usually lawyers and clerks of national standing. Meanwhile in the lower ranks there were full-time clerical officers to deal with the more routine tasks. Yet even the professionals remained hopelessly dependent on the local knowledge and connections of the gentry. Thus in the inquisition *post mortem* of Hugh Venables in 1415 it was a jury consisting of Sir William Brereton, Sir John Poole, John Donne and others which furnished the information necessary for the proper performance of the escheator's duties.[50]

Many other important offices remained firmly in the hands of local families. The five sheriffs of Cheshire between 1408 and 1427 were Sir William Brereton, Sir Lawrence Merbury, John Legh of Booths, Hugh Dutton and Richard Warburton.[51] Likewise Sir Richard Hoghton, Sir Thomas Gerard, Sir John Bold, Sir Nicholas Longford, Sir Robert Urswick, Sir Richard Radcliffe of Radcliffe and Sir Robert Lawrence all served as sheriffs of Lancashire during this period.[52] Matthew Mere and Richard Manley, between them, held the office of escheator in Cheshire for most of Henry IV's reign, while Robert Halsall and William Bradshaw acted in the same capacity in Lancashire in Henry V's reign.[53] Other administrative posts in the region were shared among the gentry, some on a more or less hereditary basis. Sir Richard Hoghton was chief steward and Ralph Radcliffe was receiver of the duchy of Lancaster estates in the region, while Sir Henry Hoghton and Sir Thomas Tunstall were the stewards of the hundreds of Blackburn, Amounderness and Lonsdale.[54] Sir William Stanley was steward of Halton, while William Venables was

[49] *Ches. R.R.*, I, p. 38; II, p. 375.
[50] P.R.O., CHES 3/28 (1).　　　　　　[51] P.R.O., CHES 19/3–5.
[52] R. Somerville, *History of the Duchy of Lancaster*, part I (London, 1953), pp. 461–2.
[53] *Ches. R.R.*, I, p. 38; Somerville, *Duchy of Lancaster*, p. 465.
[54] *Ibid.*, pp. 499–500.

constable of Chester Castle.[55] Sir Robert Urswick was master forester of Amounderness, John Donne forester of Delamere, and Ralph Davenport serjeant of the peace in the hundred of Macclesfield.[56] All these positions of public responsibility involved interaction with many other families. In the space of a few years as sheriff or escheator, for example, a gentleman would have acquainted himself with the business of every major landlord of his county.

Furthermore, these permanent positions represent only a fraction of the administrative load borne by the gentry families of the Northwest. More significant socially were the numerous *ad hoc* commissions instituted from time to time to deal with specific problems. In the period between 1416 and 1418, for example, three Cheshire commissions were appointed to levy subsidies. Among those chosen as commissioners were Sir Thomas Grosvenor, Sir William Brereton, Sir Lawrence Fitton, Sir William Stanley and nineteen others from the present sample.[57] Similarly in 1419 Henry V appointed a commission which included Sir Robert Urswick, Sir Henry Hoghton, Sir John Stanley, Robert Lawrence and Ralph Standish to arrange a loan from the Lancashire community.[58] Manifestly the collection of subsidies involved both close contact with the persons liable for assessment and a certain measure of trust and co-operation between the members of the commission.[59]

Commissions of array, on the other hand, turned the knights and gentlemen of the shire into brotherhoods-in-arms. In 1402 a Lancashire commission to raise an army against Owain Glyndŵr included Sir Richard Hoghton, Sir Thomas Southworth, Ralph Standish, Robert Lawrence and Richard Radcliffe.[60] In the years 1404 and 1406 two such commissions were instituted in Cheshire, and some twenty-four of the present sample served on them.[61] In the latter case the commissioners were specifically required to lead their levies to the Welsh border. Nor was Wales the limit of the common military experience of the local gentry. As early as the 1390s members of the two samples can be found serving together under John Stanley's father in Ireland.[62] In 1399 Sir John Poole, Lawrence Fitton, William Stanley, Thomas Grosvenor, William Brereton and Philip

---

[55] *Ibid.*, p. 510; *Ches. R.R.*, I, p. 90.

[56] Somerville, *Duchy of Lancaster*, p. 506; *Ches. R.R.*, I, p. 155; II, p. 493.

[57] P.R.O., CHES 2/89, m. 6; CHES 2/90, m. 6; CHES 2/91, m. 6.

[58] *C.P.R. 1416–1422*, p. 252.

[59] A mise-book dating from 1406 contains a list of the sums due from each vill, with the initials of one of the commissioners alongside each entry: J.R.U.L., Tatton MSS., no. 345.

[60] *La. P.R.*, p. 531.

[61] P.R.O., CHES 2/77, m. 4d; CHES 2/78, mm. 2, 4.

[62] E.g. Henry Hoghton, William Stanley and John Bold: P.R.O., E 101/247/1, E 101/41/18.

Egerton were among those leading Cheshire archers in Richard II's last Irish expedition.[63] A campaign on the Scottish border in 1400 involved large contingents of knights and archers from the Northwest. The commissioners of array for Lancashire included Butler, Hoghton, Tunstall, Atherton, Southworth, Lawrence and others from the sample, while the Cheshire levies were officered by fifteen of the gentlemen from the Macclesfield group.[64] In the years after the gatherings of 1412 and 1414 many local gentlemen saw active service together in France. Among those present on the Agincourt campaign were at least nine knights and fourteen gentlemen from the two groupings. Meanwhile Butler, Southworth, Robert Legh and Ralph Davenport were casualties at the siege of Harfleur.[65]

Military adventures in distant lands inevitably assisted the development of an *esprit de corps* within each county community. In both palatinates this sense of corporate identity was in any case already well-established. The earldom of Chester, in particular, had a virtually independent position within the kingdom, possessing its own separate chancery, exchequer and judicature which, housed in Chester castle, represented in miniature those institutions at Westminster.[66] In the middle ages it did not send representatives to parliament and accordingly remained exempt from national taxation. The mise of Chester was a customary levy, raised each time the earldom changed hands. If further subsidies were to be raised, the consent of the county community was sought. In 1389 two knights represented the shire in treating with the king concerning a subsidy of 3,000 marks.[67] In 1436 twenty-nine gentlemen, including the aged Sir Lawrence Fitton, Randle Mainwaring, Hugh Dutton, John Donne, Henry Spurstow, Thomas Starkey, Lawrence Warren, John Kingsley and Robert Davenport, were summoned to the royal council at Chester to discuss various matters and especially the granting of a subsidy 'in the name of the whole commonalty of Chester'.[68] The county court, when suitably afforced by the presence of the earl and local notables, could assume parliamentary status.

The franchisal privileges of the county palatine of Lancaster were neither as extensive nor as well-entrenched as those of its neighbour. Indeed palatine status seems to have added little to the liberties of the shire. Yet

[63] P.R.O., CHES 2/73, m. 2.

[64] *La. P.R.*, p. 528; *Cheshire Sheaf*, third series, item 4302.

[65] N. H. Nicolas, *History of the Battle of Agincourt and the Expedition of Henry the Fifth into France* (London, 1832), *passim*.

[66] See M. Sharp, 'Contributions to the history of the earldom and county of Chester, 1237–1399', unpublished Ph.D. thesis, University of Manchester, 1925.

[67] *Ches. R.R.*, I, p. 96.          [68] *Ches. R.R.*, II, p. 671.

a number of factors still made Lancashire society more cohesive politically than the average county. With an independent chancery, exchequer and judicial system Lancashire was far more self-contained institutionally than most other shires. At the same time its physical remoteness, its homogeneity as a feudal unit, and its direct relationship with its royal lords, all contributed to its political identity. Unlike their neighbours, however, Lancashire men were not exempt from national taxation, and were required to send representatives to parliament. Whether or not knights of the shire were actually elected in any genuine sense at the county court, parliamentary representation remained an important facet of the shire's corporate life. Even if the knights of the shire were often the nominees of the duke of Lancaster, the local gentry assembled to go through the forms of election, and doubtless to make their feelings known to the candidates.[69] The knights chosen to represent the shire were almost always prominent members of the county community. Robert Lawrence and John Stanley, the members elected in 1414, were by no means the only gentlemen in the gathering to serve in this fashion. Sir Richard Hoghton and Sir Thomas Gerard were veteran parliamentarians from the 1380s, while Sir Henry Hoghton, Sir Robert Urswick, Sir Nicholas Atherton, Sir William Butler and Sir Richard Radcliffe of Winmarleigh had also earlier served as members of parliament. Several more, including Nicholas Butler, Richard Shirebourne and Richard Radcliffe of Radcliffe, were to gain parliamentary experience in the following decades.[70] In the representation of the opinions of their fellow-countrymen, and in the dissemination of information on their return to the Northwest, these men at least would have developed a keen sense of the political identity of their county community.

Undoubtedly the most dramatic phase in the formation of a collective political consciousness in the two county communities was the decade spanning the end of the fourteenth and beginning of the fifteenth centuries.[71] During the last years of his reign Richard II embarked on a deliberate policy of building his earldom of Chester into a veritable bastion of royal authority. The elevation in status to the principality of Chester

---

[69] See H. G. Richardson, 'John of Gaunt and the parliamentary representation of Lancashire', *B.J.R.L.*, 22 (1938), 175–222.

[70] Roskell, *Lancashire Knights, passim.*

[71] See in general R. R. Davies, 'Richard II and the principality of Chester 1397–9' in F. R. H. du Boulay and C. M. Barron (eds.), *The Reign of Richard II. Essays in Honour of May McKisack* (London, 1971), pp. 256–79, and A. L. Brown, 'The reign of Henry IV. The establishment of the Lancastrian regime' in S. B. Chrimes, C. D. Ross and R. A. Griffiths (eds.), *Fifteenth-Century England. Studies in Politics and Society* (Manchester, 1972), pp. 1–28.

in 1397 was symbolic of the high favour he showed to the people of the shire in more material ways. By 1399 the position of Richard II's Cheshire favourites had become so invidious that, according to one contemporary chronicler, 'the whole kingdom cried vengeance on them'.[72] The usurpation of Henry IV in that year inevitably changed the situation. The men of Cheshire lost many of the offices and annuities bounteously bestowed by the old king, and there was even an attempt to curtail the ancient privileges of the palatinate. At the same time, in building up his own political power-base, Henry IV showed great favour to his tenants from the duchy of Lancaster. During his reign, Lancashire men were almost as successful as their Cheshire neighbours under Richard II in obtaining access to royal patronage. Superficially at least the change of dynasty in 1399 brought about a dramatic reversal in the political fortunes of the two counties. The restless condition of Cheshire, with its abortive rising in 1400 and its participation in the Percys' revolt of 1403, certainly suggests that the local gentry acutely felt the eclipse of royal favour. Meanwhile the new king's Lancashire retainers rallied to the crown in these troubled years, and it is not entirely fanciful to picture the two county communities on opposite sides of the field at Shrewsbury.

The decade spanning the end of the fourteenth and beginning of the fifteenth centuries was well within the living memories of the gentlemen in both samples. The Cheshire men had spent their formative years in this dramatic phase of the county's history. The youthful Ralph Davenport, John Donne, Adam Bostock and John Legh of Booths had been retained by Richard II with annuities ranging from £5 to £20 and had risen to become commanders of four of the seven *vigiliae* into which the royal bodyguard was divided. Similarly Sir John Poole, Sir William Stanley, Sir William Brereton and eight others from the sample were retained with substantial fees, while several more occur among the names listed as *sagittarii de corona*.[73] Although there was no determined resistance to Bolingbroke's advance across England in 1399, no more than a few Cheshire men deserted the king at this time. Outflanked by the Lancastrians' seizure of the city of Chester, and with the Cheshire bodyguard stranded in Ireland or South Wales, the loyalists in the region had to bide their time. Involved in the rising of 1400, planned to coincide with the conspiracy of the three earls, were many of the old king's local retainers, including Donne, Legh of Booths and Robert Davenport.[74]

[72] *Chronicon Adae Usk*, ed. E. M. Thompson (London, 1904), p. 26.
[73] P.R.O., E 101/41/10; *Ches. R.R.*, I, pp. 154, 138, 45, 292, 385, 495, 54, 128, 273, 523, 472; Cheshire R.O., DDA/1533/31/2; *Ches. R.R.*, I, pp. 73, 505, 531, 223.
[74] *C.P.R. 1399–1401*, p. 295.

Even more serious was the county's contribution to the Percys' rebellion of 1403, and among the local rebels who survived the defeat at Shrewsbury were Sir Thomas Grosvenor, Poole, Stanley, Sir Lawrence Fitton, John Kingsley, Robert Toft, Donne, Legh and Bostock.[75] Even as late as 1406 Kingsley could still be accused of spreading the rumour that Richard II was in Scotland, 'as well and as prosperous as he ever was', and of conspiring to kill Henry IV and the prince of Wales.[76]

Most of the members of the Lancashire sample, on the other hand, found the change of dynasty congenial to their interests. The high proportion of knights in the county in 1414 is perhaps an indication of the favour already shown to the gentlemen of the palatinate. A sizeable Lancashire contingent joined Bolingbroke soon after his landing in 1399, and Sir Richard Hoghton, Sir William Butler, Robert Lawrence and Robert Urswick were retained by the new king as early as November of that year.[77] During the following years some twenty-one of the thirty-eight in the sample were retained, for in 1405 letters were sent requiring them to join the royal host at Worcester.[78] Undoubtedly most of the retainers fought with the king at Shrewsbury, and Sir Nicholas Atherton and Ralph Standish were among the many Lancashire men rewarded with grants of rebels' lands.[79] Sir William Atherton, Sir Thomas Gerard, Sir Thomas Tunstall, Sir Henry Hoghton, Sir John Southworth, Standish, Richard Radcliffe and Lawrence were likewise probably in close attendance, for a few days after the battle they were appointed to raise more troops in Lancashire against the earl of Northumberland.[80] Many other Lancashire men, like Sir John Bold and Henry Scarisbrick, held military commands in the Marches during the troubled period of Glyndŵr's and the Percys' revolt.[81]

Thus the collective involvement of the local gentry ranges across the whole spectrum of political activities. From the routine tasks of administration to the pursuit of military glories overseas, the gentry of the region shared in the public responsibilities of their class. From being the most loyal and favoured of the king's subjects, the leaders of the local communities could also turn to taste the heady water of rebellion. Manifestly all these activities, and not least the staging of an armed uprising, demanded the existence of a framework of trust, consensus, and

[75] *C.P.R. 1401–1405*, pp. 256, 253, 331, 264–5. For a detailed assessment see P. McNiven, 'The men of Cheshire and the rebellion of 1403', *L.C.H.S.*, 129 (1979), 1–29.

[76] P.R.O., CHES 25/10, m. 34.

[77] P.R.O., DL 42/15, ff. 7d, 8, 6, 13d.   [78] P.R.O., DL 42/16, f. 128.

[79] *C.P.R. 1401–1405*, pp. 252, 247.   [80] *Ibid.*, p. 292.

[81] *Royal Historical Letters during the Reign of Henry the Fourth*, ed. F. C. Hingeston (2 vols., R.S., 1860, 1865), II, pp. 22–4.

co-operation. The very real differences which on occasion divided members of each county community cannot of course be glossed over. Competition for office, rivalry in the field and differing allegiances could always split the county élites into hostile factions. Neither the Cheshire nor the Lancashire gentry were entirely homogeneous in their political loyalties, and it is salutary to note that two of the latter, namely Hamo Mascy of Rixton and Thomas Bradshaw of Haigh, joined the rebellion of 1403.[82] It is clear, however, that both county communities were sufficiently flexible to provide the framework for a wide range of political and administrative operations, and sufficiently resilient to accommodate fruitfully such potentially divisive elements.

By the detailed analysis of two social occasions – the settlement of a property dispute at Macclesfield in 1412 and the election of knights of the shire at Lancaster in 1414 – it has been possible to document some of the complex networks of relationship operating among both the Cheshire and Lancashire gentry. Sustained by the solidarities of kinship and class as well as by its corporate status and collective responsibilities in the realm at large, the county community was manifestly a social unit of immense utility, both at a personal and institutional level. Within its ambit a wide range of social needs could be satisfactorily met, and each form of collective activity in turn served to reinforce the overall solidarity of the group. The social lives of Cheshire and Lancashire gentlemen were strikingly unspecialised and unfragmented: individuals associated with each other not merely in one, but in a whole variety of capacities. This made the county community a face-to-face society of considerable cohesiveness. Even though their association was completely informal, its members were readily identifiable not only within the shire but also at a governmental level. Indeed through the county community a new chain of personal connection was established between the king and his subjects. In the absence of a magnate of real stature in the Northwest at this stage, the county community was the medium through which chains of connection could be established between the royal household and the lesser gentry. Later in the fifteenth century the rising house of Stanley proved more effective brokers between court and country, and took on many of the other functions of the county community. Like their counterparts in other parts of the realm, the two gentry oligarchies were to be split asunder and submerged in the swelling tide of aristocratic clientage.

[82] *C.P.R. 1401–1405*, pp. 258, 256.

*Chapter 3*

# LESSER SOLIDARITIES

The larger units in the social geography of the Northwest provided the frameworks within which the wealthier and more mobile sections of the population operated. The social horizons of other groups and classes were necessarily far more closely circumscribed. While peasants from all over the region shared common dialect-forms, cultural traditions and economic conditions, and while villagers from different parts of the shire doubtless felt some degree of solidarity, to a large extent their lives were lived out within far smaller units. In the following sections it is intended to identify, and to assess the significance of, some of these lesser communities in the Northwest.

I

Even for the gentry class involvement in communities of the size of the shire could never have been total. For many local lineages the towns of Chester and Lancaster were a hard day's ride from their homes, and frequent intercourse with neighbours of similar rank tended to be the pattern. Such observations have even greater relevance for the lower orders, and not merely the peasantry. Despite their attendance at the county courts and their occasional involvement in the wider community, the social worlds of the lesser gentry and yeomanry could be surprisingly small. Marriage alliances and other relationships were often confined to the immediate locality, and contact with the county community mediated through a more powerful neighbour. John Snelson of Snelson, Thomas Starkey of Wrenbury, Thomas Cotton of Cotton and the many other lesser gentry who were accepting the liveries of Randle Mainwaring early in the reign of Henry VI were men of this sort.[1] Nor did the lesser gentry and yeomanry of the Northwest lack convenient frameworks within which to interact. Just as the demands of county administration gave shape and consistency to the social life of the leading lineages, so the solidarities

---

[1] P.R.O., CHES 29/133, m. 37. Starkey and Cotton were with Mainwaring at Macclesfield in 1412.

of men of lesser rank were patterned on the smaller units of administrative, feudal and ecclesiastical geography.

In the Northwest the most important sub-division of the shire was the hundred or wapentake, of which there were thirteen: Broxton, Nantwich, Northwich, Macclesfield, Bucklow, Edisbury and Wirral in Cheshire, and West Derby, Salford, Blackburn, Leyland, Amounderness and Lonsdale in Lancashire. While the hundreds had lost much of their earlier importance by the fourteenth century, and while some were highly artificial in geographical terms, these ancient divisions were still of consequence in the organisation of local life.[2] Given the palatinate status of Cheshire and Lancashire, and the consequent devolution of government, the hundreds assumed even greater administrative significance in the region than in most other parts of the kingdom. In addition to the customary bailiff and his subordinates, each hundred had its own coroner to keep pleas of the crown until the next eyre. In terms of judicial competence the hundred court in Cheshire was in some respects the functional equivalent of the county court elsewhere: it received justices in eyre, though from Chester rather than from Westminster. Such sessions were attended by many local notables, as were the courts assembled for the sheriff's tourn. In the latter meetings presentments were made by panels of twelve freeholders, many of whom were gentlemen. The new judicial and administrative procedures developed during this period continued to find the hundredal framework useful. When county commissions were established for arraying an army, levying a subsidy, restoring law-and-order or whatever, responsibilities were always divided on a hundredal basis.[3] In Cheshire each hundred paid a fixed proportion of the mise, while in Lancashire the hundred also served as the unit for taxation, even in the feudal aid of 1431.[4] Similarly in the arraying of an army the men of each hundred were summoned to some convenient centre where the commissioners could select the fittest soldiers. Even on campaign the Cheshire levies seem to have been organised on a hundredal basis, and it is perhaps significant that Richard II's bodyguard was divided into seven *vigiliae*, matching the number of hundreds in the county.[5]

2  In general see H. M. Jewell, *English Local Administration in the Middle Ages* (Newton Abbot, 1972). More specifically, see Sharp, 'Earldom of Chester'; G. H. Tupling, 'The royal and seignorial bailiffs of Lancashire in the thirteenth and fourteenth centuries' in *Chetham Miscellanies*, new series VIII (C.S., n.s. 109, 1945); R. B. Smith, *Blackburnshire. A Study in Early Lancashire History* (University of Leicester, Department of English Local History, Occasional Papers no. 15, 1961).

3  E.g. the various commissions instituted in Broxton hundred in 1392, 1398, 1399, 1400, 1402, 1403, 1406, 1416, 1417, 1418: *Ches. R.R.*, I, pp. 63, 101; II, p. 94.

4  J.R.U.L., Tatton MSS., no. 345; *Feudal Aids* (6 vols., H.M.S.O., 1899–1920), II, pp. 92–6.

5  P.R.O., E 101/42/10. Since the bodyguard was recruited from the Cheshire levies raised in August 1397, it is possible that the seven *vigiliae* evolved from the seven hundredal units,

The structure of local government not only provided occasions for social contact between men of a particular hundred but also imposed collective responsibilities on the entire community. Thus the gentlemen and other freeholders of the hundred were compelled to develop a corporate identity. Though the evidence is more limited, the lesser gentry and yeomanry of the hundred, like their more illustrious neighbours at the county level, tended through the arrangement of marriages and the exchange of services to interact as a community. The twelve jurymen from the sheriff's tourn at Bucklow in 1425 constitute a useful sample: Geoffrey Mascy, John son of Richard Legh, William Holford, Roger Mullington, Thomas Legh of Northwood, John Domville, Richard Ashton, Richard Cocker, John Stathum, John Danyers of Grimsditch, Hugh Huet and Richard Whitington can all be traced acting together in various other contexts.[6] A grant by Thomas Legh in 1420 was witnessed by John son of Richard Legh, Whitington and others.[7] In 1435, in a dispute involving John son of Richard Legh, Ashton and Stathum acted as sureties that he would accept the arbitration of Domville, Thomas Legh, Mullington, Danyers and others.[8] Hundredal units of considerable antiquity, like Blackburnshire, or with natural boundaries, like Wirral or Amounderness, were doubtless even better integrated as communities than the more recent and artificial divisions like Bucklow. Whatever governmental needs it served, the community of the hundred was always something more than the product of administrative convenience. In both Cheshire and Lancashire the communities of various hundreds can be found taking positive action in the assertion of their rights or the defence of their interests. During the reign of Edward III the community of Broxton hundred appointed two serjeants to plead on its behalf before the justices of *trailbaston* at Chester; the men of West Derby hundred took collective action against the extortions of their bailiff; and the communities of Bucklow and Northwich wrangled over the size of their respective contributions to the mise.[9]

While the community of the hundred can be regarded as including all the freeholders in the division, in practice there were varying degrees of immunity from hundredal administration, and correspondingly varying degrees of commitment to the notion of community.[10] In the western part of Bucklow hundred, for example, there were numerous villages

though they soon seem to have lost their local character. J. L. Gillespie, 'Richard II's Cheshire archers', *L.C.H.S.*, 125 (1975), 1–39, suggests that the seven-fold division might rather relate to the number of night-watches in a week.

[6] P.R.O., CHES 19/5, m. 8d.

[7] J.R.U.L., Cornwall Legh MSS., deed 80.     [8] Chester R.O., Earwaker MSS., 1/139.

[9] *B.P.R.*, III, p. 165; Manchester Central Reference Library, Farrer MSS., 50/18/4; P.R.O., CHES 29/64, m. 4.

[10] See in general W. O. Ault, *Private Jurisdiction in England* (New Haven, Conn., 1923).

which, as members of the barony of Halton, were largely exempt from the jurisdiction of the hundred court. Even though the feudal geography of the Northwest had lost much of its force and coherence, it was still of consequence in the social life of the region. Local landholders continued to gravitate around the traditional honorial centres. The Lancashire knights and gentlemen who held lands of the baron of Warrington can be traced performing homage even in the sixteenth century, while the barony of Newton in Makerfield also served as the natural meeting-place for tenants of the fee.[11] The remarkable elasticity of such relationships even in the fifteenth century is attested by the frequent presence of local gentlemen at Swineshead, the Lincolnshire seat of the barons of Manchester.[12] Not unnaturally, feudal bonds often cut across administrative boundaries. In the Northwest almost all the baronies had dependencies in more than one hundred, though significantly none embraced land outside the region. The barons of Kinderton, for example, had tenants in Bucklow, Edisbury, Nantwich and Northwich hundreds. Yet by this period most baronies had relinquished direct control over their more distant members, and franchisal rights tended to be limited to the manors in close proximity to the honorial centre. In this regard the ancient baronies differed little from the non-baronial franchises in the region. The royal lordships of Frodsham and Macclesfield enjoyed wide immunities, as also did the manors of such well-favoured monasteries as Vale Royal and St Werburgh.[13] In all such cases homage and certain perquisites were exacted from feudal tenants over a fairly wide area,[14] but direct franchisal control was restricted to the immediate locality of the capital fee. Again, these franchisal units tended not to straddle boundaries, but rather to constitute autonomous sub-divisions of the hundred. Indeed, to a surprising degree, feudal ties served to reinforce the significance of the hundred as a unit of social identification. The barony of Clitheroe and

[11] W. Beamont (ed.), 'Homage roll of the manor of Warrington' in *Lancashire and Cheshire Miscellanies*, I (L.C.R.S., 12, 1885). From the witness-lists to a series of eleven deeds drawn up at Newton in Makerfield between September and December 1368, it is possible to identify knights and gentlemen in regular attendance at this baronial centre. Most of the transactions were between John Langton, baron of Newton, and John Haydock of Haydock, and the frequent attenders were Henry Scarisbrick (nine occasions), Adam Kenyon (nine), Ralph Bickerstaffe (eight), John Rainford (eight), Sir William Butler (six), Sir William Atherton (five) and Sir Thomas Lathom senior (four): J.R.U.L., Legh of Lyme Muniments, M/2/12–27.

[12] Town Hall, Manchester, Manchester Corporation MSS., 51/6, 52/29 and 52/74.

[13] Ault, *Private Jurisdiction*, pp. 240–66; P.R.O., CHES 19/3, m. 17.

[14] For records of homage paid by Robert Grosvenor to the abbot of Vale Royal, Ranulf Merbury to William Danyers, and John Nowell to Thomas Hesketh see *The Ledger Book of Vale Royal Abbey*, ed. J. Brownbill (L.C.R.S., 68, 1914), p. 62; P.R.O., DL 30/3/46; *English Historical Documents*, vol. IV, 1327–1485, ed. A. R. Myers (London, 1969), pp. 1117–18.

the lordship of Macclesfield were more or less conterminous with the hundreds of Blackburn and Macclesfield, while such centrally-placed and reasonably compact baronies as Manchester and Nantwich doubtless added considerably to the internal cohesion of the hundreds of Salford and Nantwich.

While the importance of administrative geography needs little stressing, and the continued influence of feudal relationships is apparent in a number of contexts, the exact significance of the larger ecclesiastical divisions cannot be readily established. On the one hand many ecclesiastical boundaries were of greater antiquity, and reflected more fundamental social cleavages than their administrative or feudal counterparts. It has already been suggested that the archdeaconry of Chester, with its inclusion of anglicised areas west of the Dee and its exclusion of lands north of the Ribble, in some ways constitutes a more coherent field of investigation than Cheshire and Lancashire in their entireties. On the other hand, whatever the original logic of their boundaries, ecclesiastical divisions were never of great consequence in the integration of such large areas. Dioceses, archdeaconries and deaneries obviously provided, frameworks within which the clergy operated, and institutional structures of which the laity had to take cognisance, but there is no evidence of corporate responsibilities and common identities among their lay inhabitants. Yet, when ecclesiastical and secular boundaries coincided, the former must have given greater definition to the geography of social life. The deaneries of Wirral, Macclesfield, Nantwich, Blackburn and Leyland were, with only slight variations, conterminous with the hundreds of the same name while the deaneries of Malpas, Middlewich, Warrington and Manchester were more or less equivalent to the hundreds of Broxton, Northwich, West Derby and Salford. Undoubtedly the frequent occurrence in the hundred courts of groups of villagers prosecuting the rural dean for his extortions is perhaps indicative of a fusion of identities.[15]

While the evidence is necessarily more limited, it seems that more informal bonds were also important in shaping the social geography of the Northwest. As centres of communication, the towns were clearly of pivotal importance. The larger boroughs, providing goods and services unobtainable in the countryside, functioned as meeting-places as well as markets for the local population. When the town was also a hundredal, baronial or ecclesiastical centre, commercial and administrative functions tended to reinforce each other. The borough of Nantwich was not only a prosperous market-town, attracting buyers and sellers from a wide hinterland, but also the centre of a hundred, a barony and a deanery. Many local towns in fact owed their existence and survival to seignorial

---

[15] E.g. in Macclesfield hundred: P.R.O., CHES 19/3, m. 17.

patronage and administrative convenience. Elsewhere formal ties, whose institutional logic had long been forgotten, continued to bind town and hinterland. Thus, according to ancient custom, twenty neighbouring villages provided judgers at the borough court of Northwich, and seventeen local villages performed similar services at Middlewich.[16] There were other traditional associations of importance in the structuring of social life in the region. It is noteworthy that some hundred courts were not held in towns, but rather at such customary meeting-places as Bucklow Hill, Golborne Ford, Witton Chapel and so on.[17] Meanwhile the significance of such sites as Sandiway, where the Cheshire folk gathered in 1403 to await the return of Richard II, or Billinge Hill, where the Blackburnshire men assembled on a number of occasions, can be noted, if not explained.[18]

Generally speaking, the hundred was the only large unit of abiding consequence in the organisation of social life in the Northwest. The tenurial, ecclesiastical and commercial structures were not without influence, but for the most part their impact was contained within the all important hundredal system. Given that in Anglo-Saxon times hundred courts, like county courts, dealt with both ecclesiastical and civil business, it is hardly surprising that there was a fair degree of congruence between hundreds and deaneries. At the same time it was natural for the *capita* of baronies, parochial centres and boroughs to arise in close proximity, especially given early seignorial interest in the endowment of churches and the establishment of boroughs. Where honorial *caput*, parish church and market were not established in a single settlement, there were often significant clusterings of vills, each fulfilling a different function in the district. Thus the barony of Dunham Massey, the borough of Altrincham and the parish church of Bowdon, sited in neighbouring but separate townships, all served the same hinterland, and doubtless reinforced the district's sense of solidarity. Yet, while acknowledging the importance of the hundred and the relative consistency of some of the other divisions, it is important not to present too monolithic a model of the social geography of the region. Since governmental, feudal, ecclesiastical and natural boundaries were rarely in complete accord, there remained a flexibility and richness in the structuring of social relations which cannot be ignored. Given all the variables that have to be taken into account, it is apparent that few villages could have shared identical social locations.

[16] *A Middlewich Chartulary*, part I, ed. J. Varley (C.S., n.s. 105, 1941), pp. 27–31.

[17] P.R.O., CHES 19/3, *passim*.

[18] M. V. Clarke and V. H. Galbraith, 'The deposition of Richard II', *B.J.R.L.*, 14 (1930), 177; A. R. Myers, 'An official progress through Lancashire and Cheshire in 1476', *L.C.H.S.* 115 (1963), 3n.

II

The smallest territorial units in the region were the parish, the manor and the vill or township. In some respects these three terms all allude to a single social entity, the village or perhaps borough, as seen from an ecclesiastical, tenurial or governmental perspective. At this stage it seems hardly necessary to assemble detailed evidence to prove that villages, or towns for that matter, were real communities. The statement that sizeable sections of the local population were born and married, lived, worked and died within the confines of a single village surely needs little corroboration. Much detailed research has been done in recent decades by W. O. Ault, J. A. Raftis and others on the collective obligations imposed upon the communities of the parish, manor and vill, and on the complementary process by which villages assumed corporate identity through taking common action in their own interest.[19] Since village life in the Northwest is rather poorly evidenced, there is an obvious temptation to read into the local situation the better-documented findings of researchers elsewhere. Such an approach, even if it were not positively misleading, would forgo the opportunity to ask certain fundamental questions of the local evidence. It would certainly be rash to assume too hastily that the structure of manorial life so well attested in the Midlands and elsewhere is an appropriate model. The Northwest cannot be readily categorised as *champion* country, with a preponderance of nucleated settlements and open-field farming. Nor was it a region with a high degree of congruence between village, parish and manor. Local parishes were typically large, containing on average half-a-dozen townships, while neither county was heavily manorialised in the classical meaning of the term. For all these reasons, there is some value in assembling the evidence, sparse as it is, regarding local village life, and to assess the significance of the elemental communities of parish, manor and vill in regional society.

Whatever has been concluded about the larger ecclesiastical divisions, the parish obviously constituted a social unit of considerable importance in the Northwest. The parish church itself provided both a symbolic focus for the loyalties of the local populace and a material expression of their common identity. Apart from the church's spiritual role, most of the community's *rites de passage* were enacted under its auspices.[20] From the evidence of inquisitions *de aetate probanda* it is apparent that baptisms were

---

[19] W. O. Ault, *Open-Field Farming in Medieval England. A Study of British By-Laws* (London, 1972); Raftis, *Tenure and Mobility*.

[20] In general see J. Bossy, 'Blood and baptism: kinship, community and Christianity in western Europe from the fourteenth to the seventeenth centuries' in D. Baker (ed.), *Sanctity and Secularity. The Church and the World* (Studies in Church History 10, 1973), pp. 129–43.

social events of considerable consequence, attracting not only large numbers of parishioners but also friends and kinsmen from farther afield.[21] Weddings and funerals were also important occasions in the parish's social calendar. Indeed the church was the venue for many more obviously profane activities. Disputes between neighbours were resolved by oaths sworn after mass, as at Macclesfield church in 1412 or at Leigh church in 1430 and 1435.[22] Unlicensed markets, entertainments and other boisterous activities were commonly held in churchyards, and the major festivals were occasions for conviviality among parishioners. While the parishes had not all the administrative responsibilities later laid on them, there were still numerous communal obligations to fulfil. The parishioners, through their elected churchwardens, were responsible for the upkeep of the church and for various other tasks of a religious, educational or charitable nature. Even the arrangement of seating in the church seems to have been a matter of great common concern, judging from the survival of documents listing the allocation of benches in Ashton under Lyne and Frodsham churches.[23] More important, the parishioners had to make presentments regarding moral misdemeanours to the archdeacon and his officers,[24] and in the secular sphere to assist in the apprehension of criminals. Certainly the hue and cry was sometimes raised on a parochial basis, as in Sandbach after the murder of Hugh Bostock of Hassall early in Henry VI's reign.[25] Meanwhile responsibilities of the parish with regard to sanctuary-seekers were even clearer: the parish of Runcorn was collectively fined for allowing one to escape in the early fifteenth century.[26] Such corporate obligations, reinforced by the threat of ammercement, all doubtless contributed to the cohesiveness of the parish as a social unit.

Where the parish and township were conterminous, involvement in parochial affairs was probably regarded as another facet of the common business of the village community. Indeed, in the history of local government in pre-industrial England, it is possible to detect an increasing tendency to merge the responsibilities of parish and township. Since in Cheshire and Lancashire the single-township parish was the exception

---

[21] E.g. inquisition transcribed in Ormerod, *History of Cheshire*, III, pp. 254–5.

[22] *Local Gleanings relating to Lancashire and Cheshire*, vol. I, ed. J. P. Earwaker (Manchester, 1880), pp. 146–9.

[23] W. M. Bowman, *England in Ashton under Lyne* (Altrincham, 1960), pp. 167–8; *Cheshire Sheaf*, third series, item 688.

[24] Chetham Library, Manchester, Raines MSS., vol. XI, p. 39.

[25] P.R.O., CHES 19/5, m. 11.

[26] Cheshire R.O., DDX 1320 (Transcript of Chamberlain of Chester's Account, 4–5 Henry IV).

rather than the rule, there can have been far less identity between the two administrative units.[27] In the large, sprawling parishes of the Northwest travel to church would be extremely arduous, especially when it was located in some remote church-hamlet like Prestbury, Astbury, Rostherne or Whalley. To a certain extent it would have perhaps been more appropriate to consider such parishes in the context of the larger social units, for some were as extensive as hundreds elsewhere. Yet even in the larger parishes there is clear evidence that the churches served as symbols of solidarity for their dependent villages. The churchwardens and gentlemen of the parish of Manchester came together on numerous occasions in the 1420s to participate in the collegiation of the church.[28] There were longstanding rivalries between the parishioners of Prestbury and Stockport which on occasion resulted in violence.[29] Meanwhile humble men and women in the parish of Ormskirk joined together to subscribe towards the salary of an additional priest.[30]

To move from the parish to the manor in a study of the social geography of the Northwest is to enter a less obscure but more confused field. In comparison with other parts of England, it appears that neither Cheshire nor Lancashire was heavily manorialised, except in D. Sylvester's limited, and largely topographical sense.[31] While most villages and many hamlets were held as manors, it would seem that such key features of manorialism as heavy labour services were never very widespread.[32] The typical manor in the region seems to have consisted of a manor-house with a small home-farm and park, and a clustering of peasant households from which rents were drawn. This is not to deny the existence of manors of the classical type. The estates of St Werburgh's abbey around Chester and in Wirral hundred, the properties of Vale Royal abbey, and the lands of the duchy of Lancaster on both sides of the Mersey all maintained a certain degree of manorialisation. In parts of the region subject to vigorous seignorial regimes, the manor itself could clearly become a social unit of vital significance. Yet it is noteworthy that, as in the case of some parishes, the important manors tended not to be conterminous with individual village settlements. Probably because of low population densities, vills and hamlets were often grouped together around monastic granges or some central manor like Halton or Widnes. Significantly this larger conception

---

[27] In general see Sylvester, *Rural Landscape of Welsh Borderland*, pp. 164–89.

[28] Manchester Cathedral, MS. 26.

[29] P.R.O., CHES 25/12, m. 8.

[30] Transcribed as an appendix to J. P. Rylands (ed.), 'The Exchequer lay subsidy roll, 1332' in *Lancashire and Cheshire Miscellanies*, II (L.C.R.S., 31, 1896).

[31] D. Sylvester, 'The manor and the Cheshire landscape', *L.C.A.S.*, 70 (1960).

[32] See below, Chapter 6.

of the manorial estate had its own impact on the social geography of the region, and tenants from different villages on a single estate can often be found acting in concert. Thus the peasant farmers of Disley, Yeardsley, Whaley, Shrigley, Pott, Kettleshulme and Rainow, all dependencies of the manor of Macclesfield, jointly petitioned the Black Prince regarding agistment in Handley.[33] Even more interesting, tenants from two of the larger ecclesiastical estates can be found taking concerted action against their manorial lords. Bondmen from the manors of Over and Darnhall embarked on extensive legal proceedings against the abbot of Vale Royal, while villeins from various manors belonging to St Werburgh's abbey conspired together at the time of the Peasants' Revolt of 1381.[34]

Despite its importance in some regards, it would be misleading to treat the manor as the elemental community in local society. After all, perhaps as many as a half of the townships in the region would not have possessed their own manor court. The hallmoots at Halton, Widnes, Macclesfield and elsewhere performed this function for scores of townships, while lesser lordships extended manorial jurisdiction over several vills each. Even in the villages where manor courts were held, the significance of manorial organisation must not be over-estimated. In such cases the manor court can in any case be regarded as an assembly of the village community as much as an instrument of seignorial discipline. There seem to have been few local lords taking a close interest in the cultivation of their demesne-lands, and labour services were not at all widespread in the region by the period under discussion. Given that the lords had fewer valuable rights to enforce, it is likely that much of the initiative for the courts was coming from the villagers themselves. The obstruction of pathways, the overstocking of pastures and so on were more often the concern of the peasant than the lord, and while the profits of justice went to the latter it was the customary laws of the village which regulated the court's activities.[35]

In the Northwest it is therefore the township or vill which constituted the basic form of social organisation. This might be either a borough, a village with nucleated settlement, a hamlet of dispersed settlement, or even groups of hamlets and isolated farms. Yet, whatever its status or size, the township remained the elemental community and the natural unit for

[33] P.R.O., CHES 17/13, m. 34.

[34] *Vale Royal Ledger Book*, pp. 37–42; P.R.O., CHES 25/8, m. 57.

[35] Apart from the records of the large royal estates, few court-rolls have survived from local manors in this period. There is some documentation, however, for the Cheshire manor of Over Peover and the Lancashire manors of Sefton and Hale, and village by-laws are attested in the latter two communities: J.R.U.L., Mainwaring MSS., roll 4; Lancashire R.O., DDM/7/449; *Three Early English Metrical Romances*, ed. J. Robson (Camden Soc., first series 18, 1842), pp. xxxviii–xliii.

judicial and administrative purposes. Since taxes were collected township by township it is possible to make a fairly comprehensive list of village communities in the Northwest. In Cheshire over four hundred vills contributed to the mise, while in Lancashire south of the Ribble there were nearly three hundred effective townships. Whether or not the village was conterminous with manor or parish, it had definite communal obligations. Each village elected a constable or pair of constables, who were responsible for keeping the peace as well as more general duties, and whose activities were overseen at the hundred and county courts.[36] Likewise the village was responsible for presenting criminals and testifying at coroners' inquests.[37] In Cheshire it was even the responsibility of the villagers to apportion the tax burden among themselves.[38] Needless to say, the townships with the status of boroughs showed even greater vitality in their corporate life. Having attained their charters of liberties, the towns had the privilege of electing a wide range of officials and of administering justice in the name of the corporation. In Chester the civic community was further divided into wards, each with its own officers and administrative responsibilities.[39]

Unfortunately there is too little evidence to support a detailed discussion of the functioning of the village community in the Northwest. In the last resort it must simply be assumed that local townships and vills were more than merely haphazard clusterings of households or units of administrative convenience.[40] Local village communities were certainly well able to take the initiative in matters of common concern. Thus husbandmen from Helsby can be found taking united action in a boundary dispute with the men of Frodsham.[41] In 1416 there is evidence of Cheshire villagers putting up a stubborn resistance to the collection of the mise. As the tax-collectors passed from township to township distraining goods, the villagers forcibly recovered them, claiming that only the people who had consented to the subsidy ought to be required to contribute. In the fragmentary record of

---

[36] The constables of Hollingworth, Dukinfield, Newton, Northenden, Bollin, Pownall, Chorley, Butley and Rode all appeared at the Macclesfield hundred court in 1424: P.R.O., SC 2/256/5. For elections of constables see W. Beamont, *An Account of the Rolls of the Honour of Halton* (Warrington, 1879), p. 7; J.R.U.L., Mainwaring MSS., roll 4; *Metrical Romances*, p. xli.

[37] Four men from each of the four nearest vills had to attend a coroner's inquest: e.g. P.R.O., CHES 29/96, m. 24.

[38] Thus Robert son of Hugh Holt was assessed by his neighbours to pay 4s towards the mise of Titherington: P.R.O., CHES 17/14, m. 9d.

[39] R. H. Morris, *Chester in the Plantagenet and Tudor Reigns* (Chester, 1894).

[40] For a detailed analysis of a village community in Huntingdonshire see E. B. Dewindt, *Land and People in Holywell-cum-Needingworth. Structures of Tenure and Patterns of Social Organisation in an East Midlands Village, 1272–1457* (Toronto, 1972).

[41] P.R.O., CHES 25/11, m. 8.

these disturbances the village clearly emerges as the elemental unit of social identification, and at Baguley at least, the uprising was led by the two constables, Hugh Stanilands and John Mascy. The tax revolt also throws into relief other features of the social geography of the Northwest. Groups from the villages made their ways to parochial centres such as Audlem, Wynbunbury and Nantwich where church bells were rung to summon the entire parish to arms. Meanwhile in the Macclesfield area villagers from all across the hundred allegedly gathered together in armed array to resist the tax-collectors.[42]

While the village community in the Northwest lacked the overall cohesiveness of its counterpart in the Midlands, its vital role in regional life cannot be contested. Despite their lack of formal corporate status, villages can be found acting as corporations in a variety of contexts. Indeed an individual's affiliation to a village community and its particular location in a wider network of interlocking and overlapping solidarities, decisively patterned his relations with the outside world. The immense importance of social geography in structuring access to opportunities for patronage is illustrated in later chapters. In the assessment of an individual's social position in late medieval England it will be shown to be as necessary to discover his geographical provenance as his socio-economic status.

[42] P.R.O., CHES 25/11, mm. 9–11d.

*Chapter 4*

# THE POPULATION

A discussion of Cheshire and Lancashire society in the later middle ages cannot proceed very far without some quantitative conception of the population. Of course, it is impossible to assess the population of medieval England with any degree of precision. Until the sixteenth and seventeenth centuries, there was scant interest in the compilation or estimation of population figures, and not until the early nineteenth century was it considered necessary to institute a census. Nevertheless the absence of records directly relating to population should not discourage historians from making informed estimates from such material as has survived. Indeed in projects of this nature it is essential to obtain a fairly realistic impression of the demographic scale of the society under discussion. At the same time it is felt that studies of this type can make a useful contribution to larger-scale projects, and in the following sections it is hoped at least to improve on the estimates presented by J. C. Russell in his pioneering work on the demography of medieval England.[1]

I

Any assessment of the population of late medieval England must begin with the evidence of the poll-tax returns of 1377, 1379 and 1381. The poll-tax of 1377, which demanded four pence of every man and woman over the age of fourteen, has particular value for the demographer. Although certain parts of the kingdom, including the palatinate of Chester, were exempt from the tax, the returns of the 1377 levy amount to a fairly thoroughgoing appraisal of the adult population of England at the accession of Richard II. It is acknowledged, of course, that population totals in the late fourteenth century were well below the levels which obtained in the kingdom prior to the Black Death.[2] Yet it is clear that the poll-tax returns of 1377 can at least provide minimum figures

---

[1] J. C. Russell, *British Medieval Population* (Albuquerque, 1948).
[2] For a masterly discussion of population trends after the Black Death see J. Hatcher, *Plague, Population and the English Economy 1348–1530* (London, 1977).

Table 1. *J. C. Russell's estimated population of England in 1377*[3]

| | |
|---|---:|
| Laity in the poll-tax | 1,355,555 |
| Clergy in the poll-tax | 30,641 |
| Estimate for Cheshire | 15,503 |
| Estimate for Durham | 13,091 |
| Estimates of mendicant friars | 2,590 |
| | 1,417,380 |
| Add fifty per cent for children | 708,690 |
| | 2,126,070 |
| Add five per cent for indigent and untaxed persons | 106,303 |
| Estimated total | 2,232,373 |

for the population of England, and that reasonable estimates and multipliers can be devised for the sections of the community omitted from the assessment. At the same time, since total receipts were enrolled shire by shire, it has proved a fairly straightforward task to compile minimum figures for individual counties and to establish relative population densities across England.

The enrolled totals from the poll-tax of 1377 have been in print for some time,[4] but it was left to J. C. Russell to make a full analysis of the figures for demographic purposes. After conducting certain statistical experiments to test for obvious errors in enumeration, he devised multipliers for children and indigent persons, made estimates for exempted areas, and added from the separately levied clerical poll-tax. His conclusions appear in Table 1.

On the whole Russell's multipliers for the numbers of children and indigents in the population have been seen to be too conservative.[5] Yet his total population figure of two and a quarter million has been widely quoted,[6] and it is worth pursuing his estimates for the Northwest. In the case of Lancashire, the reasoning was straightforward. A figure of 23,880 tax-payers in 1377 became an estimated total population of around 37,000. With regard to Cheshire, the argument was more tendentious. Russell's procedure was to assume an analogous population density both sides of

---

[3] Russell, *British Medieval Population*, p. 146.

[4] J. Topham, 'Subsidy roll of 51 Edward III', *Archaeologia*, VII (1785), 337–47.

[5] E.g. J. Krause, 'The medieval household: large or small?', *Ec.H.R.*, second series IX (1956–7), 420–32.

[6] E.g. P. Ziegler, *The Black Death* (London, 1969), pp. 232–5.

the Mersey, and to compute the Cheshire population at the Lancashire rate of 12.7 tax-payers per square mile. After adding in a figure of 2,500 for the city of Chester, he arrived at an estimate of 15,503 hypothetical tax-payers, and thus some 24,000 men, women and children for the southern shire.[7] Adding together the two estimates, it is apparent that Russell envisaged a population in the two counties of some 60,000 souls.

Without for the moment challenging Russell's faith in the comprehensiveness of the poll-tax, his assumption regarding the relative population densities of Cheshire and Lancashire must be called into question. Given that the poll-tax returns can be most reliably used to plot population distribution, it is particularly disappointing that his work in this field is riddled with errors and inconsistencies. With regard to Cheshire and Lancashire, for example, at one stage he assumed analogous population densities of 12.7 tax-payers or 19.7 persons per square mile, but at another point posited figures of only 11.5 persons for the former and 26.2 persons for the latter.[8] This strange conclusion was reached by 'multiplying the Domesday figures by the gain made by the counties between 1086 and 1377', despite the fact that his Lancashire estimates for 1086 were based on Cheshire figures, just as his Cheshire estimates for 1377 were based on Lancashire figures.[9] Without doubt R. A. Pelham's earlier study remains the best guide to the distribution of the population in the late fourteenth century.[10] His map bears graphic witness to the sharp contrast between the population densities of Lancashire, with its 12.7 tax-payers per square mile, and the Southeast and East Anglia, where figures in excess of forty were common. Unfortunately Pelham did not venture an estimate for Cheshire, but his map does suggest the logic of averaging the population densities of the four adjacent counties: 12.7, 17.5, 18.6 and 23.1 tax-payers per square mile for Lancashire, Shropshire, Staffordshire and Derbyshire respectively.[11] According to this formula Cheshire would have domiciled 18.0 tax-payers per square mile, and Russell's estimate of its total population would need to be increased by at least a third to around 33,000.

To assume equivalent population densities in Cheshire and Lancashire is unwarrantable, even for the most arbitrary statistician. Bringing other

---

[7] Russell, *British Medieval Population*, pp. 144–5.    [8] *Ibid.*, p. 313.

[9] *Ibid.*, p. 312. The calculations are further confused by the fact that Russell had no figures for Lancashire at the time of Domesday, and arrived at his estimated total by assuming a population density analogous with Cheshire and Yorkshire: *ibid.*, pp. 52–4.

[10] R. A. Pelham, 'Fourteenth-century England' in H. C. Darby (ed.), *An Historical Geography of England before A.D. 1800* (Cambridge, 1936), p. 232.

[11] Russell's procedure of not including the larger towns (which were separately listed) in the county totals has been followed: Russell, *British Medieval Population*, pp. 144–5.

neighbouring counties into the calculation is salutary, but is still not entirely satisfactory. Other evidence must be sought as to the comparability of the two counties in the region. Physical factors would certainly suggest a much higher population density in Cheshire than in Lancashire: the latter had a much higher proportion of land lying above the 500 foot contour, and its northern areas might have been as sparsely populated as neighbouring Westmorland, with its 9.4 tax-payers per square mile. The clerical poll-tax for the archdeaconry of Chester in 1379 lends rather more precision to this sort of comparison.[12] The returns record the presence of 342 clergymen in Cheshire as opposed to only 167 in Lancashire south of the Ribble. Since the two halves of the archdeaconry of Chester were more or less equivalent in size, and there is no reason to suppose that under-enumeration was more prevalent north of the Mersey,[13] these figures are directly comparable. Assuming that the ratio of clerk to layman was reasonably constant, the population density of Cheshire, including the city of Chester, might have been twice as high as Lancashire, implying at least 26,000 tax-payers. When all the other multipliers have been included in the calculations, this figure provides a total population figure of around 41,000 for Cheshire, and over 77,000 for the combined populations of Cheshire and Lancashire.

II

J. C. Russell clearly under-estimated the population of the Northwest in 1377. Even accepting his evaluation of the poll-tax material, there are grounds for raising his estimate for the region by as much as a third. Yet it is by no means clear that his assessment of the quality of the poll-tax evidence has any validity. His assumption that five per cent is sufficient allowance for under-enumeration is particularly tendentious. His detailed calculations on the incidence of terminal groats is irrelevant to the problem of tax-evasion, and the well-attested zeal of the tax-collectors in Shrewsbury seems the only solid evidence of its limited scale.[14] Initially it was hoped to make a systematic appraisal of the poll-tax material by

---

[12]  P.R.O., E 179/15/6a, E 179/271/4. An edition of the returns has been published in Bennett, 'Lancashire and Cheshire clergy', pp. 22–30.

[13]  There were over twice as many parishes in Cheshire as in south Lancashire, and this ratio matches the relative numbers of clergymen. A rather higher proportion of the beneficed clergy of Lancashire was omitted from the returns, but this phenomenon can be more plausibly attributed to absenteeism than tax-evasion: *ibid.*, pp. 4–5.

[14]  W. G. D. Fletcher, 'The poll-tax for the town and liberties of Shrewsbury, 1380', *Transactions of the Shropshire Archaeological and Natural History Society*, second series II (1890), p. 27.

collating the names of tax-payers in 1377 with the names of persons recorded in the later poll-taxes and other sources. Unfortunately such an investigation is not really feasible in any village in the Northwest. Cheshire was exempt from all three lay poll-taxes, and Lancashire provides detailed returns only for limited areas and for the assessments of 1379 and 1381. Nevertheless sufficient material has survived to cast considerable doubt on the more optimistic evaluations of the 1377 poll-tax.

In the first place it is unclear whether the totals enrolled in 1377, upon which historians have depended for population estimates, actually represent the entire tax-paying population. In an age when public officials were only marginally honest and even less efficient it remains probable that leakages occurred between the collection of the tax and the enrolment of the returns. In fact, where evidence permits this supposition to be tested, a high discrepancy can sometimes be found between the enrolled total and the number of named tax-payers. The clerical poll-tax returns for the archdeaconry of Chester in 1379 provided the names of 509 tax-paying clergymen, whereas according to the enrolments used by Russell the clerical population numbered a mere 271. Nor is it likely that this latter figure is merely a scribal error. The total numbers of clergymen in the assessments of 1377 and 1381 were 498 and 308 respectively, and in all dioceses the 1379 figures were the lowest of the three levies.[15] Although it is improbable that discrepancies on this scale occur throughout the whole corpus of the poll-tax material, the possibility of large-scale under-enumeration at the time of enrolment must be countenanced.

The fact that the poll-tax returns of 1379 list the names of more local clergymen than the levy of 1377 suggests the need for a re-assessment of the relative comprehensiveness of the three poll-taxes. It has been generally assumed that the first levy was the most complete, and that its enrolled receipts provide the surest foundation for population estimates. Certainly it is apparent, both from the chronicle sources and from the figures, that the poll-tax of 1381 was subject to widespread evasion and indeed armed resistance. In Lancashire nearly two-thirds of the tax-payers in 1377 successfully avoided the 1381 imposition.[16] Since the poll-taxes of 1377 and 1381 were strict *per capita* levies, it is possible to make an appraisal of their relative comprehensiveness from the totals themselves. With regard to the graded assessment of 1379, such a straightforward comparison is impossible. Since individuals might be assessed at sums ranging from four pence to as many pounds, its receipts cannot be readily converted

[15] Russell, *British Medieval Population*, pp. 134–7.
[16] The number of Lancashire tax-payers in 1381 was 8,371, as opposed to 23,880 in 1377: P.R.O., E 359/8c, m. 6d.

into demographic data and accordingly have been somewhat neglected. At the same time the fact that husband and wife were taxed jointly has led to the assumption that this assessment was the least comprehensive of all the levies. Demonstrably a fair evaluation of the poll-tax of 1379 must depend on a thorough examination of the returns.

Poll-tax returns from 1379 survive for over forty villages and hamlets in Lancashire, and provide the names of 1,375 tax-payers. Since this group of villagers together contributed rather less than an eighth of the total receipts for Lancashire, it can be presumed that the total number of tax-payers exceeded 11,000.[17] Of course, most women and children under the age of sixteen were excluded from the levy of 1379, and so adjustments must be made before the figures can be usefully compared to the total of 1377. As an allowance for women and the missing age-group of fourteen to sixteen, it is appropriate to double the figure of 11,000. Such a procedure would bring the total for 1379 well within the range of the 23,880 tax-payers recorded in 1377.[18] The evidence of the clerical poll-tax returns is also instructive: the number of clergymen listed in the 1379 returns is not only comparable with, but actually in excess of the total from 1377.

Given the rough comparability of the population estimates derived from the first two poll-taxes, it is clearly feasible to test the comprehensiveness of the total in 1377 through a detailed scrutiny of the schedules from 1379. With regard to the clerical population of the Northwest, for example, it is possible to detect quite a number of omissions from the latter assessment: there are some twenty beneficed clergymen missing; the fragmentary returns from 1377 furnish the names of fifty more chaplains; and the ordination-lists and other local sources record the names of dozens of clerks who appear in neither levy.[19] Of course, nominal linkage is a problem. At the same time, many of the missing parsons were absentees, while some of the elusive clerks had doubtless moved on, been promoted elsewhere or simply died. Yet the suspicion remains that the total of 509 from the 1379 returns, and more especially the total of 498 from 1377, is a gross under-statement of the clerical population in the archdeaconry

---

[17] Lancashire poll-tax returns from 1379 survive in P.R.O., E 179/130/24 (various vills in West Derby hundred), E 179/130/28 (various vills in Blackburn hundred), E 179/130/27 (unclassified list of tax-payers from Lonsdale hundred), E 179/240/308(5) (part of vill of Formby). The total receipts from the above returns, excluding Lonsdale, were £38 14s 10d. The total receipts for the entire county were £314 4s 1d: P.R.O., E 359/8b, m. 23d.

[18] There were a small number of women who were individually assessed in 1379, but they almost all seem to have been widows.

[19] Bennett, 'Lancashire and Cheshire clergy', 3, based on P.R.O., E 179/45/16 and Lichfield R.O., B/A/1/4–5.

of Chester. A figure of nearer 600 would be more plausible, and would imply a rate of under-enumeration of almost twenty per cent.[20] A critical assessment of the lay poll-tax returns points in the same direction. Liverpool, for example, had some eighty-six recorded tax-payers in 1379, but only forty-eight in the much evaded levy of 1381. Yet the latter survey produced a dozen names wholly omitted from the more comprehensive returns two years earlier.[21] Contemporary rent-rolls, which record the existence of over 160 burgages in the town, likewise suggest a rather higher population.[22] Judging from the proportion of new tax-payers noted in 1381 and the number of burgage-tenancies, an estimate of twenty-five per cent under-enumeration in Liverpool might even be unduly conservative. In all the Lancashire villages for which two sets of returns have survived, the select band of contributors in 1381 similarly included men who had escaped notice in the fuller assessment of 1379: at Eccleston the proportion was around ten per cent, at Atherton fifteen per cent and at Rixton with Glazebrook twenty-five per cent.[23] Other local evidence likewise undermines confidence in the thoroughness of the tax-collectors in rural areas. The list of subscribers to the stipend of a priest in Ormskirk in 1366 indicates a much larger population in the parish than would be expected from the poll-tax totals.[24] An Eccleston rent-roll, compiled in 1373 but kept up-to-date until the reign of Richard II, provides the names of a dozen customary tenants missing from the levy of 1379.[25] Meanwhile the 'Order of Seating in Ashton Kirk' indicates a population of over 400 for the single-parish township of Ashton under Lyne in 1422, a population twice as large as the highest poll-taxes projections for the borough of Liverpool.[26]

Unfortunately the dearth of manorial records from Lancashire prevents a more systematic evaluation of the poll-tax returns, but the scraps of evidence available are sufficient to cast grave doubts on Russell's optimistic assessment of their comprehensiveness. Obviously a new estimate of the rate of under-enumeration must await more studies of other localities, but it must be stressed that in this respect Lancashire does not appear untypical.

---

[20] Bennett, 'Lancashire and Cheshire clergy', 3–4.

[21] The total for 1381 has been adjusted by omitting dependent females. The Lancashire returns for 1381 survive in P.R.O., E 179/130/24 (West Derby hundred) and E 179/133/29 (Salford hundred).

[22] There is an extent of Liverpool in 1346 in *Lancashire Inquests, Extents and Feudal Aids*, part III, 1313–1355, ed. W. Farrer (L.C.R.S., 70, 1915), pp. 69–73, and a rental from *c.* 1408 in Lancashire R.O., DDK/B/1542.

[23] P.R.O., E 179/130/24.    [24] Transcribed in *Lancashire and Cheshire Miscellanies*, II.

[25] Lancashire R.O., DDSc 25/1.

[26] Transcribed in Bowman, *Ashton under Lyne*, pp. 73–9.

In terms of the demographic size of communities, for example, Lancashire as revealed in the levy of 1379 has a profile not entirely dissimilar to the West Riding of Yorkshire in 1377; fourteen per cent as opposed to fifteen per cent with populations of under 50; forty-nine per cent as opposed to thirty-eight per cent between 51 and 100; thirty-two per cent as opposed to thirty-seven per cent between 100 and 200; and five per cent as opposed to ten per cent over 200.[27] Needless to say, the repercussions of raising the estimate for under-enumeration from Russell's five per cent to a figure of the order of twenty-five per cent are far from negligible for the demography of late medieval England. Even using Russell's unduly modest multiplier for children under fourteen years old, it would make the total populations of Cheshire and Lancashire over 48,000 and over 44,000 respectively, giving a grand total of more than 93,000 for the Northwest.[28]

III

While estimates of total population from tax records are notoriously hazardous, their potential for providing information about relative population densities is more widely acknowledged. It is usually assumed that under-enumeration and tax-evasion occurred at fairly uniform rates across the countryside and that the tax liabilities of particular areas correlate well with the size of their population. Of course, neither premise inspires complete conviction: in capitation taxes, like the poll-tax in Lancashire, the proportion of people escaping assessment would have been higher in the towns than the countryside, while traditional levies based originally on moveables, like the mise in Cheshire, inevitably reflect old wealth rather than new life. Yet, bearing these problems in mind, it is hoped that the tax records can at least provide a rough guide to the distribution of the population in the Northwest.

In a survey of this sort the relationship between town and countryside is a natural focus of interest. Unfortunately, the evidence available for an assessment of the size of the larger local towns is extremely limited. Manifestly the city of Chester was the only urban centre of any real stature in the region, but even its approximate population remains a matter of conjecture. Russell offered an estimate of 2,500 hypothetical tax-payers

---

[27] The Staffordshire, Yorkshire and Northumberland figures are based on Russell's calculations from the 1377 returns: Russell, *British Medieval Population*, p. 308. The Lancashire figures are based on the 1379 tax-paying population, trebled to include women and children.

[28] If similar rates of under-enumeration obtained in other parts of the realm, and if a more generous multiplier for children under fourteen is appropriate, the total population of England in 1377 would have approached three millions: see brief discussion in Hatcher, *Plague, Population and English Economy*, pp. 13–14.

on the basis of an assumed equivalence between Chester and such towns as Bury St Edmunds and Newcastle upon Tyne. After adding in fifty per cent for children, and a further twenty-five per cent for under-enumeration, this would give a total population of over 4,600, as compared to 44,000 for the rest of Cheshire. Given that the city of Chester's mise assessment was a tenth of that of the rest of the county, and that at least six out of seventy or so Cheshire parish churches lay within its precincts, this figure seems to be of roughly the right order of relative magnitude.[29] It is improbable that any other town in the region was even a quarter of its size. In Lancashire, the borough of Preston might have had a population of 1,000,[30] but the poll-tax returns for Wigan and Manchester suggest no more than 400 inhabitants each. In Cheshire, Nantwich had a mise assessment of only a fifth that of the city of Chester, and most other towns paid even more modest sums. In truth the tax records do not reveal any great difference in terms of size between most towns and the larger villages. The poll-tax returns of 1381, for example, record tax-paying populations in boroughs ranging from 99 at Wigan, 91 at Manchester, 81 at Liverpool, 70 at Warrington right down to 42 at Newton in Makerfield, but also list 115 tax-payers at Withington, 79 at Scarisbrick and 78 at Lathom, all relatively undistinguished villages.[31] Similarly many boroughs contributed less to the mise than some neighbouring villages. In Bucklow and Macclesfield hundreds, for instance, none of the six townships assessed at more than £3 – Cheadle, Mobberley, Lymm, High Legh, Hale and Over Whitley – were boroughs, while Knutsford, Stockport, Macclesfield and other chartered towns all contributed sums of less than £2.[32] While both taxes probably under-estimated the capacity of towns, it would be unwise to maintain on demographic grounds a rigid divide between town and countryside in the Northwest.

While comparisons between the populations of individual communities are necessarily tendentious, it remains possible to plot in general terms the distribution of the population across the region. Within Cheshire the mise assessments of individual townships provide a useful guide to relative population densities. When the positions of townships assessed at rates higher than thirty shillings are plotted on a map, definite patterns emerge. For the most part such communities were situated along the main river valleys. To the northeast there was a chain of such settlements – including

---

[29] Six Chester parishes had incumbents in 1379: Bennett, 'Lancashire and Cheshire clergy', 23–4.

[30] There were over three hundred Preston men in the guild merchant in 1397: *Preston Guild Rolls, 1397–1682*, ed. W. A. Abram (L.C.R.S., 9, 1884), pp. 1–7.

[31] The 1381 figures, of course, include females as well as males, unlike the 1379 figures.

[32] The mise assessments are taken from J.R.U.L., Tatton MSS., no. 345.

Table 2. *Mise assessments for three Cheshire parishes*

| St Oswald's, Chester | £ | s | d | Mottram in Longdendale | £ | s | d |
|---|---|---|---|---|---|---|---|
| Bache | | 6 | 5 | Mottram | | 12 | 9 |
| Great Boughton | 2 | 0 | 0 | Godley | | 5 | 7 |
| Church Heath | | 3 | 3 | Hattersley | | 9 | 7 |
| Lea Newbold | 1 | 2 | 4 | Hollingworth | | 8 | 9 |
| Newton | 1 | 9 | 8 | Matley | | 5 | 7 |
| Saighton | 3 | 16 | 10 | Newton | | 7 | 2 |
| Wervin | 1 | 0 | 0 | Stalybridge | | 17 | 7 |
| Iddinshall | | 6 | 8 | Tintwistle | 1 | 2 | 5 |
| Blacon with Crabwall | | | | | | | |
| (part) | 2 | 4 | 10 | | | | |
| Croughton | 1 | 0 | 10 | | | | |

| St Mary on the Hill, Chester | £ | s | d |
|---|---|---|---|
| Marlston | | 9 | 8 |
| Lache | | 7 | 2 |
| Mollington Banaster | 1 | 0 | 0 |
| Upton | 1 | 6 | 4 |
| Moston | | 16 | 8 |

Total assessment for 10,800 acres in southwest Cheshire: £17 10s 8d

Total assessment for 10,500 acres in Northeast Cheshire: £4 9s 5d

Lymm, Mobberley, Knutsford, Wilmslow and Macclesfield – along the Bollin and its main tributaries. In central Cheshire there were strings of wealthy townships along the Weaver and the Dane: Halton, Runcorn and Frodsham at the estuary of the former river; Dutton, Over Whitley, Lostock Gralam further upstream; Northwich at the confluence of the two rivers, with Middlewich and Congleton higher up the Dane, and Church Minshull and Nantwich further along the Weaver. Predictably the anciently settled lowlands around Chester and Wirral, and more especially the fertile Dee and Gowy basins, appear to have been the wealthiest areas of Cheshire. Despite their being smaller in terms of acreage than most eastern villages, the townships in these parts were generally more highly taxed. A comparison between the tax liabilities of parishes of equivalent size from the Chester area and northeast Cheshire is instructive. On the one hand there are the two Chester parishes of St

Table 3. *Numbers of tax-payers in certain Lancashire vills in 1379*

| West Derby hundred | | Blackburn hundred | |
|---|---|---|---|
| Rixton with Glazebrook | 33 | Walton le Dale | 75 |
| Westleigh | 30 | Cuerdale | 25 |
| Atherton | 66 | Samlesbury | 49 |
| Hindley | 55 | Balderstone | 21 |
| Liverpool | 86 | Osbaldeston | 8 |
| Ince in Makerfield | 27 | Mellor with Eccleshill | 12 |
| Huyton with Roby | 29 | Clayton le Dale | 17 |
| Windle | 25 | Salesbury | 9 |
| Parr | 26 | Wilpshire with Dinkley | 21 |
| Pennington | 36 | Billington | 35 |
| Eccleston | 39 | Pleasington | 18 |
| Ashton in Makerfield | 58 | Livesey | 35 |
| Lowton with Kenyon | 49 | Witton | 5 |
| Bickerstaffe | 40 | Blackburn | 42 |
| Knowsley | 31 | Little Harwood | 10 |
| | | Great Harwood | 29 |
| | | Rishton | 34 |
| | | Oswaldtwistle | 27 |
| | | Ditton | 20 |
| | | Ribchester | 32 |
| | | Thornley with Wheatley | 25 |
| | | Chipping | 25 |
| | | Whalley | 14 |
| | | Pendle Chase | 36 |
| | | Rossendale Chase | 22 |
| | | Trawden Chase | 6 |
| Total: 15 vills/630 tax-payers | | Total: 26 vills/652 tax-payers | |

Oswald and St Mary on the Hill, which together embraced some 10,800 acres of fertile lowlands outside the city boundary. On the other hand there is the parish of Mottram in Longdendale, containing 10,500 acres (excluding moorland) of dour countryside in the northeastern corner of the shire (see Table 2). These figures suggest that the lowlands in the neighbourhood of Chester were four times as densely populated as the bleak Pennine uplands of Longdendale.

Similar contrasts in the distribution of the population can be detected in Lancashire. The poll-tax returns of 1379 provide evidence for only forty vills in West Derby and Blackburn hundreds, but useful comparisons can be made. Since the former hundred was situated on relatively good agricultural land in southwest Lancashire while the latter was situated on predominantly pastoral terrain to the northeast, the two sets of figures are worth listing in their entirety (see Table 3). It is striking that the fifteen West Derby vills had almost as many tax-payers as all the twenty-six Blackburnshire vills. With an average of forty-two as opposed to twenty-two tax-payers per vill, there can be little doubting the greater density of settlement in the southwestern lowlands as opposed to the eastern uplands. A more comprehensive series of poll-tax returns might have helped to reveal more complex and variegated patterns in the distribution of the Lancashire population. Even from the extant material, another interesting feature can be discerned. Though no figures from the levy of 1379 have survived for Preston, Wigan or Warrington, the significance of the main highway linking the towns is apparent. Of the five vills with more than fifty tax-payers in the surviving returns, four are situated along this important thoroughfare.[33]

Through an assessment of the fragmentary evidence available it has been possible to offer some quantitative conception of Cheshire and Lancashire society. It has been argued that Russell seriously under-estimated the size of the population in the Northwest, and after making more generous allowance for the density of settlement in Cheshire and adding in twenty-five per cent rather than five per cent for under-enumeration in the poll-tax, a new estimate of 93,000 has been proffered. Since this latter figure has only allowed a multiplier of fifty per cent for children under fourteen, and since this multiplier is increasingly regarded as minimal by demographic historians, a total population of over 100,000 in the Northwest at the beginning of the reign of Richard II might well be nearer the mark.

Inevitably this assessment of the local population has tended to be static. Needless to say, it must be stressed that population levels were subject to violent fluctuation, and in view of the recurrent demographic crises in this period it would be unwise to allow estimates from 1377 to stand for the whole age. Unfortunately there is very little choice. All that can be done is to chronicle the impact of the plague in the region. After the Black Death and the epidemics of the 1360s, in the Northwest as elsewhere, villages decayed, tenancies remained unfilled, and labourers wasted little time in pressing for higher wages. In the ecclesiastical sphere, a large proportion of benefices fell vacant, profits from mortuary fees soared, and

---

[33] Walton le Dale and Ashton in Makerfield actually straddle the highway, while Hindley and Atherton are situated in close proximity.

new cemeteries were authorised for the burial of the stricken.[34] Plague remained endemic throughout the period under discussion. Adjustments made to the rent-roll at Newbold Astbury late in the reign of Richard II indicate an exceptionally high turnover of tenants over a comparatively short period of time.[35] Even more stark is the evidence relating to an epidemic at Bosley a few miles to the north. Some time between the drawing up of two rentals, one in 1400 and the other around 1410, over seventy per cent of the tenancies changed hands, most not even remaining in the tenure of the same family. To make the nature of the catastrophe explicit, the rental was sombrely followed in the cartulary by a hymn imploring Christ to save the world from the scourge of the plague.[36] In all likelihood the village had suffered in the wake of the national epidemic of 1407. There were certainly casualties in other parts of the region at this time: William Maghull of Maghull allegedly died of the pestilence five years after the battle of Shrewsbury.[37]

The significance of demographic change in the development of English society has long been recognised, and the crises of the late fourteenth century have been seen to represent something of a watershed.[38] Whatever the validity of assigning primacy to demographic data, it is clear that regional studies will continue to reveal wide local variations in the timing and scale of population movements, and in their relationship to economic and social change. From the limited evidence available, it is difficult to credit the Black Death with really fundamental changes in the structure of Cheshire and Lancashire society in the period under discussion. After all, patterns of economic and social organisation in the region were still largely geared to low population densities on the eve of the great plague. Large-scale demesne cultivation seems never to have been prevalent in the Northwest, while arable husbandry and open-field systems never completely predominated over mixed farming, woodlands, pasture and enclosures. The decline of the great seignorial and ecclesiastical estates, so fraught with significance elsewhere, doubtless passed unnoticed in many parts of the region. Of course, there were some important new developments. The process of internal colonisation was slowed, though not completely arrested, and in some areas land went out of cultivation, but it is probable that local depopulation was more a phenomenon of the

---

[34] See in general J. F. D. Shrewsbury, *A History of Bubonic Plague in the British Isles* (Cambridge, 1970), pp. 75–6, and Ziegler, *Black Death*, pp. 190–1 and 196–7. More specifically, see R. S. France, 'A history of plague in Lancashire', *L.C.H.S.*, 90 (1938), 1–175.

[35] P.R.O., SC 11/8.

[36] B.L., Cotton MSS., Cleopatra D VI (Macclesfield Cartulary), ff. 7–7d, 202–3d.

[37] Lancashire R.O., DDK 1406/8.

[38] E.g. J. T. Rogers, *A History of Agriculture and Prices in England* (Oxford, 1866).

second quarter of the fifteenth century than the late fourteenth century.[39] Possibly the Northwest, unlike many more anciently settled regions of England, retained throughout the fourteenth century some of the demographic dynamism of an expanding, 'frontier' society, and accordingly was better placed to recoup its losses in the first generations after the Black Death.[40] This is not to claim that population levels ever reached their earlier heights, or that traditional structures were ever fully established. Rather, it is suggested that alongside the evidence for rural depopulation in some areas must be set signs of new vigour. In the fifteenth century a number of villages and towns in east Cheshire and southeast Lancashire continued to prosper and expand.[41] In any case, any overall decline in the area under cultivation must be regarded as a retreat from marginal lands, and a reflection of an increasingly healthy relationship between men and resources. At the same time there can be little doubt that the uneven and volatile nature of population movements greatly encouraged personal mobility. Certainly many hundreds of local men left their homes seeking opportunities as labourers, craftsmen, clerks and soldiers in other parts of the realm, and a great number never returned.[42] Any assessment of demographic conditions in the Northwest must take account of its considerable expatriate population.

[39] There was a steady rise in aggregate rents at Halton and Whitley between 1375 and 1425: P.R.O., DL 29/4/34–5, 60. For a detailed reconstruction of the situation on one Cheshire manor see P. H. W. Booth and J. P. Dodd, 'The manor and fields of Frodsham, 1315–74', *L.C.H.S.*, 128 (1978), 27–57.

[40] There is also evidence of a demographic rally in other parts of England in the last decades of the fourteenth century: Hatcher, *Plague, Population and English Economy*.

[41] E.g. see G. H. Tupling, 'The pre-Reformation parishes and chapelries of Lancashire', *L.C.A.S.*, 67 (1957), 1–16.

[42] See below, Chapters 7, 8 and 9.

## Chapter 5

# LANDED SOCIETY

While the value of obtaining some quantitative conception of Cheshire and Lancashire society in the later middle ages is obvious, it needs stressing that such a concern would have seemed alien to contemporaries. It is true enough that princes and lords were aware of the value of a prolific population, and could appreciate the grave consequences of the demographic crises of the fourteenth century. Yet, in so far as men had a conception of the social structure, their terms of reference were qualitative. In the traditional view, society was an ordered hierarchy in which the various ranks maintained degrees of power and influence totally unrelated to their numerical size. If numerical significance were attached to the population, it was more as a reflection of the status of the lords who commanded their allegiance. Indeed the concept of nobility and the institution of lordship permeated the entire social structure, welding together the disparate orders into a single system of deference and patronage. For the most part individuals and groups were evaluated according to their positions on this hierarchical scale. While statistical information is vital to an understanding of many aspects of the social process, it must be appreciated that the social system of medieval England was primarily an ideological construct.

In proceeding with this study of regional society it is therefore important to examine some fairly direct and tangible expression of its value-system. Without doubt it is the tenurial hierarchy which most nearly expressed in material terms the moral order of late medieval England. It is indeed instructive that landholding provided so much of the terminology of rank and status. The concepts of lordship and serfdom were rooted in particular forms of tenure, while the institutions themselves were anchored in a differential access to landed resources. Indeed a general distinction can be drawn between landholders who held their estates in return for secure and honourable services and tenants who farmed their lands in return for more onerous rents in cash, kind or labour, between landlords who could afford to live as rentiers and who held courts for their dependent tenantry and the peasants who lived by their own labour and who were subject to manorial discipline. Accordingly the tenure of manorial property can be taken as a convenient criterion in defining membership of what might be loosely termed a landowning class, and the manor itself can be regarded not merely as an economic unit through which the lords 'ensured the flow of income',[1] but also as a visible expression of the political, social and moral dominance of the landed élite. In the following sections landed society is approached largely through a consideration of the various institutions and families holding manorial property in the Northwest.

I

It was noted earlier that English society in the later middle ages has been studied almost exclusively from the perspective of the greater landlords. Without doubt this approach has served to over-estimate the importance of the large estate in the rural scene, and nowhere is this more apparent than in Cheshire and Lancashire. Sparsely populated and economically under-developed, the Northwest could boast no important seignorial households and few large monastic establishments, nor a sizeable commercial sector to stimulate large-scale demesne-farming. It has already been suggested that the region was never as thoroughly manorialised as most other parts of the kingdom, at least not in the classical sense. Yet most local villages were at some stage styled as manors, and a detailed study of landed society must commence with the tenure of manorial property in the region.

The researches of G. Ormerod, W. Farrer and others have made it possible to reconstruct in some detail and at little cost in labour the structure of landed society in the Northwest at any given point in time.[2] Thus the large and populous hundred of West Derby in Lancashire contained some sixty-seven reasonably distinct manorial units in the period under discussion. This sample grouping of manors can be divided roughly into four main classes according to the nature of their tenure: six (nine per cent) remained as demesne of the duchy of Lancaster; two (three per cent) were in the tenure of non-resident baronial families; eight (twelve per cent) were in the possession of religious institutions; the remaining fifty-one (seventy-six per cent) were in the hands of local gentry families. From rough calculations for other hundreds, it seems that the West Derby figures reflect conditions right across the region. In Broxton, Nantwich, Northwich, Bucklow, Edisbury, Macclesfield, Salford and Leyland hundreds well over three-quarters of the manors were in the tenure of the

---

[1] Hilton, *West Midlands*, p. 124.
[2] For the detailed manorial histories on which this analysis is based, see Ormerod, *History of Cheshire*, and *V.C.H. Lancaster*, *passim*.

gentry. The hundred of Wirral, where the abbey of St Werburgh possessed vast estates, and the hundred of Blackburn, where Whalley abbey was a major landowner and vast acreages lay under the forest jurisdiction, were to some extent exceptional, but even in these divisions over half the manors lay in the hands of the local gentry. Out of the fifty-four identifiable manors in Wirral, thirty-seven per cent were monastic properties, while fifty-seven per cent belonged to gentry families. Out of the sixty vills in Blackburnshire listed by R. B. Smith for the early fourteenth century,[3] some thirty per cent were part of the demesne of the honour of Clitheroe, later the duchy of Lancaster, four per cent were held by local monasteries, while sixty-six per cent were tenancies of local gentlemen. Looking at the region as a whole, it would appear that the resident gentry held over three-quarters of the manors, leaving less than a quarter under royal, aristocratic or ecclesiastical control.[4]

This introductory survey has provided some statistical impression of the character of landed society in the Northwest. Even these findings do not do full justice to the overwhelming preponderance of small over large estates in the region. In a later section it is suggested that most of the manors in the possession of local families were held singly or in pairs rather than in larger conglomerations. Further, most of the monastic holdings were isolated manors and granges. The eight manors in West Derby hundred in the possession of religious institutions included Burscough and Holland, the home-farms of local priories; Wigan, Winwick and Prescot, the glebes of local rectories; and three small properties belonging to Whalley abbey, the Hospitallers and Merivale abbey in Warwickshire. Nor do the figures give a full impression of the landed wealth of the resident squirearchy. Thus the rectory of Wigan was virtually part of the Langton patrimony, while other ecclesiastical properties also lay at the disposal of local lineages. Moreover the earls of Chester, dukes of Lancaster and other non-resident lords were increasingly relinquishing direct control of their estates in the Northwest. On both sides of the Mersey royal manors were

---

[3] Smith, *Blackburnshire*, pp. 42–4.

[4] Though the manors held by the untitled Cheshire and Lancashire 'barons' have been included among the gentry holdings, the proportion of land in the Northwest held by resident gentry families was far higher than in most other regions, where the church was the greatest landowner. Even in 'gentry-dominated' Buckinghamshire and Rutlandshire the landed wealth of the gentry (only half of whom were in any case residents) was only narrowly greater than that of the church: J. Cornwall, 'The early Tudor gentry', *Ec.H.R.*, second series XVII (1964–5), 461. Meanwhile in Richmondshire, very much a lay enclave in north Yorkshire, gentry families still held only around 43% of the manors, though to their holdings might be added the estates of some of the local baronage: A. J. Pollard, 'The Richmondshire community of gentry during the Wars of the Roses' in C. Ross (ed.), *Patronage, Pedigree and Power in Later Medieval England* (Gloucester, 1979), pp. 43–7.

leased, and baronial properties purchased, by local gentlemen. Indeed the general trend throughout the later middle ages was towards a total control of the landed resources of the region by resident gentry families. It is necessary at this point to discuss the position of the various classes of landlord in more detail.

II

Throughout the middle ages the paramount landlords in the Northwest were the earls of Chester and the lords of Lancaster. In the decades following the Norman Conquest Cheshire and the area later known as Lancashire were granted as fiefs to two of William the Conqueror's closest companions. Through a long and chequered history the earls of Chester and the lords of Lancaster, in addition to their extensive estates in other parts of the kingdom, managed to consolidate their holdings and to acquire franchisal rights in their respective shires. Although the two lordships reverted to the crown from time to time, they were retained as territorial units and used to endow members of the royal family. From the late thirteenth century the earldom of Chester became a part of the appanage of the king's eldest son. At the beginning of the period under discussion it was held by Edward, the Black Prince. At the same time the duchy of Lancaster, as the lordship was styled from 1351, had passed to another son of Edward III, John of Gaunt. By a curious series of circumstances, the lordships of Chester and Lancaster were never far removed from crown control throughout the later middle ages. For much of their reigns Richard II, Henry V and Henry VI were without direct male heirs, and accordingly the earldom of Chester remained in their hands. After the death of John of Gaunt in 1399, the duchy of Lancaster also descended with the crown, though again its administration continued to be kept distinct.

Within the Northwest the pre-eminence of the earls of Chester and the dukes of Lancaster was uncontested. In Cheshire the former had acquired almost all the rights of the crown, and had developed an independent chancery, exchequer and courts of law at Chester. In Lancashire the latter built upon the achievements of earlier lords and gained further franchisal rights within the region. Both shires were recognised as counties palatine, with large measures of autonomy from crown control. Their semi-independent status was accentuated by their unusual tenurial structure. In the feudal hierarchy the earl of Chester and the duke of Lancaster stood within the limits of their shires in the same position as the king within the kingdom, and accordingly relations between the chief lords and their lesser tenants were unusually direct and uncomplicated. Even humble yeoman farmers from the forest of Macclesfield can be found travelling down to London to perform homage to the Black Prince for their lands and offices.[5] Indeed the value of feudal perquisites kept the royal lords keenly interested in local affairs. In addition to military obligations, there were the profits of relief, wardship and marriage, accruing from the two palatinates. Simply in their private capacities as feudal lords they had valuable interests to guard and maintain in every village in the region. If it is remembered that wide-ranging administrative and judicial powers of a public nature were also in their hands, some impression can be gained of the immense influence of the Black Prince, John of Gaunt and their successors in the region.

Alongside their rights as feudal overlords and franchise-holders, the earls of Chester and the lords of Lancaster retained direct proprietary interests in the two counties. From the first they retained certain profits for their own use, most notably the fee-farms of Chester, Liverpool, Wigan, Preston and Lancaster and the returns from the Dee mills.[6] Then there were those parts of the region which had never been sub-infeudated. The manors of Frodsham, Shotwick and Macclesfield in Cheshire, and the manors of West Derby and Salford in Lancashire, were retained as demesne throughout much of the middle ages. Even more significant were the tracts of land, presumably uncleared or uncultivated in the earlier period, which were designated as forest. The Cheshire forests of Delamere and Macclesfield, and the Lancashire chases of Blackburnshire and Bowland remained important reserves of profit and power for their royal lords. Even estates which had been granted out could escheat, and be reincorporated into the demesne of the two lordships. Thus in the early fourteenth century the Lancashire baronies of Clitheroe, Widnes and Penwortham and the Cheshire barony of Halton, each with their own demesne-lands, had passed into the hands of the lords of Lancaster. All in all there were several score villages and hamlets which remained in the direct control of the royal lords. Although it is impossible to be precise, around ten per cent of local peasants would have owned either the earl of Chester or the duke of Lancaster as their manorial lord.

While the earls of Chester and the dukes of Lancaster retained strong territorial interests in the region, there was little scope for the intensive demesne cultivation typical of large seignorial estates in other parts of the kingdom. Neither the terrain nor the climate were particularly suited to arable farming, and the value of a home-farm to an absentee lord was limited. In such circumstances stock-breeding and dairy-farming were

---

[5] E.g. in 1362 John son of Richard Sutton and William son of Robert Hulme performed homage to the Black Prince in Kennington and London: *B.P.R.*, III, pp. 450–1.
[6] Somerville, *Duchy of Lancaster*, p. 94; P.R.O., SC 6/787/9, m. 1.

doubtless of greater significance. In the honour of Clitheroe a number of
well-stocked vaccaries had been established at the beginning of the
fourteenth century, and the dairy-farms continued to be an important
source of revenue well into the period under discussion.[7] The Black
Prince's stud-farm at Macclesfield was successful for a time, and from his
Cheshire stock herds of cattle were driven south to feed his household
or perhaps even to swell the markets in London.[8] The timber, turves and
coal found on royal manors were also sources of local profit. Yet,
increasingly from the late fourteenth century, the royal lords came to
surrender their direct interests in the regional economy, and to lease out
manorial assets, first on a piecemeal but later on a wholesale basis, to local
farmers.

During the later middle ages it is evident that more and more of the
powers and profits accruing from royal estates in the Northwest were
passing into the hands of local families. Since there had always been
Cheshire and Lancashire men employed in seignorial administration, this
was not an entirely novel development. Yet by the end of the fourteenth
century the process was virtually complete, with local gentlemen holding
most of the more prestigious positions and lucrative leases. Thus in Henry
V's reign Sir Richard Hoghton was chief steward of the Lancastrian estates
in the region, while Sir Thomas Tunstall, Sir Henry Hoghton and Sir
James Harrington were the stewards of the hundreds of Lonsdale,
Amounderness, Blackburn, Salford and West Derby as well as several
manors and parks.[9] In Cheshire there were fewer positions of this nature
left to be filled. Most of the forestships had been the hereditary preserves
of local families for many generations.[10] The most valuable prize still
outstanding was the stewardship of the lordship of Macclesfield, customarily held with the surveyorship of the Cheshire forests. In the fourteenth
century this lucrative office was bestowed on a succession of nobles and
knights from outside the region.[11] Indeed the first local knight to be
advanced to the stewardship of Macclesfield was Sir John Stanley in
1403.[12] He was followed in 1414 by his son and namesake, and in 1439

[7] Tupling, *Rossendale*, pp. 17–27, 31–3.

[8] *B.P.R.*, III, pp. 76, 349, 393, 419, 423. The Macclesfield stud-farm was still well-stocked in
1380: P.R.O., SC 6/787/11, m. 6.

[9] Somerville, *Duchy of Lancaster*, pp. 492–3, 499–503, 507.

[10] E.g. Donnes of Utkinton in Delamere and Stanleys of Storeton in Wirral: *Ches. R.R.*, I,
pp. 154–5; J.R.U.L., Rylands Charters, R72927/1306. See also B. M. C. Husain, 'Delamere
Forest in later medieval times', *L.C.H.S.*, 107 (1955), 23–59, and R. Stewart-Brown, 'The
disafforestation of Wirral', *L.C.H.S.*, 59 (1907), 165–80.

[11] For the appointments as stewards of Macclesfield of Sir John Chandos, Sir Nigel Loring,
the earl of Stafford, Sir Thomas Clifford, Sir Thomas Wednesley and Sir Hugh Despenser,
see *B.P.R.*, III, p. 122; *Ches. R.R.*, I, pp. 297, 111, 511, 145.     [12] *Ibid.*, p. 446.

the office became virtually hereditary with a grant of the stewardship to Sir Thomas Stanley and his son in joint survivorship.[13] Meanwhile Sir John Savage and his successors succeeded in establishing a dynastic interest in the parkership of Macclesfield.[14]

Nor was the tenure of office the only means by which local men were able to profit from the royal estates in the region. From the earliest times the earls of Chester and the lords of Lancaster had found it expedient to lease parts of their demesne, or even entire manors and lordships. In his study of Rossendale, G. H. Tupling has chronicled in some detail the leasing of the vaccaries in the honour of Clitheroe to local men in the later middle ages.[15] From the late fourteenth century the demesnes of Drakelow in Cheshire were regularly leased to members of the Bulkeley family, while the farms of Ulnes Walton and Leyland in Lancashire came to be regarded almost as part of the patrimony of the Faringtons of Worden.[16] Whether local gentlemen made fortunes from such leases is perhaps to be questioned, but there is no doubt that an increasingly large proportion of the revenues of the two palatinates was being diverted into their pockets. While local officials continued to receive the fees for duties rendered obsolete through the leasing of demesnes, the profitability of the estates was further reduced through lavish patronage. Vast sums were assigned from the revenues of the palatinates as annuities for local men. On occasion entire manors were granted to particularly favoured retainers.[17] In the first six months of his reign Henry V retained some eighty-six Lancashire gentlemen, and granted them annuities totalling over £1,100 from the duchy of Lancaster.[18] It would seem that this sum represented about half of the king's income from his Lancashire estates.[19]

Indeed it is tempting to conclude that during the period under discussion the earls of Chester and the dukes of Lancaster were administering their estates in the Northwest largely for the benefit of the local gentry. While such a conclusion has some plausibility, it must be remembered that grants of offices, annuities, and favourable leases were instruments of patronage, designed to reward past, and secure future, services. Accordingly it is extremely difficult to compute the costs and benefits of the entire arrangement. What is certain is that the operations of patronage were necessarily discriminatory, adding to the fortunes of

---

[13] *Ches. R.R.*, II, pp. 666, 484.    [14] *Ches. R.R.*, I, p. 292; *Ches. R.R.*, II, pp. 484, 487.

[15] Tupling, *Rossendale*, pp. 32–3.

[16] *Ches. R.R.*, I, p. 352; *Ches. R.R.*, II, p. 221; *V.C.H. Lancaster*, VI, p. 11n.

[17] E.g. the manor of Shotwick was granted to Sir Hugh Calveley for life: Ormerod, *History of Cheshire*, II, p. 571.    [18] P.R.O., DL 42/17, ff. 2d–8.

[19] Based on figures in the duchy of Lancaster *valor* of 1419: Somerville, *Duchy of Lancaster*, p. 188.

certain families at the expense of others. While a large number of local men appear to have profited in the years when Richard II and Henry V were actively building up their followings in the region, at other times the prizes were far less widely distributed. Inevitably local families with influence at court were able to mediate to a greater degree the flow of patronage into the region. There can be little doubt that the rapid rise to regional eminence of the Stanleys of Lathom in the fifteenth century was in large measure a function of the ability to act as brokers between court and country.[20]

III

The extensive territorial interests of the earls of Chester and the dukes of Lancaster rather pre-empted the growth of other aristocratic power-bases in the Northwest. Indeed neither Cheshire not Lancashire could boast a resident noble house during the period under discussion. Even in earlier times the lords of Chester and Lancaster, like most members of their class, preferred to reside closer to the centres of political power and influence. In any case there were few other magnates with important territorial possessions in the Northwest. While the lords of Chester and Lancaster had created baronies, surprisingly few were acquired by families from outside the region. In Lancashire a fortunate marriage early in the fourteenth century secured the return of the Lacy baronies of Clitheroe, Penwortham and Widnes to the chief lord, leaving only three baronies south of the Ribble in the hands of vassals: Warrington and Newton in Makerfield held by the Butlers and Langtons, both Lancashire families, and Manchester held by outsiders, the De La Warres of Swineshead in Lincolnshire. In Cheshire the situation was fairly similar. The baronies of Kinderton, Shipbrook and Stockport were held by the local families of Venables, Vernon and Warren. The baronies of Nantwich and Malpas were sub-divided, but despite the moieties of the Suttons and Audleys from Staffordshire local interests seem to have predominated.[21] The barony of Dunham, the ancestral seat of the Masey family, was acquired by the Stranges of Knockin in Shropshire during this period, but by the 1430s it was in the hands of several Cheshire claimants.[22] Meanwhile the barony of Halton passed back with the rest of the Lacy inheritance to the duchy of Lancaster. Only the barony of Montalt, held by the earls of Salisbury, remained as a bastion of aristocratic power in the region, and even this lordship can be regarded as the exception that proves the rule:

[20]  See below, Chapter 10.
[21]  Ormerod, *History of Cheshire*, III, pp. 421–6; II, pp. 601–5.
[22]  Ormerod, *History of Cheshire*, I, pp. 520–9; *Ches. R.R.*, II, p. 225.

its territorial base lay outside Cheshire and in any case it was soon to pass under the sway of the Stanleys of Lathom.[23] Indeed the noble families having interests in local baronies – the Montagues, Stranges, De La Warres, Suttons and Audleys – constitute almost all the major non-resident landowning families. The FitzAlans, Greys of Ruthin, Lovells, Ferrers's of Groby and Dacres of Gilsland were the only other absentee landlords of any substance.

Demonstrably there were important factors working against the consolidation of aristocratic fortunes in the Northwest in this period. In the first place the local holdings of noble families were doubtless considered too poor and remote to serve as residences, and their best interest lay in amassing properties close to their main seats. In any case the economic climate was against large-scale demesne-farming, and all across the country landlords were cutting their losses by leasing outlying manors to local farmers. The palatine status of Cheshire and Lancashire posed further problems for outsiders holding property in the region. At the best of times it was difficult for absentee lords to maintain property interests against local opposition, but to prosecute and defend cases in the Northwest was a prospect to daunt even the most litigious noblemen. Accordingly it is not surprising that so many aristocratic houses were finding it more convenient to sell or let to farm their local estates. In Cheshire, the earls of Salisbury certainly divested themselves of their interests during this period: the manor of Neston was acquired by Sir John Stanley and the manor of Bosley by the royal clerk, John Macclesfield.[24] The earl of Arundel, likewise, sold the manors of Dunham on the Hill, Mickle Trafford and Hoole to William Troutbeck in the 1420s.[25] The earl of Huntingdon sub-let his farm of the town of Northwich to Sir Richard Winnington in 1395.[26] Lord Grey of Ruthin granted Sir Hugh Holes the manors of Rushton, Eaton and Tarporley on a long lease in 1387.[27] Lord Strange of Knockin sold the manor of Bidston to Stanley around 1397, and soon after relinquished control of the barony of Dunham.[28] In Lancashire Ferrers of Groby leased moieties of Chorley and Bolton to John Audlem in 1388, and Dacre of Gilsland similarly let to

---

[23] *Ibid.*, p. 671.

[24] *Ibid.*, p. 354; J. L. C. Bruell, 'An edition of the cartulary of John de Macclesfield', unpublished M.A. thesis, University of London, 1969, items 23, 161; *Ches. R.R.*, II, p. 482. In 1391 Sir John Mascy of Puddington led an armed assault on the castle of Hawarden, but was subsequently pardoned and appointed its steward: Bruell, 'Edition of cartulary of John de Macclesfield', item 38.

[25] *Ches. Pleas*, pp. 79, 85; *Ches. R.R.*, II, pp. 24, 719, 461.

[26] *Ches. R.R.*, I, pp. 241, 531.     [27] *Ches. R.R.*, II, p. 371.

[28] *Ches. R.R.*, I, p. 445; Ormerod, *History of Cheshire*, I, pp. 520–9; *Ches. R.R.*, II, p. 225.

farm the manor of Eccleston.[29] Around 1400 the earl of Ormond relinquished control of the barony of Weeton to the enterprising Stanley, who probably secured it in exchange for his Irish acquisitions.[30] Throughout the region the territorial influence of non-resident nobles was dwindling to insignificance, and newly powerful local families were gaining at their expense.

In the structure of landed society the aristocratic element was clearly negligible in the Northwest. Even in 1375 less than three per cent of local manors were held by noble families, and this percentage declined further in the fifteenth century. The limited importance of the aristocracy in local society is attested in other ways. Whereas in most shires commissions of the peace and the like were normally headed by noblemen, in Cheshire and Lancashire the leading members were usually only knights. Nor is there much evidence of aristrocratic leadership in more informal matters. In his heraldic dispute with the Scropes of Masham, Sir Robert Grosvenor could find no magnate to vouch for him, and had to rely on the depositions of some two hundred knights and gentlemen. Similarly, whereas disputes elsewhere were often referred to the adjudication of a nobleman, local settlements were made by panels of gentlemen. Prior to the rise to pre-eminence of the Stanleys of Lathom in the second quarter of the fifteenth century, social leadership in the region was largely vested in the two county communities.[31]

Yet it must not be concluded that there was no contact between peers of the realm and Cheshire and Lancashire men. Nobles retaining property interests in the region maintained regular contact with local agents and tenants. Gentlemen from the Manchester area seem to have been regular visitors at Lord De La Warre's mansion at Swineshead in Lincolnshire.[32] Even more interesting, it is possible to document the presence of a whole group of Cheshire men two hundred miles from their homes in the earl of Salisbury's castle at Carisbrooke.[33] Since local soldiers acquired great prominence in the fourteenth century, aristocratic commanders seem to have been particularly anxious to maintain relations with the region. While the earls of Chester and the dukes of Lancaster had first call on their

---

[29] *V.C.H. Lancaster*, VI, pp. 246–7; Manchester Central Reference Library, Farrer MSS., 51/1/18, p. 890; *V.C.H. Lancaster*, VI, p. 162.

[30] *C. Ch. R. 1341–1417*, p. 436. In 1399 Stanley granted his manor of Blackcastle, Co. Meath to James, earl of Ormond: *Calendar of Ormond Deeds*, part II. 1350–1413, ed. E. Curtis (Irish Manuscripts Commission, 1934), no. 340.

[31] Bennett, 'County community', 36, 38.

[32] Town Hall, Manchester, Manchester Corporation MSS., 51/6, 52/29, 52/74.

[33] The Cheshire men included Sir Robert Legh, Sir John Mascy of Tatton, Peter Legh and Robert Downes: Bruell, 'Edition of cartulary of John de Macclesfield', item 23.

services, local soldiers can be found serving in the retinues of all the leading magnates of the realm. The tenure of local office also provided noblemen with the opportunity to build up their followings in the Northwest. Thomas Mowbray, earl of Nottingham and Sir Henry Percy were two lords who, while serving as justices of Chester, developed close relations with local gentry.[34] If the regional society was remarkably unaristocratic in complexion, it must not be assumed that local knights and gentlemen did not often move in more exalted circles.

IV

Of all the main classes of landlord in late medieval England, the church remained the wealthiest. Many churchmen were deemed to command resources on a scale comparable with even the most affluent secular lords. In the poll-tax of 1379 the abbot of St Werburgh's, Chester, was assessed at £4, the statutory rate for peers of the realm.[35] The abbots of Whalley and Vale Royal at £3 each, and the abbot of Combermere and the prior of Norton at £2 each, were likewise taxed on a scale commensurate with the baronage. Indeed no local layman was required to contribute more than £1. This was the assessment of Ralph Langton, baron of Newton in Makerfield and several other knights holding estates worth more than £40 per annum.[36] Significantly, there were numerous lesser churchmen, including the priors of Birkenhead and Burscough, and the rectors of Stockport, Rostherne and Standish, whose incomes were assessed at the same rate. Even more remarkable, the rectory of Wigan was valued at 200 marks, and its youthful parson, James Langton, was assessed at thirty shillings, half as much more again as his father, the baron of Newton.[37] Clearly the leading churchmen in the region could command resources well in excess of most of the local gentry.

Ecclesiastical incomes were derived very largely from the possession of landed estate. Tithes, probate and mortuary fees, oblates and so on were all important sources of income, but the tenure of manorial property was the hallmark of the well-endowed religious establishment. The abbey of St Werburgh, Chester was undoubtedly the richest landlord in the region. Founded soon after the Norman Conquest on the site of an earlier religious house, the Benedictine convent not only stood heir to the properties of

---

[34] *C.P.R. 1391–1396*, p. 573; *Ches. R.R.*, I, pp. 326, 379–80.

[35] Bennett, 'Lancashire and Cheshire clergy', 22–8.

[36] P.R.O., E 179/130/24, E 179/130/28.

[37] Bennett, 'Lancashire and Cheshire clergy', 7. For a fuller account of the Langtons and the rectory of Wigan see G. T. O. Bridgeman, *The History of the Church and Manor of Wigan*, vol. I (C.S., n.s. 15, 1888).

its collegiate predecessor but also benefited from the piety of successive earls of Chester.[38] By the time of Domesday Book the manors of Saighton, Boughton, Newton, Wervin, Ince, Sutton, Eastham and Bromborough, some of the most highly valued manors in Cheshire, were already in its possession, and in the following centuries it amassed lucrative holdings in the city of Chester, the Dee–Gowy lowland, Wirral and elsewhere. Since its estates included some of the most populous and fertile lands in the region, the Benedictine convent enjoyed unrivalled prosperity and prestige. Yet several Cistercian monasteries might well have possessed larger acreages. Despite its marginal location in a detached portion of Lancashire, Furness abbey with its vast tracts of countryside and its extensive liberties must be acknowledged as the second most substantial ecclesiastical landlord in the region.[39] Within the archdeaconry of Chester, the Cistercian abbeys of Whalley, Vale Royal and Combermere and the house of Augustinian canons at Norton were the next most important establishments. Whalley owned vast acreages in the bleak moorlands of Blackburn hundred; Vale Royal held a compact estate centred upon the manors of Darnhall and Over; Combermere drew its wealth from extensive properties in south Cheshire; and Norton was possessed of substantial holdings in and around the lordship of Halton.[40] Even the more modestly endowed priories of Burscough, Birkenhead, Holland and Penwortham were able to acquire manorial properties in their immediate neighbourhoods.[41] In addition to the holdings of local monasteries, there were the estates attached as glebe to parish churches or in the possession of religious institutions from other parts of the kingdom. All in all about twelve per cent of local manors were in the possession of the church. Although this was probably not as high a proportion as is found in other regions, it still represented a significant hold by ecclesiastical landlords on the rural economy of the Northwest.

Despite the survival of a great deal of evidence relating to the endowment of local monasteries, there is very little documentation regarding the management of their properties. The lack of this sort of

---

[38] See Jones, *Church in Chester*, pp. 59–60; R. V. H. Burne, *The Monks of Chester* (London, 1962).

[39] *V.C.H. Lancaster*, II, p. 128.

[40] Bennett, 'Lancashire and Cheshire clergy', 22–3; *The Coucher Book or Chartulary of Whalley Abbey*, ed. W. A. Hulton (4 vols., C.S., o.s. 10, 11, 16, 20, 1847–9); *Vale Royal Ledger Book*; J. Hall, 'The Book of the Abbot of Combermere, 1289–1529' in *Lancashire and Cheshire Miscellanies*, II (L.C.R.S., 31, 1896); W. Beamont, *History of the Castle of Halton and the Abbey of Norton* (Warrington, 1873).

[41] *The Cartulary of Burscough Priory*, ed. A. N. Webb (C.S., third series 18, 1970); R. Stewart-Brown, *Birkenhead Priory and the Mersey Ferry* (Liverpool, 1925); *V.C.H. Lancaster*, II, p. 111; *Documents relating to Penwortham Priory*, ed. W. A. Hulton (C.S., o.s. 30, 1853).

source material is perhaps instructive, since manorial records survive in such abundance for the larger religious establishments elsewhere. It might reflect considerably less interest among the monasteries of the region in demesne cultivation. Doubtless most houses retained a home-farm to supply the immediate needs of the brethren, but there is no evidence of large-scale production for the market. Significantly the holdings of most local monasteries were extremely localised, and any outlying possessions were typically let to farm. In so far as monasteries were interested in the commercial exploitation of their estates, stock-rearing took priority over arable farming. Whalley abbey and other Cistercian houses in the region prided themselves on their large flocks of sheep, and some of their wool certainly found its way into the export market. In this respect St Werburgh's abbey remained the great exception. Undoubtedly Benedictine traditions of estate organisation, the size and value of its properties, and the close proximity of the markets of Chester all served to encourage it to retain arable land in demesne cultivation for much longer than other religious houses in the Northwest. While the trend towards commutation and a rentier economy was well advanced, it was still involved in the direct exploitation of some of its lands in 1431.[42] Several generations after its dissolution a local antiquarian recalled that the manor of Newton 'was once one of those sweet morsels that the Abbot and his Covent [*sic*] kept for their own wholesome provision'.[43]

By the fourteenth century the age of generous benefactions to the church had long since finished. Interestingly enough, Holland priory, founded by Sir Robert Holland during the reign of Edward II, was the last Benedictine house to be established in medieval England, and it was far from lavishly endowed.[44] During the period under discussion pious laymen continued to make gifts to the church, but the sums involved were far more modest than in earlier generations. Many local testators left sums of money to the four orders of friary, but few made bequests to monasteries. The first duke of Lancaster's gift of cottages and land to Whalley abbey was to be used solely to maintain a female recluse to pray for his soul.[45] Indeed all the most substantial benefactions in this period were directed toward the enrichment of the secular church. Thus funds were bequeathed to rebuild and beautify many parish churches, and colleges were endowed at Bunbury and Manchester.[46] Still, the involve-

[42] P.R.O., SC 11/901.
[43] D. King, *The Vale Royal of England, or the County Palatine of Chester* (London, 1656), p. 54.  [44] *V.C.H. Lancaster*, II, p. 111.
[45] *H.M.C.*, Various Collections, vol. II (1903), pp. 11–12.
[46] *C.P.R. 1385–1389*, pp. 310, 444; Manchester Cathedral, MSS. nos. 25–31.

ment of monks from St Werburgh's, Vale Royal, Norton and Birkenhead, as well as local friars, in Sir Thomas Dutton's schemes for a chantry chapel in Warrington indicates that the various sections of the church were not entirely inimical to each other's interests.[47]

In the main time was running against ecclesiastical landlords in the Northwest. After the Black Death profits from land declined, and while some gentry families recouped their losses through inheritance, few monasteries were able to increase the size of their estates. The declining demand for grain further reduced the profitability of estates still trying to produce for the market. D. Jones has cited the diminishing value of the tithes raised by the dean of St John's, Chester, from Shocklack, Farndon, and Stoke parishes to illustrate the problems facing landlords in this period.[48] After all, the church was faced on the other hand by mounting labour costs. Where labour services were still enforced, there was restiveness among the tenantry. There were major disturbances on the estates of St Werburgh's abbey in 1381, and thirteen years later the convent complained that 'the rents and services which their tenants and serfs used to pay had been irrevocably diminished and withdrawn under pretext of pestilence', and that in addition coastal erosion had reduced their income from Wirral, 'the land from which they were wont to derive the greater part of their victuals'.[49] There were other difficulties for ecclesiastical landlords in the region: in 1400 the Carmelite friars bewailed losses incurred through the murrain and border raiding, while the dean of St John's protested about the deleterious effects of the Welsh wars.[50]

Declining incomes from land, compounded by mismanagement and burdensome obligations, brought many monasteries to the verge of bankruptcy. As early as 1362 the Black Prince intervened in the affairs of St Werburgh's 'in consideration of the damage and loss which has befallen the said house by the bad government' of the last abbot.[51] In 1415 the house was again seized after it had been brought to the king's attention that it 'was charged with great annuities, pensions and corrodies, and debts, and its goods and jewels [were] wasted, and many of its manors, lands and possessions improvidently demised at farm and otherwise alienated'.[52] In 1418 the new abbot was obliged to mortgage the manor of Weston on Trent in Derbyshire to Thomas Langley, bishop of Durham, in return for a loan of 800 marks.[53] During Richard II's reign it was also

---

[47] Cheshire R.O., DLT, Liber C, f. 167d.

[48] Jones, *Church in Chester*, p. 78. In some respects his figures are misleading. The church of Stoke was leased for £20 in 1385, but it was the church without the glebe which was leased for £15 6s 8d in 1392: *Ches. R.R.*, I, pp. 452–3.  [49] *C.Pap.L.*, IV, p. 533.

[50] *C.Pap.L.*, V, p. 270; Jones, *Church in Chester*, p. 77.  [51] *B.P.R.*, III, p. 444.

[52] *C.P.R. 1413–1416*, p. 353.  [53] *C.C.R. 1413–1419*, p. 518.

discovered that the abbot of Vale Royal had wasted and impoverished his house, while in 1412 the chamberlain of Chester and others were instructed to administer the revenues of Combermere abbey which 'was so impoverished and so greatly in debt'.[54] Legal and illegal harassment from local gentry families added to the misfortunes of the monasteries. Many heads of religious houses found it expedient to buy the support of local notables. Thus the prior of Norton granted an annuity of £3 to Sir Lawrence Dutton.[55] The abbot of Vale Royal was far less successful in his choice of protector, judging from the anxious tone of advice sent him regarding Sir John Stanley's spurious claims to the advowson of Kirkham.[56]

v

In the Northwest over three-quarters of the manors were in the hands of local gentry families. Since royal, aristocratic and ecclesiastical estates often came under their effective control, it is far easier to under-estimate than to over-estimate the domination of the local countryside by members of this class. Of course, not every Cheshire and Lancashire village had its own resident gentry family. After all the more important lineages held more than one manor. The poll-tax returns of 1379 provide some impression of the distribution of gentry seats. In over half of the seventeen villages in West Derby hundred for which returns have survived, there is evidence of a resident lord of the manor. Sir William Atherton at Atherton, Sir Peter Gerard at Ashton in Makerfield, Hugh Bradshaw at Westleigh, Henry Scarisbrick at Scarisbrick and John Eccleston at Eccleston were among the lords assessed at £1, while there were other *armigeri* at Rixton with Glazebrook, Hindley, Ince in Makerfield, Lowton with Kenyon, Bickerstaffe and Aughton, and two substantial franklins at Parr. Knowsley, Huyton, Pennington and Windle were the only villages populated solely by peasant-farmers. Even in the poorer and less populous Blackburn hundred, a third of the townships could still boast a resident lord. Most important was Ralph Langton at Walton le Dale, but other notables included Thomas Molyneux at Cuerdale, Thomas Hesketh at Great Harwood, Thomas Banastre at Osbaldeston, Richard Rishton at Rishton, and John Towneley at Dutton. In some villages there were even two or three gentlemen in residence. All in all, in the forty-one Lancashire townships for which returns have survived, there were six knights and *armigeri* assessed at £1 each, and some thirty other squires, *armigeri* and

[54] Ormerod, *History of Cheshire*, II, p. 150; *Ches. R.R.*, I, p. 120.
[55] Cheshire R.O., DLT, Liber C, f. 159.
[56] *Vale Royal Ledger Book*, pp. 36–7.

franklins.[57] Since the surviving poll-tax material accounts for only an eighth of the population, it can be estimated that there were around forty knightly houses of the first rank, and some two hundred and forty gentry families of lesser means in the shire. Given that the population of Cheshire was a little larger than Lancashire, it is reasonable to infer that its gentry families were even more numerous. In Tudor times William Camden wrote that although Cheshire was less fertile than most other counties 'yet it always produc'd more Gentry than any of them'.[58] Even after the Industrial Revolution has completely transformed the region, the survival of so many timber-framed houses testifies to the former importance of the gentry class on both sides of the Mersey.

While the range of their connections and interests must never be under-estimated, the gentry families of the Northwest ultimately depended for their status and prestige on their positions in the local community. Sir Robert Grosvenor of Hulme, for example, was no backwoods squire. He had served on several continental campaigns. Even Geoffrey Chaucer recollected seeing his shield hanging outside an armourer's shop in London.[59] Yet it was in his native region that his real credit was based, and it was to two hundred Cheshire and Lancashire gentlemen that he turned to attest the heraldic rights of his lineage. After all, families like the Grosvenors, Venables, Vernons, Butlers, Mascys and Molyneuxs had been seated in the region since the Norman Conquest, and over the centuries had assumed almost prescriptive rights to social eminence in the two counties. Many other local lineages proudly bore as surnames the names of the villages over which from time immemorial they had exercised lordship. For many generations the Halsalls, Radcliffes, Stand-ishes, Swettenhams, Breretons and Ashtons had been patrons of the churches as well as manorial lords of the villages whose names they bore. The local stature of such dynasties, and particularly such prolific families as the Leghs, Davenports, Mascys, Radcliffes and Harringtons, cannot be gauged merely by reference to their wealth and political influence. The testimonies recorded in the Scrope–Grosvenor dispute provide some conception of the impression made by one such lineage on the local scene. According to the evidence, there were few places in Cheshire where men would not have been confronted with the Grosvenor coat-of-arms of *azure*

---

[57] P.R.O., E 179/130/24, 28. Gentry seats were clearly far thicker on the ground in the Northwest than in many other regions. According to similar calculations based on poll-tax returns, only around 16% of Yorkshire (West Riding), 12% of south Staffordshire and 10% of Gloucestershire townships had resident squires: P.R.O., E 179/206/49; R. H. Hilton, *The English Peasantry in the Later Middle Ages* (Oxford, 1975), p. 27.

[58] Camden, *Britannia*, p. 555.

[59] Stewart-Brown, 'Scrope and Grosvenor controversy', 10.

*a bend or*: it was featured on windows in the minster and *frater* of St Werburgh's, Chester; it was painted on altar-pieces in the Franciscan convent and Combermere abbey; it was engraved in stone at Norton priory and Vale Royal abbey; it was featured in stained glass in the parish churches of Aldford, Davenham, Lymm, Middlewich, Mobberley, Stockport, Tarvin and Waverton; it was depicted in numerous other chapels and manor-houses across the shire; and it was even painted on an old stone cross on the highway between Knutsford and Warrington.[60]

It is rather curious that the historian has more detailed information on the symbolic representations of the Grosvenors' ancestral worth than on its material foundations. While it is possible to trace the descent of most manors in the Northwest, and accordingly to assess in general terms the property holdings of gentry families, there is little firm evidence from which to draw conclusions regarding their incomes. A fair number of inquisitions *post mortem*, half-a-dozen rentals of varying utility, and a pitiful handful of manorial accounts and extents are all that survive to assist in the illumination of this obscure field. In the last analysis it is impossible to add a great deal to the fairly generalised assessments of landed income found in fiscal, legal and literary records.[61] Thus in the late middle ages an income of between £5 and £10 seems to have been regarded as the minimum compatible with gentle status. Higher up the scale there are two other figures to which contemporaries attached significance. Traditionally the tenure of property worth £20 a year was regarded as equivalent to holding a knight's fee. While men in this category were no longer distrained for knighthood, it is possible to depict them as constituting the bulk of the squirearchy. By the period under discussion an annual income from land of £40 had become a more significant threshold, marking a useful divide between landed families of perennial stature, whose members were frequently knighted, and the rest of the gentry. Significantly the Lancashire gentlemen with incomes over £40 were assessed at far higher rates than their neighbours in 1379, and the six individuals in this category included the only two knights listed in the returns, William Atherton and Peter Gerard, the unknighted baron of Newton in Makerfield, Ralph Langton, and three substantial squires, John Eccleston, Hugh Bradshaw and Henry Scarisbrick, the latter two of whom had sons knighted in this period.[62]

There were over six hundred gentry families in Cheshire and Lancashire,

---

[60] *Ibid.*, pp. 17–19.
[61] E.g. see H. L. Gray, 'Incomes from land in England in 1436', *E.H.R.*, XLIX (1934), pp. 623ff, and T. B. Pugh, 'The magnates, knights and gentry' in Chrimes, Ross and Griffiths (eds.), *Fifteenth-Century England*, esp. p. 97.   [62] P.R.O., E 179/130/24, 28.

and it can be assumed that almost all enjoyed incomes in excess of £5 per annum. Judging from the poll-tax returns, only about a hundred lineages held estates worth more than £40 a year, but above this line the variation could be considerable. Obviously the inquisitions *post mortem*, with all their limitations, must be brought into service to provide more specific information regarding the size, value and geographical distribution of gentry holdings. Serviceable returns have survived for less than a quarter of the gentlemen who assembled at Macclesfield in 1412 and Lancaster in 1414. While it is doubtless unduly representative of the upper echelons of the county communities, this select group of nineteen landlords provides a useful sample for detailed consideration. The wealthiest of their number was almost certainly Sir William Butler, baron of Warrington, whose Lancashire estate was valued at almost £200. Most of his landed wealth was centred on Warrington, with its dependent manors of Bewsey, Sankey and Burtonwood, but he also held the valuable manor of Layton on the Fylde coast.[63] Next in order of affluence came Sir Thomas Gerard of Brynn, with lands valued at £150 a year, including two-thirds of the manor of Ashton in Makerfield and other manorial properties at Brindle, Windle and Skelmersdale; Sir William Atherton, with an annual income of £100 from the manor of Atherton, the other third of Ashton and other estates; and Hugh Venables, baron of Kinderton, whose chief manor and other lands around Middlewich and Northwich were deemed to be worth almost £100 a year.[64] Below this opulent minority came other members of the knightly class: Sir Lawrence Fitton of Gawsworth with lands worth over £80 in the Macclesfield area; Sir Thomas Tunstall with Lonsdale properties valued at more than £60; and Adam Bostock whose estates in Bostock, Huxley and Wettenhall also brought in around £60 a year.[65] Still among the knights, actual and potential, were William Bradshaw of Westleigh, Henry Langton, Sir Thomas Grosvenor and Sir Nicholas Longford with estates worth £52, £46, £43 and £40 respectively.[66] With patrimonies valued at between £20 and £40 a year were other members of the squirearchy, including in order of affluence Sir Richard Hoghton of Hoghton, Nicholas Hesketh of Great Harwood and Rufford, Richard Bulkeley of Cheadle, John Donne of Utkinton and John Manley of Manley.[67] Beneath the line of £20 a year came three gentlemen from widely different backgrounds. John Whitmore, the scion of a rising

---

[63] *Lancashire Inquisitions*, I, pp. 112–14.
[64] *Ibid.*, pp. 123–4, 107–9; P.R.O., CHES 3/28.
[65] *Ches. R.R.*, II, pp. 278–9, 64; *Lancashire Inquisitions*, I, pp. 115–16.
[66] *Ibid.*, pp. 109–11, 137–9, 114–15; *Ches. R.R.*, II, pp. 324–5.
[67] *Lancashire Inquisitions*, I, pp. 145–7, 126; *Ches. R.R.*, II, pp. 104–5, 211, 507.

mercantile family, possessed the manor of Thurstaston and property in Chester to the total value of £18; Sir Richard Radcliffe of Winmarleigh allegedly died seised of nothing more than the manor of Astley valued at £10; and Sir Henry Hoghton, a younger son who had made his way through military and administrative service, held properties worth a mere £5 a year.[68]

It was hoped to compare the valuations given in the inquisitions *post mortem* with the assessments recorded in extents, rent-rolls and accounts. Unfortunately the two sets of documentation hardly ever seem to survive for the same village. Nevertheless manorial records can at least provide an additional perspective on the economic position of the local gentry. Thus according to the inquisitions *post mortem* the nineteen members of the sample together held thirty-seven complete manors. Since their combined estimated value was £760 a year, it is evident that the average manor in the region was reckoned to be worth a little over £20 a year. This figure finds some corroboration from the few surviving extents. Late in the reign of Edward III the Lancashire manors of Worsley and Ince Blundell were appraised in some detail, revealing annual values of £58 and £13 respectively.[69] In 1390 the Cheshire manors of Thornton and Helsby were valued prior to a division among the heirs of Sir Peter Thornton, and total receipts of approximately £20 and £15 were recorded.[70] Extant rent-rolls, on the other hand, suggest rather higher returns for the average manorial holdings. Tenants at Ashton under Lyne paid rents totalling over £80 in 1422, while their fellows at Great Barrow were paying over £50 a generation earlier.[71] Perhaps more significantly, the rentals of five widely dispersed Cheshire manors – namely Over Peover, Baddiley, Newbold Astbury, Witton and Bosley – all totalled around £30, as did the assized rents at Bickley and Marbury.[72] On a number of manors, like Aston juxta Mondrum, Church Minshull and Dutton, rent-rolls record totals of £10 and less,[73] though it is difficult to know whether these figures represent half-yearly instalments. There are other problems in the use of rentals. Obviously by their very nature they constitute optimistic evaluations of the lord's rights, but at the same time they do not record all the sources of his income. In any case no firm conclusions can be based on such a

[68] *Ibid.*, p. 790; *Lancashire Inquisitions*, II, pp. 32–4, 12–13.

[69] Manchester Central Reference Library, Farrer MSS., 50/21/21.

[70] J.R.U.L., Cornwall-Legh MSS., no. 792.

[71] Bowman, *Ashton under Lyne*, pp. 73–9; P.R.O., DL 29/4/42.

[72] J.R.U.L., Mainwaring MSS., roll 1; P.R.O., SC 11/8; Cheshire R.O., DVE/R/1; B.L., Cotton MSS., Cleopatra D VI, ff. 7–7d; Cheshire R.O., DCH/B/17–30; Shropshire R.O., Bridgewater Estates, Marbury bailiff's accounts.

[73] B.L., Additional Charters, nos. 50886, 51504.

small sample. Almost certainly the average local manor was worth more than £20 a year, but the evidence is too slender to offer an alternative estimate.

Given the limitations of the extant source material it would be even more hazardous to draw any firm conclusions regarding the composition of landed incomes in the Northwest, or to attempt to chart at all precisely the changing relationship between the lord and his estate which is so significant a feature of rural life in the later middle ages. Yet a few tentative observations can be offered. The few surviving extents indicate that even in the late fourteenth century profits from the demesne still constituted an important element in the gentry incomes. In the larger manors of Worsley and Helsby the demesne-lands accounted for a third of the total profits, while on the smaller manors of Ince Blundell and Thornton the proportion was almost exactly a half. Obviously, while the general economic climate was unfavourable to large-scale demesne-farming, most local lords were continuing to maintain home-farms to provide for their immediate needs. A number of inquisitions *post mortem* record crops growing in the fields. After his rebellion in 1403, Sir John Mascy of Tatton was found to hold eight acres of wheat, eight of rye, twenty-one of oats, one of barley and half of peas.[74] Similarly in 1427 John Whitmore had twenty-two selions sown with wheat, twenty with barley and twenty-two with peas.[75] Other factors perhaps helped to keep demesne profits as a significant item in landed incomes. On some manors at least a shortage of tenants served to swell temporarily the lands in the lord's hands, and even to stimulate the permanent extension of the demesne through enclosure. Significantly, the demesne at Worsley was worth twice as much in the reign of Henry VI as it was in 1376, while the rents had fallen by about twenty per cent.[76] Still, there is also ample evidence of lords increasingly leasing out their demesne-lands. Since the values of the Worsley, Ince Blundell, Thornton and Helsby demesnes were expressed in terms of a sum for each acre, it is possible that even they were normally let to farm, while most of the demesne-lands had been leased at Great Barrow, Newbold Astbury, Haslington, Picton, Hurleston and Aston juxta Mondrum by around 1400.[77] Likewise when John Macclesfield acquired the manors of Bosley and Christleton around the same time, he found the demesne in the former leased to peasant-farmers and the latter in decay through defect of tenants.[78]

---

[74] Ormerod, *History of Cheshire*, I, p. 442.   [75] P.R.O., CHES 29/133, m. 24d.

[76] Manchester Central Reference Library, Farrer MSS., 51/10/1.

[77] P.R.O., DL 29/4/42, SC 11/8, E 163/6/41; B.L., Additional Charters, no. 50886.

[78] B.L., Cotton MSS., Cleopatra D VI, f. 7d; Staffordshire R.O., Stafford MSS., 1/2/52.

Even if it were possible to establish with some exactitude the scale and composition of incomes from land in the Northwest, there would remain major problems in accurately assessing the material fortunes of particular individuals or families. Inquisitions *post mortem* often give a wholly misleading picture of the property interests of local landlords. In addition to holdings in distant shires passing unnoticed, the main estate itself was subject to continuous fragmentation and reunification through temporary grants and leases to widows, younger sons, trustees and others. Thus the patrimony of the Bulkeleys of Cheadle was far more extensive than the lands worth £27 a year found to be in the hands of Richard Bulkeley in 1454. Since around 1391 a third of the estate had been in the possession of his mother, by then the wife of Randle Mainwaring, and a further 20 marks worth of rents had been granted to his uncle.[79] Many other estates were likewise burdened with annuities and pensions. The manor of Worsley was subject to a pension of 5 marks while the manor of Ince Blundell, valued at only £13 a year, was encumbered with annuities amounting to over £11. Since individuals could benefit as well as lose from such arrangements, it is almost impossible to draw up, complete balance-sheets. The property interests of particular gentlemen have to be laboriously collated from a variety of sources. Thus Randle Mainwaring, who did not succeed to his patrimony until after the deaths of two elder brothers in 1410, contrived to enjoy throughout his long life an income from land far in excess of any ancestral endowment. His marriage brought him control of a third of the Bulkeley estate, and he purchased the wardship and marriage of the young heir. He shared in the farm of the royal manor of Frodsham, and leased the demesnes of Drakelow for life. Thenceforward he proved singularly adept at obtaining profitable leases and wardships. In 1415 he took to farm the serjeanty of the peace in Macclesfield hundred during the minority of his son-in-law, John son of Ralph Davenport. In the 1420s he had control of the inheritance of another son-in-law, William Bromley, and after his untimely death he leased the wardship of his grandson, John son of William Bromley. Around the same time he acquired the custody of the lands of the Fouleshursts and Beestons.[80]

It is clear that personal circumstances could drastically alter the fortunes of individuals and families. The longevity of Randle Mainwaring and his

---

[79] *Ches. R.R.*, II, pp. 104–6; *Ches. R.R.*, I, p. 72.
[80] J.R.U.L., Mainwaring MSS.; *Ches. R.R.*, I, p. 72; *C.P.R. 1391–1396*, p. 507; *Ches. R.R.*, I, pp. 316–17; *Ches. R.R.*, II, pp. 493, 90, 37, 291. For Randle Mainwaring's petition for the wardship of Richard Bulkeley see J. A. Tuck, 'Richard II's system of patronage' in du Boulay and Barron (eds.), *Reign of Richard II*, p. 11.

wife, coupled with the premature deaths of two elder brothers and two sons-in-law, brought him temporary control of a far larger proportion of the landed wealth of the shire than that to which his house was traditionally entitled. Demographic factors alone ensured a high degree of differentiation within the landowning class, with large amounts of land being continually redistributed through wardship and marriage. The tendency of non-resident landlords to lease out their manors added to the property available to astute local proprietors and ambitious newcomers. The varied fortunes of landed families in the Northwest can be illustrated by reference to the thirteen Lancashire gentlemen assessed at half a mark or more in the poll-tax of 1379.[81] Sir William Atherton, Sir Peter Gerard, Ralph Langton, Henry Scarisbrick, Thomas Hesketh and John Eccleston represented dynastic continuity in the shire. On the other hand, Adam Bickerstaffe was the last of his lineage, with his estates passing to a cadet of the Athertons, and Hugh Bradshaw of Westleigh's line terminated with his son. Conversely, Richard Mascy of Rixton and Roger Bradshaw of Aughton were younger sons, acquiring their estates through marriage and ultimately founding their own dynasties. Thomas Molyneux, also holding land in right of his wife, failed to leave heirs after his death at Radcot Bridge. Henry Bradshaw and William Aughton likewise seem not to have established new lines. While much of the fluidity in landed society was attributable to demographic chance, there was considerable latitude for enterprising individuals to establish footholds in it.

In later chapters the various other means by which gentry families were able to differentiate their fortunes are discussed. Discreet involvement in trade and industry, investment in clerical or legal education, military and administrative service, all brought opportunities for material advancement. Yet the acquisition and retention of landed estate remained their ultimate concern. Men of all backgrounds who amassed money through trade or the professions sought to convert their riches into land. Given the conservatism of the landed society, and the strong pressures working against individual advancement, their ambitions were not easily fulfilled. Indeed in the Northwest there were few gentry families who made dramatic advances in terms of their landed wealth in this period. This is not to maintain that the profits to be made through careerism were not substantial. A major problem was that much of the wealth amassed filtered back into the region in a rather diffuse form, bringing modest gains to wide circles of clients and dependents. Another problem was probably the local resentment experienced by ambitious careerists. Predictably younger

---

[81] P.R.O., E 179/130/24, 28. For details see *V.C.H. Lancaster*, *passim*.

sons of the gentry and adventurers from all ranks found it least troublesome to buy their way into landed society in other parts of the kingdom. The establishment by Cheshire and Lancashire men of new landed dynasties in other parts of the realm is certainly a well-attested phenomenon. In their genealogical studies local scholars have amply documented the extraordinary prolificness and mobility of such families as the Radcliffes, Hollands, Shaws and Pilkingtons.[82] A pioneering piece of research by W. W. Longford long ago drew attention to the establishment of branches of the Osbaldeston, Lawrence and Molyneux families in the Cotswolds region in the fifteenth century.[83] Indeed the Northwest's reputation as a 'seed-plot of gentility' finds some corroboration in the heralds' visitations of the Tudor period. Thus a brief survey of the returns for Gloucester, Nottingham, Oxford, Warwick and Dorset reveals that cadets of the Cottons, Pooles, Carringtons, Grosvenors, Leghs, Radcliffes, Gerards and other local families acquired manors in these shires during the later middle ages.[84]

[82] C. P. Hampson, *The Book of the Radclyffes* (Edinburgh, 1940); B. Holland, *The Lancashire Hollands* (London, 1917); R. C. Shaw, *The Records of a Lancashire Family* (Preston, 1940); J. Pilkington, *History of the Pilkington Family, 1066–1600* (Liverpool, 1894).

[83] W. W. Longford, 'Some notes on the family of Osbaldeston', *L.C.H.S.*, 87 (1935).

[84] *The Visitation of the County of Gloucester*, ed. J. Maclean and W. C. Heane (Harleian Soc., Visitations, 21, 1885), pp. 45–6, 125; *The Visitations of the County of Nottingham*, ed. G. W. Marshall (Harleian Soc. Visitations, 4, 1871), pp. 72, 9–10; *The Visitations of the County of Oxford*, ed. W. H. Turner (Harleian Soc. Visitations, 5, 1871), p. 202; *The Visitation of the County of Warwick*, ed. J. Fetherston (Harleian Soc. Visitations, 12, 1877), pp. 76, 385, 81, 149; *The Visitation of the County of Dorset*, ed. J. P. Rylands (Harleian Soc. Visitations, 20, 1885), pp. 45, 63.

## Chapter 6

# THE PEASANTRY

The distinction between those persons living off rents and those labouring to wring a livelihood from the soil is reasonably easy to maintain. Contemporaries would have regarded this division as the fundamental cleavage in the social order. Even in the more economically developed regions, the proportion of the populace engaged in trade, industry and the professions was small, and such groups had no fixed place in the ordered hierarchy of landed society. Yet, while there are good grounds for dividing the rural population into two main categories, there are no firm guide-lines as to how they might be labelled. The landed classes present the least problems. Lords of the manor were of gentle rank or above, and visibly set apart by their life-style and interests. It is far less easy to give definition to that great residual class, the common folk of the countryside. The terms used in the Lancashire poll-tax returns in 1379 to refer to the nine out of ten men who were not gentlemen, craftsmen or servants, cannot be readily translated into the terminology of class. In West Derby hundred they were called '*cultores*', while in Blackburn hundred they were named '*incolae et laboratores*'. Despite misgivings about the appropriateness of the label, in this chapter they will be termed 'peasants'.

It is not suggested that the peasantry was a homogeneous class. Indeed it is a basic proposition of this chapter that there was considerable variation in status and wealth among peasant families, both between different areas and within the same manor. All that is being claimed is that the initial frame of reference has to be the entire residual population of the countryside, and that 'the peasantry' is a convenient term to use to embrace the wealthier freeholders and cottagers as well as the more easily categorised customary tenants.[1] Increasingly, official sources identify three main groups on the land: yeomen, husbandmen and labourers. Unfortunately the names of representatives of these groups can rarely be collated with actual tenancies, and accordingly such categories can play

---

[1] For the essential unity of the 'peasant' class see Hilton, *English Peasantry in Later Middle Ages*, Ch. 3.

little part in this study. Yet the growing precision in the terminology of class is itself indicative of a gradual re-ordering of rural society during the period under discussion.

I

Historically speaking the most important differences among the peasantry were derived from their varied forms of tenure and legal status.[2] During the thirteenth century a fairly rigid distinction had been drawn between free and unfree tenures, and a peasant's status depended on the nature of his holding. While the fortunes of freeholders varied enormously, all enjoyed certain advantages over the villeins, serfs or bondmen, as the unfree tenants were variously called. Freeholders had protection in the royal courts against landlords, and theoretically were free to realise the full economic potential of their land and labour. In contrast villeins bore the full weight of the manorial regime, being bound to the soil and typically paying heavy dues in rent and services. Needless to say, tenurial conditions, both in theory and practice, varied enormously from manor to manor as well as from region to region and indeed were subject to transformation over time. Thus it would be extremely rash, especially in view of the sparsity and ambiguity of local evidence, to make too many firm statements regarding the situation in the Northwest in this period. All that can be offered at this stage are a few inferences drawn from studies of tenurial conditions elsewhere which can be illustrated from the fragmentary local record.

Thus some historians have observed correlations between patterns of settlement and land-utilisation and forms of peasant-tenure. R. H. Hilton associated a high incidence of free tenures with 'the availability of land for colonisation, [a] strong pastoral element in the economy and the absence of large-scale early manorialisation'.[3] Conversely, widespread villeinage has been frequently linked with anciently settled *champion* country. Without doubt the Northwest approximates much closer to the former model, and there are strong grounds for assuming that villeinage was never as significant there as in many parts of the Midlands. No evidence has been found that week-works, often regarded as the hallmark of bondage, were ever exacted by local landlords. The extensive opportunities for internal colonisation and assarting almost certainly added to the bargaining power of customary tenants in the region. Yet serfdom remained a feature of local society throughout the fourteenth century. From the limited material available it is possible to document the existence

[2] In general see R. H. Hilton, *The Decline of Serfdom in Medieval England* (London, 1969).
[3] *Ibid.*, p. 23.

of villein tenures, and to chronicle their transformation into customary tenures in which the peasants acquired 'the advantages usually associated only with free tenure and status'.[4]

Even prior to the Black Death it is possible that unfree status was not the lot of most local peasants, and that even on manors where serfdom was recognised many of the obligations were not strictly enforced. Still, references to villeinage are by no means uncommon, especially on the larger estates and in the more anciently-settled lowland areas. At the beginning of the fourteenth century there was villeinage on the estates of the abbeys of St Werburgh and Vale Royal as well as on the demesnes which later constituted the lordship of Lancaster. Indeed servile tenancies were the norm in numerous villages around Chester and in Wirral, at Darnhall and Over in the Weaver valley, on the lordships of Halton and Widnes, at West Derby and elsewhere in southwest Lancashire, and in several important manors in Amounderness and Lonsdale.[5] In addition bond tenures existed on some of the manors held by local gentlemen, since *nativi* are mentioned at Scarisbrick in 1361, Frankby and Upton in Wirral in 1362, Cuerdley in 1370, Buerton in 1388 and Hooton in 1403.[6] Yet it is by no means clear what actual disabilities and obligations such terminology implies. On the whole it does not seem that heavy labour services were being enforced, or that villeins were required to suffer all the other penalties attendant on their status. The harshest conditions evidenced in the region were on the estates of Vale Royal abbey. According to custumals drawn up in the early fourteenth century, bondmen lost a proportion of their goods to the abbot at their death, and during their lives they 'must work for him at his will, and he will pay them for their work at his own will',[7] but even this regime provoked determined and resourceful resistance to the abbot's pretensions in the 1330s. For several years the tenants undertook a vigorous campaign against the abbot's officers and impleaded their lord in the highest court of the land, before being finally reduced to manorial discipline.[8] Even then the abbot's victory was short-lived: men at Darnhall were termed tenants at

---

[4] *Ibid.*, p. 31.

[5] P.R.O., CHES 25/8, m. 57; *Vale Royal Ledger Book*, pp. 117–22; W. Beamont, *An Account of the Rolls of the Honour of Halton* (Warrington, 1879), pp. 14, 17–18; *Lancashire Inquests, Extents and Feudal Aids*, III, pp. 186, 173–6. Note also bondmen on the earl of Arundel's manors of Dunham on the Hill and Mickle Trafford in 1301: *Two FitzAlan Surveys*, ed. M. Clough (Sussex Record Soc. 67, 1969), pp. 84–8.

[6] Lancashire R.O., DDSc/43a/91; *B.P.R.*, III, pp. 464–5; J.R.U.L., Arley Charters, 5/6; *V.C.H. Lancaster*, III, p. 394; J.R.U.L., Rylands Charters, R72927/1721.

[7] *Vale Royal Ledger Book*, pp. 117–22.

[8] *Ibid.*, pp. 37–42. For an analysis of this movement see R. H. Hilton, 'Peasant movements in England before 1381', *Ec.H.R.*, second series II (1949), 128–9.

will, and at the dissolution compulsory boon-works were allegedly a distant memory.[9]

In all likelihood the demographic crisis of the fourteenth century dealt the death blow to serfdom in the Northwest. With vacant holdings in many villages, manorial lords would have found it difficult to resist demands for improved tenurial conditions. Unfortunately the transition from bond tenancies to freer forms of customary tenure cannot be chronicled with any exactitude. In 1351 the duke of Lancaster made a new covenant with tenants at Widnes, Appleton, Denton and Upton, remitting some services in return for rents of a shilling per 'long measure' acre. According to the new customs, the villagers were to be quit of all servile dues, excepting heriot and other fines on the transfer of land, which were henceforward fixed at reasonable rates.[10] Landlords right across the region found themselves having to accept a similar attrition of their rights. In 1394 the abbot of St Werburgh's complained that his tenants had taken advantage of the new conditions to secure lower rents and fewer services.[11] Even though servile obligations continued to be recorded at Halton, Runcorn and some other Lancastrian estates, there is little evidence of their being ruthlessly exploited. Tallage was not arbitrary, but a fixed sum rendered every third year, while payments for chevage, leyrwite and merchet occur only rarely in the ministers' accounts.[12]

Elsewhere the old Benedictine monasteries led the rearguard action against the decline of serfdom, and in this regard the Northwest conforms to the national pattern. St Werburgh's abbey, with its rich manorial properties in close proximity to the civic market, was the only local institution which could hope to emulate the policies of estate-management pursued by its sister houses elsewhere. Even though heavy labour-services might never have been in force on its estates, the convent strove hard to keep its dependent peasantry tied to the soil, and to assert its seignorial rights to the full. Thus in 1380 the county court-rolls make reference to two *nativi* of St Werburgh's, Thomas Jackson of Wervin and Richard Forster of Bromborough, whose goods and chattels were forfeit to the abbot.[13] Then at the time of the Peasants' Revolt there is evidence of unrest among its villeins. Following a royal proclamation expressly forbidding such assemblies, a number of *nativi* 'with force and arms congregated at Lea juxta Backford...in contempt of the lord king and in affray, and in disturbance of the peace, and to the manifest terror of his people both

[9] Ormerod, *History of Cheshire*, II, p. 150; J. Youings, *The Dissolution of the Monasteries* (London, 1971), pp. 227–8.

[10] P.R.O., DL 42/16, f. 92d.

[11] *C.Pap.L.*, IV, p. 533.

[12] P.R.O., DL 29/4/32–42, DL 29/5/43–60.

[13] P.R.O., CHES 29/83, mm. 13d, 6d.

Table 4. *The tenancies of rebels on the St Werburgh's estate*

| Rebels named in 1381 | Principal holdings recorded in 1398 |
| --- | --- |
| Hugh Harvey | Two bovates in Childer Thornton |
| Thomas Paine | Land in Ince or Upton (?) |
| Robert Hudson of Little Sutton | Two bovates in Little Sutton |
| William Reeveman | A little land in Great Sutton |
| William Brown | Four bovates (two freehold) in Newton |
| William Haineson | Land in Overpool (?) |
| Henry Russell | Three bovates in Whitby and Overpool |
| Richard Cotton | Four bovates in Whitby |
| Adam Lees | Two bovates in Great Sutton |
| Robert son of John Overpool | Land in Overpool (?) |
| John Reeveson | Land in Saighton (?) |
| Richard Sutton | Two bovates in Little Sutton |
| Robert Gardiner of Upton | Two bovates in Little Sutton |
| Thomas son of John Wervin | Land in Benefield (?) |
| William Lee of Newton | Three bovates (one freehold) in Newton |
| Robert Lees of Whitby | Four bovates in Whitby, two in Great Sutton |

in the said city and in the said county, and to the annihilation and destruction of the abbot and his convent and the goods of the said house and church'.[14] While the aims of this rising were not recorded, its context suggests that villeinage was a major issue.

Yet it is by no means clear that the movement can be classed as a local echo of the Peasants' Revolt. The Cheshire men certainly could not have shared the other rebels' resentment of the poll-tax. It is more probable that the *nativi* of St Werburgh's were following an earlier tradition of peasant resistance by conspiring to take concerted legal action. After all there were no specific allegations of violence, and it was doubtless a tactic of the wily abbot to link their activities with the recent disturbances in the Southeast. Perhaps some of the Cheshire men had been inspired by the general ferment, but the objectives of this particular group must have been more limited and localised. The fortunate survival of both the names of the sixteen alleged rebels in 1381 and a rental of the St Werburgh's estate for 1398 allows further insights into the character of the rising (see Table 4).[15]

[14] P.R.O., CHES 25/8, m. 57.    [15] B.L., Additional MSS., no. 36764.

Drawn from a number of adjacent manors, namely Great Sutton, Little Sutton, Childer Thornton, Whitby and Newton, most of the rebels appear seventeen years on as leading members of their respective communities. Cotton, Russell and Lees rank as three of the most substantial tenants at Whitby, while Brown and Lee both farmed freeholds as well as customary bovates at Newton. In 1381 all the accused were of sufficient repute to find freemen to put up bail of £40, and judging from their later condition none seem to have been punished with great severity. The picture emerges of responsible men of solid means, who were finding their dues and disabilities irksome and were aiming at their reduction or abolition through legal action rather than armed rebellion. Interestingly enough, there is some evidence from a later custumal that labour-services at Great Sutton, Little Sutton, Whitby and Overpool were rather more onerous than elsewhere on the St Werburgh's estate.[16] When this document was drawn up in 1431, the tenants were still termed *nativi*, and obliged to perform two days' ploughing, one day's mowing and six days' reaping. This was probably their position in 1381 but fifty years later such conditions doubtless appeared less threatening.

Villeinage in the Northwest, as in other parts of the kingdom, 'was never abolished; it withered away'.[17] Whatever is concluded about the status of most of the local tenantry prior to the Black Death, rentals and other sources from the late fourteenth century onwards acknowledge two main categories of tenant, the *tenentes ad voluntatem* and the *terminarii*. As far as can be ascertained, the tenants 'at will' were closer in evolutionary terms to true villeinage. According to M. M. Postan, the tenants for life at the lord's will were villeins who had been granted their concessions on a temporary basis.[18] Landlords, unwilling to forgo their seignorial rights in perpetuity, had created large numbers of these life leases. On the whole tenancies at will were the most precarious and least attractive of the customary tenures, and constituted an intermediary stage between villeinage and leasehold proper. On a number of manors tenants at will had still to perform minor labour-services. At Ashton under Lyne they were required to plough for two days, harrow for a day, shear for four days and perform carting services, while their fellows at Worsley had remarkably similar obligations.[19] Tenants at will can be found right across the region, and throughout the period under discussion: at Newton in Makerfield and Walton le Dale in 1362, Sefton in 1368, Bispham in 1369,

---

[16] P.R.O., SC 11/901.    [17] Hilton, *Decline of Serfdom*, p. 31.

[18] M. M. Postan (ed.), *The Cambridge Economic History of Europe*, vol. I. 'The Agrarian Life of the Middle Ages', 2nd edn (Cambridge, 1966), pp. 615–16.

[19] Manchester Central Reference Library, Farrer MSS., 50/21/21; Bowman, *Ashton under Lyne*, pp. 73–9.

Chorley in 1371, Ince Blundell in 1375, Darnhall in 1385, Helsby in 1389, Altrincham, Dunham and Hale in 1401, Leyland in 1412 and so on.[20] Apparently life tenures at the will of the lord had developed in an exceedingly random fashion, and were subject to considerable local variation.

References to *terminarii*, or tenants for terms of years, span more or less the same geographical and chronological range. Exactly what conditions led to leases for life on one manor and leases for terms of years on another cannot be ascertained with any certainty, but the significance of the distinction is attested by an extent which alludes first to tenants at will on the manor of Helsby and then refers to *terminarii* at neighbouring Thornton le Moors.[21] Doubtless forms of leasehold developed fastest on manors where the demesne had been anciently let to farm, like Frodsham, or where new ploughlands had been created, as at Drakelowe.[22] Yet there were *terminarii* at Eccleston in 1373, Dutton, Barnton, Keckwick and elsewhere in 1389, Newbold Astbury in 1388, Bosley in 1400, Aston juxta Mondrum and Church Minshull in 1405, Haslington and Picton in 1407, High Legh in 1416, Litherland in 1417, Christleton in 1418, Over Peover in 1425 and so on.[23] Unfortunately there is little evidence regarding the conditions of leasehold tenure for terms of years. It is known that the Bosley tenants held their lands on leases of twelve years, and that the Drakelowe tenants held their farms for twenty years, but whether in practice the position of the *terminarii* was always preferable to that of the tenants at will is difficult to ascertain.

Indeed all that can be concluded regarding customary tenures in the Northwest is that conditions were fluid, but steadily improving. While the exact nature of customary tenures was to become a critical issue in the sixteenth century, at this stage demographic forces still worked to the advantage of the peasant-farmer. With little population pressure on the land, few landlords were in a position to exploit fully their legal rights, and most tenants at will could feel secure in their holdings. As more and more peasants became leaseholders, with the terms of their holdings

---

[20] *V.C.H. Lancaster*, III, p. 143; *Lancashire Inquisitions*, II, p. 98; Lancashire R.O., DDM/17/36; *V.C.H. Lancaster*, VI, pp. 101, 132; Ormerod, *History of Cheshire*, II, p. 150; J.R.U.L., Cornwall-Legh MSS., no. 792; Cheshire R.O., DLT, Liber C, ff. 208–10; Lancashire R.O., DDF/110.

[21] J.R.U.L., Cornwall-Legh MSS., no. 492.

[22] Ormerod, *History of Cheshire*, I, p. 50; P.R.O., SC 6/793/3.

[23] Lancashire R.O., DDSc/25/1; B.L., Additional Charters, no. 51504; P.R.O., SC 11/8; B.L., Cotton MSS., Cleopatra D VI, ff. 7–7d; B.L., Additional Charters, no. 50886; P.R.O., E 163/6/41; Chester R.O., Earwaker MSS., 1/140; Liverpool R.O., Plumbe Tempest Deeds, A1/9; Staffordshire R.O., Stafford MSS., 1/2/52; J.R.U.L., Mainwaring MSS., roll. 1.

recorded and protected in the manorial courts, customary tenure lost all taint of servility. This process was particularly well advanced on the large royal estates. The tenants on the ancient demesnes of Macclesfield, Widnes, West Derby and Clitheroe held their lands for fixed rents and entry fines.[24] More important, they were able to demise and sub-let their holdings at will, and apart from the formalities of submission to the hallmoot court the properties became 'practically as negotiable as freeholds'.[25] Other developments served to blur the distinction between the old customary freeholds and the old villein tenures. The increasing tendency for families of all ranks to farm both free and bond tenures tended to impugn the servile character of specific holdings. As labour-services became less onerous for tenants in villeinage, the obligations and liabilities attached to free tenancies, particularly in the sphere of local government, must have seemed the more burdensome. Indeed by the end of the fourteenth century the main advantage which the freeholder had over the customary tenant was the level of his rent. Many paid nominal rents for quite substantial holdings, and were clearly in a far better position to make capital gain from their farms. While there were few peasants in the region whose legal status was so depressed as to seriously limit their economic capacity, obviously individuals varied considerably in their opportunities to make material advances on their fortunes.

II

If little is known regarding the tenurial status of most Cheshire and Lancashire peasants, even less is known of their material condition. The dearth of detailed manorial records has been lamented in other contexts, but the limited value of the governmental records and private deeds to this particular enquiry must also be admitted. The meagre survival of inventories, potentially such a valuable source, is particularly disappointing. The list of the goods of Richard Forster of Bromborough, a *nativus* of St Werburgh's, is the only inventory found for this period in the court-rolls, and is thus worth reciting in full.[26] Drawn up early in 1380, it recorded crops of wheat, rye, barley, beans, peas and oats valued at forty shillings; a two-year-old ox, a cow, a young heifer, four sheep, one sow, four piglets and a mare; four bee-hives worth forty pence; and various household utensils valued at ten shillings. Such were the modest possessions of a

[24] P.R.O., SC 2/255/1–12; P.R.O., DL 42/16, f. 92d; R. Syers, *The History of Everton* (Liverpool, 1830), p. 387; T. D. Whitaker, *An History of the Original Parish of Whalley and Honour of Clitheroe*, ed. J. G. Nichols and P. A. Lyons, 4th edn (2 vols., 1872, 1876), I, pp. 265–7.

[25] Tupling, *Rossendale*, p. 75.     [26] P.R.O., CHES 29/83, m. 6d.

Table 5. *Average holdings/rents on four manors of the St Werburgh's estate in 1398*

| Manor | Number of tenancies | Average holding (in bovates) | Price per bovate | | Average rent for total holding | | |
|---|---|---|---|---|---|---|---|
| | | | s | d | £ | s | d |
| Saighton | 14 | 1.8 | 4 | 6 | | 8 | 1 |
| Wervin | 11 | 3.8 | 5 | 7 | 1 | 1 | 2 |
| Whitby | 12 | 2.7 | 9 | 5 | 1 | 5 | 5 |
| Newton | 8 | 2.0 | 15 | 6 | 1 | 11 | 0 |

probably not untypical Cheshire peasant in the late fourteenth century. Since Forster was a villein, he was subject to more onerous exactions than most of his fellows, but he was not necessarily the poorer on that account. Much more depended on the opportunities available in particular areas, and the ability of individuals to turn them to material advantage. Given the meagreness of relevant documentation, it is not possible to give an adequate account of the peasant economy in the region. Yet some impression can be offered of the range of fortunes evident among local families.

The most basic source of economic differentiation within the peasant class was the varying proportion of income paid in rent. Even the most cursory glance at contemporary rent-rolls must unnerve the historian seeking consistency between villages in the rents charged for the standard customary holding. Even among neighbouring manors on the St Werburgh's estate, there were considerable differences. While the bovate was the standard tenurial unit in all the nineteen or so villages featured in the rental of 1398, and while in each village it was let at a standard rate, the level of rent per bovate ranged from 4s 6d at Saighton, 5s 7d at Wervin, 9s 5d at Whitby to 15s 6d at Newton.[27] The explanation for this variation does not seem to lie in different standards of measurement or qualities of soil. If the size or productivity of the bovate did vary it ought to be possible to find a corresponding variation in the number of bovates in the average holding in different villages. While the average tenancy does in fact range from 1.8 to 3.8 bovates, there is no correlation between its size and the level of rent. Rather, the introduction of the new variable accentuates the differences between the four manors (see Table 5). Thus

[27] B.L., Additional MSS, no. 36764.

the average tenant at Saighton was paying only a third of the rent of his fellow at Whitby, and only a quarter of that at Newton. Perhaps the heavier rents on the latter manors incorporated commuted labour-services and levies in kind, but there is no evidence from the later custumal that the tenants of Saighton and Wervin were particularly burdened in this manner. To some extent the differences in the levels of rent must also reflect market forces. All the manors were fairly close to Chester, but while Newton's position as a virtual suburb must have greatly enhanced the value of its fields, Saighton's dangerous proximity to the Welsh border might account for its exceptionally low rents. However the variation is to be explained, a basic fact about peasant conditions remains clear: even within the context of a single, reasonably compact estate, the levels of rent differed considerably. In such circumstances the proportion of income paid in feudal dues of all kinds can scarcely have been constant.

Furthermore, there is reason to assume that conditions on other local manors would have been even less standardised than on the St Werburgh's estate. The large monastic corporations were more eager and better placed than most landlords to keep the customary tenancies as discrete units of uniform value and bearing uniform charges. On other estates the levels of rent might well have been even more variable. Analysis of the more standardised holdings recorded in other rentals certainly reveals at least an equivalent sort of range. Thus the average *terminarius* at Thornton and tenant at will at Helsby paid less than ten shillings a year in rent, while the average *terminarius* at Newbold Astbury and tenant at will at Ashton under Lyne paid over twice that amount.[28] In addition to the customary holdings, account must be taken of the larger number of freeholds and assarts found in other parts of the region. Many freeholders paid purely nominal rents, like Agnes Faysand who held a messuage and five selions at Great Barrow in return for a rose.[29] Such villagers were in a far better position to accumulate capital than their neighbours with customary tenancies. Similarly, outside areas of ancient and intensive cultivation, new land was often available to enterprising peasants at fairly advantageous rates. In the forest of Macclesfield new enclosures were let out at eight pence a 'long measure' acre, and even in the 1380s and 1390s approvements could amount to five acres a year.[30] There were even more startling developments on the sparsely-settled estates of the honour of Clitheroe in Lancashire. Throughout the period considerable acreages were parcelled out of the waste in the forest of Rossendale, and acquired by local farmers at the low rent of four pence an acre.[31] While many of the assarts cannot

[28] J.R.U.L., Cornwall-Legh MSS., no. 792; P.R.O., SC 11/8; Bowman, *Ashton under Lyne*, pp. 73–9.     [29] P.R.O., DL 29/4/42.
[30] E.g. in 1390: P.R.O., SC 2/254/12.     [31] Tupling, *Rossendale*, p. 35.

Table 6. *Tenancies on four manors of the St Werburgh's estate in 1398*

| Manor | Number of bovates | Number of tenants | Average holding |
|-------|-------------------|-------------------|-----------------|
| Saighton | 3 | 5 | 1.8 |
|  | 2 | 3 | — |
|  | $1\frac{1}{2}$ | 1 | — |
|  | 1 | 1 | — |
|  | $\frac{1}{2}$ | 4 | — |
| Wervin | 6 | 3 | 3.8 |
|  | 3 | 8 | — |
| Whitby | 4 | 3 | 2.7 |
|  | 3 | 3 | — |
|  | 2 | 6 | — |
| Newton | 2 | 8 | 2.0 |

have been of prime agricultural land, many thought it worth while to consolidate and extend their holdings by piecemeal enclosure, some perhaps to build up conveniently sized units for tillage and others no doubt to increase pasturage for cattle and sheep. Some enterprising farmers in Macclesfield forest were even able to sub-let parts of their holdings to realise an income from rents five times larger than their own capital charges.[32]

The varying proportion of income exacted in rent was not the only source of economic differentiation among the peasantry. In most villages there was a remarkable range in the size of the holdings. Evidence from the manors of St Werburgh's abbey is again instructive in this context. Even though on this estate there must have been considerable pressure working against the fragmentation of holdings, by the late fourteenth century the bovates in most villages were distributed among the tenants in a very uneven fashion. The distribution of customary tenancies at Saighton, Wervin, Whitby and Newton can be seen in Table 6.

In three of the manors there is evidence of considerable differentiation. At Saighton the polarisation between the larger and smaller holders – between holders of three bovates and holders of half a bovate respectively – was particularly pronounced. In other parts of the region, where tenancies were not based on the traditional bovate, there was often even more variation in their size. At Ashton under Lyne in 1422 there can be found, amidst large numbers of holdings of a miscellaneous nature, some forty-five

[32] E.g. Roger Jodrell; J.R.U.L., Jodrell Charters, no. 6c.

Table 7. *Rents paid for the forty-five standardised tenancies at will at Ashton under Lyne in 1422*

| Basic rent for tenement | Number of tenants |
|---|---|
| 50s and above | 1 |
| 45s and above | 0 |
| 40s and above | 1 |
| 35s and above | 4 |
| 30s and above | 4 |
| 25s and above | 7 |
| 20s and above | 7 |
| 15s and above | 8 |
| 10s and above | 7 |
| 5s and above | 6 |

fairly standardised tenancies, each held in return for a specific rent, a few labour-services and a present at Christmas. Leaving aside the additional lands that many of the tenants leased, there was still great diversity in the rents, ranging from Robert Wright who held his tenement for 56s 11d, a service and a present worth 1s 8d, to Robert Chadwick who held his tenement for 5s, a service and a present worth 4d. Between these two customary tenants there were forty-three other tenants as in Table 7, while above and below the main body of tenants there were many more prosperous leaseholders and humble cottagers. Grouping the customary tenants at Ashton under Lyne into three classes according to the size of their rents, the fifteen most substantial tenants paid on average 34s 11d, the fifteen middling tenants paid on average 20s 11d, and the fifteen smallest holders paid on average 10s 10d.

Given such wide differences in the size of rents, it can be safely assumed that the acreages cultivated by individual farmers varied as greatly. Unfortunately rentals which record acreages are rather uncommon, and only two have survived from the region in this period. The earlier of the pair, a rental of Newbold Astbury from the beginning of Richard II's reign,[33] presents the most problems for this analysis. Since it merely lists acreages alongside the names of farmers, it is not always clear which were the holdings of resident cultivators. Then again, it itemises a number of fields, meadows and so on, noting their acreage and value but without naming the tenant. In the other rental, listing the tenants at Bosley in

[33] P.R.O., SC 11/8.

Table 8. *Holdings by acreage at Newbold Astbury and Bosley*

| Holdings in statute acres and in local long measure | | Number of tenants | |
|---|---|---|---|
| | | Newbold Astbury | Bosley |
| Statute acres | Local long measure | | |
| 60 and above | 41.3 and above | 0 | 2 |
| 55 and above | 37.9 and above | 1 | 0 |
| 50 and above | 34.4 and above | 0 | 1 |
| 45 and above | 31.0 and above | 1 | 1 |
| 40 and above | 27.5 and above | 1 | 0 |
| 35 and above | 24.1 and above | 0 | 4 |
| 30 and above | 20.6 and above | 2 | 3 |
| 25 and above | 17.2 and above | 5 | 6 |
| 20 and above | 13.7 and above | 4 | 5 |
| 15 and above | 10.3 and above | 4 | 6 |
| 10 and above | 6.8 and above | 5 | 4 |
| 5 and above | 3.4 and above | 4 | 1 |
| Less than 5 | | 1 | 0 |
| Total number of tenants | | 28 | 33 |

1400,[34] it is easier to focus attention on actual holders of messuages, and to discount more miscellaneous holdings. Table 8 therefore under-estimates the size of tenancies in both Newbold Astbury and Bosley, but more strikingly in the former than the latter.

Still, in both villages there is evidence of considerable variation in the acreages farmed. At Newbold Astbury the ten leading tenants held an average of 35 statute acres, while the ten smallest farmers averaged slightly less than 10 acres. At Bosley the top third of the tenantry farmed an ample average of 45 acres, while the bottom third cultivated holdings of around 15 acres. In both places there were individuals who held tenancies far beyond their own needs and capabilities. John Jauny of Bosley and Robert Peyke of Newbold Astbury, for example, were farming 90 and 55 acres respectively, and both must have either sub-let to, or employed the labour of their neighbours. At the other end of the scale there were a number of individuals apparently holding only one or two acres who must have had other means of livelihood. Assuming a rough comparability in quality of land, however, the average farmer in these two villages seems to have been better endowed than his fellows in other parts of the country. With

[34] B.L., Cotton MSS., Cleopatra D VI, ff. 7–7d.

forty-nine per cent of the tenants holding between 15 and 30 acres, and twenty-six per cent holding over 30 acres, the proportions of medium-sized and large holdings are greater than are usually evidenced elsewhere, while the proportion of small holdings (twenty-five per cent) is correspondingly smaller.[35]

There can be little doubt as to the importance of the Black Death to both the progressive amelioration and the increasing differentiation of peasant fortunes. Detailed studies in many other parts of England have revealed high mortality-rates, leaving often unbreachable gaps in the ranks of the tenantry. The consequent shortage of labour was bound in the long run to work to the advantage of most sections of the peasant class, and the large number of vacant holdings inevitably enabled the more enterprising survivors to add to their tenancies on a scale hitherto unimaginable. It is not within the chronological scope of this study to offer a detailed assessment of the social and economic effects of the Black Death in the region. Yet it is important to note that the period under discussion witnessed not only the slow and undramatic process of adjustment to lower population levels, but also the continual recurrence of plague in more localised, but none the less devastating outbreaks. Significantly enough the rentals of both Newbold Astbury and Bosley were rapidly rendered obsolete by local epidemics. When a new rent-roll was drawn up in the former village in 1399, all but four of the twenty-five tenants of twenty years' earlier had disappeared:[36] In the latter township the rental drawn up in 1400 was totally redundant by the end of the decade. A mere ten of the original thirty-three messuage-holders had survived the epidemic which had swept across the region around 1407.[37]

The fortunate survival of the two pairs of rentals provides the opportunity to consider more closely the impact of the demographic crises. Predictably enough, some of the survivors were able to profit from the situation by extending the scale of their holdings. William Benet and Matthew Moreton increased their acreages at Newbold Astbury by fifty per cent. Both Henry and John Hordren doubled the size of their farms at Bosley, and several energetic newcomers managed to take over multiple tenancies. Yet no farmers found it profitable to increase their holdings beyond certain limits. At Newbold Astbury in 1399 there were two large tenancies in decay for want of takers, while at Bosley the median tenancy

[35] Cf. Hilton, *English Peasantry in Later Middle Ages*, pp. 39–40; Harvey, *Westminster Abbey and its Estates*, pp. 288–90; J. Hatcher, *Rural Economy and Society in the Duchy of Cornwall 1300–1500* (Cambridge, 1970), p. 139; Dewindt, *Land and People in Holywell-cum-Needingworth*, pp. 112–13.

[36] Both rentals are to be found in P.R.O., SC 11/8.

[37] B.L., Cotton MSS., Cleopatra D VI, ff. 7–7d.

of the more substantial third of the farmers rose only to thirty-one acres, though it must be noted that the average is somewhat deflated by the break up of John Jauny's ninety-acre holding.

At the same time as demographic factors were bringing an improvement in the ratio of man to land and livestock, so various other, not entirely unrelated, developments were serving to add to the proportion of land under direct peasant control. The rising costs of labour and the falling price for agricultural produce would have served as the death-blow to large-scale demesne-cultivation in a region in which it had never had more than an attenuated existence. Needless to say, the letting to farm of demesne-lands and other manorial assets provided increased opportunities for local peasant enterprise. At Newbold Astbury John Cotton gained the lease of the manor and forty acres of demesne-land for £2, William Sherman acquired twenty acres for £1, while two other tenants formed smaller portions. On the manor of Bosley Cecilia Huester leased the demesne for 43s 4d, and John Jauny, in addition to his ninety-acre holding, had the lease of the watermill for £1. At Rushton secondary demesne leasings amounted to two-fifths of the manorial profits for the absentee Greys of Ruthin.[38] Even on the tightly administered manors of St Werburgh's abbey there were valuable demesne leases, sometimes as at Ince and Whitby in 1398 held by the entire village community and sometimes as at Upton in 1431 in the hands of an individual.[39] At Ashton under Lyne various manorial assets as well as numerous parcels of land were let to farm.[40] Jack Spencer leased the bailiwick, that is the profits of tolls, markets, fairs and so on, for ten shillings a year, while Robert Walker and Roger Smith, both substantial tenants, had the farms of the fulling mill and the smithy.

### III

Demonstrably the Cheshire and Lancashire peasantry was a differentiated class, both in terms of legal and tenurial status and real economic condition. Conditions of peasant life varied considerably not only from manor to manor but also from household to household within a single community. The arrangements for seating in Ashton under Lyne church indicates that the villagers themselves were acutely conscious of fine gradations in status and condition: the wives of the leading freeholders and more substantial customary tenants occupied the front benches, while the wives of the lesser tenants were relegated to the back pews.[41] Furthermore it should be noted that in this study attention has been

[38] P.R.O., DL 29/4/42.
[39] B.L., Additional MSS., no. 36764; P.R.O., SC 11/901.
[40] Bowman, *Ashton under Lyne*, pp. 73–9.       [41] *Ibid.*, pp. 167–8.

confined almost entirely to the least differentiated sections of the peasant class, the customary tenants with the more standardised holdings. If there had been sufficient documentation to support a detailed analysis of the wealthier freeholders on the one hand and the poorer cottagers, sub-tenants and landless labourers on the other, the picture of peasant conditions presented could have been even more varied and confused.

Needless to say, there were limitations on the extent to which individual peasants could differentiate their fortunes in this period. Within the village community there were doubtless strong pressures working towards the maintenance of some sort of social equilibrium, which at the very least might have ensured that no villager starved while his fellow enjoyed abundance. In addition purely economic factors served in some measure to minimise the polarisation between rich and poor. As soon as their holdings became too large to be cultivated by family labour, the more substantial peasant-farmers were forced to compete with the greater landlords for sub-tenants and hired hands in adverse market conditions. In contrast, as long as labour was at a premium and there were still vacant tenancies on most manors, only the aged and infirm needed to fall back on the charity of their neighbours. While there is little detailed information regarding the fortunes of the rural proletariat, their position was assuredly better than at any other stage prior to the eighteenth century. While the new economic climate of the late fourteenth century certainly brought increased opportunities for economic differentiation, the most important effect of the Black Death was the wholesale amelioration of the material conditions of all classes living by their own labour.

The more enterprising peasants were certainly able to achieve modest capital accumulation. Yeoman farmers like Richard Byrnes and Thomas Patrick, who took on the lease of the manor of Aston juxta Mondrum, and Roger Brown, who farmed demesne-land at Great Barrow, were obviously men of weight in their own communities.[42] Even bondmen could hope to make savings: Richard Webb of Frodsham left goods worth £7 at his death, and no less than 8s 8d was expended on his wake.[43] Presumably some of his neighbours put their savings to more productive uses, though not necessarily on the land. William Frodsham, chamberlain of North Wales, and John Nicholson, citizen of Chester, were both the sons of Frodsham men.[44] Given the intense conservatism of village society, and the general sluggishness of the rural economy, many ambitious families found it more attractive to invest their energies and savings in crafts, commerce and careerism. The Ormerods were freeholders

[42] B.L., Additional Charters, no. 50886; P.R.O., DL 29/4/42.
[43] Booth and Dodd, 'Manor and fields of Frodsham', 35.
[44] B.L., Additional Charters, nos. 50590, 50580.

at Cliviger, but close family members included a wright, a chapman and a tradesman established at Southampton in the 1420s.[45] Thomas Castle and Richard Archer, serfs at Halton, were willing to pay the fines necessary to allow their sons to be ordained for the priesthood, while the Winwicks of Huyton and the Leyots of Hale were among the many yeomen who reaped rich dividends through investment in clerical careerism.[46] In view of the legion of utterly undistinguished names among the Cheshire and Lancashire men serving as archers on the continent, it must be assumed that even larger numbers of yeomen and husbandmen sought to advance their fortunes through occasional soldiering.[47]

In later chapters there are numerous other examples of peasant families diversifying their fortunes through involvement in various trades and professions, but the documentation rarely permits an assessment of their advancement at the local level. One Cheshire yeoman family whose rise to gentry status is fairly well chronicled, however, is Jodrell of Disley and Whaley. Originally modest freeholders in northeast Cheshire, there is evidence of their early and profitable involvement in the French wars. William Jodrell held only thirteen acres in the forest of Macclesfield when he is first noticed in the records shortly after the Black Death.[48] In 1355 he can be found serving as an archer under the Black Prince in Aquitaine, while his kinsman was one of a group of local bowmen who found a prize worth £8 on the field of Poitiers.[49] In the following decades he added substantially to his holdings in Whaley and elsewhere, and by his death his annual rent totalled £3, indicating a farm of ninety 'long measure' acres.[50] Roger Jodrell, who took over his father's tenancies in 1376, also seems to have taken to soldiering, and at some stage entered the service of Richard II. Styling himself as a squire, he paid 100 marks for his marriage to the heiress of Robert Thornton, a merchant of York in 1395, and along with his new wife he was granted property in Coventry by the king in 1397.[51] Meanwhile he continued to add to his acreage in the forest of Macclesfield, apparently in order to sub-let it at a handsome profit. In 1418 he made a jointure for his son and daughter-in-law of some sixteen acres which had been sub-let for £3 a year, and for which he paid only twelve shillings.[52] By the end of his life in 1423 he had consolidated a manorial estate just outside the forest boundary at Whaley, and

---

[45] P.R.O., PL 15/2, m. 13.  [46] *B.R.U.O.*, III, p. 2063, II, p. 1143.
[47] E.g. see the names of local archers in P.R.O., E 101/39/9.
[48] J.R.U.L., Jodrell Charters, no. 1.
[49] J.R.U.L., Jodrell Charters, no. 2; *B.P.R.*, IV, p. 254.
[50] J.R.U.L., Jodrell Charters, no. 7.
[51] J.R.U.L., Jodrell Charters, nos. 13, 18; *C.P.R. 1396–1399*, p. 62.
[52] J.R.U.L., Jodrell Charters, no. 6c.

established the claims of his lineage to gentility. In his will he made provision for some eight sons and two unmarried daughters, and his gifts of 'body armour' and 'a fishing boat in the land of Gower' testify to the range of interests which had contributed to advancing the fortunes of his house.[53]

[53] J.R.U.L., Jodrell Charters, no. 35.

*Chapter 7*

# TOWNS, TRADE AND INDUSTRY

The pursuit of a craft or engagement in commerce perhaps represent the most elemental forms of social mobility. Almost all stable agrarian societies manage to maintain a measure of specialised commodity production and a more or less developed system of exchange. A reasonably compact, centralised and politically mature state like England in the middle ages was well placed to develop a fairly sophisticated market sector, which could both draw its strength from, and in turn further stimulate regional specialisation. While the vast majority of English tradesmen operated on a fairly localised scale, the economic integration of the nation cannot be overlooked in a study of this nature. Even the humblest chapman or artisan in the Northwest was potentially linked into a network of opportunities which embraced the entire kingdom.

Geographical mobility was in many respects a necessary preliminary to social advancement. To the commercial classes, freedom of movement was absolutely vital. Demonstrably the low-born but ambitious tradesman had first to emancipate himself from manorial discipline, and in earlier times had sought the comparative freedom of chartered towns. Furthermore, if the best opportunities were to be obtained, it was often necessary to travel to find the best markets for the particular commodity or skill to be sold. In real life as in popular myth, few enterprising men could resist the lure of London. Finally, there can be little doubt that the successful merchant found it easier to register social advancement in more distant parts. Even if opportunities for rapid capital formation were available in his native region, there were strong pressures operating in local communities to hold him to the station in which he was born. In a consideration of trade and industry as avenues of social mobility it is clearly necessary to extend the field of reference far beyond the geographical confines of one region.

While few successful tradesmen ever secured complete acceptance as country gentlemen, it must not be assumed that the impact of the commercial sector on the social structure was minimal. There is a tendency to dwell on the spectacular achievements of individuals like Dick

Whittington, but perhaps more significant are the more modest fortunes of innumerable lesser men and the cumulative gains of entire families and communities. Through quiet investment in real estate, the unassuming tradesman might at least be able to secure the recognition of his heirs as landed gentlemen, and sizeable estates could be built up over several generations. Similarly the wealth and influence of a successful merchant might be diffused among a wide circle of kinsmen, friends and compatriots, providing opportunities for advancement through patronage and connection. In this respect it is important not to take too narrow a view of the commercial classes. After all, gentlemen were not averse to arranging marriages with tradespeople, or having their younger sons apprenticed to a trade. More important, men of all ranks can be found involved in some measure in commercial enterprise, and it is often as difficult to draw the line between the business-minded landlord and the propertied merchant as it is between the resourceful peasant and the rural craftsman. Thus, even though vast fortunes were rarely accumulated in a single generation, and even less rarely converted directly into enhanced social status, there is no reason to deny the importance of trade and industry as a source of economic differentiation. In late medieval England the commercial sector represented the broadest avenue of advancement, accessible to all who were enterprising, able to amass a little capital and free to travel.

Obviously there was considerable variation in the conditions of people involved in trade and industry at this time. There was a world of difference between the wealthy merchant freighting ships for trade with Bordeaux and the itinerant peddler carrying his wares around the countryside, or between the well-patronised London goldsmith and the humble village blacksmith. Other distinctions need perhaps to be drawn between full-time tradesmen and persons with more limited commercial interests, and between manufacturers, retailers, wholesalers and financiers. Nevertheless certain aspects of the life-style and status of all traders and craftsmen help set them apart as a distinctive class. All were concerned more or less directly with the manufacture and marketing of goods, and were at least one stage removed from the primary process of cultivating the soil. All were more than averagely mobile, both personally and in terms of their capital, and tended to gravitate around the larger settlements, where more specialised pursuits could be maintained and wider-ranging connections established. Indeed the towns, which engrossed so much of the commercial and industrial life of the kingdom, provide a natural focus for the study of this nascent bourgeoisie.

Despite a great deal of research on towns, trade and industry in medieval England, precious little has been written on the commercial sector as a source of social mobility. It is rather disappointing that Sylvia Thrupp's pioneering study of the merchants of London has not provoked further discussion on this topic, nor stimulated regionalised studies of those sections of the population seeking advancement through trade and industry.[1] In this chapter it is hoped to make some contribution towards remedying this defect through a consideration of the Cheshire and Lancashire evidence. First of all there is a general survey of the towns in the region. Then there is a discussion of the occupational structure of those sections of the local population engaged in commerce and manufacturing. Next an account is provided of the activities of entrepreneurs and tradesmen whose interests extended into other parts of the kingdom. Finally it is intended to offer some general observations regarding opportunities for social advancement through trade and industry, and to discuss the relationship between the commercial sector and landed society.

I

Prior to the Industrial Revolution urban development in the Northwest was slow and followed well-established patterns.[2] The exigencies of the landscape determined the main lines of communication and centres of potential growth. Salt was always a vital commodity of trade, and in all likelihood the profuse web of saltways issuing from the Cheshire 'wiches' and enmeshing most of northern Britain was of considerable antiquity. With their sound strategic sense and their ambitious military engineering, the Romans gave greater definition to the human geography of the region. Established as the northwestern outpost of their empire, Chester never ceased to be a vital cornerstone in the defences of lowland Britain. Commanding the gateway to northern Wales as well as providing access to the Irish Sea, it was from the first well served with roads, which in more propitious times bore merchants as well as soldiers. A vital corridor southwards connected it with other garrison-towns along the Welsh borderland. In one direction Watling Street provided a direct route to London, while in the other it fed back out across the Cheshire Plain to Manchester and York. By this means it was also linked to parallel thoroughfares running northwards through the region: the one cutting

[1] Thrupp, *Merchant Class* is the seminal work in this field. For rare attempts to view the commercial sector in a wider social setting see Hilton, *West Midlands*, ch. 7, and A. F. Butcher, 'The origins of Romney freemen, 1433–1523', *Ec.H.R.*, second series XXVII (1974), 16–27.

[2] See in general Freeman, Rodgers and Kinvig, *Lancashire, Cheshire and the Isle of Man*; G. H. Tupling, 'Markets and fairs in medieval Lancashire' in J. G. Edwards, V. H. Galbraith and E. F. Jacob (eds.), *Historical Essays in Honour of James Tait* (Manchester, 1933), pp. 345–56.

through the densely forested and poorly drained lowlands to the strategic fort at Lancaster, the other boldly traversing the eastern uplands through Manchester and Ribchester in a more direct route to Carlisle. Through all the vicissitudes of the centuries following the withdrawal of the legions, these avenues of communication never ceased to be used. While few sites were occupied continuously from Roman times, most of the important local towns developed upon this basic grid. Chester, Lancaster and Manchester were Roman foundations; Middlewich, Northwich and Wigan grew up around Roman staging-posts; Warrington, Preston and Stockport arose at Roman river-crossings. Maps and itineraries from the fourteenth century reveal that the region had filled out somewhat. New roads leading to new towns, like the road from Chester to Liverpool via the Birkenhead ferry, are in evidence. Yet the basic pattern of development had changed surprisingly little in the intervening millennium.

By the time of the Black Death the region boasted several dozen boroughs and market-centres, but a fair number were towns in little more than name.[3] Few had developed more than a modicum of corporate strength and commercial prosperity. In terms of status, the city of Chester enjoyed a lonely eminence. An important military site, a major port and communications centre, a provincial capital, it had acquired unique civic liberties from a succession of indulgent earls. With its burgeoning mercantile community, it had developed communal institutions and a guild structure of considerable sophistication. Its nearest rivals lay in northern Lancashire, where Lancaster and Preston vied for precedence. Like Chester, both functioned as markets, ports and county towns, and possessed facilities for the registration of debts, but ducal patronage of the old castle-town failed to prevent its rival capitalising on its greater centrality. Significantly, Preston was the only town outside Chester to house a functioning guild merchant. Further south along the main thoroughfare, Wigan was developing as an important mart as well as a natural meeting-place for the southern half of Lancashire. In 1350 it acquired the right to keep a seal 'for recognisances of debts' on account of the 'frequent concourse at the said borough, as well of merchants as others, for the sake of trading and otherwise'.[4] The possession of this important facility set the four leading urban centres somewhat apart from other towns.

---

[3] Among the many studies of individual towns, Morris, *Chester in the Plantagenet and Tudor Reigns*, J. Hall, *A History of the Town and Parish of Nantwich* (Nantwich, 1883), H. Heginbotham, *Stockport Ancient and Modern* (2 vols., London, 1882, 1892), H. W. Clemesha, *A History of Preston in Amounderness* (Manchester, 1912), C. S. Davies, *A History of Macclesfield* (Manchester, 1961) and W. B. Stephens (ed.), *History of Congleton* (Manchester, 1970), have proved particularly valuable.     [4] *C.P.R. 1348–1350*, p. 553.

Yet there were other boroughs with considerable potential for development. While Chester and Preston were the only communities with organised guilds, Nantwich and Liverpool as well as Lancaster and Wigan had the right to form such associations. With its salt-springs and its location in the heart of rich dairying country, Nantwich was an important centre for marketing and processing agricultural goods, the hub of a network of ancient saltways, and straddled the main lines of communication with the Midlands and the Southeast. On the northern bank of the Mersey estuary, Liverpool was not only the market for a prosperous hinterland but also a port to rival Chester in the coastal and Irish trades. Among the other major boroughs, Middlewich, Northwich and Knutsford were well-established market-towns in central Cheshire, Congleton, Macclesfield and Stockport were poised for expansion on the Pennine fringe, and Clitheroe was strategically placed in the upper reaches of the Ribble valley, the easiest route across the central Pennines. There were many lesser boroughs, whose markets served narrowly circumscribed areas and whose fortunes remained inordinately dependent on their status as hundredal, honorial or parochial centres. Small chartered boroughs like Over and Roby certainly testify more to seignorial ambition than to economic potential.[5] Meanwhile some substantial settlements prospered without the possession of borough charters. Warrington and Manchester were important market-towns with sizeable trading and manufacturing communities, but both had their claims to borough status challenged in this period.

Even by contemporary standards Cheshire and Lancashire towns were not large. With its six functioning parish churches, and its division into wards, the city of Chester was wholly exceptional. With an estimated population of over four thousand, it dwarfed its nearest rivals. While Preston might have boasted a community of a thousand souls, almost all other local towns counted their inhabitants in three figures. In truth there was little difference in population size between many boroughs and the larger villages.[6] In distinguishing between town and countryside, occupational structure is perhaps a surer guide than demographic scale. The poll-tax returns of 1379 provide valuable data on the numbers of merchants and tradesmen in different communities.[7] Unfortunately detailed material is extant for only one major town in the region, but its

[5] The borough of Over was the creation of the abbot of Vale Royal: *Vale Royal Ledger Book*, *passim*. The borough of Roby was founded by Sir Thomas Lathom as late as 1372: M. Bateson, 'The creation of boroughs: Charters of Deganwy, Dunster, Higham Ferrers, Bolton, Warton and Roby', *E.H.R.*, XVII (1902), 284–96.

[6] P.R.O., E 179/130/24; E 179/133/29.    [7] P.R.O., E 179/130/24; E 179/130/28.

Table 9. *The occupational structure of three Lancashire vills in 1379*

|  | Liverpool | Walton le Dale | Atherton |
|---|---|---|---|
| Gentlemen | 2 | 6 | 1 |
| Peasant cultivators | 26 | 69 | 45 |
| Trademen | 49 | 0 | 3 |
| Servants | 9 | 0 | 17 |
| Total population | 86 | 75 | 66 |
| Status of vill | Borough | Village | Village |

profile can be profitably contrasted with those of the two largest villages (see Table 9).

Obviously Liverpool, with over half its tax-payers designated as merchants and craftsmen, exhibited a much higher degree of occupational specialisation than either Atherton, with its three smiths, or Walton, with no full-time artisans, and can be set apart with some conviction as a functioning urban centre. The new borough of Roby, on the other hand, must be deemed to have failed the same test. The two vills of Huyton and Roby, grouped together in the tax returns, produced only twenty-nine tax-payers, none of whom were full-time tradesmen.

In a study of this nature the actual location of trade and industry accordingly represents the main focus of interest. In the absence of material of the quality of the poll-tax returns for most of the region, evidence regarding the distribution of merchants and craftsmen in the region must be derived from inferior sources. Since from the reign of Henry V it was mandatory to record the occupation and residence of all persons involved in legal actions, court-rolls can provide some useful insights. While appearances in legal records cannot have been entirely random, it is fair to assume that, given large enough samples, the tradesmen named in the court-rolls provide some indication of the relative size of the commercial and manufacturing sector in different localities. Thus the fine series of Cheshire county court-rolls between 1415 and 1425 provide the names of exactly four hundred local merchants and craftsmen,[8] and their places of residence can be listed as in Table 10.

Again, the commercial hegemony of the city of Chester is strikingly evidenced, with nearly half the sample residing in its precincts. While

---

[8] The sample has been compiled from all the merchants and craftsmen named in P.R.O., CHES 25/11, CHES 25/12, mm. 1–12, CHES 29/123, CHES 29/125, CHES 29/129, CHES 29/130.

Table 10. *Geographical distribution of Cheshire merchants and craftsmen*

|  | Number | Percentage of sample |
|---|---|---|
| Chester | 187 | 46.75 |
| Nantwich | 42 | 10.50 |
| Knutsford | 18 | 4.50 |
| Stockport | 14 | 3.50 |
| Middlewich | 13 | 3.25 |
| Other boroughs | 37 | 9.25 |
| Other villages | 89 | 22.25 |
| Totals | 400 | 100.00 |

Chester tradespeople lived in closer proximity to the halls of justice, their greater prominence in the records does seem to reflect the enormous scale of their contribution to local trade and industry. The showing of Chester's three closest rivals is more surprising. Head and shoulders above others was Nantwich, where ten per cent of the sample plied their trade. Next in importance were two other seignorial boroughs in east Cheshire, Knutsford and Stockport. While there are no institutional grounds for ranking these three towns so highly, the court-roll evidence accords well with the apparent vigour of their connections with London.[9] A number of other boroughs, including the royal boroughs of Middlewich, Northwich and Macclesfield, also hold respectable positions in the table. Although smaller numbers make the rankings far less reliable lower down the scale, it does seem that most boroughs, including such modest townships as Malpas, Halton and Over, had larger trading populations than all but the most exceptional villages. Yet it is still noteworthy that nearly a quarter of the sample lived outside the chartered boroughs. While rural tradesmen probably were not of the same substance as their colleagues in the towns, their quantitative importance in commerce and manufacturing must not be overlooked. Needless to say, some large villages such as Sandbach, Bunbury and Lostock rivalled the smaller boroughs in terms of the number and range of their resident craftsmen.

---

[9] See Bennett, 'Social mobility', 65–6.

II

Occupational structure remains the surest guide to urban functions, but it would still be most inappropriate in a study of this nature to draw too rigid a divide between town and countryside. Even relatively prosperous boroughs maintained sizeable sections of the population engaged in agriculture, while small hamlets sometimes boasted one or two craftsmen. Certainly in a discussion of trade and industry as avenues of social mobility, it would be ill-advised to treat the urban sector in isolation. Rural traders and craftsmen had access to shops or stalls in market-towns, just as enterprising burgesses organised cottage-industries and invested in real estate in the surrounding countryside. Labour and capital certainly moved both ways, if only to meet seasonal market demands. In the following section it is intended to look more closely at the range of trades pursued in town and countryside, and to uncover some of the channels by which men on the land became involved in the commercial and manufacturing sector.

Given the free status of the greater part of the local peasantry, it can be assumed that most villagers with the inclination and opportunity were able to supplement their incomes through rural crafts. A significant proportion of the population doubtless depended for its livelihood on wage-labour. Much of this employment, of course, was of a purely agricultural nature, but there was a great deal of semi-skilled work like carting and droving which was very much on the margins of the primary process. Then there were numerous other occupations integral to village life. Most communities had their smiths, millers, carpenters, brewers and bakers, even if only on a part-time basis. Since the craftsmen were assessed at a higher rate than ordinary villagers, those identified in the poll-tax returns of 1379 must have been the more prominent of their profession, like the two carpenters, the fletcher, cooper, walker and tailor at Ashton in Makerfield, the two potters and the turner at Knowsley, and the three weavers at Rixton with Glazebrook. All in all, resident craftsmen were recorded in three-quarters of the villages of West Derby hundred. With the exception of shepherds, none occur in the surviving returns for Blackburn hundred, although whether this was a function of the greater poverty of the region or a reflection of the different terms of reference of the tax-collectors cannot be ascertained.[10]

The range of skills and crafts pursued in the countryside was considerable, as can be evidenced from the Cheshire court-rolls. Most villagers seem to have had mills and smithies. Millers are attested at Bickley, Sutton,

[10] P.R.O., E 179/130/24; E 179/130/28.

Over Peover, Mickle Trafford, Leighton and elsewhere, and smiths at Doddington, Appleton, Lostock, Lymm, Sandbach, Cheadle and Bramhall. In addition there were wrights of various sorts at Warburton, Whatcroft, Leftwich, Chorley, Bostock, Mollington Banastre, Romiley and Aldford; a cartwright at Mobberley, a carpenter at Morley, a turner at Godley, a harper at Warmingham and fletchers at Kinderton and Timperley. Among the victualling trades, there were butchers at Walgherton, Stathum, Bradley, Grappenhall, Whitley, Hassall and Sandbach, salters at Duddon and Smallwood, a baker at Mere, and a mustardmaker at Witton. Tailors were common, as at Tarvin, Over Alderley, Edge, Pownall, Wilmslow, Weston, Warmingham, Lachford, Clotton, Over Tabley, Nether Peover, Lostock, Lymm and elsewhere. The textile industry was also in evidence, with weavers at Kingsley, Styal and Witton, a linen-weaver at Newhall, a huester at Sandbach, a chaloner at Leighton, walkers at Hyde and Tintwistle, and even a draper at Rostherne. More miscellaneous, there was a chapman at Agden, a collier at Romiley and a minstrel at Bunbury.

In the towns there was obviously greater variety and specialisation in the occupational structure. The Cheshire court-rolls record the names of some forty-two Nantwich townsmen between 1415 and 1425. Among the victuallers, there were seven butchers and a grocer. In leather-processing there was a skinner, seven shoemakers, a corviser and two saddlers. In textiles and allied trades there were two drapers, a chaloner, seven weavers and two tailors. Then there was a goldsmith, an ironmonger, a cartwright, a barber, a fletcher, three masons, a thatcher and two wallers working on the salt-pans. Although the evidence for other boroughs is rather limited, general conclusions can be made regarding the sorts of trades pursued in local towns. While there is little evidence of leather-workers in villages, for example, most boroughs supported a number of craftsmen in this field. Thus there were shoemakers and sometimes glovers at Chester, Nantwich, Knutsford, Stockport, Middlewich, Halton, Northwich, Congleton and Tarporley. Another industry in which the towns enjoyed a virtual monopoly was fine metalwork. There were cutlers at Macclesfield and Knutsford, and goldsmiths at Stockport as well as at Nantwich and Chester. With regard to textiles the contrast between town and countryside was rather less well marked. In the Northwest, as elsewhere, it was probably more economical to have the wool spun, the yarn woven and the cloth fulled outside the chartered boroughs. Already Cheshire villages and hamlets situated close to the fast-flowing Pennine streams were growing in importance as manufacturing areas.[11] Yet the vast majority

[11] E.g. see the references to numerous weavers of wool and linen in north Cheshire villages in the reign of Richard II: P.R.O., CHES 19/2, mm. 44–7.

of full-time textile-workers were still to be found in the towns. More specialised ancillary trades, such as dyeing, certainly seem not to have developed in rural settings.

Naturally enough, Chester housed the richest assortment of merchants and craftsmen in the region. The names of its streets and 'rows' – Ironmonger Street, Cooks' Row, Baxter Row, Butter Shops, Flesh-monger Lane, Saddler Row, and even Love Lane – bear graphic witness to the range of its trades in this period.[12] Merchants and craftsmen in the city were sufficiently numerous to form specialised guilds. By the time of the Black Death the drapers, tailors, tanners and shoemakers had formed separate companies, and by 1422 the ironmongers, carpenters, bowyers, fletchers, coopers, stringers and hoopers were also organised as guilds.[13] Needless to say, there is far more evidence regarding the occupational structure of Chester than any other town in the region. The records of admissions to the freedom of the city provides the names and occupations of one hundred and forty citizens in the period 1393 to 1493,[14] but this source has an in-built bias in favour of the wealthier or better-connected tradesmen who were admitted to full citizenship. More representative of the Chester trading community as a whole are the 187 merchants and craftsmen named in the county court-rolls, to whom a further 59 tradesmen from the mayor's book for Henry V's reign can be added to make a total of 246.[15] The occupations of this sample grouping, perhaps as many as a quarter of the city's independent tradesmen, are shown in Table 11.

Of course, this classification of the various trades is in some respects artificial. Many of the butchers, for example, were also skinners, and more closely associated with the leather industry than with victualling. At the same time the vintners and the drapers might be more reasonably grouped with the merchants than with humble artisans in similar lines of business. Yet this survey does give some impression of the range and relative size of occupational groupings in Chester.

While the existence of large numbers of local tradesmen can be profusely documented, exceedingly little is known about their economic position. Information on prices charged by craftsmen and wages claimed by journeymen is extremely hard to find in the region in this period. Even if more such data were available, there would be much that would remain obscure. It cannot be hoped to compute, for example, the profit margins

[12] J. McN. Dodgson, 'Place-names and street-names at Chester', *J.C.A.S.*, 55 (1968), 29–61.

[13] Morris, *Chester in the Plantagenet and Tudor Reigns*, p. 411; E. K. Chambers, *English Literature at the Close of the Middle Ages* (Oxford, 1945), p. 23.

[14] *Chester Freeman Rolls*, passim.

[15] The additional names have been extracted from Chester R.O., MB 3.

Table 11. *Occupational structure of Chester in the reign of Henry V*

| Occupation | Number | Percentage of sample |
|---|---|---|
| Merchants and shipmen | | |
| Merchants | 6 | |
| Shipmen | 4 | 4·0 |
| Victuallers | | |
| Vintners | 3 | |
| Spicers | 1 | |
| Bakers | 21 | |
| Millers | 20 | |
| Fishers | 5 | |
| Butchers | 12 | 25.2 |
| Wood and metalworkers | | |
| Goldsmiths | 4 | |
| Cutlers | 5 | |
| Ironmongers | 2 | |
| Spurriers | 1 | |
| Plumbers | 1 | |
| Smiths | 3 | |
| Cartwrights | 2 | |
| Wheelmakers | 1 | |
| Coopers | 2 | |
| Carpenters/Wrights | 7 | |
| Glaziers | 1 | |
| Stringers | 1 | |
| Sheath-makers | 1 | |
| Harpers | 1 | 13.0 |
| Leather tradesmen | | |
| Barkers | 2 | |
| Curriers | 5 | |
| Saddlers | 3 | |
| Girdelers | 1 | |
| Shoemakers/Corvisers | 15 | |
| Glovers | 6 | 13.0 |
| Clothing and textile tradesmen | | |
| Drapers | 2 | |
| Tailors | 8 | |
| Hosiers | 4 | |
| Capmakers | 1 | |
| Weavers | 42 | |
| Linen-weavers | 3 | |
| Broiderers | 1 | |
| Dyers/Huesters | 6 | |
| Chaloners | 5 | |

Table 11. *cont.*

| Occupation | Number | Percentage of sample |
|---|---|---|
| Shearmen | 5 | |
| Cardmakers | 2 | |
| Walkers/Fullers | 17 | 39.0 |
| Professional and clerical workers | | |
| Lawyers | 1 | |
| Scriveners | 1 | 0.8 |
| Menial and semi-skilled tradesmen | | |
| Barbers | 5 | |
| Tinkers | 3 | |
| Waterleaders | 2 | |
| Carters | 1 | |
| Drovers | 1 | 4.9 |
| Total | 246 | |

of a retailer, the productivity of a craftsman, or the number of days a journeyman could expect to be in employment. Perhaps all that can be claimed at this stage is that at best a handsome livelihood could be gained through involvement in trade and industry, and at worst the prospects still appeared alluring to many agricultural workers. When itinerant bands of Welsh labourers were able to demand wages of five pence a day in Nantwich, it can be assumed that even the humblest local journeyman was able to earn comparable if not superior rates.[16]

Access to the opportunities presented by the commercial sector, of course, remains the fundamental problem. Demonstrably too little is known about the organisation of small-scale trading and manufacturing enterprises to make more than a few general observations.[17] At the lowest levels of involvement, among part-time craftsmen in the villages and unskilled labourers in the towns, there could have been few formal restrictions on employment. While a few rural tradesmen might have completed apprenticeships in towns, the vast majority would have learned their crafts informally from family or friends. By the same token the rural

[16] Hugh Welshman of Nantwich was apparently inciting other Welsh labourers to demand higher rates of pay: P.R.O., CHES 19/5, m. 5.

[17] Court-rolls occasionally provide some information, e.g. the disputes between Richard Walker of Wilmslow and Richard Lister of Stockport, and between Richard Edgeley and John Fresby, huester of Macclesfield, both of which concern the detention of quantities of woollen cloth: P.R.O., SC 2/254/14 and SC 2/255/1.

craftsman required little in the form of capital investment, and the journeyman or piece-worker had no immediate need to acquire plant and stock. At higher levels of enterprise, naturally enough, the opportunities were more restricted. To be apprenticed to a master craftsman in Chester, Preston, Nantwich or some other town, and then to become established in a trade, required financial backing.[18] Yet it was certainly not beyond the means of an enterprising peasant to put his son to a trade. There is no evidence that the trading classes recruited at all extensively from the local squirearchy, and the surnames of tradesmen suggest that the overwhelming majority were of low birth. The presence in Chester of many merchants and artisans of Welsh and Irish origins also tends to corroborate the notion that entry into trade was relatively open. Edmund Eulowe, a well-connected citizen of Chester in Henry V's reign, was not only Welsh by birth, but also a villein from the lordship of Ruthin.[19]

Far more important than wealth and status in determining access to commercial opportunities was personal connection. David Eulowe, a mayor of Chester in the late fourteenth century, was probably responsible for sponsoring the careers of Edmund Eulowe and other kinsmen and compatriots. The Hawardens, another prolific lineage, also hailed from the Welsh Borderlands. Both John and William Hawarden were wealthy merchants who served as mayors of Chester in the early fifteenth century. Richard and William son of Richard Hawarden, two weavers, were also relatives. Henry Hawarden, David son of John Hawarden, Hopkin Hawarden and other tradesmen with the same surname were likewise kinsmen or compatriots.[20] It is often difficult to disentangle genealogical and geographical connections. The manifold links between the city of Chester and Hale in Lancashire are particularly interesting. William Mawer of Chester held property in Hale, and his will was witnessed by Richard Hale of Chester as well as a number of villagers of Hale.[21] Another Chester tradesman with a tenancy in this village was John Hale, the son of William Hodgson, a customary tenant on the manor of Hale.[22] Richard and John Hale, possibly brothers, were closely associated in the fulling industry. Stephen and Maurice Hale, two weavers of Chester, also might have been kinsmen, and collaborators in an allied trade.

[18] See two surviving indentures of apprenticeship for this period, relating to Preston and Nantwich respectively: *De Hoghton Deeds and Papers*, ed. J. H. Lumby (L.C.R.S., 88, 1936), no. 310; *Cheshire Sheaf*, third series, item 8398.

[19] P.R.O., CHES 25/11, m. 18.

[20] P.R.O., CHES 25/12 and CHES 29/129; Chester R.O., MB 1 and MB 3.

[21] *Norris Deeds*, nos. 608 and 609.

[22] Lancashire R.O., DDIb, Box 1 (unclassified). For William Hodgson see the Hale manorial records in *Three Early English Metrical Romances*, p. xl.

While even the most friendless labourer could conceivably amass sufficient savings to establish himself in a craft, most aspiring tradesmen were dependent on the patronage of others. Still, it must not be assumed that such sponsorship was only available to the chosen few. The circle of an individual's potential patrons extended far beyond the immediate family to embrace not only kinsmen but also godparents, family-friends, fellow-parishioners and manorial lords. William Laghok of Speke probably owed his admission into the Chester trading community to the good offices of the Erneys family, lords of the manor of Speke as well as prominent city merchants.[23] Similarly in outlining the links between Chester and Hale, it is worth noting the career of the notable royal clerk, John Leyot. A generous benefactor of his native village of Hale, he was also for nearly thirty years the holder of the richest benefice in Chester.[24] The significance of linkages of this sort are difficult to evaluate. Yet, in the absence of quantifiable data, individual case-studies are all there is to rely on. Nor does the possibly unrepresentative character of such cases make them valueless. An account of the particularly distinguished career or the specially efficacious connection merely serves to delineate the potentialities of the patronage system. Thus the achievements of humble local tradesmen who managed to prosper at a national level have considerable relevance: they define the realms of the possible and at the same time pre-suppose hundreds of more modest success-stories.

III

It would be a grave error to assume that the activities and interests of local tradesmen were at all confined to their native region, or that the traffic in goods and services between the two counties and other parts of the kingdom was negligible. In the first place there was a considerable transit trade. The port of Chester handled a large share of the trade with Ireland, exporting cloth and other manufactured articles from as far afield as Coventry and Yorkshire and importing such raw materials as wool, flax and hides. Then again the region straddled important trade-routes with North Wales and Cumbria. Though much of this commerce was in the hands of outsiders, a number of local towns greatly benefited from their location on major arteries of trade. Drawing raw materials from the under-developed Celtic fringe, Chester and certain other towns developed as entrepôts in textiles and leatherwork. The importing of flax likewise seems to have fuelled the development of the linen cloth industry in the

[23] *V.C.H. Lancaster*, III, pp. 132–3; *Chester Freeman Rolls*, p. 1.
[24] He was dean of St John's, Chester from 1394 until around 1422: *B.R.U.O.*, II, p. 1143.

Manchester area.[25] At the same time Chester was able to build up a market for luxury goods in North Wales and Ireland, re-exporting finished cloth and fine leatherwork as well as wine, spices and other exotic products.[26]

Nor was the Northwest completely without its own resources. From the Cheshire brine-springs came one of the most basic articles of trade, and local salt found its way across the Pennines, south into the Midlands, westwards into Wales and across the sea to Ireland. The towns of Nantwich, Middlewich and Northwich owed much of their prosperity to this vital commodity, and many of the main arteries of commerce in the region had been pioneered by the pack-horses of Cheshire salters. Perhaps salt went some way towards compensating for certain natural deficiencies. The region was not particularly good for wheat-growing, and it imported grain more often than it produced surpluses. Both counties were better suited for stock-rearing and dairying, and in some areas vaccaries and stud-farms were major sources of seignorial income. During the Black Prince's time herds of cattle were driven south for royal consumption, and it is probable that even more passed through private hands to the markets of the Midlands and Southeast. Of course, in the development of a meat trade the region was fortunate in having at hand plentiful supplies of salt, the standard preservative. At Chester meat and fish could even be imported, salted for preservation, and then re-vended elsewhere. The proximity of the brine-springs to rich dairying areas also must have stimulated cheese-making. While there is little evidence regarding its sale in other parts of the kingdom, Cheshire cheese had acquired a national reputation by the sixteenth century.

Local pastoralists provided other commodities of trade. The hides of their animals went to supply a burgeoning leather industry. Since skins could not be left long in their raw state, there were tanners to prepare the leather in most larger towns, and sizeable numbers of shoemakers, saddlers and other leather-workers. Some places even developed their own specialisms, like glove-making at Congleton.[27] Wool was another source of wealth. While the region was not noted for the quality or quantity of its wool, sheep-fells from local Cistercian houses do seem to have found their way on to the national market. More important, local wool fed a growing native textile industry. Perhaps its distance from the major outlets for English wool served to stimulate cloth-making in the region even prior

[25] For linen weaving in the villages to the south of Manchester see P.R.O., CHES 19/2, mm. 44–45d.

[26] For a full assessment of the commercial life of Chester see K. P. Wilson, 'The port of Chester in the later Middle Ages', unpublished Ph.D. thesis, University of Liverpool, 1965.

[27] Stephens, *History of Congleton*, p. 54. See also D. M. Woodward, 'The Chester leather industry, 1558–1625', *L.C.H.S.*, 119 (1968), 65–111.

to the national shift from wool to cloth exports. Fulling mills early became a feature of the landscape on the western slopes of the Pennines, and spinning and weaving for the market became additional sources of income for many local towns and villages. By the 1390s cloth was being transported across the Pennines for export. The Shaws of northeast Cheshire was one family company to prosper through this trade, and syndicates of local clothiers can even be traced freighting ships in Hull.[28]

While the Northwest was fairly generously endowed with such natural resources as timber, coal, and iron, and while it was able to export some cloth, leather and other goods, its balance of trade with the rest of the kingdom can scarcely have been healthy. Whether the region was even self-sufficient in food is debatable, but it was certainly heavily dependent on outside suppliers for a whole range of commodities, including both luxury and essential items. Fine cloth, specialised metalwork and many other manufactured items doubtless had to be brought from London, Coventry, York or elsewhere. Then there were the goods which had to be imported. Spices were virtually indispensable. Gascon wine was the staple of Chester's overseas trade in this period, but with it came oil, wax and other foreign produce. Indeed there is a problem of how the region made up for what appears to be a gross trade deficit. The solution would have to be that there was an outflow of capital. This is not so improbable as it might first seem. Although impossible to calculate, the earnings, fees and emoluments accruing to local men from outside the region were considerable. At times literally thousands of local gentlemen, soldiers and clerks were on the royal pay-roll alone.[29]

Local tradesmen played their part in the process by which the Northwest shared in the wealth of the more commodious parts of the realm. Wherever trading connections were established, the region was represented by groups of merchants and craftsmen. Links with major trading partners like Coventry were particularly strong. A large number of local merchants felt it worth their while to join the prestigious Trinity Guild, including Adam Ingram, John Coly, John Armourer, John Arrow, Roger Porter, Richard Hawarden, Robert Bradley, Robert Hope, Thomas Peacock and John Madeley from Chester, and other tradesmen from Preston, Warrington and Northwich.[30] Some local craftsmen seem to have resided permanently in Coventry. The Molyneux of Sefton deeds

---

[28] R. C. Shaw, 'Two fifteenth-century kinsmen: John Shaw of Dukinfield, mercer, and William Shaw of Heath Charnock, surgeon', *L.C.H.S.*, 110 (1958), 15–30. See also J. Lister (ed.), *The Early Yorkshire Woollen Trade* (Yorkshire Archaeological Soc., record series 64, 1924), *passim*.

[29] See below, Chapter 10.    [30] *Register of Trinity Guild, Coventry, passim*.

testify to a sizeable colony of townsmen from villages in southwest Lancashire including Richard Furness and Thomas Walton alias Crosse, both of whom held land in Walton on the Hill, and William Walker and John White, a baker, two sons-in-law of John Orshagh of Ince Blundell.[31]

Cheshire and Lancashire men seem to have established themselves in almost all the larger towns of the kingdom. The evidence for this veritable diaspora is fragmentary and diffuse, but the chance survival of odd pieces of information sometimes provides more useful insights than vast quantities of more standardised material. The will of Henry Kelsall, a clothier of Reading, for example, documents an otherwise unknown connection between this rapidly developing textile town and his native Knutsford.[32] In a similar fashion the existence of James Merbury, a local adventurer who married into an important Bristol trading firm, is only known from testamentary evidence.[33] Deeds and court records similarly recover from oblivion William Faurokeshaw of Worcester, tailor, who hailed from Rainford; Hugh Marthall of Nottingham, a native of Congleton; William Laghok of St Neots in Huntingdonshire who originated from Speke; and John Ormerod of Southampton whose nearest kinsmen were small-time chapmen and artisans around the hamlet of Ormerod in Lancashire.[34] Across the Pennines, likewise, local men settled and prospered. Wills have survived to attest the Lancashire provenance of such prominent merchants of York as Nicholas Blackburn and John Radcliffe, while charters document Cheshire interests in Hull and Beverley.[35] In the towns of North Wales and Ireland local tradesmen seem to have been particularly advantaged. In Wales, the Bolds and Bulkeleys were only two of many families who built up fortunes in and around Caernarfon, Conwy and other castle-towns.[36] Across the Irish Sea, the Prestons, originally from Lancashire, were well-advanced along the path that would bring them a peerage, while numerous others sought to emulate their achievements.[37]

Needless to say, the uncontested centre of the commercial and industrial life of the kingdom was London. With a population far outstripping

---

[31] Lancashire R.O., DDM/51, DDM/34/18.

[32] *Cheshire Sheaf*, third series, item 4215.　　　　[33] *Ibid.*, item 4557.

[34] *Lancashire Pleas*, p. 67; *H.M.C., Various Collections*, II, pp. 18–19; *Norris Deeds*, no. 172; P.R.O., PL 15/2, m. 13.

[35] *Testamenta Eboracensia. A Selection of Wills from the Registry at York*, vol. II, ed. J. Raine (Surtees Soc., 30, 1855), pp. 17–21, 92–3; J.R.U.L., Arley Charters, 24/21, 24/25 and 24/34.

[36] Jones-Pierce, 'Caernarvonshire in the later Middle Ages'.

[37] *Calendar of the Gormanston Register*, ed. J. Mills and M. J. McEnery (Royal Soc. of Antiquaries of Ireland, 1916). For Macclesfield men in Dublin see Bruell, 'Edition of the cartulary of John de Macclesfield', item 111.

regional capitals, with its political prestige and close proximity to continental markets, it dominated the national economy. Yet it must not be concluded that its prosperity was wholly at the expense of provincial tradesmen. The web of commercial connections spun from the metropolis sooner or later drew in members of all the more prominent mercantile families, many of which invested in its fortunes by establishing branches in London. Similarly, given the high mortality-rates in the city, there was a continuous demand for artisans and labourers from the countryside. Judging from the evidence of admissions to London guilds, a fair proportion of these immigrants came from Cheshire and Lancashire. One in eleven of the new apprentices in the skinners' and the tailors' guilds in the late fifteenth century was a native of the region, whose population after all constituted only one thirty-sixth of the nation as a whole.[38]

While it is impossible to be certain, it seems that immigration from the Northwest into London began on a really large scale in the decades around 1400. The rise of aldermanic families of local provenance can be taken to reflect, at an interval of a few generations, this process. Prior to the late fourteenth century no local tradesmen seem to have achieved eminence in London. Thomas Knolles, grocer and alderman from 1393 to 1435, was probably the first Cheshire man to achieve aldermanic rank in the capital. He was followed by Nicholas Aughton, a stockfishmonger of Lancashire provenance, who attained the dignity shortly before his death in 1415. Still, the real invasion of the civic oligarchy did not begin until the middle of the fifteenth century, with the elections of William Wettenhall, a grocer from Nantwich, in 1438, Philip Malpas, a draper from south Cheshire, in 1448, and Hugh Wiche, a mercer and another native of Nantwich, in 1458. Indeed from this time until well into the sixteenth century the region was continuously represented on the aldermanic council. Thomas Oulegreve, a skinner from Knutsford, and George Ireland and John Crosby, both grocers from southwest Lancashire, were aldermen in the 1460s and 1470s. Among the members of this august corporation in the last quarter of the fifteenth century were Edmund Shaw, a goldsmith and native of northeast Cheshire, Hugh Pemberton, a tailor from south Lancashire, and John Percival, a tailor from Macclesfield.[39]

Cheshire and Lancashire tradesmen did not achieve positions of eminence in the civic community overnight. The fortunes of men like Sir Hugh Wiche and Sir Edmund Shaw in the late fifteenth century were

---

[38] Thrupp, *Merchant Class*, appendix C.

[39] *Ibid.*, appendix A. The Cheshire provenance of Philip Malpas is suggested both by his name and his association in 1418 with Hugh Malpas of Checkley and William Malpas of Chester: *Ches. R.R.*, II, p. 574.

built on foundations laboriously laid by kinsmen and compatriots in earlier decades. Even in the relative obscurity of the London trading community around 1400 some of the important connections can be traced back. Nicholas Aughton, alderman of London in 1415, was almost certainly related to another stockfishmonger, Gilbert Aughton, operating in the city in the 1380s. At about the same time a whole group of other merchants from the Liverpool area, including William Liverpool, girdeler, John Formby, brewer, and John Tippup, mercer, seem to have become established in the capital.[40] Nor were William Wettenhall and Hugh Wiche the only Nantwich tradesmen to prosper in London. Thomas Wiche, a fishmonger who died in 1425, was the latter's kinsman, as in all likelihood was William Wiche, another fishmonger.[41]

The avenues through which tradesmen came to establish themselves in London cannot be documented in any detail. Purely commercial channels must always have been the most significant. It is instructive that over half the Cheshire and Lancashire men who became aldermen of London or who became apprentices in the tailors' and skinners' companies were of burgess stock. It was clearly advantageous for trading families in the provinces to have sons established in the capital. Nor were men of this sort lacking in the money and connections to put their policies into practice. Thus the career of Nicholas Aughton as an alderman and stockfishmonger of London might be seen as the ultimate achievement of a family firm which began with fishermen on the Lancashire coast. A chance reference to a kinsman's involvement in trade with Ireland adds further detail to the picture.[42] The textile industry also seems to have been important in linking local tradesmen with London. Thomas Knolles, William Wettenhall and George Ireland were grocers, and the latter at least was involved in the wholesale export of wool. Philip Malpas was a draper, and two later aldermen from the region were tailors. Yet sometimes moving into the capital involved a change of business. Edmund Shaw was the son of a local clothier, but he was apprenticed in London as a goldsmith.[43]

There was also movement into trade and industry from other walks of life. London contained a large population of courtiers, lawyers, soldiers, clerks and other functionaries, and such men played a considerable role

---

[40] They witnessed a deed together in London in 1413: Wigan R.O., Crosse Deeds, no. 122. Note also John Liverpool, citizen and jeweller of London, and Hugh Liverpool, citizen and mercer of London: *C.Pap.L.*, v, p. 120; P.R.O., CHES 29/98, m. 4d.

[41] *Cheshire Sheaf*, third series, item 4043.

[42] *C.P.R. 1385–1389*, p. 114. On the other hand, the Aughtons in commerce might have owed their fortunes to the Aughtons in soldiering and administration: see below, Chapter 10.

[43] Shaw, 'Two fifteenth-century kinsmen', 20.

in introducing new blood into the mercantile community. In some cases it is difficult to distinguish between merchants and other careerists in London. Thus Richard Clitheroe from Lancashire pursued interests which straddled both the city and the court. An esquire in the household of Richard II, he also held appointments which accorded well with commercial concerns. From 1392 he was changer and assayer of money at Calais, from 1395 measurer of woollen cloths and canvas bought and sold in London, and from 1398 collector of the customs. In Henry IV's reign he became a buyer for the royal household, and served on occasion as sheriff of Kent, escheator of Northumberland and admiral.[44] While such a man cannot be classed as a merchant, the nature of his interests makes his social status somewhat marginal. It is instructive that among the apprentices to the mercers' company in the 1390s were two other Clitheroes, Ellis and John.[45] They were almost certainly relatives of Richard Clitheroe, and owed their start in life to his credit in the city. A chance local reference proves conclusively that Ellis was the nephew and heir of a proven kinsman, John Clitheroe, the chancery clerk.[46]

Doubtless many other tradesmen from the Northwest depended upon the patronage of local careerists associated with the capital. It would be interesting to speculate, for example, how dependent Thomas Knolles' fortunes were on the availability of lucrative military contracts from his kinsman, Sir Robert Knolles. In so far as the first local success-stories in London begin in the late fourteenth century, it seems reasonable to adduce political factors as major determinants of opportunities in trade and industry. From the reign of Richard II onwards there were numerous Cheshire and Lancashire men in the royal service who were in a position to sponsor their kinsmen and compatriots in the city. Sir John Stanley and John Macclesfield, for example, both held key positions in the royal household, and were well able to secure valuable custom for their friends. The Tildesleys were certainly one local family able to capitalise on their connections in the metropolis. Christopher Tildesley was a goldsmith in London, who was appointed to the king's works and attached to the great wardrobe in 1398, significantly during the keepership of John Macclesfield.[47] His appointment by the crown was more or less contemporaneous with the rise of Thomas Tildesley, a serjeant-at-law, who served on various commissions in the city in this period. At his death

---

[44] *C.C.R. 1392–1396*, p. 314; *C.P.R. 1391–1396*, p. 603; *C.P.R. 1396–1399*, p. 185; *C.P.R. 1399–1401*, pp. 19, 308; *C.P.R. 1401–1405*, pp. 386, 452; *C.P.R. 1405–1408*, p. 171.

[45] J. M. Imray, '"*Les Bones Gentes de la Mercerye de Londres*". A study of the membership of the medieval mercers' company' in A. E. J. Hollaender and W. Kellaway (eds.), *Studies in London History presented to Philip Edmund Jones* (London, 1969), pp. 153–78.

[46] Lancashire R.O., DDIn/12/5.    [47] *C.P.R. 1396–1399*, p. 319.

in 1410, the latter left the sum of £5 to Jack Tildesley the younger to make him an apprentice in some honest craft.[48] Whether this youth was apprenticed as a goldsmith is uncertain, but there were certainly other members of the family in the trade. Dennis Tildesley was enrolled as an apprentice to Christopher Tildesley in 1397, becoming his own master in 1406. Richard Barton, another local goldsmith operating in London at this time, took on Hugh Tildesley as an apprentice in 1414. Meanwhile another Christopher and an Adam Tildesley had been admitted as apprentices to the company in 1409 and 1410 respectively.[49] Indeed there was a virtually unbroken succession of Lancashire goldsmiths in the capital during the fifteenth century. In the 1440s Edmund Shaw of Stockport was apprenticed to Robert Butler, very probably a Lancashire master. In later decades he rose to prominence as a warden of the goldsmiths, master of the mint, lord mayor of London and privy councillor.[50]

Although it is possible to follow the fortunes of individual tradesmen, it is rather more difficult to assess how far opportunities in London were available to members of the lower orders. While in theory apprenticeships were open to all young men of free birth, and while even villeins were tolerated in some companies, financial backing was always a necessity. In 1393 the goldsmiths ruled that a premium of at least £5 should be demanded of the parents of apprentices, but in all likelihood individual masters adjusted the fee to the means of the family. Thomas Tildesley left £5 for a kinsman to be apprenticed, while the abbot of St Werburgh's apparently paid £10 to have a youth placed with a London tailor.[51] Although such sums constituted substantial outlays for families of less than gentry stock, it seems not to have prevented the entry into honourable crafts of many young men from lower down the social scale. Many yeoman farmers and provincial townsmen undoubtedly viewed the apprenticeship of a son to a London master as an investment worthy of material sacrifice. The fathers of local apprentices to the tailors' and skinners' companies in the late fifteenth century included two merchants, five yeomen, one husbandman, one shearman and one drover as well as five gentlemen.[52] Doubtless many young men depended on patronage from outside the immediate family. Successful careerists were often willing to sponsor younger relatives, neighbours and friends. It even seems that religious houses like St Werburgh's and Vale Royal assisted in the placement of apprentices.[53] Certainly William Wiche, registrar to the

[48] P.R.O., PROB 11/2A.

[49] J. Lunn, *History of the Tyldesleys of Lancashire* (Altrincham, 1966), pp. 19–21.

[50] Shaw, 'Two fifteenth-century kinsmen', 20.

[51] P.R.O., PROB 11/2A; Thrupp, *Merchant Class*, p. 214.

[52] *Ibid.*, p. 391.  [53] Bennett, 'Social mobility', 81, 93n.

abbot of St Albans, was instrumental in establishing several of his Cheshire kinsmen in trades in London.[54]

It cannot be pretended that the streets of London were paved with gold. Only a proportion of the young men entering apprenticeships emerged as masters, while few master craftsmen achieved more than a modest livelihood. Young Robert Hilton of Chester absconded from his master and took sanctuary in Westminster Abbey and even Christopher Tildesley had to involve himself in litigation over the terms of his apprenticeship.[55] Once qualified as a master craftsman, substantial capital was required to set up in business. Again, the availability of patronage was a crucial factor, although capital could be laboriously amassed from high-interest loans and savings from daywork. The fortunate young tradesman might make a profitable marriage. George Ireland acquired control of nearly £3,000 through his betrothal to a wealthy widow.[56] A number of other merchants from the Northwest succeeded in amassing considerable fortunes during their life-times. Christopher Tildesley was a creditor of Henry IV, and his loans to the crown were sometimes in the order of £1,000.[57] The wealth of other merchants can be judged from the scale of their legacies. William Wettenhall left gifts worth £500; Philip Malpas made many lavish bequests, including half a mark each to five hundred poor householders; and Hugh Wiche was able to leave his wife £3,000.[58] Moreover, such sums represent only fractions of their total estates. Many merchants had in any case already invested some of their riches in land. Thus Thomas Knolles had purchased the manor of North Mimms in Hertfordshire, and William Wettenhall, George Ireland and other local merchants similarly acquired manorial properties in the Home Counties.[59] There can be no doubt that the spending-power of such tradesmen was substantially in excess of even the wealthiest gentry families in the Northwest. Furthermore, their role as creditors of the crown and leaders of the civic community made the wealthier merchants influential in the kingdom at large. Among the natives of the Northwest, Hugh Wiche, George Ireland, John Crosby and Edmund Shaw were all knighted for their services to the realm.[60]

[54] *Cheshire Sheaf*, third series, item 4043.
[55] *Calendar of Letters from the Mayor and Corporation of the City of London*, ed. R. R. Sharpe (London, 1885), pp. 164–5; Lunn, *Tyldesleys*, p. 19.
[56] Thrupp, *Merchant Class*, p. 107.
[57] Lunn, *Tyldesleys*, pp. 19–21.
[58] Thrupp, *Merchant Class*, pp. 128, 178; Hall, *Nantwich*, p. 84.
[59] Thrupp, *Merchant Class*, pp. 130, 128, 350.
[60] *Ibid.*, appendix A.

IV

So far a general survey of the opportunities for material improvement through trade and industry has been presented. By adopting a regionalised perspective it has been possible to offer a fuller and more balanced assessment than could have been obtained from studies of particular towns, trades or industries. Although Cheshire and Lancashire were comparatively poor and remote counties, displaying few visible signs of commercial development, a substantial section of the population do seem to have been able to acquire wealth through commerce and manufacturing. The variety of crafts pursued in the region, the range of interests and connections apparent among expatriate tradesmen, and the size of the fortunes amassed by the more successful merchants all indicate that trade and industry were far more significant as avenues of social advancement than might at first have been anticipated. By way of conclusion it is intended to discuss the degree to which tradesmen were able to convert profits into improved social status, and to assess in general terms the impact of the trade on landed society.

First of all, it must be stressed that commercial enterprise was not simply the means of livelihood of a distinctive class, but rather another dimension of the entire social order. Members of all classes were able to profit, even if only on a fairly limited or humble scale, from trade and manufacturing. In the countryside it is difficult to draw a line between the peasant with his handicrafts and the rural tradesman with his smallholding, and distinctions higher up the social scale are often equally blurred. Roger Jodrell was one of many prosperous freeholders with mercantile connections. He was married to the daughter of a prominent York merchant, and he and his wife were members of the Trinity Guild at Coventry.[61] Many old-established landed families were interested in the commercial and industrial development of their estates. As late as 1372 Sir Thomas Lathom attempted to create a borough at Roby, and other local lords sought to maximise profits from fulling-mills, coal-mines, salt-springs and the like.[62] Local knights and gentlemen with military or administrative commissions were particularly well-placed for commercial dealings. Sir David Cradock, a native of Nantwich, served for a time as mayor of Bordeaux, an office which would surely have lent itself to profitable involvement in the lucrative Gascon trade.[63] Sir John Stanley, variously

---

[61] J.R.U.L., Jodrell Charters, nos. 18 and 35; *Register of Trinity Guild, Coventry*, p. 65.

[62] E.g. coal was mined at Worsley, Pemberton and Westleigh in Lancashire: Manchester Central Reference Library, Farrer MSS., 51/10/1, transcript from Bridgewater MSS.; J.R.U.L., Legh of Lyme Muniments, N1/58; *V.C.H. Lancaster*, III, p. 423n.

[63] Y. Renouard, *Bordeaux sous les Rois d'Angleterre* (Bordeaux, 1965), p. 569.

steward of the royal household and lieutenant of Ireland, was likewise strategically positioned to advance his own or his friends' trading interests. It is perhaps significant that he was a boat-owner as well as a leading burgage-holder in Liverpool, fast developing as a major port for the Irish trade.[64]

Indeed nothing could be more mistaken than to assume that local towns were the preserve of tradespeople. Many urban centres owed their prosperity to their administrative and social functions, to their law courts and churches, and to other facilities of a non-economic nature. Naturally enough, most professional men had residences in towns. Sir Hugh Holes, William Troutbeck and other lawyers and bureaucrats held property in Chester. Many landed gentlemen also felt the need for town-houses. Richard Mascy of Sale made his will in 1407 'in his house or hospice in Bridge Street, Chester', while Sir Thomas Grosvenor had a house in Fleshmonger Lane.[65] Some lineages seem to have seen the investment possibilities of burgage property. The Stanleys, Bolds, Halsalls, Leghs and Savages acquired large burgage-holdings in Liverpool and Macclesfield during the period under discussion.[66] This development was mirrored by the process by which many merchants, seeking ultimately to live as rentiers, ploughed back part of their wealth into the rural as well as the urban land market. The Whitmores and Hawardens of Chester, the Moores of Liverpool and the Alcocks of Macclesfield, though continuing to hold municipal office, acquired country estates and began slowly to merge with the landed gentry. In some towns there is evidence that the middle ranks of the burgess class were being squeezed between the aspirations of wealthy patrician families and the ambitions of outsiders. Thus in Liverpool the tenurial structure of the borough was radically transformed between the Black Death, when there were as many burgesses as burgages, with most shopkeepers and artisans holding a burgage each, and the reign of Henry IV, when there were half the number of burgage-holders, with much larger tenancies in the hands of men whose interests transcended the borough.[67] This invasion of the towns by the local gentry, and the absorption of the leading burgesses into the county élite, sets in broader perspective the related process by which the parliamentary representation of boroughs ceased to be predominantly bourgeois in character. Sometimes this development has been viewed with disfavour, as involving the progressive stifling of communal independence

[64] *C.P.R. 1405–1408*, p. 329; *C.P.R. 1408–1413*, p. 437; P.R.O., CHES 25/11, m. 3d; Lancashire R.O., DDK/B/1542.

[65] J.R.U.L., Cornwall-Legh MSS., deed 871; Eaton Hall, Chester, Eaton Charters, no. 419.

[66] Lancashire R.O., DDK/B/1542; Cheshire R.O., DCH/R/4 (unclassified).

[67] *Lancashire Inquests, Extents and Feudal Aids*, III, pp. 69–73; Lancashire R.O., DDK/B/1542.

and the haemorrhaging of capital from town to countryside. Yet it must also be recognised as a valuable stage in the commercial education of the landed gentry, a development with portentous consequences for the future.

When assessing the relationship of merchants and craftsmen to the traditional social order, it must be asked how far tradesmen really did constitute a self-contained, hereditary class. While it can be argued that the mercantile communities in London and some other large towns were growing in self-consciousness, there seems little doubt that most townsmen regarded themselves more as temporarily misplaced members of rural society. The demographic realities of urban living as well as the ideological hegemony of feudalism long maintained such attitudes. With their higher than average mortality-rates, urban populations in the late fourteenth century sustained themselves largely through large-scale immigration from the countryside. Few prominent Liverpool families survived the epidemics of the period, while over two-thirds of the Preston aldermen in 1397 were first-generation guildsmen.[68] Given the origins of many merchants and craftsmen, the number and strength of the bonds linking town and countryside need occasion no surprise. Even native townsmen were in little danger of being marooned in an exclusively bourgeois environment. Many burgesses sought country girls as brides, and even proud knightly houses were not entirely averse to exchanging status for wealth by allying with trading families. Often it was through a marriage alliance that the ambitious merchant began that slow and stealthy process by which country estates were acquired and new landed dynasties established.[69]

In any final estimate of trade and industry as avenues of advancement, it is necessary to consider how successful merchants were in making the transition to landed gentility. Superficially at least Cheshire and Lancashire tradesmen seem fairly modest in their achievements. Mercantile families resident in the region like the Whitmores, Hawardens, Moores and others had to build up their landed fortunes slowly, extending their estates through marriage as much as investment. Their counterparts in London, naturally enough, were able to amass property on a more spectacular scale. Thomas Knolles and William Wettenhall, for example, were particularly avid speculators: the one purchased the manor of North Mimms in 1428, and immediately raised the rents; the other was accused of obtaining the

---

[68] *Preston Guild Rolls*, pp. 1–7.
[69] E.g. the marriages arranged between the son of John Eulowe of Chester and the daughter of John Donne of Utkinton, and between the grandson of John Whitmore and the daughter of Sir William Atherton: *Ches.R.R*, I, p. 153; Lancashire R.O., DDLi/14 (unclassified).

manor of Clapham by underhand means.[70] Yet men of this ilk rarely put down roots, and surprisingly few founded enduring lineages. Significantly, their dynastic ambitions met with least success in their native region. Both Christopher Tildesley and William Wettenhall were active in the local land market, but no permanent interests were established.[71] Presumably there were strong pressures against affluent upstarts acquiring lordships, and such prejudices were most stubborn when local men returned to vaunt their gains before former neighbours. On the whole the Home Counties, with their proximity to London, their more fluid land markets, and their shorter memories, were more attractive areas for investment for men on the make.

All too often the apparently substantial fortunes amassed by tradesmen proved in the long term ephemeral. Certainly few noble dynasties were founded on the basis of commercial wealth in this period. There are a number of explanations for this phenomenon, some of which have already been touched upon. It can be claimed that marriage late in life, to aged widows or heiresses of degenerate stock, coupled with the higher mortality-rates in the towns, limited the effective fecundity of the trading classes, and indeed all socially-mobile groups. Moreover the existence of various social pressures, which tended to encourage the dissipation of newly-acquired fortunes both before and after the death of the original founder, has to be assumed. Yet it must not be concluded that commercial wealth had little impact on the structure of landed society in the region. While vast fortunes could rarely be converted wholesale into landed status, more modest savings might have been more easily digested. The gains and losses in wealth and power made by an individual were often diffused among a wide network of dependants. Accordingly it is as appropriate to consider the changing fortunes of entire families, affinities and communities as of individual careerists. Thus the achievements of successful merchants must not be assessed solely in terms of their thwarted territorial ambitions but more properly in terms of their capacity to aid numerous kinsmen and friends to make more modest advances on the land. While the life of the grand seignior remained the ultimate goal, most merchants had to realise their dreams vicariously.

[70] Thrupp, *Merchant Class*, pp. 130, 129.
[71] J.R.U.L., Clowes Deeds, no. 724; *Ches. R.R.*, II, p. 782.

## Chapter 8

# THE CHURCH

In theory the church provided an honourable career structure open to all the talents. Given the requisite ability and dedication, even the humblest ploughboy might rise to become an eminent abbot or bishop. Needless to say, his climb to the top would be far more arduous than the gentle slope encountered by the young nobleman. The positions at the summit were in any case limited in number and strongly contested. Yet, when all the injuries of class and obstacles to progress have been noted, it remains substantially true that the church in late medieval England provided an avenue of advancement viable to men of all ranks. There were, after all, no absolute restrictions on members of the lower orders obtaining an education or entering the priesthood. Moreover, even the poorest curate enjoyed a measure of privilege and esteem denied the layman. Nor were opportunities for material profit lacking at any level of the ecclesiastical hierarchy. With the possible exception of the mendicants, most clergymen could expect to make at least modest advances on the fortunes to which their birth entitled them.

The church was by no means a monolithic institution, and the clergy were far from homogeneous as a class. In the following discussion of clerical careerism, therefore, two rather different perspectives are adopted in turn. In the first place the church is viewed as a self-contained body providing in various ways for the spiritual needs of the faithful. Within this framework it will be possible to discuss both the churchmen directly engaged in liturgical and pastoral work and the church bureaucrats and scholars whose specialised experience and knowledge were vital to the functioning of organised religion. Secondly the church is seen as a more open-ended institution, organically linked to, and performing far wider functions in a particular social system. Thus it can be regarded as a major pillar of the establishment, supplying through its wealth and traditions of learning both an educated administrative élite and the means to maintain it in secular employment. In this context the clergy can be treated less as a body of men distinguished by religious vocation and more as aspirants to secretarial and administrative careers. While individual clergymen cannot always be ascribed categorically to either group, the distinction between clerks who were largely immersed in the life of the church and clerks who were almost totally engaged in secular employment is useful to maintain in a study of this nature.[1]

I

The clerical poll-tax returns of 1379 provide a useful survey of the men who served the local church at the beginning of the period under discussion.[2] There were then resident in the archdeaconry of Chester 78 rectors and vicars, 276 chaplains, 28 other clerks and 114 monks and canons. Virtually all these men were either ordained to the priesthood or in monastic orders, and with the exception of a few aristocratic parsons and secular clerks can be regarded as the local religious establishment. Thus in Cheshire and Lancashire south of the Ribble there seem to have been at least five hundred benefices, chaplaincies and other livings for churchmen. More significant, since the resident clergy were almost entirely natives of the region, no account being taken of absentee incumbents, this figure testifies to the number of openings typically available to men of the region. Leaving aside for the moment the vast army of laymen in the service of religious institutions as well as mendicants and other indigent clerks, the proportion of the adult male population ministering to the spiritual needs of the region is remarkable. Apparently the local church was providing livings with assessable incomes for as many as one in fifty Cheshire and Lancashire men.

The five hundred or so clerical tax-payers in the region were for the most part men of comfortable means. Judging from their assessments, the abbots of St Werburgh's, Vale Royal and Whalley were far richer than any local laymen. Such magnates played an important role in the political and social life of the region, even on occasions serving as justices of Chester.[3] Outside the cloister the rectories of Wigan, Stockport and Standish, valued at 200 marks, £90 and £80 respectively, enabled their privileged incumbents to lead lives scarcely distinguishable from their patrons at the manor-house. Many affluent parsons took a vigorous part

---

[1] In general see A. H. Thompson, *The English Clergy and their Organisation in the Later Middle Ages* (Oxford, 1947); W. A. Pantin, *The English Church in the Fourteenth Century* (Cambridge, 1955); P. Heath, *The English Parish Clergy on the Eve of the Reformation* (London, 1969). For clerks in the royal service, see T. F. Tout, 'The English civil service in the fourteenth century', *B.J.R.L.*, 3 (1916), 185–214; J. L. Grassi, 'Royal clerks from the archdiocese of York in the fourteenth century', *Northern History*, 5 (1970), 12–33.

[2] Edited in Bennett, 'Lancashire and Cheshire clergy', 22–30.

[3] E.g. *Ches. R.R.*, I, p. 94.

in local life, serving as trustees, arbiters, counsellors and leaders of public opinion. In 1403 the rectors of Dodleston, Pulford, Davenham, Rostherne, Hawarden and Handley were prominent among the Cheshire rebels against the king.[4] Even unbeneficed chaplains, the vast majority of whom paid six times as much tax as ordinary householders, were able to afford luxuries denied to all but the wealthiest of their parishioners. John Toft, a chaplain in the service of the rector of Rostherne, owned a furred cloak and gown, two beds with linen and blankets, and a small quantity of silverware and a number of books.[5]

Of course, it is never really possible to compute clerical incomes fully or exactly. Apart from the inadequacies of official valuations of church livings, there is the problem of assessing more miscellaneous sources of profit. Almost all clergymen would have received fees for various sorts of clerical employment, while many continued to work part-time on the land or developed a flair for business. Thomas Sharpe, chaplain who was outlawed in 1386, owned little besides livestock and grain.[6] Roger Manchester, the rector of the poorly-endowed church of Radcliffe, similarly had additional sources of income. He held property in Manchester, and in an inventory of his goods a herd of almost forty cattle took precedence over a small collection of books.[7] Doubtless some clergymen were able to add ancestral holdings to their glebes. Others found themselves involved in the world of real estate through their activities as trustees and executors, and became active participants on their own account in the local land market. Whatever their original means and interests, clergymen were well placed to advance themselves through timely influence and informed investment.

Needless to say, the livelihoods of local churchmen might range from the opulent to the fairly meagre. The point is that for the vast majority there is evidence of material improvement in their economic position. Given the wealth and influence of the larger religious houses, for example, it is remarkable how few monastic leaders had exalted social backgrounds. Henry Sutton, abbot of St Werburgh's from 1387 to 1413, appears to have been a native of either Great or Little Sutton, two manors in the possession of the monastery, a few miles north of Chester.[8] Richard Wiche, prior of Norton from 1370 to 1409, was at best of bourgeois stock. Two other

---

[4] *C.P.R. 1401–1405*, p. 264.  [5] *Cheshire Sheaf*, third series, item 4469.
[6] *Lancashire Inquisitions*, I, p. 40.
[7] *H.M.C., Various Collections*, II, p. 16.
[8] William Bebington (d. 1349) and John Saughall (d. 1455) were two other abbots of Chester who seem to have originated from the abbey's Wirral estates; Burne, *Monks of Chester*, pp. 101, 77, 127.

contemporaries – John Wrightington, prior of Burscough from 1385 to 1407, and Robert Fazacreley, prior of Holland from 1389 to 1403 – might be more plausibly connected with lesser gentry families, but with no great certitude. The priors of Birkenhead between 1375 and 1425 – Roger Didsbury, Robert Handbridge and John Wood – likewise bear names which carry little assurance of high breeding. The background of one of their successors, Richard Norman, can be documented with interesting circumstantial detail. Of low birth, he began his career in the service of an Austin friar. After slaying his master in the course of an argument, he went on a pilgrimage to Rome to secure absolution. Seeking spiritual consolation, he entered Birkenhead priory around 1420, where he was elected prior some twenty years later.[9]

Similar opportunities for advancement were available to humble clerks outside the cloister. Over two-thirds of Cheshire and Lancashire parishes in 1379 were in the hands of parsons whose surnames preclude the possibility of gentle birth.[10] Admittedly the poorer churches had more than their share of low-born incumbents, while some rich rectories, like Wigan, Standish and Halsall, were the hereditary preserves of gentry families. Still, many lay patrons were willing to use their advowsons to promote talented clerks from among their tenantry. Sir William Brereton and John Domville of Brimstage presented Nicholas Penne of Brereton and John Brimstage to the churches of Tilston and Mobberley, and the presentments made by the Fouleshursts to Woodchurch in Wirral likewise reveal the importance of tenurial connections.[11] Religious houses were even keener to nurture local talent, and even prize livings could fall to worthy candidates from the lower orders. Roger Belgreve, Richard Madeley, William Warmingham and Richard More, whose churches at Astbury, St Mary on the Hill, Chester, Bebington and Bowdon were valued at 95, 90, 50 and 44 marks respectively in 1379, were all men of modest origins, who attained their livings only after years of service as stipendiary priests.[12]

It is in any case unwise to draw too rigid a distinction between the beneficed clergy and the large number of apparently unbeneficed priests. In view of their equivalent tax assessment of two shillings a head, there can have been little perceived difference in the incomes of the poorer parsons and the vast majority of chaplains. Again, it seems significant that of 276 tax-payers in this category few bore surnames of any distinction,

[9] Stewart-Brown, *Birkenhead Priory*, pp. 83–7.
[10] Bennett, 'Lancashire and Cheshire clergy'.
[11] *Ibid.*, 10; Ormerod, *History of Cheshire*, II, p. 523.
[12] Bennett, 'Lancashire and Cheshire clergy', 25–6.

while Thomas Porter, Adam Mason, Henry Smith, John Walker, Nicholas Baker, Richard Cooper, Henry Herdsman and the many other chaplains with occupational surnames were demonstrably of humble stock.[13] When ordination-lists record the place of origin of clerks, it is possible to be even more confident in establishing their social background. Of the seventeen local ordinands for whom such details were recorded at Lichfield in the 1370s, none was of gentle birth, six were the sons of townsmen, four were the sons of clerks in minor orders, and the remaining seven were presumably the sons of either yeomen or husbandmen.[14]

Of course, young men could not enter the church without some sort of financial backing. The problem is to assess the scale of the investment required in the initial stages of a clerical career. At the most basic level bondmen were compelled to pay fines to their lords for the privilege of taking the cloth. At Halton in 1367 Thomas son of Thomas Castle and Thomas son of Richard Archer each paid forty pence to enter the church.[15] Still, such fines were scarcely prohibitive, and applied only to a small fraction of the population. Then there was the business of obtaining the rudiments of education. Private tuition would have been ruinously expensive to most families, and schools were few and far between in the region, being limited to such centres as Chester and Preston.[16] Most boys doubtless learned to read and write in less formal settings, acquiring basic literacy from a local parson or curate, perhaps in return for service. In any event the educational demands made on aspiring priests were minimal, and bright young men probably proceeded to holy orders without incurring undue expense in this field. Finally, each ordinand had to demonstrate to the bishop that he had an assured livelihood as a priest. The privileged few had independent means or had already secured preferment, and were ordained to the title of their own patrimony or benefice. The vast majority had no immediate prospects of institution to a church, but for some reason managed to secure ordination to the title

---

[13] *Ibid.*, 25–6.

[14] Lichfield R.O., B/A/1/4–5. This conclusion matches R. B. Dobson's findings regarding the social origins of Durham monks. He maintained that most 'came from the middle ranks of urban and rural society' and that it was 'improbable that more than a very few' were 'members of a cadet line of a country gentry family': R. B. Dobson, *Durham Priory 1400–1450* (Cambridge, 1973), p. 58. This view must be contrasted with the claims of R. H. Hilton that 'not many' of the clergy 'seem to have sprung from families lower in the social scale than the gentry': R. H. Hilton, *Bond Men Made Free. Medieval Peasant Movements and the English Rising of 1381* (London, 1973), p. 212.

[15] Beamont, *Account of Rolls of Halton*, p. 14.

[16] *Ches. R.R.*, I, p. 196; *Preston Guild Rolls*, p. 9. There is also evidence of schools at Lancaster and Clitheroe: N. Orme, *English Schools in the Middle Ages* (London, 1973), pp. 307, 300. Note also Cardinal Langley's foundation at Middleton: Storey, *Thomas Langley*, p. 6.

of a local monastery.[17] In all likelihood the system had become something of a formality by the late fourteenth century, and religious houses had no reason to fear that they were underwriting large numbers of unemployable priests. Though some expense was almost certainly incurred at the ordination ceremony, there is no evidence that ordinands had to lodge money with a monastery in return for the title. Again, the conclusions reached regarding their social origins are consistent with the view that only modest outlays were required.

It is easier to concede that the men serving the church in the Northwest were not particularly advantaged in status, wealth and connection, when it is realised that by comparison with the careers of other local clerks their achievements were wholly pedestrian. Of the five hundred or so resident clergymen taxed in 1379, all of whom doubtless lived in comparative ease, none advanced their careers significantly in later life.[18] In truth successful ecclesiastical careers rarely began with pastoral work in the provinces, and such clerks had already missed out on the high roads to advancement, which led outside the region. The absence of a clearly defined career structure through which talented clerks could be promoted from parochial backwaters to the centres of ecclesiastical power was always the major problem. Ambitious young men needed patrons and contacts outside their own communities, and the sons of leading gentry families were doubly advantaged by the greater resources and wider connections of the governing élite. Yet the prospects for ambitious clerks of more humble birth making their way in other dioceses were not so bleak. In all probability it was as advantageous to be a kinsman or friend of an influential churchman, as to be the scion of a landed family. Naturally, once one generation of Cheshire and Lancashire clerks found high preferment in the church, another found it easier to progress in their wake. Whatever the nature of the contacts mobilised, or the scale of the sacrifices made, a surprisingly large number of local churchmen can be shown to have achieved positions of eminence in Christendom at large.

Of all the channels through which clerks moved in search of advancement, those cut by the monastic orders were perhaps the most institutionalised. With their wide territorial interests, educational facilities, and patronage of churches, religious houses had a long tradition of seeking out, training and promoting local talent. At the same time their connections with monasteries in other regions, not least the leading houses of their order and their university colonies, enabled them to offer far wider opportunities to their more apt brethren. Certainly many Benedictine monks from the Northwest attained prominence in other convents,

---

[17] Bennett, 'Cheshire and Lancashire clergy', 14–17.     [18] *Ibid.*, 18–19.

though it can rarely be ascertained what had saved their careers from provincial oblivion. Thomas Prestbury, abbot of Shrewsbury and chancellor of Oxford University, was possibly a native of Prestbury in Cheshire: the monks of St Werburgh's, the lords of Prestbury, were responsible for the maintenance of scholars at Oxford.[19] A strong regional presence was certainly established at the famous Benedictine abbey of St Albans. Nicholas Radcliffe, a champion of orthodoxy against Wycliffe while at Oxford, was archdeacon of St Albans for twenty years until his death around 1400.[20] Among his contemporaries at the convent was William Wiche, a native of Nantwich. Though not a professed monk, he served as registrar for three successive abbots, and like Radcliffe his burial in the cloister was commemorated in the monastery's annals.[21] Even John Wheathamstead, twice abbot of St Albans and noted as both a scholar and statesman, merits a mention in a study of local careerism. The son of Hugh Bostock, a Cheshire man who settled at Wheathamstead in Hertfordshire at the end of the fourteenth century, he long continued to maintain contact with his kinsmen in the Northwest.[22]

Strictly speaking, the cloistered life placed severe constraints on the mobility of regular clergymen. The rules of the mendicant orders, on the other hand, came near to canonising rootlessness. Instituted early in the thirteenth century to minister more directly to the spiritual needs of the community, the various orders of friars might have lost much of their idealism by this period, particularly in respect of their vows of poverty, but their dynamism cannot be doubted. Their popularity as purveyors of spiritual counsel and consolation is attested by the large number of bequests to them in local wills, while their reputation in the world of learning is reflected in the steady stream of able recruits into the Franciscan, Dominican and Carmelite convents at Chester and the Augustinian convent at Warrington.[23] Certainly the more proficient brethren were fairly rapidly provided with opportunities for further study at university.

---

[19] *B.R.U.O.*, III, p. 1517; Burne, *Monks of Chester*, p. 122.

[20] *B.R.U.O.*, III, p. 1539.

[21] '*De Altaribus, Monumentis, et Locis Sepulcrorum, in Ecclesia Monasterii Sancti Albani, Quaedam Annotationes*' in *Chronica Monasterii Sancti Albani*, vol. 5, ed. H. T. Riley (R.S., 1870), pp. 443, 436.

[22] C. E. Hodge, 'The Abbey of St Albans under John of Wheathamstede', University of Manchester, Ph.D. thesis, 1933. In 1434 Wheathamstead acted as an arbiter in a dispute involving his Cheshire kinsmen: *Cheshire Sheaf*, first series, item 356.

[23] Lichfield R. O., B/A/1/6, ff. 140–56. See also J. H. E. Bennett, 'The grey friars of Chester', *J.C.A.S.*, 24 (1921), 5–85; 'The white friars of Chester', *J.C.A.S.*, 31 (1935), 5–54, 'The black friars of Chester', *J.C.A.S.*, 39 (1952), 29–58, and W. Beamont, 'History of Warrington Friary' in *Chetham Miscellanies*, old series IV (C.S., old series 83, 1872).

In the late fourteenth century three members of the Warrington convent alone attained doctorates in theology at Oxford; Geoffrey Banastre, John Wiche and John Banaster.[24] Despite their formal poverty, ambitious friars might aspire to positions of power and influence. William Appleton, a Franciscan, was a native of Appleton in north Cheshire, a manor belonging to the duchy of Lancaster. As confessor, steward and physician of John of Gaunt, he was a fit target for the peasants' wrath in 1381.[25] Two other local friars attained episcopal office. Roger Cradock, a Franciscan and the son of a Nantwich tradesman, served as bishop of Waterford from 1350 and bishop of Llandaff from 1362, while Thomas Radcliffe, an Augustinian, had become a doctor of theology and prior provincial of his order by 1426, and bishop of Dromore by 1429.[26]

While the regular clergy retained an invidious eminence in the scholastic world, the secular clerks flocked to the universities in greater numbers. By the late fourteenth century university degrees were becoming widely valued as passports to promotion both outside and inside the church. Many leading gentry families in the Northwest were willing to put suitable sons through university, especially when there was a suitable benefice available to finance the whole enterprise. The Radcliffe clan, in particular, showed a keen awareness of the value of education sending at least three of their scions to Oxford on the proceeds of local benefices.[27] Other Lancashire gentlemen followed their lead: Alexander Standish, Nicholas Tildesley and Richard Stanley were all presented to benefices in lieu of scholarships by ambitious kinsmen, and sought study-leave before proceeding to ordination.[28] Many men of middling rank also regarded the education of an intelligent son as an attractive investment. Ralph Erghum and Robert Hallum, the sons of townsmen from Preston and Warrington, certainly justified such faith. Beginning their studies at Oxford as unbeneficed clerks, both men reached the peak of their careers as bishops of Salisbury.[29] In the countryside modest freeholders, like the Mottrams of Mottram St Andrew and the Leyots of Hale, seem to have been able to afford to send their sons to university.[30] Doubtless some really dedicated clerks even paid their own way, whether through savings from local employment, by casual work at the universities, or on the proceeds of a first benefice. William Warmingham nursed scholastic ambitions as

[24] *B.R.U.O.*, III, pp. 2149, 2099, 2150.
[25] Beamont, *Account of Rolls of Halton*, p. 16.
[26] *B.P.R.*, III, pp. 58, 63, 69, 71; *B.R.U.O.*, III, p. 1540.
[27] *Ibid.*, pp. 1538–40.          [28] *Ibid.*, pp. 1758, 1921, 1762.
[29] *B.R.U.O.*, I, pp. 644–5; F. D. Hodgkiss, 'Robert Hallum', unpublished M.A. thesis, University of Manchester, 1931; *B.R.U.O.*, II, pp. 854–5.
[30] *B.R.U.C.*, p. 415; *B.R.U.O.*, III, pp. 2189–90.

an unbeneficed chaplain in Cheshire for twenty years: immediately upon his preferment to Bebington in 1400 he forsook his parish for the spires of Oxford.[31]

Opportunities for a university education were never entirely dependent on personal wealth, whether inherited or laboriously saved. Patronage played a considerable role in providing access to the schools for wider sections of the population. In addition to material benefits to be derived from sponsoring able young men, benefactors of individual students and founders of lavish colleges alike found inspiration in the belief that to maintain poor and deserving scholars was a work of signal merit. In the Northwest, Thomas Booth of Barton, Thomas Tilson of Rushton by Tarporley and Richard Fitton of Pownall all bequeathed sums to specified individuals, for the most part kinsmen, to finance their studies.[32] Two successful Lancashire clerks, who doubtless had personal experience of the privations of scholastic life, made endowments on a grander scale. In 1360 John Winwick from Prescot left scholarships of eight pence a week for twenty poor scholars of canon or civil law at Oxford, while in 1399 Ralph Erghum from Preston bequeathed a considerable proportion of his estate 'in the exhibition of poor scholars at Oxford, especially for boys of my chapel and other clerks who are or were of my household'.[33] In all likelihood these men had been supporting kinsmen and friends in their studies for some time, and there can be little doubt as to their contribution to local traditions of clerical careerism in this period.

Wealthy benefactors wishing to make a more permanent endowment for the maintenance of scholars might found a college. John Winwick had intended to endow such an establishment, but no other local philanthropist in this period had the means and inclination to fulfil his ambition. Yet Cheshire and Lancashire clerks were often able to benefit from the generosity of others. William Wykeham's lavish foundations at the beginning of Richard II's reign provided a whole new range of opportunities to aspiring churchmen. Despite preference being given to natives of Winchester diocese, young men from the Northwest were among the first to benefit from his endowment of twin institutions providing scholarships for matriculants and undergraduates. John Farington from Lancashire and John Fitton from Cheshire were pioneers for their respective counties, being admitted to New College in the 1380s. In the

[31] *Ibid.*, pp. 1993–4.

[32] E. Axon, 'The family of Bothe (Booth) and the Church in the fifteenth and sixteenth centuries', *L.C.A.S.*, 53 (1938), 32–82; *Cheshire Sheaf*, third series, items 4058 and 4275.

[33] F. Crooks, 'John de Winwick and his chantry in Huyton Church', *L.C.H.S.*, 77 (1925), 26–38; *B.R.U.O.*, I, p. 645.

following decades William Hornby, Roger Farington, Nicholas Wildboar, Richard Rishton, Andrew Holes and Henry Fitton can be traced proceeding as Winchester scholars to New College. All these clerks held their fellowships until their preferment to benefices, two even parting with churches in the college's gift.[34] If the careers of the more notable alumni are any guide, New College was as distinguished by the quality of its education as by its generous provision for its own. Though of different generations, John Fitton and Andrew Holes followed parallel courses in their careers: both served as chamberlains at the papal court and both ended their days in the congenial office of chancellor of Salisbury cathedral. It is surprising that the younger man went no further. Briefly keeper of the privy seal under Henry VI, and consistently commended by popes and princes, he narrowly avoided being raised to a bishopric. A doctor in canon law from Padua, an assiduous collector of manuscripts, a noted humanist, his historical reputation has become that of 'a neglected harbinger of the English Renaissance'.[35]

Traditionally university colleges had restricted their role to providing places to a select number of scholars in the higher faculties. There was naturally great competition for fellowships, and local graduates found few doors open to them in the early days. With its strong northern associations, Queen's College showed some favour to men from parts of Lancashire lying within the archdiocese of York.[36] Robert Hothersall and Richard Ulverston both held fellowships in the 1390s, the former teaching theology until his death in 1414, and the latter acquiring notability as the author of the *De officio militari* and the English submission on the reform of the church at the council of Pisa.[37] Another Lancashire theologian, William Farington, also had rooms in the college at this time.[38] His elder brother was a prominent chancery clerk, whose connection with Bishop Wykeham presumably secured the admission of two younger Faringtons to New College. A generation later, Archbishop Chichele's new foundation at All Souls' provided a fellowship for Richard Penwortham, the kinsman of the archbishop's Lancashire registrar.[39] It is unfortunate that the networks of patronage operating in Oxford cannot be reconstructed with any precision, particularly in the decades before and after 1400 when Lancashire clerks attained such prominence in the university. William

---

[34] In general see A. F. Leach, *A History of Winchester College* (London, 1899), and T. F. Kirby, *Winchester Scholars* (London, 1888). For the careers of local Wykehamists, see *B.R.U.O.*, II, pp. 670, 737–8, 965, III, pp. 2115, 1620, II, pp. 949–50.

[35] J. W. Bennett, 'Andrew Holes. A neglected harbinger of the English Renaissance', *Speculum*, XIX (1944), 314–35.

[36] *V.C.H. Oxford*, III, pp. 132–3.

[37] *B.R.U.O.*, II, p. 940, III, pp. 1928–9.

[38] *B.R.U.O.*, II, p. 666.

[39] *B.R.U.O.*, III, pp. 1459–60.

Farington and Richard Ulverston both held high academic office in these years, while Robert Hallum crowned his scholastic career with the chancellorship of the university of Oxford between 1403 and 1407.[40]

A number of local graduates financed their advanced studies from the proceeds of ecclesiastical benefices. The more fortunate had acquired livings even before graduation, and were able to proceed unhindered to the faculties of law or theology. George Radcliffe, the son of Sir Ralph Radcliffe of Smithhills, was in this happy position, and his legal studies were paid for by a succession of choice benefices, some in the Northwest and some in the gift of an old family friend, Bishop Langley of Durham.[41] Nicholas Rishton from Dunkenhalgh and John Leyot from Hale, who gained their first benefices soon after graduation, were sufficiently successful as canonists to ease the paths of their 'nephews'.[42] Nicholas Rishton junior and Richard Leyot were advanced to benefices as young men, and both successfully completed the arduous path to a doctorate in laws: the former spending eight years in civil law, five years in canon law and twelve years in practice at the court of Arches before his inception in 1444.[43] Few others could have been so fortunate. While there were no unbeneficed masters of arts resident in the Northwest in 1379, there were always some local clerks in this position in the university towns. At Oxford William Ashton had his baccalaureate in civil law two years before his first promotion.[44] At Cambridge Adam Mottram, the first known Cheshire alumnus, was a bachelor of canon law and a petitioner for papal graces twelve years before finding preferment.[45] Of course, records of their earlier institutions might have been lost, and it is hard to imagine either man in want: the one was an executor of John Winwick's charities and the other was prominent in the service of Bishop Courtenay. Yet their disappointments can be allowed to stand for the wholly undocumented failures whose number it is impossible to fathom.

Few churchmen were able to afford to take a non-utilitarian view of their studies. For most local clerks, the arts degree was a vital professional qualification, assuring them accelerated promotion in the ecclesiastical hierarchy. Even well-connected churchmen saw the advantages to be derived from a university degree. Though the son of a local grandee, Richard Stanley appeared a more credible candidate for the archdeaconry

---

[40] *B.R.U.O.*, ii, p. 666, iii, p. 1929, ii, p. 854.
[41] *B.R.U.O.*, iii, p. 1539.
[42] *Ibid.*, pp. 1620, 2189–90.   [43] *Ibid.*, pp. 1620, 2190.
[44] *B.R.U.O.*, i, p. 64.
[45] *B.R.U.C.*, p. 415. Adam Davenport, King's Hall fellow in 1372 and subsequently chancellor of Philippa, queen of Portugal, might well have been a Cheshire man, and, if so, an early sponsor of Adam Mottram: *ibid.*, p. 178.

of Chester on his return from Oxford.[46] Masters of arts were in some demand in all areas of diocesan administration. Henry Penwortham found employment as Archbishop Chichele's registrar and treasurer.[47] Canon and civil lawyers had even better prospects. Local jurists were prominent in the Canterbury administration throughout this period: Adam Mottram as chancellor under Archbishop Courtenay; Robert Hallum as registrar under Courtenay and chancellor under Arundel; Matthew Ashton junior as commissary-general under both Arundel and Chichele.[48] Theologians were rather less well represented in the upper echelons of the church. Nevertheless two local theologians, William Farington and John Fitton, were advanced to the chancellorship of Salisbury cathedral in the early fifteenth century.[49]

Some ambitious graduates furthered their careers in the church by entering the papal service. It was common form for unbeneficed schoolmen, like Adam Mottram, to have their names entered in the roll of petitioners for papal graces, but probably the most effective means of attracting the attention of the pope was through personal attendance at the curia. First at Avignon and later at Rome, there was always a significant number of English clerks strategically placed to provide audiences for their kinsmen and compatriots, while for the enterprising careerist there was a great deal of lucrative work to be done in the representation of suits. Richard Winwick and John Thelwall were two local clerks with some credit at Avignon in the 1360s.[50] Even more opportunities opened up for men from the Northwest with the advent of the schism. John Leyot was a vigorous espouser of the Urbanist cause: in addition to more material benefits Urban VI granted three hundred days' indulgence to everyone praying for the repose of his soul.[51] Nicholas Rishton senior had found favour at the papal curia as early as 1389: he made the schism the subject of a determination in the Oxford theology faculty in 1396; he was papal chaplain and auditor of causes at the apostolic palace in 1398; and in 1409 he laboured for the reunification of the church at the council of Pisa.[52] By this stage Robert Hallum was also prospering at Rome, being the papal nominee for several English sees from 1404 until his provision to Salisbury in 1407. Consecrated in Italy by Gregory XII, he also served on the English legation at the councils of Pisa and Constance and was offered a cardinal's

[46] *B.R.U.O.*, III, p. 1762.
[47] *Register of Henry Chichele*, I, p. clxxi; *B.R.U.O.*, III, pp. 1459–60.
[48] *B.R.U.C.*, p. 415; *B.R.U.O.*, II, pp. 854–5; *B.R.U.O.*, I, p. 64.
[49] *B.R.U.O.*, II, pp. 666, 737–8.
[50] *C.Pap.L.*, IV, p. 9; *C.C.R. 1354–1360*, p. 636; *C.P.R. 1377–1381*, p. 374.
[51] *B.R.U.O.*, II, p. 1143.  [52] *B.R.U.O.*, III, pp. 1619–20.

hat by John XXIII.[53] Among the numerous other local conciliarists, John Clitheroe, a clerk in the papal camera, was advanced to the bishopric of Bangor in 1423.[54]

The church rewarded such distinguished servants well. All offices in the ecclesiastical hierarchy had their own fees and perquisites, but in addition valued clerks could expect to be rewarded with benefices by episcopal collation or papal provision. Adam Mottram, whose preferment was so long delayed, was granted a succession of prebends in the 1390s, and having made his selection of the more choice livings, ended his days in the congenial position of precentor of Salisbury cathedral in 1415.[55] Henry Penwortham was also able to acquire a rich harvest of benefices: in 1426 he obtained dispensation to hold another benefice in addition to the rectory of Lyminge, the free chapel of Whittlesford Bridge, and a canonry and prebend at Wells.[56] Local graduates with influence at the papal curia were even more successful as pluralists. In 1389 Nicholas Rishton secured papal provision to the canonry of Lichfield, notwithstanding his canonry and prebend at Crediton, his rectory of Warfield and numerous other expectative livings. In 1405, after fifteen years of further preferment, he clearly felt the need to rationalise his holdings and obtained papal dispensation 'to resign as often as he pleased for purposes of exchange his benefices present or future, with and without cure'.[57] Andrew Holes, whose career at the Roman curia began in the late 1420s, similarly accumulated great wealth from ecclesiastical sources, a fair proportion of which went into the purchase of a considerable library. Apparently reluctant to assume the responsibilities of episcopal office, he died in 1470 burdened with the chancellorship of Salisbury, the archdeaconries of York and Wells, several prebends and two parish churches.[58]

Few other churchmen had qualms about accepting election to the episcopate. From the late fourteenth century onwards a surprisingly large number of local clerks attained episcopal rank. Roger Cradock from Nantwich led the way, serving as bishop of Waterford from 1350 and bishop of Llandaff from 1362.[59] Ralph Erghum from Preston held the sees of Salisbury from 1375 to 1388, and Bath and Wells from then until his death in 1400.[60] Thomas Langley from Middleton was raised to the bishopric of Durham in 1406, and ruled his northern palatinate until

[53] *B.R.U.O.*, II, pp. 854–5.
[54] *B.R.U.O.*, I, p. 444.                       [55] *B.R.U.C.*, p. 415.
[56] *C.Pap.L.*, VII, p. 471.                      [57] *B.R.U.O.*, III, pp. 1619–20.
[58] Bennett, 'Andrew Holes', 314–35.
[59] *C.Pap.L.*, III, p. 339; J. le Neve, *Fasti Ecclesiae Anglicanae 1300–1541*, vol. XI. The Welsh Dioceses, ed. B. Jones (London, 1962), p. 21.
[60] *B.R.U.O.*, I, pp. 644–5.

1437.[61] Meanwhile Robert Hallum from Warrington presided over a distinguished chapter at Salisbury between 1407 and 1417.[62] Two other Lancashire clerks acquired minor dioceses in the 1420s: John Clitheroe held Bangor from 1423 to 1435, while Thomas Radcliffe held Dromore from 1429 to around 1446.[63] Finally William Booth began a remarkable career which not only brought him the bishopric of Lichfield from 1447 and the archbishopric of York from 1452, but also established the fortunes of a remarkable dynasty of clerical careerists.[64] Of course, not all these prelates owed their promotion to their services to the church. Langley and Booth had made their careers in the royal administration, while Erghum's election to Salisbury and subsequent translation to Bath and Wells reflected the rise and eclipse of the Lancastrian faction. Yet none proved entirely unworthy of their office. A fine scholar and a noted reformer, Hallum has an almost unimpeachable record as a bishop. Cradock and Radcliffe, both mendicants, can be assumed to have had some aptitude for pastoral work. Erghum and Clitheroe had doctorates in law. Even Langley and Booth proved capable diocesans, and patrons of learning. In its appointments to bishoprics, the crown as often lost men of talent to the church as it gained tame prelates.

II

In the study of clerical careerism it is impossible to draw a clear line between the spiritual and temporal domains. The conflicts of loyalties experienced by some prominent churchmen are all too evident, but the ambivalence was no less real among the lower echelons of the clergy. Strictly speaking, clerical status connoted an education rather than a spiritual calling. Since the church had a virtual monopoly in learning, and since scholars were required to accept the tonsure, dress and discipline of the clerical order, young men with purely secular ambitions were intermingled from the first with aspiring churchmen. Both classes of clerk doubtless shared similar opportunities and constraints in their acquisition of a basic education and their entry into minor orders. Indeed it is very difficult to establish a point of departure for their divergent career structures. After all, the choice between employment in the church or in some secular field was influenced as often by the availability of patronage and position as by personal inclination. Perhaps the vast majority of clerks were impelled by circumstance to some early commitment. Most men with a religious vocation took monastic vows or sought ordination to the

---

[61] Storey, *Thomas Langley*.     [62] *B.R.U.O.*, II, pp. 854–5.
[63] *B.R.U.O.*, III, p. 1540.     [64] Axon, 'Family of Bothe (Booth)', 32–82.

priesthood as a necessary first step in their careers. Young men with more secular ambitions, or simply wishing to keep their options open as long as possible, sought employment of a secretarial or administrative nature. Obviously the more affluent and better connected clerks could afford to postpone such decisions until much later. Private incomes, family benefices or exhibitions at the schools bought the more fortunate careerists time to assess their own aptitudes and evaluate the opportunities available to them. Still, few commitments were wholly irrevocable: many clerks in secular employment later sought ordination to make themselves eligible for ecclesiastical preferment, while some priests and schoolmen subsequently found themselves seduced into the service of temporal lords.

It is hard to estimate the number of local openings available to clerks seeking work outside the church. The clerical poll-tax returns certainly give the impression that the vast majority of clergymen were ordained priests, and probably these parsons and chaplains did a fair amount of clerical work in their spare time. Yet it is possible to document a distinctive class of clerks in secular employment. The palatinates of Chester and Lancaster maintained their own bureaucracies, in which clerks found not only routine work but also executive office. The chamberlain of Chester and the chief officers at the chancery and exchequer of Lancaster, of course, were appointed from outside the region, but a fair number were natives of the Northwest. John Woodhouse, chamberlain of Chester, was included in the poll-tax of 1379 in his capacity as dean of St John's, Chester. It does not seem that he was a local man, but he certainly adopted the city of Chester as his home.[65] Thomas Thelwall, chancellor of the county palatine of Lancaster at this time, was unquestionably of Cheshire provenance, though he had first served a long apprenticeship quill-pushing at Westminster.[66] William Hornby, a younger colleague, worked his way up through local channels, serving first as receiver for the duchy of Lancaster in the region and later as chancellor of the exchequer at Lancaster.[67] In the lower echelons of the palatinate administrations, there were more positions available to local clerks. Each chief officer had his own clerical assistants, while offices like the clerkship of the Dee mills could be extremely lucrative. Outside government circles, there were opportunities for gainful employment wherever there were accounts to be rendered, legal proceedings to be recorded, or contracts to be drawn up.

[65] Jones, *Church in Chester*, pp. 125–6.
[66] *C.P.R. 1374–1377*, p. 455.
[67] *John of Gaunt's Register 1379–1383*, ed. E. C. Lodge and R. Somerville (2 vols., Camden Soc., third series 56 and 57, 1937), I, pp. 30, 216, II, p. 253.

Many clerks found comfortable livings in the larger towns. Roger Saughall, a notary of Chester, was sufficiently prosperous to contribute half a mark in the poll-tax.[68] William Middwall, an unbeneficed clerk assessed at four pence in 1379, later became clerk for recognisances of debt at Wigan; William Dutton held a similar office at Preston.[69] Some clerks occur so regularly in the property transactions of particular towns – like John Rossendale in Macclesfield, Henry Gille in Warrington and Richard Newton in Newton in Makerfield – that it can be surmised that they were employed as permanent town clerks.[70] In the countryside, the more substantial landed families offered clerical positions in their households. Thomas Charnock found employment with the Stanleys of Lathom, while Hugh Malpas crossed the county line to serve the Talbots of Blackmere.[71]

The range of incomes enjoyed by clerks in secular employment must have been considerable. The salaries and perquisites accruing to the chief clerical officers of the palatinates were on an entirely different scale to the paltry fees obtained by many scribes. In addition the better connected clerks were able to obtain preferment to benefices. Lay patrons, from the king downwards, valued clerical skills the more highly in that their services often involved only indirect costs. John Woodhouse found handsome provision as dean of St John's, while Roger Saughall acquired the vicarage of Acton to supplement his notarial income.[72] Many lesser clerks had good cause to view their benefices as a reward for services to their patron. Unfortunately, since such men had a vested interest in proceeding to the priesthood, they rapidly become indistinguishable in status, if not in life-style, from other churchmen. Still, some successful clerks doggedly remained in minor orders, presumably because they nursed dynastic ambitions. Adam Kingsley began his career as a clerk in the Cheshire administration, but his appointment to the escheatorship placed him in an ideal position to develop secular interests, and at the same time rendered his clerical status inconsequential. Married with children, he was able to amass sufficient wealth to ensure the acceptance of his heirs as landed gentry.[73] As clerk of the Dee mills, Henry Strangeways of Manchester

---

[68] Bennett, 'Lancashire and Cheshire clergy', 23. For three notarial colleagues of Saughall see P.R.O., CHES 25/8, m. 11.

[69] Manchester Central Reference Library, Farrer MSS., 50/27, ff. 45, 56.

[70] Chester R.O., Earwaker MSS., 2/281–3; J.R.U.L., Legh of Lyme Muniments, M/6/29, M/6/31; M/1/110, M/1/114.

[71] Lancashire R.O., DDFi/8/5; Shropshire R.O., Bridgewater Estates, Marbury bailiff's accounts.

[72] Jones, *Church in Chester*, pp. 125–6; Ormerod, *History of Cheshire*, III, p. 347.

[73] See Bruell, 'Edition of cartulary of John de Macclesfield', items 314, 315, 118 etc.

was able to provide his son with the legal education which would assure his lineage fame and fortune.[74] In many ways such men were a dying breed. In earlier generations amphibious careers of this sort were more common, and quasi-clerical dynasties abounded. With the increasing laicisation of law and administration from the late fourteenth century onwards, careerists of their ilk felt less need to seek the security of the tonsure and the cloth.

While some clerks could attain a degree of wealth and standing through secular employment in the region, the best opportunities lay in positions closer to the centres of power and influence in the realm. Again, the mobilisation of clerical talent depended very largely on personalised networks of patronage and connection. The more prominent Cheshire and Lancashire lineages certainly had the right sorts of contacts, and used them to facilitate the advancement of their protégés. In addition the special relationship between the two palatinates and princes of the blood provided many lesser families with access to powerful sponsorship. During his tenure of the earldom of Chester, the Black Prince showed most interest in the local soldiery, but some clerks prospered through the connection. John Scolehall, the prince's yeoman, was able to secure the advancement of his clerical kinsman, Randle Scolehall, through the good offices of his lord.[75] Even John Alcock, the prince's stock-keeper at Macclesfield, had sufficient leverage to have his son placed in the royal service. Apparently inherited from the Black Prince by Richard II, John Alcock junior alias John Macclesfield set out on a spectacular career leading through the privy seal office to the keepership of the great wardrobe.[76] Meanwhile the duchy of Lancaster had an even more impressive record of nurturing clerical talent. William Appleton, John of Gaunt's *éminence grise* in 1381, might well have been hand-picked from the lordship of Halton, while Thomas Langley, the old duke's executor in 1399, seems to have been introduced into the Lancastrian service by his kinsman, Thomas Radcliffe.[77] Ralph Erghum and William Ashton, both chancellors of the duchy of Lancaster at this time, doubtless commended themselves as Lancashire men as well as doctors of civil law.[78]

[74] Strangeways was accused of extortion in 1400: Morris, *Chester in the Plantagenet and Tudor Reigns*, p. 105; J. S. Roskell, 'Sir James Strangeways of West Harlsey and Whorlton. Speaker in the Parliament of 1461', *Yorkshire Archaeological Journal*, 39 (1956–8), 455–82.

[75] *B.P.R.*, III, p. 485; Jones, *Church in Chester*, pp. 164–5.

[76] For career of John Macclesfield see Bruell, 'Edition of cartulary of John de Macclesfield', who unfortunately missed Cheshire R.O., DCH/R4 wherein the royal clerk is identified conclusively as John son of John Alcock.

[77] Beamont, *Account Rolls of Halton*, p. 16; Storey, *Thomas Langley*, p. 3.

[78] *B.R.U.O.*, I, pp. 644–5, 64.

Needless to say, the greatest opportunities available to secular-minded clerks were in the service of the crown. Not only did the king need clerks in his own immediate entourage, but there were also posts in the government departments which had been detached from court and housed at Westminster. By the early fourteenth century the royal clerks accredited to the chancery, exchequer and privy-seal office constituted a more or less permanent civil service. Each department had its own trained personnel, administrative procedures and professional traditions, and there can be little doubt as to the immense corporate power wielded by these clerical bureaucrats.[79] Naturally enough, recruitment into their ranks was highly selective, but men from the Northwest were represented among them from early in the reign of Edward III. Since Lancashire clerks pioneered this form of careerism for the region, some of their success must be attributed to the influence of the lords of Lancaster in the central departments of state. It is doubtless significant that Henry Haydock and John Winwick, both natives of south Lancashire, first appear as royal clerks in 1331, a short while after the political rehabilitation of the Lancastrians.[80] The former established himself in the chancery, and in 1353 secured a place among the twelve senior clerks of the first form, while the latter found employment in the privy-seal office, and rose to become keeper of the privy seal from 1355 to 1360, and even for a time acting chancellor of England.[81]

The professional achievements of Haydock and Winwick set the stage for a more systematic infiltration of the royal administration in the second half of the fourteenth century. Matthew Ashton senior, a close associate and probably a kinsman of Winwick, rapidly joined him at the privy-seal office.[82] Thomas Thelwall and Robert Farington likewise probably owed their careers at Westminster to the Winwick circle. Both rose to become chancery clerks of the first form, and traded on their expertise to obtain key positions outside the capital: Thelwall as chancellor of the county palatine of Lancaster and Farington as treasurer of Ireland.[83] Meanwhile local interests at Westminster continued to be well represented. In the privy-seal office John Macclesfield was securing promotion in Richard II's household, first as a private secretary and then as keeper of the great

---

[79] In general see Tout, 'English civil service' and B. Wilkinson, *The Chancery under Edward III* (Manchester, 1929).

[80] *C.P.R. 1330–1334*, p. 82; *C.C.R. 1330–1333*, p. 423.

[81] *C.P.R. 1350–1354*, pp. 114, 397; Wilkinson, *Chancery under Edward III*, p. 167. T. F. Tout, *Chapters in the Administrative History of Medieval England* (6 vols., Manchester, 1923–35), V, p. 36, VI, p. 53. [82] *B.R.U.O.*, I, p. 64.

[83] *C.P.R. 1358–1361*, p. 281; *C.P.R. 1374–1377*, p. 455; *C.P.R. 1367–1370*, p. 331; *C.P.R. 1396–1399*, p. 283; *C.P.R. 1388–1392*, p. 84; *C.P.R. 1399–1401*, p. 113.

wardrobe from 1397 to 1399.[84] At chancery John Clitheroe and Thomas Stanley were active through the 1390s. While the former later forsook the royal service for advancement at the papal curia, the latter weathered the change of dynasty and went on to hold office as keeper of the rolls and royal councillor under Henry IV.[85] Even before the revolution of 1399 brought into positions of power and responsibility Lancastrian stalwarts like Thomas Langley, who was appointed chancellor of England for the first of several terms in 1405, local clerks had succeeded in establishing firm traditions of service in the royal administration.

Although few royal clerks ever expressed satisfaction with the scale of their remuneration, the rewards of office could be substantial. John Macclesfield was granted £5 a year for his work in the privy-seal office in 1385, and £100 a year on his appointment to the keepership of the wardrobe. In addition to regular salaries, there were many more miscellaneous annuities and fees.[86] After a life-time's service to the crown, Robert Farington was lavishly rewarded in 1398: in consideration of 'his long service' to Edward III and Richard II and 'his great and dangerous labours' in Ireland, he was granted an additional £40 a year from chancery, an extra 6s 8d a day for household expenses as treasurer of Ireland, and a tun of wine each Christmas.[87] In any case such formal grants represent only a fraction of the emoluments attached to government office. Apart from taking fees for enrolling charters, issuing writs and other administrative business, royal clerks were continuously plied with gratuities by hopeful suitors and satisfied clients, and had great opportunities to manipulate governmental powers in their own interests.

For clerks in royal and seignorial administration, as for their colleagues serving the church, ecclesiastical preferment was also an important form of remuneration. The king and the leading magnates had many benefices in their gift, and found them an economical means of rewarding their clerical servants. The clerks, for their part, valued them as secure and independent sources of income, especially since benefices could usually be accumulated in plurality. In the aftermath of the Black Death, John Winwick was strategically placed to secure the choicest vacant livings, and set a formidable record for later generations of local pluralists: in 1349 he was presented to a canonry and prebend at Salisbury 'notwithstanding canonries and prebends at York, Lincoln, Wells, Southwell, and the chapel of St Mary and Holy Angels, York', and shortly afterwards he was

---

[84] *C.P.R. 1381–1385*, pp. 379, 553; *C.P.R. 1396–1399*, p. 266; Tout, *Chapters*, v, p. 230.

[85] *B.R.U.O.*, I, p. 444; J. L. Kirby, *Henry IV of England* (London, 1970), p. 258.

[86] Bruell, 'Edition of cartulary of John de Macclesfield', pp. 110–11.

[87] *C.P.R. 1396–1399*, pp. 283, 411, 315.

advanced to the treasurership of York and the rectory of Wigan, the most valuable benefices in the realm and his native region respectively.[88] An enquiry into pluralism in 1366 provides a useful survey of the holdings of some of his local protégés: Richard Winwick held a prebend at York, a canonry at Lincoln and the vicarage of Walton on the Hill, valued together at £169 per annum; Henry Blackburn, treasurer of the Black Prince, held benefices at Lincoln and elsewhere to the annual value of £140; and Matthew Ashton senior held the rectories of Shillington in Bedfordshire and Slapton in Buckinghamshire along with pensions from six religious houses to the total value of £71.[89] In the 1390s John Macclesfield amassed an income from the wardenship of St Anthony's hospital, London, the provostship of Wells and other church livings which has been estimated at £200 a year.[90] Of course, the more ambitious clerks set their sights on bishoprics. Ralph Erghum owed his election to the see of Salisbury, as also his subsequent translation to Bath and Wells, to his political credentials; Thomas Langley, a trusted Lancastrian servant and ultimately chancellor of the realm, was the royal nominee for a succession of dioceses before his installation at Durham in 1406; and, a generation later, William Booth secured first the bishopric of Lichfield and then the archbishopric of York in return for his services to the Lancastrian regime.[91]

The prime qualifications for high advancement in secular service were political loyalty and administrative expertise. For most clerks the best means of developing and demonstrating qualities of this sort was through the opportunities for personal connection and practical experience afforded by the large seignorial households or by the nascent bureaucracy at Westminster. On the whole both groups were able to trade on their backgrounds. Experienced chancery clerks like Henry Haydock and Thomas Thelwall were eagerly sought for key positions in aristocratic establishments, while outstanding protégés of noblemen like Thomas Stanley and Thomas Langley were often recruited into the royal service.[92] Yet it must not be thought that formal qualifications were of no account in secular appointments. By the late fourteenth century the crown and leading magnates were showing an increasing interest in employing university men, most especially civil lawyers. Some of the earliest local careerists seem to have anticipated this trend: John Winwick endowed

---

[88] *B.R.U.O.*, III, pp. 2063–4.

[89] *The Register of Simon de Langham, Archbishop of Canterbury, 1366–1368*, ed. A. C. Wood (Canterbury and York Soc., 1956), pp. 47, 74, 59–60.

[90] Bruell, 'Edition of cartulary of John de Macclesfield', p. 148.

[91] *B.R.U.O.*, I, p. 645; Storey, *Langley*; Axon, 'The family of Bothe (Booth)'.

[92] For cross-fertilisation between the royal and Lancastrian administrations see Tout, *Chapters*, III, pp. 42, 197–8.

scholarships at Oxford, while Matthew Ashton senior, after gaining financial security through his work in the royal administration, found it expedient to proceed to degrees in canon and civil law.[93] Though not graduates themselves, Thomas Thelwall and Robert Farington apparently encouraged their brothers to seek academic qualifications. This pattern of increasing investment in the education of younger kinsmen is apparent in almost all clerical affinities, and must attest not only the greater prestige of purely ecclesiastical careers but also the growing opportunities for dons in the secular world. John of Gaunt appointed two doctors of civil law, Ralph Erghum and William Ashton, as chancellors of the duchy of Lancaster.[94] Richard Leyot, another jurist from Lancashire, headed the chancery of the duke of Bedford from 1419 to 1425.[95] Though the royal household, the inns of chancery and many aristocratic and episcopal *familiae* continued to train and accredit clerks, the universities assumed even greater significance in the education of bureaucrats in the fifteenth century. The allegedly unlettered William Booth was a late representative of a fast disappearing type. Lawrence Booth, his half-brother, had far sounder credentials, and on his dismissal from the keepership of the privy seal he was able to retreat again to the comparative tranquillity of Pembroke College, Cambridge.[96]

The achievements of the more notable clerical careerists speak for themselves. John Winwick, the son of a yeoman from Prescot, rose to hold the great seal as well as the privy seal, and ended his days directing the negotiations leading to the Treaty of Brétigny in 1360; Ralph Erghum, the son of a Preston tradesman, reached the pinnacle of his secular career as a member of the regency council for Richard II; John Macclesfield, the son of a minor estate official at Macclesfield, was entrusted with the keepership of the great wardrobe in the last, critical years of the latter's reign; and Richard Leyot, the illegitimate son of another clerk, came to wield considerable power as the chancellor of the regent of France.[97] Demonstrably such men were able to amass considerable fortunes. Yet it is far from easy to assess how far their wealth and influence could be converted into real social advancement. Since John Macclesfield had dynastic ambitions, and since a careful record of his property acquisitions has survived, his success in establishing a new landed lineage in east Cheshire can be copiously documented.[98] The fortunes of most clerical

[93] *B.R.U.O.*, III, p. 2063, I, p. 64.　　[94] Somerville, *Duchy of Lancaster*, p. 366.
[95] *B.R.U.O.*, III, pp. 2189–90.　　[96] *B.R.U.C.*, pp. 78–9.
[97] Tout, *Chapters*, v, p. 36; *B.R.U.O.*, I, p. 645; Bruell, 'Edition of cartulary of John de Macclesfield'; *B.R.U.O.*, III, pp. 2189–90.
[98] Records of his property transactions survive not only in his cartulary but also in the Cholmondeley deeds and in the Macclesfield court-rolls: B.L., Cotton MSS., Cleopatra D VI; Cheshire R.O., DCH/R4; P.R.O., SC 2/254–5.

careerists, being dispersed among a wider number of more distant kinsmen and friends, had a more diffuse, and hence a less dramatic impact on local society. Still, the contributions of clerks like Robert Farington and William Booth to the temporal aggrandisement of their houses can often be discerned, though never fully itemised. On occasion their munificence to a wider range of their fellow countrymen is attested. In 1359 John Winwick 'in honour of God and by way of charity in aid of the estate' of Sir William Butler, agreed to take a lease on the barony of Warrington, with all its debts and encumbrances, and to pay the impecunious knight a fixed annuity of £80.[99]

III

In outlining the history of clerical careerism in the Northwest it has been necessary to range over a hundred years, from the first successes of Lancashire men in the reign of Edward III to the achievements of the Booths in the middle decades of the fifteenth century. In this section it is intended to adopt a rather sharper focus, and to look more closely at the generation of clerks who were reaching the peaks of their careers around 1400. The achievements of two men, in particular, merit detailed attention. Robert Hallum and Thomas Langley were close contemporaries, the one being born shortly before, the other shortly after 1360, and both were natives of south Lancashire, the one from Warrington and the other from Middleton. Judging from the obscurity of their parentage, neither was unduly advantaged by birth; the Hallums were at best prosperous townsmen, and the Langleys were cadets of a gentry family. Both youths proved talented clerks, and by their late thirties were poised for high preferment. From 1404 they were rivals for a number of sees until Langley secured Durham in 1406, and Hallum Salisbury in 1407. Two of the leading churchmen in the realm, they led the English delegation to the council of Pisa in 1409, and were appointed cardinals by Pope John XXIII. Though both men diplomatically declined the latter accolade, it is worth noting that their acceptance would have brought local clerks within striking distance of the throne of St Peter itself.[100]

Given the parallels between their careers, the apparent unconnectedness of their success-stories is most remarkable. While it is scarcely credible that their acquaintanceship was no older, there is no evidence that their paths crossed before 1404, or that the two were ever more than distant colleagues. Hallum's background was thoroughly ecclesiastical. He perhaps owed his basic education to the academically distinguished Augustinian

[99] *C.C.R. 1354–1360*, pp. 514–15.
[100] In general see *B.R.U.O.*, II, pp. 854–5 and Storey, *Thomas Langley*.

friary at Warrington, and in later years would have been a credible candidate for one of John Winwick's scholarships at Oxford. By the late 1380s he was progressing to the study of canon law, and was already well established in the service of Archbishop Courtenay. Thomas Langley's connections were entirely secular. In all likelihood he was attached in his youth to the household of the Radcliffes of Radcliffe, a lineage itself not undistinguished in the church.[101] In 1385, while still in minor orders, he was presented to the rectory of Radcliffe. Around this time he was introduced into the service of John of Gaunt, and henceforward his future prospects were assured.

In their largely independent courses, the careers of Hallum and Langley illustrate the varied experiences of clerks making their ways through ecclesiastical and secular employment. Hallum owed his advancement almost entirely to his reputation as a scholar and his tireless service to the universal church. By the time of his first recorded preferment in 1387, he had already spent half of his life as a scholar in Oxford, and he remained in the world of learning for as long again, attaining his doctorate in canon law and being elected chancellor of Oxford University in 1403. Still, his growing proficiency as a canonist had not gone unnoticed in the church. In 1389 he served Archbishop Courtenay as principal registrar, and in 1400 he was appointed as chancellor to Archbishop Arundel. By this stage his reputation had spread to Rome, and from 1404 he was the prime papal candidate for episcopal office. In 1406 his provision to the archbishopric of York was blocked by the king's determination to advance his own clerks, but in 1407 he was translated to the see of Salisbury. Langley, his main rival for episcopal office, just as clearly owed his progress to his secular accomplishments. Learning his trade and finding his vocation in the Lancastrian administration, by 1394 he was acting as an *aide* to John of Gaunt, and five years later was sufficiently regarded to be appointed an executor of his will. With the accession of Henry IV, further advancement was inevitable. From being the king's secretary in 1399, he rose rapidly to become keeper of the privy seal in 1401, and chancellor of England in 1405. Needless to say, his ecclesiastical preferment kept pace with his secular advancement. Despite initial opposition from Rome, he made good his institution to the deanery of York in 1403, and finally attained episcopal rank as bishop of Durham in 1406.

As prominent members of the Lancastrian episcopate, Hallum and Langley necessarily assumed new responsibilities and interests. To the donnish churchman and the royal minister alike, episcopal office brought both temporal and spiritual obligations. Hallum had to involve himself

[101] *Ibid.*, p. 2.

in affairs of state just as surely as Langley had to look to the welfare of his flock, and it is appropriate that the one severed his connections with Oxford and the other resigned the chancellorship shortly after their promotions. In some respects their careers began to converge: Hallum and Langley headed the English nation at the council of Pisa in 1409, and both served the crown on a variety of diplomatic missions. Yet informative contrasts remain. Hallum was an earnest prelate whose primary allegiance remained to the universal church. An indefatigable champion of unity and reform, he died at the council of Constance in 1417, and was buried beneath a memorial brass in Constance cathedral. Langley, on the other hand, owed his international reputation entirely to his having the confidence of successive English governments. Given the tensions between Henry IV and the prince of Wales, and later between the Gloucester and Beaufort factions, this was in actual fact no mean feat. Almost up until his death in 1437, he remained an active and trusted member of the royal council, and even resumed the burden of the chancellorship between 1417 and 1424. Yet, despite his frequent absences from his diocese, he proved a capable and conscientious bishop, and a formidable champion of the see of St Cuthbert.

The personal achievements of Hallum and Langley were immense. From the relative obscurity of their births, they rose to the pinnacles of their twin professions. Manifestly the scale of their success was wholly exceptional, but it demonstrates the possibilities apparent to ambitious clerks from the Northwest. More important, the careers of the two Lancashire prelates cannot be seen in isolation: other local careerists had pioneered the paths along which they first travelled, while many others found advancement in their wake. As bishops, Hallum and Langley were well placed to promote the careers of their protégés. At Salisbury, Hallum presided over a remarkable coterie of Cheshire and Lancashire clerks. A canon of Salisbury himself from 1395, he had been joined two years later by Adam Mottram, an old Cheshire colleague from the *familia* of Archbishop Courtenay, and shortly afterwards by Thomas Stanley and Thomas Langley, presumably royal nominees. After 1407 Hallum's influence is all too apparent in the arrival at Salisbury of a series of churchmen distinguished as much by their academic credentials as by their regional provenance: William Farington, a compatriot and associate from Oxford, was recruited from the faculty of theology to take on the chancellorship of the cathedral in 1408; Nicholas Rishton senior acquired a canonry in the same year; John Fitton, the first Cheshire Wykehamist and theologian, joined the chapter in 1410; Gilbert Hallum, a kinsman and graduate, became a canon in 1413; Richard Ulverston, the distinguished conciliarist, and Edmund Dutton, another graduate from the Warrington area, likewise gained canonries in 1416.[102] At Durham, Langley gathered around him an even larger *familia* of local clerks. Thomas Lyes and Thomas Hebden, both natives of Lichfield diocese and almost certainly Lancashire men, held key positions in the diocesan administration: the one served as registrar and vicar-general, and the other as spiritual chancellor from 1422 to 1433.[103] A whole succession of other local clerks held office as treasurers of the bishop's household and receivers-general in the diocese: John Newton, Nicholas Hulme, Richard Buckley and John Radcliffe.[104] Langley also showed himself eager to draw into his service men of learning: Thomas Hebden was a doctor of laws, and William Blackburn, John Marshall and George Radcliffe, in addition to being from southeast Lancashire, were canon lawyers.[105] Naturally, Langley's trusted compatriots had the pick of the benefices in the diocese. At his death in 1427 John Newton held the rectory of Houghton le Spring, the hospital of Sherburn, and two prebends to the total value of £300 per annum, while Langley paid his debt of gratitude to his original patrons by the handsome preferment of George Radcliffe to a series of valuable livings, culminating in the mastership of St Edmund's hospital, Gateshead.[106]

Laymen as well as clerks were able to advance their careers in the service of Bishops Hallum and Langley. While he had far fewer secular interests than his colleague, Hallum had a sizeable non-clerical contingent in his household. Among his *famuli* were Thomas Hallum, John Hallum, Thomas Sankey, John Appleton and William Boydell, all scions of families in the Warrington area.[107] Richard Hallum, his brother, was settled in some capacity in the capital, while Richard Dutton was a prominent member of the bishop's household.[108] Langley, as chancellor of the realm, royal councillor and lord of the palatinate of Durham, offered far grander prospects to his lay servants. His personal retinue was immense: on his embassy to the king of France in 1414 it included eighty-eight persons.[109] His establishment at Durham likewise provided livings for a whole range

[102] J. le Neve, *Fasti Ecclesiae Anglicanae 1300–1541*, vol. III. Salisbury Diocese, ed. J. M. Horn (London, 1962), *passim*; *B.R.U.O.*, II, p. 666, III, pp. 1620, 1928–9, II, pp. 737–8.

[103] Storey, *Thomas Langley*, pp. 169, 50, 186.

[104] *Ibid.*, pp. 74–5.

[105] *Ibid.*, pp. 169, 178–9; *B.R.U.O.*, III, p. 1539.

[106] Storey, *Thomas Langley*, p. 79; *B.R.U.O.*, III, p. 1539.

[107] P.R.O., E 154/1/32.

[108] Richard Hallum was among several local careerists buried in the Franciscan convent in London: C. L. Kingsford, *The Grey Friars of London* (British Soc. of Franciscan Studies VI, 1915), p. 122. For Richard Dutton see *Register of Henry Chichele*, II, pp. 126–30.

[109] Storey, *Thomas Langley*, p. 92.

of secular office-holders. Thomas Holden, a native of Whalley parish, was the linchpin in this formidable machine. He held office as chamberlain of the household throughout his master's long career, and in 1422 was advanced to the stewardship of Durham, the most powerful office in the palatinate and traditionally the preserve of illustrious border magnates. By his death in 1441 he had amassed a considerable fortune, and acquired estates in a number of shires.[110] Richard Rishton, presumably a kinsman of his namesake at Oxford, and Robert Strangeways, chief forester of Weardale, were two other Lancashire laymen who prospered in the bishop's service.[111] Langley might also have been an early patron of James Strangeways, the ambitious lawyer from Manchester, who in later years held office as chief justice in the palatinate of Durham, and managed to establish himself as lord of West Harlsey, a Yorkshire manor appurtenant to the bishopric of Durham.[112]

While both prelates developed many other loyalties and obligations in the course of their long careers, a fair proportion of their wealth filtered through to benefit wider sections of the local population. In his will Hallum granted his property investments to his brothers for the terms of their lives, and bequeathed sums of money totalling £500 to members of the Dutton, Mascy, Merbury, Warburton, Grimsditch and other local families.[113] Langley's personal fortune was even more considerable. In addition to being a generous creditor of the Lancastrian regime, he had sufficient capital to finance the grandiose reconstruction of Middleton church in the years before 1412, and to lend 800 marks to the abbot of St Werburgh's, Chester, in 1418.[114] The philanthropic instincts of the two bishops naturally led them to sponsor local causes. Hallum left money to have two young relatives established in apprenticeships in London, and stipulated that his properties were to be used ultimately to support colleges of scholars.[115] Langley likewise served the poor children of his native parish well by the establishment of a free grammar school at Middleton.[116]

Needless to say, through their tenure of high office in church and state, the two men had the power and influence to assist their compatriots in a wide range of matters. Hallum was certainly well able to forward local ecclesiastical suits at Canterbury and Rome. His assistance might even be

[110] *Ibid.*, pp. 93, 102; *Register of Henry Chichele*, II, pp. 579–84.
[111] Storey, *Thomas Langley*, p. 5; *Register of Henry Chichele*, II, pp. 329–30.
[112] Storey, *Thomas Langley*, p. 63; Roskell, 'Sir James Strangeways', 455 ff.
[113] *Register of Henry Chichele*, II, pp. 126–30.
[114] *V.C.H. Lancaster*, V, p. 153; *C.C.R. 1413–1419*, p. 518.
[115] P.R.O., E 154/1/32; *Register of Henry Chichele*, II, p. 127.
[116] Storey, *Thomas Langley*, p. 6.

solicited in more mundane affairs: while still a diocesan official, he was petitioned by a London merchant to mediate with an eligible widow 'and to have a look at the said woman, and to find out what goods and rents she has at present and what she will have in days to come'.[117] Thomas Langley had even more strings to pull. An early partisan and trusted servant of Henry IV, he paved the way to royal favour for many local men. Significantly his Lancashire kinsmen were among the first to lend military backing to Bolingbroke in 1399, and were later able to rely on official support in their protracted feud with the Hollands.[118] Through his services to the church, he obtained boons of a rather different nature: at Pisa in 1409 the pope granted him faculty to issue dispensations for twelve consanguineous marriages, over half of which were given to local couples.[119] Meanwhile his terms as chancellor and royal councillor opened up to local clients the myriad forms of government patronage. His role in promoting the careers in the royal administration of old neighbours, like the Booths of Barton, cannot be ascertained, but his activities as an umpire in local disputes are well documented.[120] Indeed his reputation for 'good lordship' in the region is graphically attested in an indenture of 1431. According to this agreement, James Hopwood, a Lancashire gentleman and a close friend of Langley, promised among other things to persuade the bishop 'to graunte to be gode, gracious and well willying lord' to two other local men.[121]

From the middle of the fourteenth century onwards, a large number of clerks from the Northwest can be traced pursuing successful careers both in their native diocese and further afield. The rough distinction drawn between clerks who were first and foremost churchmen and clerks predominantly in secular employment, though hard to sustain in the lower and upper reaches of clerical attainment, has made it possible to differentiate between the two wings of the profession. Judging from the records of families with traditions of clerical careerism, the former calling must have been the more prestigious. Generally speaking, senior members of clerical families distinguished themselves through administrative experience and assiduous service in a secular household or a department of state, while their younger kinsmen more typically had academic qualifications and followed careers in the church. Manifestly, attendance at

---

[117] *English Historical Documents*, vol. IV, pp. 1193–4.
[118] Manchester Central Reference Library, Farrer MSS., transcripts from Agecroft deeds, nos. 58 and 66.
[119] *Register of Thomas Langley*, I, pp. 165, 173–5.
[120] Wigan R.O., Standish Deeds, no. 129.      [121] Lancashire R.O., DDHp/39/35.

university required considerable financial backing, and one generation of careerists tended to invest in the education of the next. Wider trends can also be discerned in this pattern. With the growing laicisation of the fields of law and administration from the late fourteenth century onwards, the opportunities for clerks in secular employment began to decline. At the same time the circumstances of the schism in the universal church between 1378 and 1414 seems to have provided English churchmen with unwonted access to papal patronage. On the whole clerks with academic qualifications were better able to make the most of both developments. Masters of arts usually experienced accelerated promotion within the church, while canon lawyers predominated in the upper echelons of the ecclesiastical hierarchy. Meanwhile, in the households of the king and leading magnates, the prospects for clerks of the old school were further diminished by the growing practice of appointing specialists in civil and canon law as chief clerical officers.

Since the overwhelming majority of the more successful local clerks hailed from south Lancashire, and since some significant chains of connection can be established, there can be little doubt that careerism bred careerism. While a proper assessment of the claim must await a thorough analysis of ordination-lists in various dioceses, it does appear that Lancashire men constituted a disproportionately large, and inordinately successful contingent in the English church in the later middle ages. While the importance of clerical careerism, both in quantitative and qualitative terms, cannot be denied, its impact on regional society is rather difficult to gauge. Few clerical careerists registered social advancement in the traditional fashion. Being celibate and for the most part chaste, they rarely established new landed dynasties. In this sense the clergy remained a liminal group. Yet the wealth and influence amassed by the more notable careerists could not fail to leave its mark on the region. Though in a diffuse and undramatic fashion, the fruits of their labours inevitably served to augment the fortunes of their families and friends. Their gifts assisted modest capital formation, their loans allowed investment in office-holding, their influence facilitated business in courts, their connections provided access to wider patronage and so on. Even if the achievements of individual clerks cannot be readily translated into the idiom of social mobility, clerical careerism remained a major source of social differentiation in the local community.

## Chapter 9

## MILITARY SERVICE

Throughout the middle ages military service remained the most celebrated avenue of social advancement. Chroniclers and poets alike delighted in recording the feats of warriors whose valour was rewarded with high estate. The drama of armed combat accounts in part for the interest shown in this form of self-improvement. In tournament and battle, the brave and the desperate could stake their lives for a better future. Yet there was more to it than the thrill of adventure. To contemporaries it was inconceivable that valiant feats of arms could go unrewarded. Through his accomplishments on the field, the young bachelor demonstrated his fitness to be accepted into the highest ranks of society. Chivalry and martial prowess were taken to reflect inner nobility of character. This notion was deeply rooted in late medieval English society. After all, the upper classes were almost by definition a military caste, most of whose members traced their descent from Norman adventurers and prided themselves on the personal performance of knight's service. In this climate of opinion it was hard to deny the claims of the warrior who proved himself in the sport of kings.

While contemporary attitudes generally approved this form of advancement, the able soldier of humble birth had major obstacles to surmount. The considerable investment required in training and equipping a mounted man-at-arms effectively excluded the vast majority of men from the pursuit of chivalry. It was not unknown for some soldiers to work their way through the ranks, reinvesting their earnings in horses and armour. There were certainly several notable commanders from the Northwest who first saw active service as mere archers. Manifestly, their remarkable achievements merit close attention, and their brilliant careers can help to illumine the experience of their more obscure colleagues. Yet neither the success of a few soldiers-of-fortune in scaling the heights of the chivalric world, nor the failure of most infantrymen to rise appreciably in rank, gives an adequate impression of the importance of military service as a means of advancement. Opportunities to profit through soldiering were never wholly, nor even predominantly, confined to men with a full-time commitment to arms. Military service was a part-time occupation, and supplementary source of income for able-bodied men from all social classes. Given the spasmodic and short-term nature of their enterprise, few recruits could expect to make more than modest gains in status and wealth. Bowmen could not hope to become knights in the course of a single campaign; but the son of a husbandman could perhaps save himself enough to acquire a farm, just as the son of a gentleman could win himself an annuity. Bearing in mind the numbers of men involved, and their direct relationship to the land, the quantitative and qualitative significance of soldiering as an agent of social mobility is all too apparent.

In this chapter it is intended to discuss the military experience of men from the Northwest. In the first section it is proposed to chronicle the building up of traditions of service, to outline the main theatres of operation, and to assess the scale of the involvement. Then, there will follow a discussion of the various enticements of war, the general conditions of service, and the achievements of local soldiers. Finally, it is hoped to make some general assessment of the impact of martial enterprise on regional society, to illustrate how success and failure in the field served to variegate the fortunes of local families, and to address the vexed problem of how far it can be claimed that England, or at least Cheshire and Lancashire, profited from the Hundred Years War.

I

Traditions of military service were deeply rooted in all parts of feudal England, but nowhere more so than in the borderlands. For several centuries after the Norman Conquest Cheshire and Lancashire remained remote and vigilant marcher communities. Many of the privileges accorded the lords of Chester and Lancaster can be attributed to the exigencies of defence against the Welsh and the Scots, and the local populace long played a vital role in the security of the western and northern marches. In the late thirteenth century the men of Cheshire took a leading part in the Welsh campaigns of Edward I and the subsequent military occupation of North Wales, but their martial skills continued to be exercised in border frays for generations afterwards.[1] Nor must it be thought that Lancashire was sufficiently remote from Scotland to be denied this invigorating experience. Throughout the twelfth century the Anglo-Scottish border was in a state of flux, and even as late as Edward II's reign the Scots raided deep into the region. Needless to say, local men had

[1] H. J. Hewitt, *Cheshire under the Three Edwards* (Chester, 1967), pp. 96–9.

numerous opportunities to return the compliment on campaigns north of the border.[2] At the same time both counties were strategically placed with regard to Ireland and the Isle of Man, and served as major recruiting-grounds for military operations in this sector.[3] Manifestly, geographical factors alone predisposed ambitious men from the Northwest towards military enterprises, and by the late fourteenth century the men of Cheshire, in particular, had a reputation for their bellicose manners. As the St Albans chronicler observed: 'because of former wars and disputes among themselves they are better trained in arms, and more difficult to control than other people in the kingdom'.[4]

Originally the military capacities of the local population were wholly committed to the forward defence of their own frontiers. With the development of contract armies in the late thirteenth century, and the increasing stabilisation of the borders from Edward I's time onwards, however, local knights and archers showed themselves eager to trade on their skills and experience in other theatres of war. Their aspirations accorded well with the ambitions of successive earls of Chester and lords of Lancaster, all of whom recruited extensively in the region. Without doubt the close association with such prominent royal commanders as the Black Prince, Henry of Grosmont, John of Gaunt and Henry V was a vital factor in the consolidation of military traditions in the two palatinates.[5] Yet it must not be assumed that the martial experience of local men was confined to the enterprises of their royal lords. Even in the early stages of the Hundred Years War, local knights and archers can be traced taking service with aristocratic commanders who held neither land nor office in the Northwest, while in later decades the region not only satisfied the considerable man-power requirements of the Black Prince and John of Gaunt but also supplied large contingents for service under their brothers Lionel, duke of Clarence and Thomas, earl of Buckingham.[6]

[2] G. H. Tupling (ed.), *South Lancashire in the Reign of Edward II* (C.S., third series 1, 1949), pp. xxxvi–xxxvii; R. A. Nicholson, *Edward III and the Scots* (Oxford, 1965), p. 252.

[3] A. J. Otway-Ruthven, *A History of Medieval Ireland* (London, 1968), pp. 322–3, 340–1, 347; *Monumenta de Insula Manniae*, vol. II, ed. J. R. Oliver (Manx Soc., VII, 1861), pp. 235–46.

[4] '*Annales Ricardi Secundi et Henrici Quarti*' in *Chronica Monasterii Sancti Albani*, vol. 3, ed. H. T. Riley (R.S., 1866), p. 160.

[5] J. E. Morris, *The Welsh Wars of Edward I* (Oxford, 1901), *passim*; H. J. Hewitt, *The Black Prince's Expedition of 1355–1357* (Manchester, 1958), pp. 15–18; K. Fowler, *The King's Lieutenant. Henry of Grosmont, First Duke of Lancaster, 1310–1361* (London, 1969), p. 222; S. Armitage-Smith, *John of Gaunt* (London, 1904), *passim*.

[6] G. Wrottesley, 'Crécy and Calais' in *Collections for a History of Staffordshire*, vol. XVIII, part II (William Salt Archaeological Soc., 1897), pp. 219–60; P.R.O., E 101/28/18; *Ches. Pleas*, p. 49.

Apparently all noblemen who felt the need to have a strong military following on call valued their connections with this rich recruiting-ground. Despite Richard II's attempts to monopolise the military resources of his beloved palatinate, it can be shown that all the Lords Appellant had Cheshire men in their retinues.[7] Needless to say, many local soldiers were only too willing to operate on a freelance basis, taking service with whomsoever offered the best prospects for advancement. Some hardy adventurers even fought under foreign banners: John Carrington and Robert Arderne found lucrative employment with Gian Galeazzo Visconti, duke of Milan until his sudden death in 1402.[8]

In any case, as military traditions became ever more firmly rooted, Cheshire and Lancashire were able to boast their own distinguished commanders. Foremost among the many notable local knights who first rose to prominence in the 1340s were Sir Hugh Calveley and Sir Robert Knolles, both natives of southeast Cheshire. First attracting acclaim as the heroic survivors of the 'battle of the thirty' in 1351, the two knights were in command of their own companies at the time of Poitiers, and held them together for further enterprises after the formal cessation of hostilities at Brétigny. For over twenty years more, they continued to find congenial employment for their men, first as freebooting captains in Brittany and Castile, and later as trusted royal lieutenants in Aquitaine and elsewhere. Finally, with the resumption of war in 1369, the two veterans acquired independent commands and led official expeditions. In 1370 Knolles directed an ambitious campaign in northern France, covenanting with the king to keep four thousand men-at-arms and archers in the field for two years. In 1375 Calveley was appointed governor of Calais, and four years later joint admiral of the English fleet. Both knights led sizeable retinues in the earl of Buckingham's expedition of 1380, and continued in harness until the petering out of the war-effort later in the decade. Presumably men of iron disposition, Calveley survived until 1394, and Knolles until 1407. In the course of their long swashbuckling careers, spanning over half a century, they served as models of chivalric achievement to all the

---

[7] *Ches. R.R.*, I, p. 98. E.g. Hugh Calveley, Hugh Browe, Thomas Crewe, Nicholas Colfox and John Norbury were in the respective retinues of the earls of Buckingham, Arundel, Warwick, Nottingham and Derby: P.R.O., E 101/39/9; A. Goodman, *The Loyal Conspiracy. The Lords Appellant under Richard II* (London, 1971), pp. 120–1; *V.C.H. Warwick*, III, p. 190; Goodman, *Loyal Conspiracy*, pp. 159–62; *Expeditions to Prussia and the Holy Land made by Henry, Earl of Derby, 1390–1 and 1392–3*, ed. L. T. Smith (Camden Soc., second series 52, 1894), p. 128.

[8] W. A. Copinger, *History and Records of the Smith-Carrington Family* (London, 1907), pp. 73–7.

fighting men of the Northwest, many hundreds of whom they doubtless personally initiated into the profession of arms.[9]

At some stage in their lives most Cheshire and Lancashire gentlemen seem to have participated in some military enterprise. The depositions collected in the Grosvenor heraldic dispute of 1386–7 provide a useful point of departure in a survey of the experience of leading members of the two county communities at this time.[10] While few of the witnesses were in any sense professional soldiers, it is clear that a good number were seasoned campaigners. Their collective memory reached back at least as far as the last expedition led by Edward III in 1359–60, when Grosvenor had still been a youth and when Sir John Danyers had challenged on his behalf the right of a Cornish squire to bear the disputed arms. Many witnesses recalled Grosvenor and themselves being back in action ten years later in Sir James Audley's expedition through northern France to Gascony, sharing reminiscences of the siege of Vire in Normandy, the crossing at Nantes, the capture of Brux in Poitou, the seizure of Belle Perche, the assault on La Roche sur Yon and other encounters. According to their own testimony, Grosvenor and his friends were in harness again in 1372, though this time the expedition was aborted after their muster at Sandwich. Finally, there was the fateful Scottish campaign of 1385 in which Grosvenor first discovered that Sir Richard Scrope bore identical arms. Judging not only from the accounts of witnesses but also from extant retinue-rolls, there can have been very few local gentry families unrepresented in the royal host.[11]

Obviously the testimonies collected on behalf of Sir Robert Grosvenor do not give a comprehensive account of the military activities of local men in the 1370s and 1380s. For the most part the deponents seem only to have served in large, royal expeditions, usually in the train of the earl of Chester or his representative, and their acquaintance with soldiering must have been rather limited by comparison with the experience of some of their compatriots.[12] Calveley, Knolles and many lesser soldiers-of-fortune were more or less continuously in harness in these decades, and

---

[9] J. C. Bridge, 'Two Cheshire soldiers of fortune: Sir Hugh Calveley and Sir Robert Knolles', *J.C.A.S.*, 14 (1908), 112–231.

[10] Nicolas, *Scrope and Grosvenor*, I, *passim*.

[11] In addition to the witnesses who participated in the campaign, it is known that Sir William Brereton, Sir Robert Legh, Sir Richard Winnington, Sir Richard Venables, Sir Nicholas Vernon, Sir Lawrence Dutton and a dozen other Cheshire squires led retinues: N. B. Lewis, 'The last medieval summons of the English feudal levy, 13 June 1385', *E.H.R.*, LXXIII (1958), pp. 1–26.

[12] On this point see P. J. Morgan, 'Cheshire and the defence of the principality of Aquitaine', *L.C.H.S.*, 128 (1978), 146.

letters of protection reveal a steady flow of local men-at-arms overseas. The earl of Buckingham's expedition in 1380, for example, involved large numbers of men from the Northwest. As one of the commanders, Calveley recruited Sir Thomas Danyers, Sir Thomas Carrington, Sir John Mascy of Puddington and other notable local gentlemen, while Sir Hugh Browe and David Hulgreve, two other experienced *routier* captains, led retinues drawn almost entirely from their native Cheshire. Three years later Calveley enlisted the same knights again for the bishop of Norwich's 'crusade' in Flanders.[13] After this expensive and fruitless campaign, there were indeed no large-scale expeditions mounted on the continent for a whole generation, but there were still garrisons to be manned in Gascony and northern France. Calveley was governor of Calais in the late 1370s, and governor of the Channel Islands from 1382 until his death.[14] Sir Robert Mascy joined the garrison of Calais in 1382, while Sir John Mascy of Puddington, John Radcliffe of Ordsall, and three members of the Strangeways family were involved in the defence of Cherbourg.[15] In the south of France Sir David Cradock was mayor of Bordeaux from 1382 to 1387, and his son was still leading troops to Gascony in 1390.[16] John Carrington likewise served his apprenticeship in arms in this theatre in the last decades of the fourteenth century.[17]

In any case Cheshire and Lancashire soldiers did not limit themselves to military operations in France. On the one hand, there was gainful employment nearer home. In 1385 at least four Welsh castles had Cheshire men as their constables: Harlech, Rhuddlan, Caernarfon and Dryslwyn were under the respective commands of Richard Mascy, Alan Chanu, Robert Fouleshurst and William Hooton.[18] In the same year many hardened professionals as well as gallant amateurs took part in Richard II's Scottish expedition. Some local men had been stationed in border garrisons for some time: four members of the Starkey clan were serving at Berwick under the earl of Northumberland in 1384.[19] In 1389 Sir John Stanley, justiciar of Ireland, recruited his retinue of fifty men-at-arms and 400 archers from among his kinsmen and compatriots, and local troops likewise formed the experienced nuclei of the two royal campaigns in

[13] P.R.O., E 101/39/9; Cheshire R.O., DLT, Liber C, f. 244.

[14] Bridge, 'Two Cheshire soldiers of fortune'. Note that Calveley established Roger Merbury, his cousin, in lands and office in the Channel Islands: *C.P.R. 1391–1396*, pp. 38–9.

[15] *Ches. Pleas*, pp. 54, 53, 56; J. Harland, *Manchester Collectanea*, vol. II (C.S., o.s. 72, 1867), p. 140.

[16] Renouard, *Bordeaux*, p. 569; *C.C.R. 1389–1392*, p. 210. In 1373 at least six Gascon fortresses had Cheshire men as castellans: Morgan, 'Cheshire and the defence of Aquitaine', p. 159.

[17] Copinger, *Smith-Carrington Family*, pp. 73–4.

[18] *C.C.R. 1381–1385*, p. 549.          [19] *Ches. Pleas*, p. 56.

Ireland in 1394 and 1399.[20] On the other hand, opportunities for adventure in more exotic climes were by no means lacking in these years. From 1386 Thomas Maisterson of Nantwich and Robert Pilkington of Rivington were among the many local gentlemen who supported John of Gaunt's struggle to establish himself on the throne of Castile, while in the early 1390s Ralph Staveley, Henry Hoghton and John Norbury were among the companions of Henry of Bolingbroke on his expeditions to Prussia and the Holy Land.[21]

Needless to say, the martial energies of men from the Northwest were not always successfully channelled into the defence of the realm or enterprises overseas. All too often they were harnessed to the ends of political faction. Most notorious were Richard II's attempts to convert his earldom of Chester into a bastion of royal power. He first began to build up an armed following in the region after his aristocratic opponents had taken over the reins of government in 1386, and the royalist army which was defeated at Radcot Bridge in December 1387 was comprised almost entirely of local men.[22] Ten years later the king again looked to his loyal subjects in the Northwest to provide the military backing for his absolutist schemes. At the Westminster parliament of September 1397, in which he wrought his vengeance on the nobles who had earlier humiliated him, the assembled commons were cowed by the presence of some 2,000 Cheshire archers, allegedly with their bows bent awaiting his command.[23] In the following months, scores of Cheshire knights and squires were formally retained in the king's service, while several hundred local archers were granted the livery of the crown. From their number a permanent royal bodyguard of some 300 men was rapidly established, organised into seven 'watches' under their own local commanders, and constituting the loyal and experienced core of a veritable standing army.[24] The king also drew into his retinue many prominent Lancashire men: on a single day in 1398 he granted annuities to twenty-two

---

[20] Stanley's retinue included Sir William Hoghton, Sir Gilbert Halsall, Sir John Bold, Nicholas Orell and John Merbury: P.R.O., E 101/247/1, E 101/41/8. For royal expeditions see J. F. Lydon, 'Richard II's expeditions to Ireland', *Journal of the Royal Society of Antiquaries of Ireland*, XCIII (1963), esp. 140; Chester R.O., Earwaker MSS., 2/26, f. 100.

[21] B.L., Harleian MSS., no. 2119, f. 43; *Ches. Pleas*, p. 49; *Expeditions in Prussia and the Holy Land*, pp. 120, 134, 128.

[22] In 1398 Richard II granted 4,000 marks to the Cheshire men who had fought at Radcot Bridge: *Ches. R.R.*, I, p. 99. In addition to Sir Thomas Molyneux of Cuerdale, deputy-justiciar of Chester, there was at least one other Lancashire man in the royal army, Nicholas Orell: *ibid.*, p. 368. See also J. N. L. Myres, 'The campaign of Radcot Bridge in December 1387', *E.H.R.*, XLII (1927), 20–33.

[23] Davies, 'Richard II and the principality of Chester', *passim*; *Chronicon Adae Usk*, p. 11.

[24] For a detailed analysis of the royal retinue see Gillespie, 'Richard II's Cheshire archers'.

knights and squires from north of the Mersey, and after the death of John of Gaunt early in 1399 he doubtless hoped to bind to him the greater part of the Lancastrian establishment.[25] Given the generally harmonious relations between the king and the duke of Lancaster in the 1390s, and the impeccable records of some Lancashire soldiers in the royal service and some Cheshire soldiers in the Lancastrian service, it is inappropriate to draw too rigid a line between the factional interests of the two counties at this time. Still, there can be little doubt that the accession of Henry IV brought about, at least in the short term, a dramatic northward shift in the balance of opportunities in the region. While some two thousand Cheshire men took part in Richard II's last Irish expedition in 1399, their Lancashire neighbours were prominent among the first recruits to Henry of Bolingbroke after his return from exile.[26] While the old guardsmen straggled back to make their submission to the new king, many Lancashire gentlemen were acquiring handsome annuities from the crown. While Cheshire seethed with discontent and mounted a major rebellion in 1403, Lancashire provided indispensable military support to the new regime in its first critical years.[27]

Nothing illustrates better the importance of military careerism in the Northwest than the involvement of the local population in civil commotion and armed rebellion. According to contemporary testimony, Cheshire men were particularly prone to violence and disorder. Complaints against their depredations in other shires were frequent in the late fourteenth century, while the author of *Richard the Redeless* immortalised the outrageous behaviour of Cheshire 'brawlers' in verse.[28] While Richard II's indulgence and the immunities of the county palatine doubtless played major roles in the encouragement of cavalier attitudes towards the law, Thomas Walsingham was justified in associating their bellicose manners with their long habituation to war. He might well have had in mind the Cheshire rising of 1393. Led by Sir Thomas Talbot, who had recently returned from a Gascon command, and finding support from Sir Nicholas Clifton, Sir John Mascy of Tatton and many lesser men who had seen service in France, its main objective seems to have been to sabotage the peace-negotiations then in progress.[29] Similarly the rebellions which followed the deposition of Richard II must not be construed simply as

[25] *C.P.R. 1396–1399*, pp. 321, 324.

[26] Davies, 'Richard II and the principality of Chester', p. 278; Kirby, *Henry IV*, p. 55.

[27] McNiven, 'Cheshire and the rebellion of 1403'; Brown, 'Lancastrian regime'.

[28] *Rotuli Parliamentorum*, ed. J. Strachey (6 vols., London, 1783–1832), III, pp. 42–3; *Mum and the Sothsegger*, ed. M. Day and R. Steele (Early English Text Soc., original series 199, 1936), passus III, lines 317–65.

[29] See J. G. Bellamy, 'The northern rebellions in the later years of Richard II', *B.J.R.L.*, 47 (1965), esp. 261ff.

spontaneous demonstrations of loyalty to the old king. Both risings were organised locally by men whose military accomplishments had been well rewarded in the previous reign. In 1400 John Carrington and Robert Arderne, whose return from Gascony had been prompted by the glorious prospects available to Cheshire men at the court of Richard II, naturally joined the conspiracy of the earl of Kent to restore him to the throne. Dispatched to raise the men of Wiltshire and Dorset, they fled to Brittany on hearing of the failure of the main rising.[30] Meanwhile two other local adventurers, John and Adam Hesketh, were sent to co-ordinate the rebellion of old guardsmen and other dissidents in the Northwest, where for a time Chester castle lay under close siege.[31] In 1403 the dangerous rising led by the Percys again depended very largely on the martial-minded gentry of the region. Sir Richard Venables, baron of Kinderton, Sir Richard Vernon, baron of Shipbrook, Sir Robert Legh, Sir John Mascy of Tatton, Sir Peter Dutton, Sir Thomas Grosvenor and many other prominent Cheshire men were implicated. Needless to say, most of the known rebels had been annuitants of the late king, while some, like Sir William Stanley and Sir John Poole, had subsequently become retainers of Hotspur.[32] Assuredly there were as many hardheaded opportunists among the rebels as diehard loyalists. Insurrection was the ultimate gamble of the soldier-of-fortune.

It is instructive in this regard to note how the participants in the three local risings were treated. The leaders of the insurrection in 1393 were retainers of Richard II who rapidly recovered their fortunes after brief periods of detention, while many of their followers were merely drafted for military service overseas.[33] Henry IV similarly attempted to restore order in the region by putting to constructive uses the martial instincts of its dissident populace. Shortly after his accession he resolved to make the late king's retainers serve him at their own costs, and in 1400 he led over 500 Cheshire men in his Scottish campaign.[34] Even after his victory at Shrewsbury in 1403 he showed no inclination to be vindictive. With wholesale insurrection in Wales and further sedition in the North, he seems to have encouraged the prince of Wales in his attempts to win back the hearts of his Cheshire tenants. Although the more notable local commanders in the struggle against Glyndŵr tended to be either

---

[30] Copinger, *Smith-Carrington Family*, pp. 73–4.

[31] P. McNiven, 'The Cheshire rising of 1400', *B.J.R.L.*, 52 (1970), 375–96.

[32] 'Annales Ricardi Secundi et Henrici Quarti', pp. 366, 371; *C.P.R. 1401–1405*, p. 259; *Ches. R.R.*, I, p. 334; *C.P.R. 1401–1405*, pp. 316, 256, 264; *Ches. R.R.*, I, p. 326.

[33] Bellamy, 'Northern rebellions', p. 273; *C.P.R. 1396–1399*, p. 252; *Ches. R.R.*, I, p. 331; 'Annales Ricardi Secundi et Henrici Quarti', p. 161.

[34] *Rotuli Parliamentorum*, III, p. 439; P.R.O., E 101/42/29.

Lancashire men, like Sir John Bold, or Cheshire men with impeccable Lancastrian credentials, like John Merbury, a fair number of former rebels eventually took service with the young prince against their former Welsh allies.[35] There is a touch of irony in the reappearance of the Hesketh brothers, the fomenters of sedition in 1400, as agents for the recruitment of Cheshire men for service in South Wales.[36]

It was not the fate of local soldiers to be left to stagnate in minor garrisons or to hatch plots in their idleness. The accession of Henry V and the resumption of full-scale hostilities with France ushered in a new halcyon age for the fighting men of the region. The new monarch could not have had a more appropriate background for the task of mobilising local man-power. As prince of Wales, he had presided over the rehabilitation of the Cheshire connection, while as king, he had inherited his father's formidable Lancashire affinity. Predictably, the scale of the region's contribution to his first French expedition of 1415 was colossal. First of all, there were the official county contingents of 700 men-at-arms and archers from Cheshire and 500 archers from Lancashire.[37] In addition there was a separate contingent of 400 Cheshire and Lancashire archers attached to the royal household.[38] Finally, there were the numerous local captains who contracted independently with the king to bring their own companies of men-at-arms and archers, perhaps numbering 300 men in all.[39] Without making any allowance for the large number of local soldiers in the retinues of other captains, it is clear that the region had at least 2,000 men in arms in 1415. Though it is impossible to be precise, local men probably constituted between a fifth and a quarter of the English army at Agincourt.[40]

In the following years the Northwest continued to contribute to the war effort on a scale out of all proportion to its demographic size. In 1416 almost a thousand local soldiers were mustered at Southampton for a second expedition.[41] In 1417 Sir Robert Urswick and several other local captains can be traced mustering men, while amid a plethora of documentation produced by the commissioners of array there is a list of

[35] P.R.O., E 101/43/24; *C.P.R. 1401–1405*, p. 51; P.R.O., CHES 2/77, m. 4d.

[36] Keele University Library, Legh of Booths Charters, no. 329.

[37] Nicolas, *Agincourt*, p. 385; P.R.O., E 101/46/35.

[38] Nicolas, *Agincourt*, p. 358.

[39] E.g. Sir James Harrington, Sir John Southworth, Sir Richard Radcliffe, Sir William Butler, Sir Ralph Staveley and Sir William Legh: P.R.O., E 101/69/3/361, 363; E 101/69/5/423, 427; E 101/69/6/461, 475.

[40] Based on estimates of total numbers at Agincourt in J. H. Wylie and W. T. Waugh, *The Reign of Henry V* (3 vols., Cambridge, 1914–29), II, p. 354n.

[41] P.R.O., E 101/328/6.

the 400 archers in the official Cheshire contingent.[42] In 1418 Sir John Savage led a company of 250 of his countrymen to strengthen the garrison at Calais.[43] In the following years letters of protection reveal a continuous stream of local soldiers passing overseas in the retinues of a range of commanders: William Ashton of Croston with the king in 1419, Ralph Langton with the king in 1420, Walter Strickland with the duke of Gloucester in 1421, Robert Sale of Bedford in Lancashire with the duke of Bedford in 1422 and so on.[44] The fighting men of the Northwest not only played a pivotal role in the military operations of Henry V and his brothers, but were even accorded a sort of regimental identity. The king had his own select company of 400 Cheshire and Lancashire archers while, even more significant, garrisons in Normandy were each assigned detachments of local bowmen.[45] Naturally enough, experienced soldiers from the region came to hold key positions in the occupation of northern France. Sir John Ashton was successively *bailli* of Cotentin and *bailli* of Coutances; Sir Lawrence Warren followed him in both offices.[46] Sir Gilbert Halsall was *bailli* of Evreux and captain of Dreux; John Keighley was *bailli* of Rouen and captain of Louviers; Richard Merbury was captain of Gisors; and Peter Legh was captain of Arques.[47] Perhaps the most distinguished commander from the Northwest at this time was Sir John Radcliffe. After acquitting himself well in Normandy, he was transferred in 1419 to the strategic post of mayor of Bordeaux, and in 1423 was appointed steward of Guyenne. From then until 1436 he was supreme commander of operations in southwestern France. His reputation for chivalry and his achievement in bringing 'by hys labour in knyghthood to hys soveraign lords obeysance, within the duchie of Guyen, many dyverse cytes, townes and fortresses' even led to his nomination for election to the exclusive Order of the Garter.[48]

By 1435 the tide of war had turned decisively against the English, and the prospects for professional soldiers deteriorated rapidly. Apart from a few more desultory and inglorious expeditions, the treaty of Arras drew the curtain on a hundred years of almost continuous involvement by

---

[42] P.R.O., E 101/51/2.      [43] P.R.O., E 101/49/21, 22, 23.

[44] *C.Fr.R.*, I, pp. 616, 617, 624, 633.

[45] Wylie, *Reign of Henry V*, p. 354; *C.N.R.*, I, pp. 719–20; *C.N.R.*, II, pp. 314, 322.

[46] *C.N.R.*, I, p. 683; *C.Fr.R.*, I, p. 634; *Actes de la Chancellerie d'Henri VI concernant La Normandie sous la Domination Anglaise*, ed. P. Le Cacheux (2 vols., Rouen, 1907–8), II, pp. 268n, 328.

[47] *C.N.R.*, I, p. 744; *C.N.R.*, II, pp. 432, 437; *Actes concernant La Normandie*, I, p. 141; *ibid.*, p. 359; *C.N.R.*, II, p. 428.

[48] *C.N.R.*, I, p. 696; *C.Fr.R.*, I, p. 634; M. G. A. Vale, *English Gascony 1399–1453* (Oxford, 1970), pp. 247, 245, 97.

Cheshire and Lancashire soldiers in enterprises overseas. Their formidable record of service during the period under discussion is well illustrated by the histories of two of the many local families which, generation after generation, sent its sons to the wars. The Carringtons of Carrington were a middling gentry family, which played only a modest role in local affairs: its leading members spent most of their active lives on campaign. William Carrington, the grandsire, was knighted at the battle of Sluys in 1340, and apparently remained in harness until the 1370s. Thomas Carrington, his son, won his spurs at Najera in 1367, served as steward of Rouergue in Aquitaine, fought under Calveley in 1380 and 1383, and on his death shortly afterwards was laid to rest under a stately monument in Blackfriars, London. John Carrington, his orphaned heir, was brought up in the household of Sir John Neville in Gascony, returning to England to enter the service of Richard II in the 1390s. After his involvement in the conspiracy of 1400, he fled to the continent, ultimately finding his way to Milan, where he fought under the Visconti banner at the battle of Como and elsewhere. In the meantime George Carrington, a soldier with better political connections, had taken over his nephew's Cheshire patrimony, but his son, another John Carrington, had no intention of putting down roots. For a time stationed at Bordeaux under the duke of Exeter, he subsequently fought in Normandy with his own company of eighty-nine soldiers. By 1435 he had been knighted by the duke of Bedford, but within a few years he was dead, leaving a widow to appeal for payment of the six months' wages owing to him and his men.[49] The Maistersons of Nantwich, whose military activities are also well attested, were of burgess stock. According to a memoir written by a descendant two centuries later, Thomas Maisterson senior began soldiering in the service of the Black Prince in the 1360s. Through his valour in the vanguard at Najera, he brought himself to the notice of John of Gaunt, who promptly retained him with an annuity of £10. Thenceforward a committed Lancastrian, he returned to the continent to champion his master's claim to the crown of Castile twenty years later, and remained loyal to his old patron's son during the rebellion of 1403. Surviving until the end of Henry V's reign, he lived to see his own son prosper in the French wars. By 1427 Thomas Maisterson junior had become chamberlain of the regent of France as well as *bailli* of Caux, and in the following year his marriage to the widow of a French nobleman brought him several lordships in Normandy.[50] Needless to say, there were numerous other local lineages whose records of service stretched from Crécy, Poitiers and Najera to Agincourt,

---

[49] Copinger, *Smith-Carrington Family*, pp. 34–77; *Cheshire Sheaf*, third series, item 4206.
[50] B.L., Harleian MSS., no. 2119, f. 43; *Actes concernant La Normandie*, II, pp. 354, 362, 365.

Verneuil and beyond. In their commitment to the profession of arms, the men of the Northwest can have had few rivals.

II

This survey of the military experience of Cheshire and Lancashire men in the late fourteenth and early fifteenth centuries provides ample testimony to the importance of soldiering in local life. Given the relatively low population densities of the two counties, the numbers of soldiers raised in them are remarkable. There can have been few years when there were less than 500 local men in arms, and at times there were several thousand. Yet the mere scale of the commitment to soldiering does not adequately express its popularity. More graphic testimony can be found in the stirring ballads composed in the region in the early Tudor period, or perhaps in the apparent enthusiasm with which successive generations of local lineages responded to the call to arms. Still, it needs little pressing that men from the Northwest hoped to advance themselves through military service, and in the following section it is intended to examine the substance behind their dreams. Drawing on the experiences of local soldiers, it is proposed to consider patterns of employment, conditions of service and opportunities for profit in war, and to make some assessment of the importance of military careerism as an avenue of advancement in the later middle ages.

Far from having to fight to gain admission to the profession of arms, many men from the Northwest had to struggle if they wished to avoid conscription. In 1346 the Black Prince ordered the justiciar of Chester to raise levies 'without sparing anyone for gift or favour', but on both sides of the Mersey officials continued to accept bribes from unwilling recruits.[51] In this crucial regard soldiering differed markedly from other trades and professions. Few able-bodied men escaped basic military training in their youth, while conscripts were supplied with the tools of their trade by the commissioners of array. In truth the transition from civilian to soldier could be alarmingly rapid. Yet, while some distinguished careers might have begun with an official summons or arbitrary impressment, success in arms ultimately required not only commitment but also considerable material investment in training and equipment. Manifestly, only the most affluent lineages could afford to prepare their sons for immediate entry into the world of chivalry, but many lesser families nonetheless had respectable traditions of military careerism. The more

---

[51] *B.P.R.*, I, p. 14; *B.P.R.*, III, p. 449; Manchester Central Reference Library, Farrer MSS., 50/18/14.

prosperous freeholders were sometimes able to equip their sons as men-at-arms, while even villeins frequently owned bows and arrows. At the same time aspiring soldiers could benefit from wider patronage. Successful local commanders doubtless offered material assistance as well as seductive prospects to kinsmen and friends with military ambitions. In this fashion strong traditions of soldiering established themselves in particular localities. From the neighbourhood of Nantwich, for example, there hailed a whole succession of distinguished soldiers, both from notable landed lineages like Sir James Audley, Sir Hugh Calveley, Sir Thomas Wettenhall and Sir John Delves, and from families of burgess or yeoman stock like Sir Robert Knolles, Sir Hugh Browe, Sir David Cradock and Sir Nicholas Colfox.[52] Without doubt the ambitious soldier could have done no better than to be born in this corner of the region.

The most important condition of service for the majority of soldiers was pecuniary. Even though there were elements of enforced obligation and conscription in the recruitment of armies, the participants in almost all military enterprises could expect wages. The two expeditions to Scotland, both justified as being for the defence of the realm, illustrate the point well. In 1385 Richard II went through the forms of summoning the feudal host, but his motive was to add more men-at-arms to his pay-roll rather than to enforce unpaid military service.[53] In 1400 Henry IV relented in his earlier resolve to make the Cheshire men serve at their own costs: he ordered the sheriff to lead sixty men-at-arms and 500 archers to Newcastle where he would 'arrange wages as will content them'.[54] By this stage the rates of payment for the various ranks of soldiers were well established. From early in Edward III's reign knights were customarily paid two shillings, men-at-arms one shilling, and archers six pence a day, and these sums were still specified in the indentures drawn up between the king and local captains for the expeditions to Ireland in 1399 and France in 1415.[55] Yet there is some evidence of variation in wage-rates. Predictably enough, distinguished local commanders could virtually name their own salaries: Edward III retained Sir Robert Knolles at eight shillings a day in 1370.[56] Even lesser known captains could command wages in

---

[52] For Audley, Calveley, Wettenhall and Delves see Ormerod, *History of Cheshire, passim*; for Knolles and Browe see Cheshire R.O., DDX/364, DCH/C/868–78; for Cradock and Colfox see Hall, *Nantwich*, pp. 85–9.

[53] Lewis, 'Last summons of feudal levy, 1385'.

[54] *Calendar of Signet Letters of Henry IV and Henry V (1399–1422)*, ed. J. L. Kirby (H.M.S.O., 1978), no. 9.

[55] Chester R.O., Earwaker MSS., 2/23, f. 64.

[56] A. E. Prince, 'The indenture system under Edward III' in Edwards, Galbraith and Jacob, *Historical Essays*, p. 292.

excess of the usual rates: the Black Prince paid John Leicester three shillings a day.[57] Obviously the bargaining-power of soldiers varied to some degree according to the law of supply and demand. In 1403 Sir John Bold, captain of Conwy, was paying his men-at-arms and archers ten pence and five pence a day respectively, but in the following year, presumably in response to the deteriorating military situation, their wages were rapidly raised to traditional levels.[58] On occasion soldiers were willing to take lower rates of pay in return for more advantageous conditions of service. Richard Millington's offer of himself and two other archers at the cut-price rate of seventeen pence a day for all three in 1427 was presumably an attempt to realise greater returns from booty and other incidental profits by eliminating the middleman and making an independent contract with the crown.[59]

Even with the comparative abundance of data on wages, it remains very difficult to assess their real value. Superficially at least, soldiers' salaries appear generous. One shilling a day gave the man-at-arms an income equivalent to the revenues from a modest manorial property in the Northwest, while six pence a day for the archer was as generous as the pay of even the best qualified provincial craftsmen. While employment tended only to be seasonal, there was clear potential for modest capital formation. Most soldiers were given lump sums on enlistment, and some immediately absconded with their first quarter's wages in their pockets.[60] On their return from campaign, veterans again often received their back-pay in this form. In 1375 John Leicester accounted for over 400 marks paid to him and his company of three men-at-arms and eight archers.[61] On the other hand it cannot be pretended that arrears of wages were always dutifully paid. In 1367 the Black Prince had insufficient money to pay off his vast army in Aquitaine. Significantly it was at this time that Thomas Maisterson, one of his men-at-arms, decided to transfer to the service of John of Gaunt.[62] With English governments tottering on the brink of bankruptcy and aristocratic commanders often heavily in debt, there were many other occasions when armies were disbanded without full remuneration. Though it is difficult to be certain, however, it might well have been the captains, who had already paid their retinues, who suffered more than the common soldiers.

Fortunately most captains had other sources of regular income. In times of war and political tension in particular, the king and the leading

[57] Cheshire R.O., DLT, deed 185.
[58] P.R.O., E 101/43/24. See also Warrington Municipal Library, Bold Deeds, no. 550.
[59] P.R.O., E 101/71/2/848.      [60] P.R.O., CHES 25/11, m. 5d.
[61] Cheshire R.O., DLT, deed 185.      [62] B.L., Harleian MSS., no. 2119, f. 43.

magnates felt it desirable to have on call the nucleus of an armed following, and accordingly kept in their service a number of experienced knights and gentlemen, who in their turn contracted to bring their own companies of soldiers in times of need. In most cases a substantial retaining-fee sealed the bargain. Needless to say, local soldiers figured prominently in the retinues of the crown and aristocracy. In the 1370s the Black Prince and John of Gaunt naturally had the largest numbers of Cheshire and Lancashire men on their pay-rolls. At the time of his death in 1376 the former was paying Sir Hugh Calveley 200 marks, Sir Alan Chanu 160 marks, Sir Nicholas Vernon 50 marks and Sir John Mascy of Tatton 50 marks per annum,[63] while shortly afterwards the latter had among his numerous retainers Sir Robert Knolles, Sir Walter Urswick, Sir John Ypres, Sir Geoffrey Worsley and scores of lesser local men, each in possession of annuities ranging from a princely £100 to a modest £10.[64] Both Richard II and Henry IV followed their fathers in building up large military followings in the region by the lavish distribution of fees. Henry V stood heir to both establishments. In addition to the fees he had disbursed as earl of Chester, he granted annuities to eighty-six local men within months of his acquisition of the Lancastrian inheritance. Sir William Butler, Sir James Harrington, Sir Ralph Staveley and Sir Richard Hoghton each received 100 marks a year, while Thomas Maisterson and others were confirmed in fees first allowed them by the king's grandfather.[65] Some prominent local soldiers even amassed annuities in plurality. Henry V confirmed Nicholas Merbury, his master of the ordnance, in four annuities totalling 180 marks granted between 1400 and 1412, and even granted him a further annuity of £40 in 1415.[66] Obviously few noblemen could afford to distribute fees on this sort of scale, and in any case details of their grants rarely survive. Yet there is evidence of a number of local soldiers in receipt of annuities from aristocratic captains, ranging from Peter Legh's £10 from the earl of Huntingdon in the 1380s to Sir John Handforth's £100 from the duke of Bedford in the 1420s.[67]

Wages and annuities were the most regular form of remuneration, but the prospect of other rewards added immeasurably to the lure of soldiering. In the Hundred Years War the opportunities for plunder were golden, and even the humblest recruits were entitled to two-thirds of their

[63] *Ches. R.R.*, I, pp. 80, 105–6, 495.
[64] *John of Gaunt's Register, 1379–1383*, I, pp. 6–13. See also N. B. Lewis, 'Indentures of retinue with John of Gaunt, Duke of Lancaster, enrolled in chancery, 1367–1399' in *Camden Miscellany*, vol. XXII (Camden Soc., fourth series 1, 1964), pp. 87 ff.
[65] P.R.O., DL 42/17, ff. 2d–8.
[66] *C.P.R. 1413–1416*, pp. 42, 44, 62, 320, 321, 327.
[67] *Ches. R.R.*, I, p. 289; Earwaker, *East Cheshire*, I, pp. 240–2.

pickings. The early expeditions of Edward III, with their pillaging of rich cities like Caen and Calais and their victories at Crécy and Poitiers, brought a flood of luxuries into England, and local soldiers were certainly able to share in the spoils. In 1356 John Jodrell and other archers picked up a silver ship belonging to the king of France at Poitiers, and received £8 12s 6d for it two years later.[68] The men who remained in France to serve as *condottieri* were even more single-minded in their pursuit of profit. According to Froissart, Sir Robert Knolles amassed upwards of 100,000 crowns in the 1360s, and 'being very liberal, he was cheerfully followed and obeyed' by a large retinue.[69] During his campaign of 1370 the towns of northern France were systematically mulcted: the unidentified town of 'Maiot' alone paid him 160 gold francs in protection-money.[70] Doubtless the opportunities for freebooting declined somewhat in the decades either side of 1400. Yet the prizes to be obtained even in Wales were far from negligible. Lord Audley went to some lengths to retrieve his share of the booty acquired by local men in his service in South Wales.[71] Transport was certainly less of an obstacle to profiteers like Thomas Wilbraham who drove 200 cattle and 100 sheep home after service on the Welsh border.[72] In any case, the resumption of hostilities in France under Henry V brought a new generation of freebooters to the continent. While the king sought to protect the civilian population through rigid discipline in his army, local soldiers were well able to enrich themselves by pillaging combatants. Even as late as 1444 an archer in the service of Matthew Longworth could win himself a sword worth 37s 6d *tournois*.[73]

In addition to the portable booty to be amassed after a successful battle or siege, large numbers of prisoners were taken for ransom. The great victories of the 1340s and 1350s led to the capture of many eminent Frenchmen, including the king of France himself. Local soldiers certainly participated in some of the greatest ransoms of the time. Sir Thomas Danyers was apparently responsible for the capture of the chamberlain of Tancarville at Caen in 1346, and perhaps shared in the 20,000 nobles paid by the king for the more prominent French prisoners-of-war.[74] Some

[68] *B.P.R.*, IV, p. 254.

[69] Bridge, 'Two Cheshire soldiers of fortune', 68.

[70] *Ibid.*, p. 81; *Calendar of Ancient Deeds* (6 vols., H.M.S.O., in progress), VI, C5199.

[71] Keele University Library, Legh of Booths Charters, no. 329.

[72] *Ches. R.R.*, I, p. 279.

[73] C. T. Allmand, *Society at War. The Experience of England and France during the Hundred Years War* (Edinburgh, 1973), p. 83.

[74] Hewitt, *Cheshire under the Three Edwards*, p. 103; J. Froissart, *Chronicles of England, France and Spain*, ed. T. Johnes (2 vols., London, 1842), I, p. 157.

time around 1361 Sir Hugh Calveley managed to take captive his great rival, Bertrand du Guesclin, and received a ransom of 30,000 *écus*. When du Guesclin was again unfortunate enough to fall into English hands at Najera in 1367, Calveley chivalrously helped to pay for his release.[75] While the combatants were less distinguished and the encounters less celebrated, there were ransomable prisoners to be obtained in military actions nearer home. In 1402 Sir John Stanley and his companions held to ransom Donald O'Neill, the son of an Irish chieftain, while Sir William Stanley and Sir John Poole led eight Scots prisoners home to Cheshire.[76] In the following year Sir James Harrington was well rewarded for his capture of the earl of Douglas at the battle of Shrewsbury.[77] Of course, in the reign of Henry V military successes in northern France again brought into local hands a large number of French prisoners. Sir Robert Lawrence, Sir John Savage and David Bunbury were among the many men from the Northwest who gained valuable ransoms at this time.[78]

Successful soldiering on the borders of the realm and on the continent brought other opportunities for advancement. Many local men-at-arms were called on to command garrisons in North Wales, Aquitaine, Normandy and elsewhere, and such postings were usually sources of profit as well as power. On top of his annuity of 160 marks, Sir Alan Chanu received £40 per annum for his keepership of Rhuddlan castle.[79] At the same time castellanies offered soldiers the chance to gain experience in, and to display their talents for the varied fields of government. Richard Rotour, constable of Bordeaux from 1375 to 1379, even if his conscientiousness went unrewarded at the time, has latterly won acclaim for the neatness of his accounts.[80] Naturally, the more able captains were felt appropriate candidates for governmental posts in militarily sensitive regions. A whole series of soldiers from the Northwest served as sheriffs of Welsh counties in the later middle ages, and as *baillis* during the English occupation of Normandy.[81] Particularly distinguished knights and squires might even be selected for positions usually reserved for men of more illustrious origins. Sir Thomas Wettenhall was steward of Rouergue from

[75] Bridge, 'Two Cheshire soldiers of fortune', 27–9.

[76] *C.P.R. 1401–1405*, p. 183; *Ches. R.R.*, I, p. 326.

[77] Somerville, *Duchy of Lancaster*, p. 172.

[78] P.R.O., E 101/46/8; *C.Fr.R.*, I, pp. 612, 586.

[79] *Ches. R.R.*, I, p. 105.

[80] E. C. Lodge, 'The constables of Bordeaux in the reign of Edward III', *E.H.R.*, L (1935), 236.

[81] Local men holding office as sheriffs of Anglesey, Caernarfon and Merioneth in this period included Richard Pickmere, Ralph Barton, Roger Strangeways, Hugh Coly, John Saughall, Richard Mascy and Robert Orell: *Kalendars of Gwynedd*, ed. E. Breese (London, 1873), pp. 34–5, 49, 69.

1365 until his untimely death in 1369, while Sir David Cradock, his lieutenant in the 1360s, went on to become justiciar of North Wales and then mayor of Bordeaux.[82] William Frodsham, chamberlain of North Wales from 1393 to 1398, and Sir John Stanley, at various times lieutenant of Ireland, were likewise local careerists who had been schooled in the French wars.[83]

Cheshire and Lancashire veterans also acquired lands and lordships in border areas. Many local soldiers put down roots in the boroughs of North Wales. Roger Ince who settled at Caernarfon as a watchman in the 1380s had the distinction of having a tower named after him, while Sir John Bold's descendants enjoyed more material success around Conwy and Beaumaris.[84] On the continent their compatriots acquired handsome, if short-lived, holdings in Aquitaine, Normandy and elsewhere. In the course of their freelance operations in the 1360s, Sir Hugh Calveley was made count of Carrion in Castile and Sir Robert Knolles won himself vast estates in Brittany.[85] In 1392 Sir William Parr was granted the lordship of Ayron in Royan, while around the same time 'Gaillard' Frodsham was established in properties in the Bordelais.[86] In the reigns of Henry V and Henry VI Cheshire and Lancashire soldiers were very conspicuous among the English settlers in Normandy. Peter Chadderton, Henry Worsley and Thomas Maisterson were early recipients of lands and houses.[87] Richard Merbury was one local adventurer who purchased a fine house in the very town that his Norman ancestors had left almost four centuries earlier.[88] Some local soldiers even acquired seigneuries, though their enjoyment of the titles and revenues can only have been brief. Oliver Barton became

[82] Morgan, 'Cheshire and the defence of Aquitaine', 152–4; R. A. Griffiths, *The Principality of Wales in the Later Middle Ages. The Structure and Personnel of Government. I. South Wales, 1277–1536* (Cardiff, 1972), pp. 111–12; *Ches. Pleas*, p. 54.

[83] *C.P.R. 1396–1399*, p. 324; *Ches. R.R.*, I, p. 444. William Frodsham can perhaps be associated with 'Gaillard' Frodsham prominent in Aquitaine from the late 1360s to the 1390s: Morgan, 'Cheshire and the defence of Aquitaine', 159; *C.P.R. 1396–1399*, p. 499.

[84] K. Williams-Jones, 'Caernarvon' in R. A. Griffiths (ed.), *Boroughs of Mediaeval Wales* (Cardiff, 1978), p. 88; Jones-Pierce, 'Caernarvonshire in the later Middle Ages'.

[85] P. E. Russell, *The English Intervention in Spain and Portugal in the Time of Edward III and Richard II* (Oxford, 1955), p. 50; M. Jones, *Ducal Brittany, 1364–1399* (Oxford, 1970), pp. 48–9. Interestingly enough, work in the Aragonese archives has more or less substantiated the local tradition that Calveley married a Spanish princess: *The Diplomatic Correspondence of Richard II*, ed. E. Perroy (Camden Soc., third series 48, 1933), pp. 233–4.

[86] *C.P.R. 1399–1401*, p. 74; *C.P.R. 1396–1399*, p. 499.

[87] *C.N.R.*, I, pp. 771, 774, 778.

[88] C. T. Allmand, 'The Lancastrian land settlement in Normandy, 1417–1450', *Ec.H.R.*, second series XXI (1968), 467. The Merburys were a branch of the Vernon family: Ormerod, *History of Cheshire*, I, p. 634.

lord of Frequarie in Caux, Thomas Barton lord of Montreuil in Alençon, and William Fitton lord of St Rémy in Caux.[89] Even as late as the 1430s, Sir Bertram Entwistle proudly styled himself in a Lancashire deed viscount and baron of Bolbec.[90]

Of course, war was a lottery, and the stakes were dangerously high. Only a small proportion of soldiers could have been fortunate enough to come unscathed through more than one campaign. If there were sometimes astonishingly few casualties in battle, there were many who fell victim to the plague and other diseases of the camp. Obviously, only the survivors lived to enjoy their wages, and only the men with their limbs intact could feel the benefit. At the same time, to be able to profit from booty, ransoms, lands and office, it was vital to be continually on the winning side. Even if many local soldiers at first had little to lose, as their careers prospered so war became more of a gamble. John Jodrell, one of the bowmen who pillaged the king of France's baggage at Poitiers, lived to taste his own medicine twenty years later. Apparently settled in Poitou, he found himself held to ransom by the French and his 'horses, men, goods, houses and rents' lost through their depredations.[91] Several other successful local soldiers found themselves valuable prizes for their captors. Sir Richard Cradock was taken prisoner on the bishop of Norwich's 'crusade' of 1383, while Sir Richard Aston ignominiously fell into the hands of the Welsh rebels in 1404.[92] Nor did all the lands and offices won in war prove particularly profitable to their holders. Properties in border areas were usually in poor condition, burdened with services, and liable to be ravaged, if not repossessed, by the enemy. Some offices were also honorific liabilities. As seneschal of Guyenne, Sir John Radcliffe became a creditor of the crown to the tune of £7,000.[93] Yet too dark a picture must not be drawn. For every soldier slain in battle, there was a survivor poised to increase his share of the profits of war. John Tailor of Whatcroft might have been mortally wounded at Poitiers, but his brother was able to return to Cheshire with two men's wages in his pockets.[94] The misfortunes of Cradock and Aston likewise have their brighter side: in both cases large subventions were made from public funds to help secure

---

[89] *C.N.R.*, I, pp. 779, 782.

[90] T. D. Whitaker, *An History of the Original Parish of Whalley and Honour of Clitheroe*, 4th edn (2 vols., London, 1872, 1876), II, p. 300.

[91] Morgan, 'Cheshire and the defence of Aquitaine', pp. 150–1.

[92] E. Garton, *Nantwich. Saxon to Puritan* (Nantwich, 1972), p. 21; *Issues of the Exchequer. Henry III to Henry VI*, ed. F. Devon (London, 1837), p. 299.

[93] *C.C.R. 1435–1441*, pp. 416–17.

[94] *B.P.R.*, III, pp. 265–6.

their release.[95] Finally, when being a creditor of the crown brought untold political influence, it is scarcely appropriate to make too much of Radcliffe's plight.

Whatever the odds against the unwilling conscript ending his days as a doyen of chivalry, large numbers of local men achieved significant levels of advancement in the world of soldiering. By carefully reinvesting the profits of war in military equipment, humble foot-soldiers were able to rise slowly through the ranks. Sir Robert Knolles, whose origins were exceedingly obscure, almost certainly began his career as a bowman.[96] Sir Hugh Browe, the son of a yeoman of Tushingham, probably also first saw service as an archer, though being a kinsman of Knolles he doubtless had an easier ride to the top of his profession.[97] Sir David Cradock and Sir Nicholas Colfox, like Thomas Maisterson, were the sons of Nantwich townsmen, and presumably started out in the lower ranks: the former perhaps in the entourage of Sir Thomas Wettenhall, the latter as an archer in the retinue of the earl of Nottingham.[98] Even the scions of minor gentry families might have had to begin at the bottom. Sir William Parr and Sir Bertram Entwistle found it a long haul through the ranks, while the Merbury brothers perhaps first enlisted as bowmen.[99] Doubtless most ambitious soldiers found their advancement excruciatingly slow, but it was sometimes possible for young men to establish their fortunes in the course of a few hours or even minutes. The king and other aristocratic commanders showed a keen interest in their men, and were ever ready to reward valiant deeds. The Black Prince proved a generous connoisseur of feats of arms. Sir Thomas Danyers was handsomely rewarded for his valour in retrieving the prince's standard at Crécy, while another doughty veteran of meaner birth was later able to obtain important favours because of 'the good position he held at the battle of Poitiers'.[100] John of Gaunt knighted John Ypres for his valour in the battle of Najera in 1367, and immediately granted him an annuity of £20 to maintain him in his new estate.[101] According to local traditions, Sir John Stanley first won fame through his gallantry in a royal tournament, while Sir Ralph Standish

---

[95] Garton, *Nantwich*, p. 21; *Issues of the Exchequer*, p. 299.

[96] Bridge, 'Two Cheshire soldiers of fortune'. He probably belonged to the Knolles family of Tushingham in Malpas parish: Cheshire R.O., DCH/C/863, 867.

[97] Bridge, 'Two Cheshire soldiers of fortune', 87; Cheshire R.O., DCH/C/868–9.

[98] Hall, *Nantwich*, pp. 85–9; Morgan, 'Cheshire and the defence of Aquitaine', 152; P.R.O., E 101/41/7, cited in Goodman, *Loyal Conspiracy*, pp. 160, 192n.

[99] A John Merbury served as an archer under Sir John Stanley in Ireland: P.R.O., E 101/41/18.

[100] Hewitt, *Cheshire under the Three Edwards*, p. 103; B.P.R., III, pp. 250–1.

[101] Lewis, 'Indentures of John of Gaunt', p. 87.

gained his knighthood after helping to hack down the peasants' leader at Smithfield in 1381.[102] Many more local men-at-arms won laurels in France under Henry V and the duke of Bedford. Sir William Harrington acquitted himself well as the king's standard-bearer at Agincourt; Sir John Bromley won himself an annuity of £40 for recovering the standard of Guyenne at Corbie; and Sir John Handforth similarly gained a handsome annuity through his valour at Verneuil.[103] Even as the tide of war was turning against the English in France, Sir John Radcliffe was building himself a formidable reputation in the world of chivalry through his feats of arms in Aquitaine.

III

Obviously the profession of arms allowed a select number of men to rise through the ranks to the heights of fame and fortune. Thomas Walsingham indirectly testified to the potentialities of military careerism in his obituary of one of the most remarkable soldiers-of-fortune of the age:

> About this time [1407] died Sir Robert Knolles, a most invincible knight, whose arms the kingdom of France felt against it for many years, the duchy of Brittany feared, and the lands of the Spaniards dreaded; who, besides the fame he earned through feats of war, had a most magnificent bridge built over the river Medway near Rochester, helped provide for a house of Carmelites in London, founded a chantry at Pontefract, and completed many other projects that could have exhausted the treasuries even of kings.[104]

At the same time as offering the fortunate few such dazzling prospects, military service also provided large sections of the male population with opportunities for more modest gains. In the last years of Richard II's reign, for example, many hundreds of Cheshire men were each receiving over £9 per annum as men-at-arms and archers. The St Albans' chronicler is again instructive in his comments. Needless to say, he was outraged at the prospect of humble soldiers lording it in the company of a feckless king. With pardonable exaggeration, he opined that they 'were not of the gentry of the land, but were drawn from the soil, shoemaking or some other trade; men who at home were hardly worthy to take off the shoes of their masters, [at court] considered themselves the equals and companions of lords'.[105] Yet, while many local men proved successful soldiers, it is

---

[102]  For Stanley see 'The Stanley Poem' in *Palatine Anthology. A Collection of Ancient Poems and Ballads relating to Lancashire and Cheshire*, ed. J. O. Halliwell (London, 1850), pp. 210–22. For Standish see *Chronicon Henrici Knighton*, vol. II, ed. J. R. Lumby (R.S., 1895), pp. 137–8.

[103]  *C.P.R. 1422–1429*, p. 44; R. Holinshed, *Chronicles*, ed. H. Ellis (6 vols., London, 1807–8), III, pp. 75–6; Earwaker, *East Cheshire*, I, pp. 240–2.

[104]  *The St Albans Chronicle, 1406–1420*, ed. V. H. Galbraith (Oxford, 1937), p. 22.

[105]  '*Annales Ricardi Secundi et Henrici Quarti*', p. 208.

183

difficult to assess how readily military advancement was translated into civilian terms. In the following section it is intended to discuss the ways in which soldiers, both professional and amateur, attempted to settle back into landed society at some higher grade.

Even the penniless soldier brought home from campaign a number of assets to aid his advancement in the community. Unless he were seriously maimed, even the most humble veteran had a strong right arm and a training in combat to offer potential employers. For the returned soldiers who did not prefer the life of brigands, there was gainful work protecting the persons and properties of the local élite. At the same time, for men with interests of their own to defend or prosecute, there can be little doubt as to the value of strong-arm tactics. The author of *Richard the Redeless* gave vent to a long tirade against the Cheshire 'brawlers' who in the late 1390s 'concocted quarrels to oppress people, and pleaded with pole-axes and the points of swords'.[106] Even soldiers of good breeding were able to use their prowess in arms to overawe their peers and cow their inferiors. The Cheshire court-rolls contain numerous illustrations of their turbulent behaviour. Early in 1380, prior to their departure overseas, Sir John Mascy of Tatton, Sir Richard Mascy, Sir Roger Mascy, Sir Ralph Vernon and Sir Nicholas Vernon assembled with 200 armed men in the town of Knutsford, much to the consternation of the civilian population.[107] In 1394 Sir John Stanley with some 800 Lancashire soldiers menaced the city of Chester, aiding and abetting colleagues who were looting the abbey of St Werburgh's wine-cellar.[108] In all likelihood many of the networks of leadership and clientage forged between local captains and their companies on campaign were readily transposed into a civilian setting, to the advantage of the parties concerned. In their struggle to advance their position in local society, veterans of all ranks were able to obtain material assistance through 'livery and maintenance'.[109]

On the whole men grew in esteem through military service. In addition to a training in arms, all soldiers gained a broad education in human affairs, which doubtless distinguished them from their brothers who had remained at home. Young gentlemen, in particular, acquired an introduction to politics and polite society, as well as experience in the leadership of men, which would help to set them apart from less active members of their class. Sometimes it is possible to document a fairly definite change in status,

---

[106] *Mum and the Sothsegger*, passus III, line 317 ff.

[107] P.R.O., CHES 25/8, m. 8.

[108] Burne, *Monks of Chester*, pp. 106–11.

[109] Many returned soldiers were involved in disturbances of the peace, e.g. see P. H. W. Booth, 'Taxation and public order: Cheshire in 1353', *Northern History*, 12 (1976), 29.

as when outlaws returned from the wars as free men, or when young squires came home as fully-fledged knights to be accorded a new precedence in the local community. More often it is a matter of inferring the rise in status from the sorts of connections which the veteran could mobilise. The husbandman who had followed a local lord in adventures overseas, the yeoman who had fought in the company of the Black Prince, and the gentleman who had been a comrade-in-arms of Henry V, all stood out within their respective communities as men who were able to reach out and touch members of the classes above them. In a world in which status was at least mildly contagious, this sort of association had its own significance in the evaluation of individuals. It also had obvious material import. Large numbers of relatively humble soldiers were usually able to prevail upon their commanders, whether local gentlemen or members of the aristocracy, to intercede for them for royal pardons and other favours. The rich fund of favour generated by the successes in France in 1346 and 1347 is well documented, with local captains like Peter Wettenhall and Adam Ashurst and noblemen like the earls of Warwick and Arundel alike supporting the petitions of humble Lancashire soldiers like William Cooper of Prestwich, Roger Hilton, Adam Smith of Blackburn and Richard Entwistle.[110] Indeed there is ample evidence to suggest that soldiers generally had far more effective connections than civilians, and were better placed to obtain pardons, protection, aid in dealing with bureaucracies and other indulgences from the authorities.[111] Through their relations with powerful patrons some old campaigners succeeded in making themselves indispensable to their neighbours. Thus in the 1380s John Leicester of Tabley, a gentleman whose military experience had brought him a wealth of connections and *savoir-faire*, was able to establish himself as the useful, though expensive, 'fixer' in the affairs of Thomas Fitton of Gawsworth.[112] On a rather more modest level, veterans from the lower ranks were doubtless able to advance themselves by acting as brokers for their village communities, while on a far grander scale, commanders of the stature of Sir John Stanley were able to come close to making whole sections of the local squirearchy their clients.[113]

The ambitions of local soldiers to advance themselves in the region by trading on the prestige of their profession and the *puissance* of their connections were often formally endorsed by grants of offices. The Black Prince's register contains numerous references to humble Cheshire veterans being appointed to minor administrative posts on the basis of their war

---

[110] Wrottesley, 'Crécy and Poitiers', pp. 229, 277, 229, 237.

[111] E.g. see *B.P.R.*, III, *passim*.

[112] P.R.O., SC 2/254/14.     [113] See below, Chapter 10.

records. Thus Adam Acton was granted the bailiwick of the serjeanty of Bucklow hundred on account of his good service at Poitiers, while three other Cheshire archers were admitted as freemen of the royal town of Middlewich.[114] Experienced soldiers tended to be selected as sheriffs of the two counties, and a list of their names becomes a roll-call of some of the more notable campaigners of their generation: Sir Lawrence Dutton, Sir Nicholas Vernon, Sir John Mascy of Tatton and Sir Robert Grosvenor in Cheshire in the late fourteenth century, and Sir Richard Hoghton, Sir John Bold, Sir Ralph Staveley and Sir Robert Urswick in Lancashire in the early fifteenth century.[115] The more distinguished knights and squires might even be appointed to key positions in the royal household and the government of the realm. For a short while at the end of the reign of Edward III, Sir John Ypres served as steward of the royal household.[116] Thirty years later, two other soldiers from the Northwest, John Norbury and Sir John Stanley, likewise held office as treasurer and steward under Henry IV.[117] Needless to say, from their positions at the king's side, local soldiers were well able to consolidate their fortunes in their native Northwest.

Royal and aristocratic patronage also enabled returned soldiers to add to their territorial interests in the region. Occasionally there might be an outright grant of land. The most notable was the Black Prince's promise of £20 worth of land to Sir Thomas Danyers as a reward for his achievements at Caen and Crécy, which later materialised as the Lyme Handley estate granted to his son-in-law, Peter Legh, in 1398.[118] In the aftermath of the rising of 1403, a number of forfeited estates were granted to trusted squires like William Venables and Matthew Swettenham, but few new permanent interests seem to have been created.[119] Indeed it was far more common for retainers to be rewarded with temporary grants. Sir Hugh Calveley obtained the royal manor of Shotwick for life in 1385, while Sir Hugh Browe was given two local manors by the earl of Arundel on a similar basis in 1388.[120] Other notable soldiers had to be content with preferential leases on manors, parks and other seignorial assets in the Northwest. Still, old retainers of the lords of Chester and Lancaster tended to be first in line when valuable wardships were to be granted or let to

---

[114] *B.P.R.*, III, p. 253; *Ches. R.R.*, I, p. 60. Unfortunately the grant of the freedom of Middlewich was subsequently revoked as being contrary to the town's privileges.

[115] Ormerod, *History of Cheshire*; Somerville, *Duchy of Lancaster*, pp. 461–2.

[116] Tout, *Chapters*, IV, pp. 157–8.

[117] Kirby, *Henry IV*, pp. 258–9; M. Barber, 'John Norbury (c.1350–1414). An esquire of Henry IV', *E.H.R.*, LXVIII (1953), 66–76.

[118] *Ches. R.R.*, I, p. 292.      [119] *C.P.R. 1401–1405*, pp. 259, 257.

[120] Ormerod, *History of Cheshire*, II, p. 571; Goodman, *Loyal Conspiracy*, pp. 120–1.

farm. Thus Richard II bestowed on Sir David Cradock the wardship and marriage of John Oulton.[121] Sometimes this sort of grant might lead, through a marriage alliance, to a more permanent dynastic interest. Twenty years later the Cradocks again acquired control of the Oulton estate on the death of their former ward.[122]

In addition to prestige and patronage, many successful soldiers brought back from campaign large sums of money. Presumably a great deal of this wealth was disbursed in small sums, and cannot be traced in the records. Ambitious knights, more than most other careerists, would have sought to enhance their standing through the maintenance of large households and conspicuous consumption. Even modest yeomen probably used their savings from war as much for the purchase of fine clothes and furnishings as for productive purposes. At the same time affluent soldiers of all ranks would have felt obligations to a wide range of dependents, and some of their wealth was doubtless set aside to establish younger kinsmen in trades and professions. Yet social advancement ultimately had to be grounded in the acquisition of land. While it is impossible to chart the flow of capital from the theatres of war into the local land market, there are a few signs that ought to prove instructive. In northeast Cheshire the Jodrells can be traced steadily increasing their holdings throughout the late fourteenth century; in Malpas parish Sir Hugh Browe can be found consolidating his modest patrimony from the 1370s onwards; in Wirral and west Lancashire Sir John Stanley was buying up a series of manors in the late 1390s.[123] Quite often investments in real estate took an indirect form, as in the purchase of a marriage to an heiress or a dowager. Stanley was scarcely a penniless adventurer when he secured the hand of Isabella Lathom some time before 1385. Her first husband had been another active campaigner, Sir Geoffrey Worsley, who died in the early 1380s. His patrimony at Worsley and elsewhere in turn passed into the keeping of Sir John Mascy of Tatton, who had shrewdly invested in the marriage of the Lancashire knight's sister.[124]

On the whole there were only limited opportunities for successful soldiers to establish new landed dynasties in the Northwest. Since the heads of so many established gentry families, not to mention the hordes of younger sons, turned to soldiering as a means of advancement, it is possible that their ambitions often served to hold landed society in a sort of tense equilibrium. Ironically the prospects of advancement for local soldiers

---

[121] *Ches. R.R.*, I, p. 129. Note also the valuable wardships acquired by Sir John Mascy of Tatton in the 1390s: *Ibid.*, p. 330.  [122] *Ibid.*, p. 129.
[123] J.R.U.L., Jodrell Charters, *passim*; Cheshire R.O., DCH/C/870–8.
[124] *V.C.H. Lancaster*, IV, p. 378.

seem to have been far better in other parts of the realm. Of course, many
found themselves settling wherever their postings and rewards had taken
them. Sir Adam Ashurst, a veteran of the opening campaigns of the
Hundred Years War, was granted lands in Essex and Hertfordshire, while
Sir Nicholas Colfox, a retainer of the earl of Nottingham, was given a
life-interest in the manor of Barton Seagrave in Northamptonshire.[125]
More often, soldiers owed their association with a particular region to their
marriage to a widow or an heiress. Sir Robert Knolles' marriage brought
him life-long interests in Pontefract; Sir William Parr's fortunate alliance
to the heiress of part of the barony of Kendal established his family as
a leading Westmorland lineage; Nicholas Merbury's alliance with the
widow of Lord Latimer temporarily made him a prominent Northamptonshire landowner; Sir John Osbaldeston's match brought him fine lands
in the Cotswolds; Sir John Radcliffe's marriage secured his descendants
rich estates and a peerage in Norfolk.[126] Manifestly, from his vantage-point
at court and his connections in the world of chivalry, with his credit in
the capital and his savings from campaign, the successful soldier was able
to take his pick of the most eligible women in the country. Sometimes
more specific connections suggest themselves: Thomas Crewe, a prominent
retainer of the earl of Warwick, doubtless owed his introduction to the
widow of John Clopton and his establishment in Warwickshire society
to his lord's good offices, while John Merbury, chamberlain and ultimately
justiciar of South Wales, presumably met his two Herefordshire wives,
both wealthy widows, in the course of his official duties.[127] Of course,
most of the men paid large sums for their brides, and in this respect can
be said to have been investing in real estate. Others were more direct in
their property dealings, and can be found investing heavily in real estate
in various parts of the realm. Sir Robert Knolles acquired interests in
London and Kent as well as establishing his principal seat at Sculthorpe
in Norfolk; John Norbury purchased the manor of Bedwell in Hertfordshire as early as 1388, over a decade before his acquisition of Cheshunt
from the earl of Westmorland and his purchase of Little Berkhamstead
from Lord Botreaux made him one of the foremost landowners in the
neighbourhood; and around the same time Sir Hugh Browe first acquired
as his line's principal seat the manor of Teigh in Rutlandshire.[128]

[125] Wrottesley, 'Crécy and Calais', pp. 38, 85, 277, 200; Goodman, *Loyal Conspiracy*, p. 159.

[126] Bridge, 'Two Cheshire soldiers of fortune', 73; *C.P.R. 1391–1396*, p. 711; *C.P.R. 1408–1413*, p. 308; Longford, 'Family of Osbaldeston'; C. P. Hampson, *The Book of the Radclyffes* (Edinburgh, 1940), *passim*.

[127] *V.C.H. Warwick*, III, p. 190; Griffiths, *Principality of Wales in the Later Middle Ages*, p. 13.

[128] Bridge, 'Two Cheshire soldiers of fortune', 110–12; *V.C.H. Hertford*, III, pp. 460, 446; Barber, 'John Norbury'; *V.C.H. Rutland*, II, p. 153.

In all likelihood soldiers of relatively humble origins found it easier to gain acceptance in polite society in regions where their origins were unknown. While in the Northwest it is possible to infer the fruits of military service from the modest acquisitions of a number of landed and farming families, and from the occasional establishment of a cadet line, the more spectacular instances of social climbing by local soldiers have to be sought elsewhere. Even if the region had been more inclined to take successful adventurers to its bosom, it is unlikely that it could have fully contained the ambitions of men of the stature of Sir Robert Knolles and Sir John Radcliffe. A number of successful soldiers came to hold lands in a range of counties: John Norbury possessed estates in Middlesex and Kent as well as Hertfordshire, while John Merbury held manors in Nottinghamshire, Leicestershire, Lincolnshire, Bedfordshire, Hertfordshire, Herefordshire and Shropshire at his death in 1438.[129] Some local veterans rapidly acquired eminence in their adopted county communities; Sir Hugh Browe, Matthew Swettenham, John Merbury and Thomas Crewe were elected as sheriffs of Rutland, Northampton, Hereford and Warwick respectively in this period.[130] While marriage late in life, often to heiresses of decayed stock or ageing widows, served to ensure that the dynastic ambitions of quite a few notable soldiers were still-born, many others put down firm roots in their new neighbourhoods. The Browes remained in Rutlandshire for another generation, the Osbaldestons and their kinsmen continued to flourish in the Cotswolds, and the Norburys remained as a prominent lineage in the Home Counties throughout the Lancastrian period.[131] Meanwhile the Radcliffes of Attleborough and the Parrs of Kendal, not to mention the Stanleys of Lathom, were destined for even higher advancement in later ages.[132] More than the members of any other profession, men who had made their fortunes through the profession of arms seem to have been responsible for the region's widespread reputation as a 'seed-plot of gentility'.

The importance of soldiering as a means of differentiating the fortunes of various individuals and groups in Cheshire and Lancashire society is all too apparent. The dramatic reversals of fortune so frequent in war, the scale of the participation in military enterprises and the centrality of chivalric values in the ideology of contemporary society add immeasurably

---

[129] Barber, 'John Norbury'; Cheshire R.O., DLT, Liber C, f. 289.

[130] *V.C.H. Rutland*, II, p. 153; *C.C.R. 1409–1413*, p. 375; Griffiths, *Principality of Wales in the Later Middle Ages*, pp. 132–4; *V.C.H. Warwick*, III, p. 190.

[131] *V.C.H. Rutland*, II, p. 153; Longford, 'Family of Osbaldeston'; *V.C.H. Hertford*, III, p. 446.

[132] The Radcliffes of Attleborough were ennobled in the late fifteenth century, and the Parrs of Kendal in the sixteenth century.

to its significance in both quantitative and qualitative terms. On the whole warfare can be seen as a lottery in which the soldier not only had the chance to win rich prizes, but also by the same token to advance his relative status even further by profiting from the distress or death of his less fortunate comrades. Thus the mortal plight of John Tailor of Whatcroft on the field of Poitiers doubled at a stroke the assets of his brother, while the demise of Sir Geoffrey Worsley likewise left two wealthy heiresses as brides for his brothers-in-arms. Even if it can be shown that many local soldiers sustained considerable losses on campaign, it would not necessarily challenge the general proposition that military service was a major source of differentiation within the community.

The thesis that in some respects the entire Northwest, or at least large sections of regional society, was able to benefit from soldiering is far harder to establish. Yet, in view of the lengthy debate on the profitability of the Hundred Years War, it is worth registering a few impressions.[133] In the first place it is clear that large sums of money flowed into the pockets of local men as wages and annuities throughout this period. At the times of major expeditions several thousand Cheshire and Lancashire soldiers were on the pay-rolls of kings and noblemen. In 1375 John Leicester accounted for 400 marks spent on wages for himself, three men-at-arms and eight archers for just six months' service, and these twelve soldiers from the vicinity of Tabley represented only a minute proportion of the local population in arms.[134] In the last years of Richard II's reign his Cheshire guardsmen were earning over £5,000 a year, and in the first few months of Henry V's reign alone eighty-six Lancashire gentlemen were promised annuities totalling over £1,100 a year.[135] While it is not possible to draw up a precise profit-and-loss account of the region's involvement in war, it is worth noting that the sums expended by successive governments in wages and annuities to local men often exceeded the total revenues of the two palatinates.[136] Whatever is concluded about

---

[133] M. M. Postan, 'Some social consequences of the Hundred Years War', *Ec.H.R.*, first series XXI (1942), 1–12; K. B. McFarlane, 'England and the Hundred Years War', *Past and Present*, 22 (1962), 3–13; M. M. Postan, 'The costs of the Hundred Years War', *Past and Present*, 27 (1964), 34–53.     [134] Cheshire R.O., DLT, deed 185.

[135] P.R.O., E 101/42/10; P.R.O., DL 42/17, ff. 2d–8.

[136] For most of Richard II's reign a high proportion of the revenues from Cheshire was spent on annuities, and in the late 1390s expenditure on fees far exceeded income: A. E. Curry, 'Cheshire and the royal demesne, 1399–1422', *L.C.H.S.*, 128 (1978), 113–38; Gillespie, 'Richard II's Cheshire archers', 8–9. Though not all the annuitants were Cheshire men, the numbers of outsiders were more than matched by the numbers of local men receiving fees from the revenues of other counties. Henry V's annuities to Lancashire men in 1413 amounted to around half the annual value of the entire duchy of Lancaster in 1419; Somerville, *Duchy of Lancaster*, p. 188.

the economic effects of war in other more heavily taxed parts of the realm, it is highly unlikely that military enterprises were a financial drain on the Northwest in the period under discussion.

Of course, it would be inappropriate to evaluate the impact of soldiering on Cheshire and Lancashire society in crude, fiscal terms. Even if full data on population and price levels were available, it would still be hard to assess the social costs in the region of the drain on man-power, the cultivation of violence, and wasteful investment in armaments. On the other hand, it would be wrong to overlook some hidden social benefits. Successful soldiers might well have been instrumental in the establishment of several local commercial houses: it can be no coincidence that the first tradesmen from the region to attain aldermanic rank in London — Thomas Knolles, Nicholas Aughton and William Wettenhall — were all kinsmen of notable soldiers.[137] At the same time the achievements of the more prominent commanders and the military traditions of many local families served to integrate the region, on terms far from unfavourable to itself, into the national polity. While there is room for endless debate on the exact weighting to be assigned to all the various costs and benefits, there can be little doubt as to the side to which most local men would have tipped the balance. The popularity of the French wars among the local population is well enough attested by its participation in the rising of 1393 and its alacrity in responding to the call to arms in 1415. The intense pride in their martial prowess felt in both counties is tellingly illustrated in the chauvinistic ballads popular in the Northwest in the sixteenth century.[138] Thomas Walsingham alleged that Richard II's Cheshire guardsmen boasted to the king that 'they could protect him against all England, nay, against the world, as long as he wished to trust in their loyalty, strength and probity'.[139] In the light of the regional jingoism apparent even in Tudor times, it seems certain that it was the soldiers, and not the chronicler, who were guilty of misrepresentation.

---

[137] Thomas Knolles had the same coat-of-arms as Sir Robert Knolles and Sir Hugh Browe: *V.C.H. Hertford*, II, p. 253; Cheshire R.O., DDX/364. Aughton and Wettenhall were both from the Northwest, and were doubtless kinsmen of some of the many soldiers bearing their surnames.

[138] *Bishop Percy's Folio Manuscript*, I, pp. 313–40, III, pp. 205–14 and 233–59.

[139] '*Annales Ricardi Secundi et Henrici Quarti*', p. 237.

*Chapter 10*

# POWER, PATRONAGE AND PROVINCIAL CULTURE

Underlying all the various avenues of social advancement in late medieval England lay the concept of service. Men did not pursue their trades and professions in isolation: they drew their wealth from those sections of the community which they served. Indeed careerists remained to a surprising degree dependent for their status on their relationship to landed society. Craftsmen, clerks and soldiers who were attached to a royal or an aristocratic household commanded a great deal more respect than their counterparts on the open market. While newly made fortunes could not be easily converted into landed respectability in a single life-time, the fortunate servant might temporarily share in the eminence of his master. Another element common to all the various trades and professions, and in some regards the obverse of service, was patronage. At all stages in the careers of tradesmen, clerks and soldiers, patrons were indispensable: merchants needed lucrative contracts, clerks rich benefices and soldiers prestigious commands. Even when fortunes had been amassed, 'good lordship' was vital to ease the careerist's path to social acceptance. There can be little doubt that most social mobility was 'sponsored' in this sense. While many men were able to advance themselves, their achievements were often dependent on, and a buttress to the powers of sections of the establishment.

Personal service was not merely an element common to all the main forms of careerism. In some respects it transcended them. The king and other magnates often found it necessary to delegate wide-ranging powers to their counsellors, retainers and clerks. The more trusted and capable servants might find themselves exercising their lord's authority and representing his interests on a whole range of matters, and in such circumstances their service to a single master is the only unifying thread in an otherwise totally hybrid career. Of course, many of the men who acted as factotums in royal and aristocratic households had clerical or military backgrounds. Worldly clerks and superannuated soldiers alike can be traced holding manorial courts, checking accounts and acting as attorneys on their lord's behalf. Yet at the same time there was a growing number of laymen with an almost professional interest in government, legal business and estate-management, and in the first section of this chapter their experiences are considered in some detail. Of course, this large, amorphous class of secular officials was far from homogeneous. With their formal education at the inns of court and their corporate privileges, the men 'learned in law' were increasingly setting themselves apart as a distinct profession. Yet it remains appropriate, as well as convenient, to consider law and administration as avenues of advancement together. After all, few lay office-holders were without some knowledge of the law, while even the proudest serjeants-at-law did not disdain to become the hirelings of noble houses.

Since opportunities were so largely determined by the operations of patronage, it is intended to proceed in the second section to a general review of the relations between the people of the region and the major sources of wealth and power in the kingdom. Obviously the connections between Cheshire and Lancashire men and their royal lords will be the major focus of interest. Since the two palatinates were held by kings or the sons of kings throughout this period, local fortunes became ever more inextricably bound with national politics. Generally speaking, men from the Northwest rode high on royal favour, and at times even achieved an invidious importance in the affairs of the kingdom. Given the political vicissitudes of the reigns of Richard II and Henry IV, their special status was never entirely unchallenged. The Lancastrian revolution of 1399, in particular, threatened a dramatic check to the ambitions of the men of Cheshire, even as it promised golden opportunities for their neighbours north of the Mersey. Yet the political fortunes of neither palatinate were so narrowly based as to be completely undermined by dynastic upheaval. Through their tenure of key offices and multifarious connections within the political establishment, successful careerists put down firm roots. By the late fourteenth century local interests were well established in most fields of endeavour, and had become in large measure resistant to the poison of faction.

The special relationship between the crown and the region had other important consequences. Closeness to the court, council and central administration brought careerists degrees of prestige and influence which could not fail to have repercussions on their own communities. Indeed the ability to mediate the flow of royal patronage and to manipulate the workings of the bureaucracy and the law courts had long been a cornerstone of aristocratic power in the countryside. For the most part it served to buttress the existing power-structure, but in some circumstances, it could also destabilise local communities. Particularly favoured lords sometimes were able to mobilise the resources of the crown to advance themselves at the expense of their rivals, while on occasion careerists of more modest provenance were able to use their credit at court to build up networks of clientage in the countryside, which necessarily threatened the old county establishment. In the Northwest the Stanleys of Lathom showed unusual resourcefulness in harnessing royal authority to their own aggrandisement. In the third section it is proposed to follow the rise of this remarkable lineage from its inauspicious beginnings in Wirral to regional hegemony and ennoblement, and to chart its establishment of mutually supportive power-bases in the country and at court.

Obviously Cheshire and Lancashire society could not have remained unaffected by the changing parameters of patronage within which its more ambitious members sought to make their marks. It must never be forgotten that the relations observable at the national level are only the upper tiers of whole pyramids of favour and faction whose foundations lay deep in the countryside. Doubtless the peasant put his son to service at the local manor-house or parsonage with the same high hopes as the knight sent his son to be educated in an aristocratic or royal household. Accordingly it seems reasonable to assume that the undulatory patterns apparent on the surface reverberate through to the hidden depths. Unfortunately there are no reliable gauges by which to measure the impact on the region of the rising tide of careerism and the fickle winds of royal favour. Perhaps the cultural achievements of local men in this period provide the best weather vane. Though the fragmentary evidence available allows only the most tentative conclusions, it is hoped to demonstrate in the final section that the growing wealth and widening horizons of sections of the local community were reflected in the enrichment of major areas of provincial culture in the decades around 1400.

I

During the later middle ages the administrative life of England became increasingly institutionalised. While the king and the landed aristocracy retained in their hands enormous discretionary powers, all sections of the community found it ever more necessary to rely on professionals to undertake the complex tasks of government and estate-management, and to cope effectively with the requirements of a sophisticated legal and administrative system. Traditionally this sort of expertise had been the preserve of the clerical order, and indeed most bureaucratic functions continued to be performed by clerks. From the late fourteenth century, however, a dramatic rise in the number of lay officials in both government and private service can be observed.[1] Without attempting to explain the structural trends underlying this development, its relation to the increasing value assigned to a training in common law by all men with interests to protect and careers to make can be acknowledged. Landed gentlemen as well as their stewards and bailiffs had to acquire some understanding of legal procedures, and some even sought formal instruction at the inns of court. Indeed men 'learned in law' were increasingly setting themselves apart as professionals with their own educational standards and a monopoly over key judicial processes.[2]

The fundamental problem in differentiating between men involved in administrative and legal work is the generally unspecialised nature of much of their early training and employment. Obviously the legal profession is the most clearly defined grouping, but even its membership can be hard to establish. The chief justices of the realm and the serjeants-at-law, of course, are readily identifiable as the cream of their calling. By the late fourteenth century it can be assumed that they had served long apprenticeships at the inns of court and attained the dignity of the coif. Yet certainty regarding the credentials of less exalted operatives in the legal system is more elusive. While judges of the realm were appointed exclusively from the ranks of serjeants-at-law, justices of the peace in the shires frequently had no legal qualifications at all. Similarly, while an education at the inns of court was becoming essential for barristers, amateur advocates continued to plead in some of the central, as well as the local courts. Perhaps some of the men who appear regularly on commissions of the peace, as stewards in honorial courts, as attorneys, estate-officials and so on, had some sort of legal training. Yet, as E. W. Ives has warned, 'it would be rash to assume that every petty expert locally esteemed as "learned in the law" was an inn of court or chancery man; the humbler estate bailiffs must have learned the smattering of law essential to their trade, either by apprenticeship, self instruction, or simply by trial and error'.[3] Again, there is utility in adopting terms of reference which embrace both the embryonic legal profession and the larger, but more inchoate body of lay administrators. In truth, in some respects their vocations need to be considered in the wider context of clerical careerism. Presumably most aspiring lay administrators and common lawyers acquired their basic education as clerks in minor orders. The processes by

---

[1] For a pioneering study of lay professionalism see R. A. Griffiths, 'Public and private bureaucracies in England and Wales in the fifteenth century', *T.R.H.S.*, fifth series 30 (1980), 109–30.

[2] In general see A. Harding, *A Social History of English Law* (Harmondsworth, 1966), pp. 167–93, and E. W. Ives, 'The common lawyers in pre-Reformation England', *T.R.H.S.*, fifth series 18 (1968), 145–73.     [3] *Ibid.*, 151.

which many judicial, legal and administrative functions were being emancipated from clerical control were certainly well in train, but they were only just beginning to generate distinct career structures and professional identities for laymen. In many respects the decades around 1400 represent a watershed in this transmutation. Doubtless many of the lay administrators and common lawyers in the fifteenth century would have been secular clerks in the earlier period. Sometimes the change can be seen within a single lineage: Sir James Strangeways, ultimately a justice of common pleas, was the son of a secular clerk who held office at Chester.[4]

Young men aspiring to a career in law and administration needed support and sponsorship. Obviously the attainment of basic numeracy and literacy was fundamental, but even elementary educational opportunities could not be taken for granted by the mass of the population. Doubtless many bright youths from peasant families gained informal instruction from parish priests and the like. Later in life, such men presumably used their little learning to good effect in village affairs. To make a proper living out of legal and administrative work, however, required far longer periods of training. To qualify as a common lawyer certainly involved many years of formal education and apprenticeship, first at school and later at the inns of court at Westminster. With regard to administration and estate-management, most men learned their trade through attachment to a large household, or sometimes perhaps through military service. Naturally enough, gentry families were usually better placed than their social inferiors to have their sons established in careers. Yet men of a middling sort often had the capital and connections to ensure the advancement of a talented child. Surprisingly few of the successful lawyers and lay officials belonged to leading local lineages. Hugh Holes, Thomas Tildesley and Matthew Mere hailed from gentry families of middle rank, but were all younger sons; James Holt, John Pigot and Henry Birtles were from very minor gentry families; James Strangeways and William Chauntrell seem to have been of burgess stock; Robert Pleasington and John Shrigley were the sons of mere freeholders.[5]

The sorts of connections which brought opportunities for an administrative training or a legal education also offered openings for employment. Inevitably most careers were extremely localised, and little is known of the experiences of individuals who at village level made themselves useful

---

[4] Roskell, 'Sir James Strangeways', 455ff.

[5] See Ormerod, *History of Cheshire*, *V.C.H. Lancaster* and Earwaker, *East Cheshire*, *passim*. For Pleasington see *V.C.H. Lancaster*, VI, p. 61 n. For Shrigley see Bruell, 'Edition of cartulary of John de Macclesfield', items 409, 430.

to their lords and fellow-villagers through their knowledge of local customs and the workings of the lesser courts. Such persons were employed as bailiffs and estate-officials by their lords, and as attorneys at the hundred and county courts by their neighbours. At a rather higher level many gentlemen with legal and administrative experience made themselves indispensable to the affairs of their more distracted peers, and were even retained with modest annuities. John Leicester of Tabley, a well-connected soldier, attempted to augment his fortunes by acting for his neighbours in legal matters. In 1393 he sued Thomas Fitton of Gawsworth for £55 as fees for his counsel and aid in various dubious property transactions.[6] Geoffrey Mascy of Wincham was another gentleman with talents in this direction, who can often be traced in London, doubtless on business for his clients. In 1411 John Kingsley granted him an annuity of 13s 4d in return for 'his good counsel', and Margaret widow of Peter Legh and William Venables similarly paid him small annuities.[7] Nicholas Blundell, a Lancashire gentleman chosen to arbitrate in a local feud, modestly thought that his qualifications for the task were 'the high trust, truth and affection that they have in me, a simple man of their kin, more than for any cunning that ever was in my person'. Yet he took it upon himself to travel down to London with the counsels of the two parties to take advice from a judge of the realm and the apprentices-at-law before making his award.[8]

In addition to employment in the private sector there were scores of openings in local government for ambitious careerists. In the Northwest the justiciar of Chester might typically be a nobleman, but the chief justice of Lancaster was always a distinguished lawyer. The chamberlainship of Chester and the chancellorship of the county palatine of Lancaster were similarly reserved for professional administrators. Of course, it was usually considered appropriate to appoint outsiders to such powerful offices, though William Troutbeck, a Westmorland gentleman with considerable local interests, managed to acquire both offices in the reign of Henry VI.[9] Lower down the administrative system, local men inevitably predominated. While the sheriffs were usually chosen from among the active knights, they also tended to be men with proven administrative ability, like Sir Lawrence Merbury in Cheshire and Sir Ralph Staveley in Lancashire. With duties embracing the complex fields of land law, estate-management and accounting, the escheatorship was even less of a

---

[6] P.R.O., SC 2/254/14.     [7] Chester R.O., Earwaker MSS., 1/139.

[8] Chetham Library, Manchester, Tarbock Cartulary, ff. 10d–13.

[9] Somerville, *Duchy of Lancaster*, p. 476. Troutbeck was a kinsman of Sir William Parr: B.L., Additional Charters, no. 72999.

sinecure, and office-holders like John Scolehall, Adam Kingsley, Thomas Maisterson, Matthew Mere and Richard Manley in Cheshire, and Matthew Kenyon and James Holt in Lancashire can be regarded as virtual professionals. Indeed, from enquiring into the rights of their royal lords to handling their affairs in the law courts was a natural progression for the escheator, and it is significant to note the subsequent appointments of Maisterson, Mere and Manley as attorneys-general in the region.[10] Whether lesser offices in the royal administration, particularly coronerships, had similar connotations cannot be ascertained, but assuredly even the most modest post in local government provided some of the experience and connections necessary for further advancement.

Little is known regarding the educational backgrounds of the many lay administrators and attorneys who made their livings in the Northwest. While it is improbable that more than a minority of the more notable among them had undergone a proper legal training, it is unwise to be dogmatic. Quite a number of properly qualified local lawyers can be identified, but this knowledge is almost entirely dependent on their subsequent promotion as serjeants-at-law. Without doubt there were many other local careerists who had benefited from formal instruction in common law. Henry Scolefield was an attorney at the court of common pleas; Nicholas Blundell certainly knew his way around the inns of court; Geoffrey Mascy and Matthew Kenyon both handled legal business in London; Matthew Mere can be traced acting as *placitor* in the county court at Chester; but nowhere is there definite evidence regarding their education.[11] Yet many of the men destined to be called to the bar began their careers in just this fashion. Henry Birtles and John Pigot, for example, can both be traced serving as local attorneys in the 1380s,[12] but only with their attainment of the coif in the following decade is it possible to attest their formal qualifications as lawyers.

There was no shortage of business for the professional lawyer in the Northwest. With their palatine courts, Chester and Lancaster might well have offered a range of work unavailable in most other provincial centres. The complement of three serjeants-at-law in Chester certainly was generous, and perhaps made it easier for local men like Hugh Holes, Robert Towneley, Roger Horton, Henry Birtles and John Pigot to attain this rank.[13] In addition, other lawyers were appointed from time to time as

---

[10] *Ches. R.R.*, I, pp. 96, 100, 103.

[11] Manchester Central Reference Library, Farrer MSS., 50/18/4, m. 13; Chetham Library, Manchester, Tarbock Cartulary, ff. 10d–13; *Cheshire Sheaf*, third series, item 6820; *C.P.R. 1396–1399*, p. 552; P.R.O., CHES 29/115, m. 7d.

[12] J.R.U.L., Arley Charters, 27/15; *Ches. R.R.*, I, p. 442; Nicolas, *Scrope and Grosvenor Controversy*, I, pp. 24 ff.     [13] *Ches. R.R.*, I, pp. 96–8, 100; P.R.O., SC 6/176/3.

deputies to the justiciar, justices *una vice* and on various commissions. Thomas Davenport, Robert Ditton, Matthew Southworth, Richard Manley and others served in this fashion in Cheshire.[14] Perhaps even more significant than the official posts and salaries were the opportunities for profit in private service. William Chauntrell was granted 20 marks to maintain Sir Lawrence Warren in his disputes.[15] Even where quarrels were settled out-of-court, lawyers still found lucrative work arranging arbitrations. In the dispute between Sir Thomas Grosvenor and Robert Legh in 1412 Henry Birtles and James Holt were retained as legal counsel, while in his feud with Edward Carrington, Hugh Arderne had to hire lawyers to attend him on four love-days.[16]

While handsome livings were made in provincial practice the really spectacular fortunes could only be acquired at a national level. Since all qualified lawyers had served apprenticeships at the inns of court or chancery, most had contacts at Westminster. Several local lawyers had sufficient credit at court and in the capital not to need a long sojourn building up a practice in the region. Robert Pleasington served as John of Gaunt's attorney at the exchequer, held other posts in the Lancastrian administration, and finally rose to become chief baron on the exchequer.[17] Thomas Tildesley, a king's serjeant from 1402 to 1409, was presumably well served by his connections through his brother, Christopher Tildesley, the king's goldsmith, with the court and the mercantile community of London.[18] Others used local appointments as stepping-stones to higher office in the kingdom. Hugh Holes was a serjeant-at-law for a number of years at Chester before he was called to be a justice of the king's bench in 1394.[19] Roger Horton followed an identical path, and even succeeded his compatriot on the king's bench in 1415.[20] James Strangeways, a native of Manchester, similarly began his career in Lancashire. His close association with Thomas Langley, bishop of Durham, perhaps provided him with wider opportunities. He was a serjeant-at-law in 1411, a king's serjeant in 1415, and a justice in the court of common pleas in 1426.[21]

Many men with administrative talents could also boast careers which transcended their native region. In many cases soldiering seems to have

14 *Ches. R.R.*, I, pp. 95–103.
15 Bodleian Library, Oxford, MS. top. Cheshire B1, f. 199.
16 Cheshire R.O., DLT, Liber C, ff. 116–18; Chester R.O., Earwaker MSS., 2/664.
17 Tout, *Chapters*, III, p. 357.
18 *Select Cases in the Court of King's Bench*, vol. VII, ed. G. O. Sayles (Selden Soc., 1971), p. lxiii; *C.P.R. 1396–1399*, p. 552.
19 *Select Cases in King's Bench*, VII, p. lxii.
20 *Ches. R.R.*, I, p. 98; *Select Cases in King's Bench*, VII, p. lxii.
21 Roskell, 'Sir James Strangeways', 455 ff; Storey, *Thomas Langley*, p. 63; Somerville, *Duchy of Lancaster*, p. 451.

provided the early experience and connections, and Wales, Ireland and France proved valuable training-grounds. In the late fourteenth century two notable Cheshire soldiers, David Cradock and William Frodsham, held office as chamberlains of North Wales, while their compatriot John Merbury later served as chamberlain and justiciar of South Wales.[22] In Ireland Sir John Stanley's terms as lieutenant opened the flood-gates to local careerists, though John Shrigley had been ensconced as a baron of the Irish exchequer since 1382. By the middle of Henry IV's reign local men were well-entrenched at Dublin, with Sir Lawrence Merbury as treasurer, Henry Strangeways as chamberlain of the exchequer, John Radcliffe as second baron of the exchequer, and Ralph Standish as escheator and clerk of the markets.[23] Further afield, numerous local veterans were promoted to governmental office in Gascony, and later in Normandy.[24] Many other enterprising soldiers made their mark in an aristocratic or royal household. Sir John Mascy of Puddington served as an estate-official for the earls of Salisbury; Thomas Crewe of Sonde rose to become steward of the Beauchamp household; and Thomas Maisterson was chamberlain of the duke of Bedford.[25] Among the local careerists in the household of John of Gaunt, several were able to secure key positions in the royal administration: Sir John Ypres became steward of the royal household and Sir Robert Pleasington chief baron of the exchequer.[26] The local retainers of Henry of Bolingbroke, earl of Derby, experienced an even more dramatic transformation in their fortunes in 1399: after years of faithful service John Norbury was rapidly advanced to the treasurership in the new Lancastrian regime.[27] Yet the abilities of some men apparently put them beyond the reach of faction. Sir John Stanley, who made his debut in the royal service under the aegis of de Vere and attained invidious eminence as controller of the wardrobe in the last years of Richard II, was soon back at the centre of affairs as steward of the household of Henry IV.

The profits to be derived from administrative and legal work were considerable. The fees and perquisites of administrative office have been touched on in the context of other forms of careerism, while the fortunes of Sir John Stanley, the most successful local careerist, are to be discussed later in some detail. For the present, it is appropriate to concentrate on

---

[22] *C.C.R. 1374–1377*, p. 405; *C.P.R. 1377–1381*, p. 57; *Ches. R.R.*, I, p. 193; Griffiths, *Principality of Wales in the Later Middle Ages*, pp. 132–4, 181–2.

[23] *C.P.R. 1381–1385*, p. 168; *C.P.R. 1405–1408*, p. 203; *C.P.R. 1401–1405*, pp. 393, 403; *C.P.R. 1399–1401*, p. 48.  [24] See above, Chapter 9.

[25] Bruell, 'Edition of cartulary of John de Macclesfield', item 38; *V.C.H. Warwick*, III, p. 190; *Actes concernant la Normandie*, II, p. 354.

[26] Tout, *Chapters*, IV, pp. 157–8; III, p. 357.  [27] Barber, 'John Norbury', 66–76.

the gains to be made through the practice of law. At the upper reaches of the profession, judges of the realm could clearly command handsome salaries, with basic rates of £180 per annum for chief justices and £120 per annum for puisne justices.[28] Supplementary fees were often authorised on an individual basis. In 1381 Robert Pleasington was granted an additional annuity of £40 as chief baron of the exchequer, while in 1394 Hugh Holes was awarded a similar fee as justice of the king's bench 'to enable him to maintain his estate more becomingly'.[29] Then there were additional payments for judicial work on circuit. In 1413 Holes was allowed ten shillings a day for fifty-two days on circuit in North Wales and Staffordshire.[30] Of course, no other lawyers enjoyed regular remuneration on this sort of scale. The three serjeants-at-law at Chester were retained on salaries ranging between 5 marks and £5 per annum.[31] Still, unlike royal judges, serjeants were allowed to retain their private practices. Great landowners were willing to pay well for a skilful advocate, some even offering retaining-fees to have first call on his services. In 1391 Hugh Holes was paid 13s 4d for legal work for the earl of Stafford, and in 1429 James Strangeways was in receipt of a retainer of £2 from the duke of Clarence.[32] Even when professional pleading was not required, as in an informal arbitration, legal bills could be extremely high. Hugh Arderne paid fourteen shillings in legal fees in his settlement with Edward Carrington.[33] In truth there are good grounds for assuming that promotion to the bench was undertaken more for reasons of prestige than profit. Yet it must not be supposed that royal justices were incorruptible. In 1386 Sir Robert Pleasington was charged with peculation at the exchequer, while in 1415 Sir Hugh Holes found it advisable to obtain a royal pardon for all his offences against the statute of livery and maintenance.[34]

Contemporaries certainly had no doubts regarding the wealth of lawyers. The chief justices of the courts of king's bench and common pleas, and the chief baron of the exchequer were assessed at £5 each in the poll-tax of 1379, a sum higher than most peers of the realm, while serjeants-at-law

---

[28] *Select Cases in King's Bench*, VII, p. xv.

[29] *C.P.R. 1381–1385*, p. 7; *C.P.R. 1391–1396*, p. 403.

[30] *Select Cases in King's Bench*, VII, p. xv.          [31] P.R.O., SC 6/176/3.

[32] Staffordshire R.O., Stafford MSS., 1/2/4; Westminster Abbey, Westminster MSS., no. 12163. Fees for consultation or court appearance, and for pleading were normally 3s 4d and 6s 8d respectively: E. W. Ives, 'The reputation of the common lawyers in English society, 1450–1550', *University of Birmingham Historical Journal*, VII (1959–60), 153.

[33] Chester R.O., Earwaker MSS., 2/664.

[34] J. A. Tuck, *Richard II and the English Nobility* (London, 1973), pp. 107–8; *Select Cases in King's Bench*, VII, p. xv.

were assessed at £2 each, twice the sum demanded of the baron of Newton in Makerfield in Lancashire.[35] Predictably enough, successful lawyers can be found acquiring land on a considerable scale. Most began by investing in the marriage of an heiress or a widow, and all made it their business to watch for the best openings in the land market. Robert Pleasington apparently obtained his estates in Yorkshire through his first wife. In the 1370s he acquired large parcels of land in the vicinity of Penwortham in his native Lancashire, while the Dacres of Gilsland gave him a lease of the neighbouring manor of Eccleston in lieu of a debt of 1,100 marks. In the 1380s he purchased the manor of Burley in Rutlandshire from the Despensers. Although his properties were temporarily confiscated on account of his forceful advocacy of the Appellants' cause in 1388, his heirs were substantial landowners in three shires.[36] Hugh Holes followed a similar policy of territorial aggrandisement. He was married, or at least betrothed, three times, and each alliance brought him substantial property interests. In 1362 he was affianced to a daughter of the Bruyns of Pickmere in Cheshire. According to a carefully worded indenture, doubtless attesting an early flair for legal chicanery, he stood to gain substantial portions of the Bruyn estate if his wife did not remain chaste. In 1374 he was in the process of securing a life interest in his second wife's estate in Chester and Wirral, while a third marriage in 1386, with the heiress of John Domville, brought a title to the manors of Mobberley, Brimstage and Oxton.[37] During the following decades he can be found making even more investments. He purchased parts of the manors of Little Neston and Hargreave, obtained a grant of the manor of Rushton for life, and acquired a lease and a reversion of the manor of Elton, though it was not until after his death in 1415 that his son finally secured a full title to the estate. By this time the interests of the Holes family had shifted to the Southeast, where the manor of Oxhey near Watford had become their principal residence.[38]

There can be no doubt of the enormous advantages wielded by members of the legal profession in their quest for a position in landed society. The successful lawyer was not only wealthy but also had the skill and connections to defend his acquisitions at the local level. At the same time none can dispute the appeal of the legal profession to individuals and families who were 'attempting to assert a claim to gentility, or else to

---

[35] P.R.O., E 359/8c; E 179/130/24.

[36] *C.C.R. 1369–1374*, p. 326; *C.C.R. 1374–1377*, p. 250; *C.C.R. 1377–1381*, pp. 216, 364, 231; *C.C.R. 1381–1385*, p. 597; *C.P.R. 1396–1399*, p. 535.

[37] Cheshire R.O., DLT, Liber B, ff. 52, 54; *Talbot Deeds, 1200–1682*, ed. E. Barker (L.C.R.S., 103, 1953), nos. 88, 92, 100–1, 103, 120, 122, 129.

[38] *Ches. R.R.*, I, p. 238; Cheshire R.O., DBA/62/E/12–17; *V.C.H. Hertford*, II, p. 456.

raise their status within landed society'.[39] William Chauntrell, a lawyer of modest origins, was able to see his line well established in his native Cheshire.[40] Others tended to find it more opportune to amass estates in other parts of the realm. Despite their early interest in the local property-market, Pleasington and Holes ultimately founded their landed fortunes in Yorkshire and Hertfordshire. Sir James Strangeways likewise established himself in Yorkshire, taking as his seat West Harlsey in the North Riding.[41] Many of the local men who made their fortunes through careers in administration also eschewed their homeland. Neither Thomas Crewe nor John Merbury, for example, seem to have purchased land in Cheshire, but their landed interests in Warwickshire and Herefordshire were sufficient to secure their election as members of parliament.[42] The ambitions of the more successful lawyers and administrators from the Northwest, as with their compatriots in other callings, could not be contained within the boundaries of their native shires.

II

Fundamental to careers in law and administration, and indeed all trades and professions at this time, were the complementary processes of service and sponsorship. Accordingly it is felt appropriate to proceed to a general assessment of the operations of patronage in the Northwest, in which the various forms of service are not rigidly divorced but regarded in some measure as branches of a single *cursus honorum*. Obviously it would be fitting to commence with a consideration of the workings of sponsorship at the local level. After all it would be no exaggeration to claim that all men, except the truly destitute, had some patronage to offer, and many successful careerists owed their starts in life to the modest favours of humble kinsmen and friends. Yet, only by shifting the focus from the region to the entire kingdom is it possible to take full cognisance of the influences which shaped the more spectacular careers of the age. In this regard the operations of royal patronage naturally demand close attention, and it is intended to trace in some detail the relations between the men of the Northwest, their royal lords and successive kings of England. Of course, there is no pretence that the government of the realm was solely

[39] Ives, 'Common lawyers in pre-Reformation England', 157.

[40] Among other properties, Chauntrell acquired an interest in the barony of Dunham Massey: Ormerod, *History of Cheshire*, I, p. 529. He married the widow of Sir Nicholas Longford: Somerville, *Duchy of Lancaster*, p. 472.

[41] Roskell, 'Sir James Strangeways', 455 ff.

[42] *V.C.H. Warwick*, III, p. 190; Griffiths, *Principality of Wales in the Later Middle Ages*, p. 133.

the private business of the monarch. Whether by prescriptive, delegated or usurped rights, princes of the blood, nobles and prelates, and even senior bureaucrats all had fairly direct access to the power, authority and assets of the crown. Although it has some connotations inappropriate in this age, the concept of government patronage might be preferred in this context.

The palatinates of Chester and Lancaster were favoured by particularly close relations with the royal house in the later middle ages, both being in the hands of the ruling monarchs for over half of the period under discussion, and of princes of the blood for the rest.[43] No other region could rival the Northwest in the puissance of its connections. The principality of Wales and the earldom of Cornwall, both parts of the appanage of the heir to the throne, were set apart as colonial appendages, while most other royal lordships were small and interspersed with aristocratic estates. In so far as closeness to the royal family determined access to government patronage, the men of the region were indeed unusually advantaged. There were few local knights and squires who were not the mesne tenants of either the earl of Chester or the duke of Lancaster. Through wardship, the performance of homage, and the rendering of military service, most came into regular contact with the households of princes and kings. Many county notables and men of lesser means gained further credit with their royal lords by protecting their interests and acting as their agents in the region. Through employment in local government and estate-management, it was often possible for able careerists to bring their talents to the attention of powerful patrons, and then to secure advancement in the realm at large.

There is certainly a great deal of evidence regarding the high value that the earls of Chester and the dukes of Lancaster placed on the human resources of the Northwest. From the late thirteenth century successive lords looked to the two counties as recruiting-grounds for their retinues, and during the reign of Edward III the martial proclivities of local men were given full rein in the wars with France. Under the leadership of the Black Prince, Henry of Grosmont and John of Gaunt, knights and archers from the region gained reputations for their gallantry and prowess. While the more distinguished captains were often able to pursue independent careers, the importance of tenurial connections in providing opportunities for military service is all too evident. By the late fourteenth century soldiering was regarded as an attractive means of livelihood by large sections of the local population. While fortunes could be lost in war as rapidly as they could be won, notable warriors like Sir Hugh Calveley

---

[43] In general see Barraclough, 'Earldom and county palatine of Chester', 23–57, and Somerville, 'Duchy and county palatine of Lancaster', 59–67.

and Sir Robert Knolles made the risks appear worth taking. In addition to its other attractions, the profession of arms brought ambitious men to the attention of their royal commanders. In this fashion Sir John Delves and Sir John Ypres found themselves promoted to positions of influence in the households of the Black Prince and John of Gaunt, and many lesser men for the first time gained direct access to the founts of royal patronage.[44]

In relations between the crown and the men of the region, military concerns set the pace. From around the middle of the fourteenth century, however, the pen began to assume significance alongside the sword. Naturally enough, princes and peers looked to their lordships for skilled clerks as well as hardy warriors. Such men not only proved loyal functionaries in the provinces, but might also rise to become powerful allies in church and state. On the whole the earls of Chester played only a modest role in cultivating clerical careerism. The Black Prince showed some interest in Roger Cradock, the Franciscan friar from Nantwich who ultimately attained the bishopric of Llandaff, and he may have been instrumental in the placement of John Macclesfield in the privy-seal office. Yet no Cheshire clerk could rival in his esteem Henry Blackburn, the Lancashire man who served as his treasurer.[45] Though curious at first sight, this latter appointment is in one respect entirely fitting. By this stage traditions of clerical careerism had taken firm root north of the Mersey, and were beginning to bud and blossom along the trellis-work of the Lancastrian administration. Doubtless the lords of Lancaster saw the value of having their own clerical protégés planted in the main departments of state, and the rehabilitation of the third earl in the 1330s might well explain the apparently sudden appearance of a remarkable group of Lancashire clerks at Westminster at this time. John Winwick and Henry Haydock were the pioneers, but they were soon joined by Matthew Ashton and Thomas Thelwall, a Cheshire man, but significantly from a Lancastrian manor. With the appointment of Winwick as keeper of the privy seal in 1355, and acting chancellor in 1359, and with a new generation of clerks like Robert Farington and John Macclesfield coming into office in their turn, the central government cannot have failed to become more responsive to local interests and ambitions.[46]

In the last years of Edward III men from the Northwest came to assume

---

[44] See above, Chapter 9.

[45] *Register of Simon Langham*, p. 74.

[46] E.g. in 1391 Robert Farington secured a royal licence for Richard Hoghton to enlarge his park at Hoghton, and in 1392 John Macclesfield obtained royal pardons for three servants of Sir Richard Bold: *C.P.R. 1388–1392*, p. 459; *C.P.R. 1391–1396*, p. 31.

a wholly unprecedented importance in the affairs of the realm. In large measure this development is attributable to the influence of John of Gaunt. With the king sinking into his dotage and with the prince of Wales in failing health, the duke of Lancaster came into his own as the power behind the throne. Naturally enough, he contrived to have trusted retainers appointed to key positions in the kingdom. Sir John Ypres took over as controller of the king's wardrobe in 1368, and as steward of the royal household in 1376, while Ralph Erghum, chancellor of the duchy of Lancaster, was raised to the rich bishopric of Salisbury on his master's recommendations in 1375.[47] In spite of mounting distrust and opposition, John of Gaunt continued to advance his protégés in the opening years of Richard II's reign. Ralph Erghum was included in the council of regency established in 1377, while Robert Pleasington was suddenly appointed chief baron of the exchequer in 1380.[48] Yet it would be a mistake to assume that the fortunes of local careerists at this time were entirely dependent on a single faction. Moving in the corridors of power in the 1370s, there were a number of prominent soldiers like Sir Hugh Calveley and Sir Robert Knolles, and clerical bureaucrats like Matthew Ashton and Thomas Thelwall, who could afford to stand aloof from party politics. Of course, such men were not disposed to reject out of hand the blandishments of such a puissant prince as John of Gaunt. Knolles joined his retinue in return for an annuity of £100, while Thelwall was enticed into his service with an offer of the chancellorship of the county palatine of Lancaster.[49] The point is that men of talent and experience were usually too widely valued in the political nation to remain the creatures of faction. While a few careerists like Erghum and Pleasington did become the casualties of their own ambition, most soldiers, lawyers and clerks were able to serve the realm, and themselves, unhindered by the vicissitudes of national politics.

In the late fourteenth century Cheshire and Lancashire careerism became ever more widely based and deeply entrenched. Knights and gentlemen from the region can be found in the households and retinues of almost all members of the royal family and the higher nobility. With Sir Robert Fouleshurst and Peter Legh in the service of Queen Philippa and Princess Joan, and with Sir Hugh Browe, Sir John Mascy of Puddington, Sir Robert Legh and Thomas Crewe in the retinues of the earls of Arundel, Salisbury, Nottingham and Warwick, there was certainly

---

[47] Tout, *Chapters*, IV, pp. 157–8; *B.R.U.O.*, I, pp. 644–5.
[48] Tuck, *Richard II and Nobility*, p. 37; Tout, *Chapters*, III, p. 357.
[49] *John of Gaunt's Register, 1379–1383*, I, pp. 6ff; *C.P.R. 1374–1377*, p. 455.

no danger of local fortunes completely floundering.[50] A number of distinguished soldiers, like Knolles and Stanley, attained a degree of independence through mounting their own expeditions, while other local squires, like Carrington and Arderne, revealed their professional commitment to arms by taking service with foreign princes.[51] The clerical bureaucrats at Westminster were able to develop an even keener sense of autonomy. The clerks in the chancery, exchequer and privy-seal office represented continuity in government, and it is possible to trace whole networks of local clerks, whose positions owed more to nepotism and corporate privilege than to political faction. Robert Farington, John Macclesfield, William Aughton and Thomas Stanley, all prominent in the reign of Richard II, continued as royal clerks after the Lancastrian revolution of 1399.[52] At the same time local careerism was beginning to diversify into fields which were even less politically sensitive. Many successful soldiers and bureaucrats invested in the education of younger kinsmen. Sir Hugh Calveley had his nephews educated at Oxford, while local dons like Robert Hallum, Adam Mottram and John Fitton were building secure platforms for advancement in the church.[53] Other men from the Northwest invested in an education at the inns of court. By the 1390s, with Sir Hugh Holes a justice of the king's bench and Robert Towneley, Roger Horton, Thomas Tildesley and John Pigot among the common serjeants, the region could boast a reasonably strong representation in the legal profession. Even more remarkable, a significant number of local tradesmen first established themselves in London around this time. Again, the influence of other forms of careerism can be detected. Of the first five local men to achieve aldermanic rank, Thomas Knolles was a kinsman of the famous soldier-of-fortune, Nicholas Aughton probably had both a royal clerk and soldiers among his kin, Philip Malpas was related to a chancery clerk, William Wettenhall was a scion of a notable soldiering family, and Hugh Wiche was a nephew of the registrar of the abbot of St Albans.[54] Demonstrably all these tradesmen had older relatives who not only might have given them their starts in life but also, through the provision of lucrative contracts, ensured their subsequent prosperity.

While below the surface of national politics there was a steady

---

50 *B.P.R.*, III, p. 79; *Ches. R.R.*, I, p. 289; Goodman, *Loyal Conspiracy*, pp. 120–1; Bruell, 'Edition of cartulary of John de Macclesfield', item 38; Goodman, *Loyal Conspiracy*, p. 162; *V.C.H. Warwick*, III, p. 190.

51 Copinger, *Smith-Carrington Family*, pp. 74–5.

52 *C.P.R. 1396–1399, passim*; *C.P.R. 1401–1405, passim*.

53 See above, Chapter 8.

54 For Henry Malpas, chancery clerk, see Jones, *Church in Chester*, p. 145.

accumulation of expertise, capital and connections by local men at court and in council, their fortunes were inevitably subject to more violent oscillation. In the late 1370s it must have seemed to ambitious men from both sides of the Mersey that the best prospects for advancement lay in the Lancastrian service. Faced on the one hand by a petulant young king with his curialist confidants and on the other by a mistrustful political nation, however, John of Gaunt increasingly withdrew from public life in the following decade. Of course, he remained a powerful patron in his own right, and retained a considerable following in the region. In the 1390s he even re-emerged as a major force in national politics, and through his good offices his clients again won favour with the king. Yet in the meantime many men from the Northwest found a surer route to the founts of royal patronage. For the first time in forty years, the king of England held the earldom of Chester, and local adventurers were determined to make the most of the connection. Richard II had compelling reasons of his own for reciprocating their ardour, and from at least the time of the Scottish expedition of 1385 he developed a keen awareness of the value of the palatinate of Chester as a power-base independent of aristocratic control. Perhaps there is substance in the claim that as early as October 1386 he was plotting to use military force to crush his baronial opponents. A few days after he had withdrawn in high dudgeon from a parliament intent on impeaching his friends, the chamberlain of Chester contracted with Sir Lawrence Dutton and William Danyers to lead sixty archers in the king's service 'towards the parts of London'.[55] During the following twelve months, with the crown in commission, the king spent some time in the environs of Cheshire recruiting an armed following. In November 1387 de Vere led this army against the lords of the commission, but it was checked and routed at Radcot Bridge. Licking his wounds and quietly planning revenge, Richard II drew his own lessons from the experience. He was never to forget the loyalty of the Cheshire men at the time of his greatest humiliation.

Demonstrably Richard II built up a sizeable retinue in the region in the late 1380s, but the names of its key members can only be surmised. Presumably he depended initially on retainers he had inherited from his father, like Sir John Mascy of Tatton and Sir Lawrence Dutton, but he soon attracted into the royal service a number of younger men, prominent among whom were Sir Thomas Molyneux, Sir John Stanley, William Stanley, Peter Legh and Hugh Mascy.[56] In marked contrast to the

[55] Cheshire R.O., DLT, Liber C, f. 181.

[56] *Ches. R.R.*, I, p. 329; Cheshire R.O., DLT, Liber C, f. 159; *C.P.R. 1381–1385*, p. 50; *C.P.R. 1391–1396*, p. 34; *Ches. R.R.*, I, p. 444; Myres, 'The campaign of Radcot Bridge', 20–33; P.R.O., CHES 25/8, m. 25.

legalised butchery at Westminster, few local men seem to have suffered for their complicity with de Vere in 1387. Molyneux was the only notable casualty at Radcot Bridge. Temporarily broken and demoralised, the king's following in the region could be readily reconstituted. Stanley still had men in harness in Ireland, and his progress from king's knight to controller of the wardrobe during the 1390s is a useful guide to the gradual process of reconstruction. In many respects the king moved with more circumspection than his local retainers. The Cheshire rising of 1393, which had amongst its aims the freeing of the king from the machinations of his uncles, was led by Sir Thomas Talbot and Sir John Mascy of Tatton, both veterans in the royal service.[57] Still, the Irish expedition of 1394 was a well-contrived opportunity for Richard II to begin to re-group his following in the region, and three years later he felt ready to act. When on 13 July 1397 the sheriff of Chester was urgently instructed to raise 2,000 archers for the king's service, and when a month later the under-sheriff was required to muster them at Kingston upon Thames, it is clear that Richard II was embarking on the implementation of a long cherished and patiently planned scheme.[58]

By the end of September 1397 Richard II had effectively turned the tables on his old adversaries. Earlier in the summer Gloucester, Warwick and Arundel, the three senior Lords Appellant, were arrested, and in the parliament summoned for 17 September they in their turn were appealed and convicted of treason. The king was showing his determination to rule in his own right, and the role of the palatinate of Chester was all too apparent. To secure acquiescence in his policies, large numbers of Cheshire archers were posted within bow-shot of the assembled parliament, and dispatched to escort Arundel to the block on Tower Hill.[59] Gradually the king began to place members of his swollen retinue on a firmer footing. Beginning with Sir Robert Legh, the sheriff of Chester, on 20 August, many local knights and gentlemen were admitted to the livery of the white hart and awarded fees.[60] During the summer the king likewise seems to have determined to recruit a permanent retinue of Cheshire archers, and from 14 September a steady stream of old hands and new recruits were formally admitted to the livery of the crown. From among their ranks, there soon emerged a select bodyguard of some 300 archers, divided into seven 'watches' commanded by Thomas Beeston, Adam Bostock, Richard Cholmondeley, Ralph Davenport, John Donne, Thomas Holford and John Legh of Booths.[61] A key figure in this development was Sir

[57] Bellamy, 'Northern rebellions', 261 ff.     [58] *Ches. R.R.*, I, p. 98.

[59] *Chronicon Adae Usk*, p. 11; '*Annales Ricardi Secundi et Henrici Quarti*', p. 216.

[60] *C.P.R. 1396–1399*, p. 177; *Ches. R.R., passim.*

[61] Gillespie, 'Richard II's Cheshire archers', 1–39.

John Stanley, and his promotion to the controllership of the wardrobe in October 1397 was entirely fitting.[62] Richard II's policies and sentiments regarding the men of Cheshire at this time do not have to be surmised. On 25 September, 'on account of the great love and affection' which he had towards its people, he raised the earldom of Chester to the dignity of a principality, and to it annexed the forfeited Arundel lordships in Shropshire and the Welsh Borderlands. He had served public notice of his determination to make Cheshire, in the words of T. F. Tout, 'the inner citadel' of his kingdom.[63]

From this time until Richard II's deposition in 1399, men of the principality of Chester acquired an invidious prominence in the realm. The king granted annuities ranging from £40 to £5 to over 100 Cheshire knights and gentlemen, including members of almost all the leading county families.[64] At the same time he gave the livery of the crown, with six pence a day, to over 600 local archers, at least three-quarters of whom were not of gentle birth but of yeomen, artisan and even peasant stock.[65] Cheshire men were able to gain preferential access to the king, and found him responsive to requests for further patronage. Contemporary chroniclers waxed indignant at the king's indulgence and the guardsmen's gross presumption, while the numerous grants of offices, farms and wardships to local men tell their own tale. Sir Robert Legh and Thomas Beeston were appointed constables of Oswestry and Shrawardine castles; Thomas Holford and Richard Warburton were given profitable farms of the customs in London and Dorset; Roger Wilde and Robert Holt were granted a parkership at Drayton and a portership at York; and so on.[66] Moving around the countryside in the entourage of the king, the guardsmen also acquired an unsavoury reputation for lawlessness and rapine, and their depredations added appreciably to the unpopularity of the regime.[67] Whatever the truth of the allegations against their

---

[62] Tout, *Chapters*, IV, p. 199. Stanley seems to have deputised for Sir Baldwin Raddington, his predecessor, for some time, perhaps from as early as 1394; Burne, *Monks of Chester*, pp. 106–11.

[63] *Rotuli Parliamentorum*, III, pp. 353–4; Tout, *Chapters*, IV, p. 199.

[64] P.R.O., CHES 2/71, *passim*.

[65] Gillespie, 'Richard II's Cheshire archers', 29, argues that at least half of the archers were drawn from the gentry and yeomanry. In actual fact only a sixth of the main bodyguard bore the surnames of gentry families, and many of them were probably not closely related to their illustrious namesakes. It would be more appropriate to argue that, with a few possible exceptions, the archers were drawn from classes lower than the gentry, and that Thomas Walsingham was not entirely mischievous in alleging that they 'were not of the gentry of the land, but were drawn from the soil, shoemaking, or some other trade': '*Annales Ricardi Secundi et Henrici Quarti*', p. 208.

[66] *C.P.R. 1396–1399*, pp. 204, 212, 454, 204–5.      [67] E.g. see *Chronicon Adae Usk*, p. 23.

behaviour, local men certainly profited immensely from royal favour. In
1398 Cheshire knights, gentlemen and archers were receiving over £5,000
in wages alone, while the county community was further indulged with
a grant of 4,000 marks to be distributed among the survivors of Radcot
Bridge.[68] Many Lancashire men were also being brought on to the royal
pay-roll, and on a single day in 1398 fees to the value of £180 were granted
to five knights and seventeen squires from north of the Mersey.[69] The
sequestration of the Lancastrian inheritance after the death of John of
Gaunt offered a further chance to extend his power-base in the region.
In the summer of 1399 the nation shuddered at the immense concentration
of royal power in the Northwest, and the king's removal of his regalia
and treasure from Westminster led many to suspect that he intended to
despoil his people from bases on the fringes of the realm.[70]

In the event Richard II lost his throne, and the principality of Chester
was dismantled. Early in July 1399 Henry of Bolingbroke landed at
Ravenspur, and rapidly succeeded in making himself master of the
kingdom. Richard II returned from Ireland to find support for himself
rapidly evaporating, and was tricked into surrendering himself at
Conwy.[71] The Cheshire guardsmen who had claimed to be able to protect
the king against the whole realm were never even put to the test. The
king had left them behind in Pembroke when he had made his frantic
dash northwards through Wales. Apparently he intended to reach Cheshire
before the rebels, though he ought not to have hoped for a great deal
in that quarter. With over 1,000 of its best fighting men already with the
royal army, its military strength must have been greatly depleted. In any
case Sir Robert Legh, the sheriff of Chester, had already negotiated the
surrender of the county to Bolingbroke on 5 August. Four days later the
latter was in control of Chester castle, and had executed Peter Legh, a
Ricardian stalwart. By driving a wedge between the king and his
principality, Bolingbroke effectively paralysed opposition, but after the
initial confusion the Cheshire men made several attempts to rescue their
master and rally to his cause. In 1400 a large force of old retainers and
guardsmen launched an attack on Chester castle to coincide with the rising
of the earls of Kent and Huntingdon, while in 1403 they joined the
rebellion of the Percys virtually *en masse*.[72]

It is tempting to view the accession of Henry IV as marking a major

---

[68] P.R.O., E 101/42/10; *Ches. R.R.*, I, p. 99.    [69] *C.P.R. 1396–1399*, pp. 321, 324.

[70] '*Annales Ricardi Secundi et Henrici Quarti*', p. 239.

[71] For a local, pro-Ricardian account of events see Clarke and Galbraith, 'Deposition of
Richard II', 125–81. See also *Chronicon Adae Usk*, p. 27.

[72] McNiven, 'Cheshire rising of 1400', 375–96; 'Cheshire and rebellion of 1403', 1–29.

northward deflection in the flow of royal patronage in the region. Just as R. R. Davies has documented the strategic significance of the principality of Chester to Richard II in his last years, so A. L. Brown has pointed to the crucial role of the palatinate of Lancaster in the establishment of the Lancastrian regime.[73] Naturally enough just as the men of Cheshire were better placed to profit from royal favour prior to 1399, so their fellows from north of the Mersey expected greater benefits from the heir of John of Gaunt. While it is impossible to identify many of the men who flocked to Bolingbroke's standard in July 1399, it is known that a substantial force of Lancashire men joined him at Pontefract.[74] Sir William Parr and Thomas Langley, two of John of Gaunt's executors, were presumably among the first local men to welcome their old lord's heir. With his undoubted administrative expertise and his impeccable political credentials, Langley experienced rapid preferment, and promptly rose from royal secretary and keeper of the privy seal to chancellor of the realm. Significantly, Robert Langley of Prestwich, his kinsman, claimed to have been with Bolingbroke from his first arrival in the country.[75] Sir Richard Hoghton, Sir Robert Urswick, Sir William Butler, Sir John Ashton and several other local gentlemen can also be shown to have been in his service in the months before his coronation, since many of their annuities date from this time.[76] In the troubled months of 1403 he was certainly heavily dependent on the services of his Lancashire retainers. A letter of 1405 reveals that he had some seventy-eight knights and gentlemen on call.[77] While there was no attempt to recruit archers for a royal bodyguard, Henry IV had almost as many local gentlemen on his pay-roll as his predecessor.

Yet there is a danger in drawing too firm a line between the political fortunes of Cheshire and Lancashire at this time. While it is by no means fanciful to picture the two county communities pitched against each other at the battle of Shrewsbury, it must be stressed that the interests of local families were far more varied and diffuse than is often supposed. Obviously there were sectional interests in both shires. For each person who prospered through the 'good lordship' of the earl of Chester or duke of Lancaster, there might well be an embittered rival waiting for a fall from grace. It is not hard to find Cheshire men who resisted the blandishments of Richard II and welcomed the Lancastrian revolution, or conversely Lancashire men who were discomfited by the deposition and

---

73 Davies, 'Richard II and principality of Chester', 256–79; Brown, 'Lancastrian regime', 1–28.

74 Kirby, *Henry IV*, p. 55.

75 Manchester Central Reference Library, Farrer MSS., Transcripts from Agecroft Deeds, nos. 58, 66.

76 P.R.O., DL 42/15, ff. 7d–13d.        77 P.R.O., DL 42/16, f. 128.

joined the rebels in 1403.[78] The allegiances of local careerists were even more complex. On the whole, few tradesmen and churchmen found themselves seriously embarrassed by the change of regime. Even Christopher Tildesley, Richard II's goldsmith, kept his privileged status at court.[79] Most lawyers and bureaucrats seem not to have suffered any real interruption to their careers. Sir Hugh Holes, the first Cheshire man raised to the bench, continued to advance himself under the new dynasty. While John Macclesfield lost charge of the great wardrobe, he and other local clerks stayed on to serve the Lancastrian administration. More remarkably, Cheshire courtiers like Sir Richard Cradock and Matthew Swettenham remained in the royal household.[80] Even Sir John Stanley rode out the storm. Though he lost the controllership of the wardrobe, he was quickly entrusted with the lieutenancy of Ireland, and within a few years he was back at the heart of affairs as steward of Henry IV's household.[81]

The Lancastrian regime apparently had no wish to be vindictive. Henry IV and his son seem to have been positively anxious to win over the goodwill of as many men of talent and influence as possible. No king could govern effectively without the services of experienced administrators and bureaucrats and without the co-operation of leading members of the county communities. It might well be that the new regime feared the immense military potential of the palatinate of Chester, or at least saw the value of harnessing it to its own cause. Certainly the men of Cheshire, on whom 'the whole kingdom cried vengeance' in 1399, were treated surprisingly leniently at the time of the deposition and in 1403.[82] Perhaps it is fortunate that they had friends at court. The king's closest friend and counsellor in the early years was John Norbury, an old Cheshire soldier-of-fortune.[83] In any case, with the Welsh in open revolt, appeasement with their traditional custodians was the only sane strategy. Henry, prince of Wales was ideally placed to build bridges. Stepping into the old king's shoes as earl of Chester, he began to bind to his cause influential members of the county community. Sir John Stanley and his son, Sir Robert Legh, Sir John Mascy of Puddington, John Legh of Booths, William Mainwaring, Sir William Brereton, John Mainwaring and John Savage were early in receipt of fees.[84] At the same time, as heir to the king and duke of Lancaster, he wasted little time in committing to his

---

[78] E.g. Sir Gilbert Halsall, Thomas Bradshaw of Haigh, Geoffrey Bold and Hamo Mascy of Rixton: *C.P.R. 1401–1405*, pp. 252, 256, 258.

[79] *C.P.R. 1401–1405*, p. 319.

[80] *C.P.R. 1399–1401*, p. 108; *C.P.R. 1401–1405*, p. 257.

[81] *C.P.R. 1399–1401*, pp. 261, 92; *C.P.R. 1405–1408*, p. 65; *C.P.R. 1408–1413*, p. 90.

[82] The phrase is from *Chronicon Adae Usk*, p. 26.

[83] Barber, 'John Norbury', 66–76.

[84] *Ches. R.R.*, I, pp. 446, 293, 333, 293, 55, 218, 422.

service Lancashire men like Sir John Bold and Henry Scarisbrick.[85] Needless to say, on his father's death in 1413, he inherited not only his crown but the entire Lancastrian retinue. On a single day shortly after his accession he granted or confirmed over £1,100 worth of annuities to Lancashire men.[86] The martial-minded Henry V clearly put a high premium on the loyalties of his tenants. In the wars in France local men served him in great number and with distinction. With royal caprice buried and factionalism in retreat, the special relationship between the royal household and the two palatinates could enter on a more constructive phase.

To maintain a healthy reciprocity between the crown and the county communities, however, required skilled brokerage. Demonstrably successive kings placed a high value on their power-base in the Northwest. In their turn, local men appreciated the manner in which royal favour served to supplement their incomes and to nourish careerism. Still, there were other considerations. Both parties had a natural concern for the cohesiveness and stability of regional society. The flow of royal patronage needed close regulation. Sharp fluctuations in the levels of largesse dispensed, or sudden changes in the channels along which it poured, inevitably disrupted traditional power relations in the counties, and dangerously factionalised local politics. In all likelihood the leading men of the region saw the problem well enough. Sir Robert Legh, the sheriff of Chester, was one county notable who appears to have been disquieted by the excesses of Richard II's last years, not least perhaps because royal indulgence fed the pretensions of local favourites like his uncle, Peter Legh. In May 1399 the king was so unsure of his good faith that he made him, along with Sir Ralph Radcliffe, sheriff of Lancaster, swear a special oath of allegiance at Cardiff.[87] Three months later Legh surrendered the principality of Chester without a struggle. Yet later events suggest that he became equally perturbed by the factionalism of the first years of Lancastrian rule. Despite having his handsome annuity of £40 confirmed in 1400, he threw his weight behind the rebellion of 1403.[88] His predicament in this troubled decade illustrates well the hazards of meddling in the affairs of princes. Bobbing up and down on the waves of political fortune and in constant danger of being split asunder on the rocks of faction, the county communities needed adroit helmsmen. The royal lords of Chester and Lancaster, for their part, required the services of trusted lieutenants to bring the factious gentry united into line behind

[85] See *Royal Historical Letters of Henry IV*, II, pp. 22–4.
[86] P.R.O., DL 42/17, ff. 2d–8.
[87] *C.P.R. 1396–1399*, p. 505.    [88] *Ches. R.R.*, I, p. 293; *C.P.R. 1401–1405*, p. 259.

214

them. Unfortunately there were no resident noblemen to act as brokers between crown and community, to offer uncontested leadership in local life, and to ensure that the flow of royal patronage underpinned, rather than undermined the social order. It was this fragile link in the chain of 'good lordship' that the Stanleys of Lathom came to exploit so effectively.

### III

Through all the vicissitudes of political fortune, the house of Stanley rarely faltered in its rise to regional hegemony. At one level a review of the life of the first Sir John Stanley is a case-study in social advancement. Through his enormous success as a soldier and servant of the crown, he rose from being a landless younger son to become a powerful landed magnate. In the meantime he was lieutenant of Ireland, held high office in the households of two kings, gained election to the Order of the Garter, and achieved regal status for his lineage as kings of Man. At another level the rise of the Stanleys must be viewed in its relation to important structural developments in regional society in the Lancastrian period. Their progress from strong-arm adventurism to *noblesse oblige* is not merely an astounding success-story, it is an epic of social and political change. While the establishment of their local leadership depended on the iron determination and unfailing political acumen of Sir John Stanley and his successors, the emergence of their brand of 'good lordship' served interests far wider than their own dynastic aggrandisement.[89]

The history of the Stanleys of Lathom does not need the embellishments of myth. Still, the Stanley legend, apparently composed in the late sixteenth century, does include some authentic traditions regarding the founder of the line.[90] The poem begins with Sir John Stanley leaving his native Cheshire to seek his fortune overseas, and relates a series of adventures at the court of the Grand Turk and in the company of Sir Robert Knolles in France. Despite many elements which are wildly improbable or wholly confused, the basic thread of this narrative cannot be dismissed out of hand. The earliest reference to Stanley so far discovered is a pardon granted him in 1378 for an earlier manslaughter in Cheshire, in which reference is made to his military record in Aquitaine.[91] The poem proceeds to recount how on his return to England he won royal favour and a knighthood through his prowess in a tournament, and how back in the Northwest he won the hand of Isabella Lathom, the richest heiress

---

[89] See Bennett, 'The Stanleys in English politics'.
[90] 'The Stanley Poem' in *Palatine Anthology*, pp. 210–22; J.R.U.L., English MSS., no. 202.
[91] *Ches. R.R.*, I, p. 444.

in Lancashire, through his gallantry. Again, the basic story-line is not lacking in substance, and even the romantic frills cannot be entirely discounted. His precipitate intrusion into his wife's inheritance in the teeth of opposition from John of Gaunt in 1385 and his sudden appearance as a knight in the inner court circle around the same time are episodes redolent of high drama.[92]

A younger son of William Stanley of Storeton, Sir John Stanley owed little to his family except perhaps his status as a gentleman and his training in arms. Like many of his compatriots, he sought advancement through military service in France and elsewhere. On the fringes of the royal household from the beginning of Richard II's reign, he had attained sufficient eminence by 1386 to be selected as deputy to the new lieutenant of Ireland, Robert de Vere.[93] Apparently stationed in Dublin during 1387, he was fortunate not to have been implicated in the débâcle of Radcot Bridge. If his career suffered a brief reverse with the Appellant triumph, the resumption of power by the king in 1389 brought renewed advancement. Formally retained with a handsome annuity, he was appointed to a term as lieutenant of Ireland in his own right.[94] Back at court from 1391, he was a prominent member of the royal household throughout the decade, doubtless adding to his stature during the king's first Irish expedition of 1394. In October 1397 he was promoted to the controllership of the wardrobe, and in the following months seems to have presided over 'the systematic development of the military side of the household'.[95] Yet, despite his prominence at the court of Richard II, Stanley experienced only a brief interruption to his career in the revolution of 1399. After making his submission to Bolingbroke, he was rapidly entrusted with a second term as lieutenant in Ireland, and returned to serve as steward of the household of the prince of Wales during the troubled years of the Glyndŵr rebellion.[96] Early in 1405 he transferred to the service of Henry IV, and served as steward of the royal household, keeper of Windsor castle and trusted councillor until the king's death in 1413.[97] At the beginning of the new reign he was again appointed lieutenant of Ireland, but died shortly after assuming office allegedly from the 'venom of lampoons written by Irish poets'.[98]

In the course of his long career in the royal service, Stanley was able

---

[92] *Rotuli Parliamentorum*, III, pp. 204–5.

[93] *Ches. R.R.*, I, p. 444.

[94] *C.P.R. 1388–1392*, pp. 101, 91.     [95] Tout, *Chapters*, IV, p. 199.

[96] *Ches. R.R.*, I, p. 446. For Stanley's submission see *Historia Vitae et Regni Ricardi Secundi*, ed. G. B. Stow (Philadelphia, 1977), p. 155.

[97] Kirby, *Henry IV*, p. 259; *C.P.R. 1408–1413*, p. 90.

[98] Otway-Ruthven, *Medieval Ireland*, p. 347.

to amass immense wealth. From 1389 he was in receipt of an annuity of
100 marks from the exchequer, and from 1397 an additional 40 marks
from the issues of the earldom of Chester.[99] The salaries and perquisites
of government posts that he held were also substantial: the stewardship
of Macclesfield and the surveyorship of the Cheshire forests were expected
to bring him 100 marks per annum.[100] Presumably in all his postings there
were opportunities for unofficial profiteering. Even in his first term as
lieutenant of Ireland there were complaints against his oppressive rule, and
after his death there were petitions alleging extortions by which 'his heirs
had been greatly enriched'.[101] Stanley was also the recipient of a great
deal of royal largesse. In 1389 he was granted the lordship of Blackcastle
in Ireland.[102] Even more remarkable in 1405 he was endowed with the
lordship of Man. Though he was required to surrender his annuity of 100
marks, this prestigious lordship, worth upwards of £400, represented a
major addition to the patrimony. As king of Man, he acquired a quasi-regal
title, and his son appeared with this status as an independent signatory in
treaties signed between England and France in 1414.[103]

In the investment of his riches Sir John Stanley showed the same
perspicacity and opportunism which characterised his political career.
Whether through gallantry, wealth or political influence, he acquired the
manors of Lathom and Knowsley by his marriage, and became at a stroke
the leading landowner in southwest Lancashire. During the 1390s he made
other important acquisitions on the local land market, including the manor
of Neston from the earl of Salisbury, the manor of Bidston from the
Stranges of Knockin and the barony of Weeton from the earl of Ormond.
At the same time there is evidence of his diversifying his fortunes through
the purchase of burgages in Liverpool and perhaps even some involvement
in commerce.[104] More important, he used his wealth and influence to
make provision for the next generation. His eldest son and heir, John, was
allied to Isabella Harrington, a daughter of the powerful north Lancashire
lineage, and was early attached to the household of the prince of Wales.
Another son, Thomas, was married to the heiress of the Ardernes of
Aldford, and was soon in control of her vast inheritance in Cheshire and
Staffordshire. A third son, Richard, a clerk, was provided with the

---

[99] *C.P.R. 1388–1392*, p. 101; *C.P.R. 1399–1401*, p. 261; *Ches. R.R.*, I, p. 445.
[100] *Ches. R.R.*, I, p. 446.
[101] Otway-Ruthwen, *Medieval Ireland*, p. 347. On the other hand the Lancastrian government
did not always fully reimburse him for his expenses in Ireland: *C.P.R. 1399–1401*, p. 523.
[102] *Calendar of Ormond Deeds*, no. 291.
[103] *Monumenta de Insula Manniae*, II, pp. 235–46; III, pp. 1–9.
[104] *C.P.R. 1399–1401*, p. 345; *Ches. R.R.*, I, p. 445; *C.Ch.R. 1341–1417*, p. 436; Lancashire
R.O., DDK/B/1542; *C.P.R. 1405–1408*, p. 329; P.R.O., CHES 25/11, m. 3d.

revenues of local churches to finance his studies at the university of Oxford, whence he returned to hold the locally powerful office of archdeacon of Chester.[105]

Despite this vast patrimony it must not be thought that the lineage's power in the region was solely a function of its landed wealth. Rather, it must be stressed that Sir John Stanley's ability to accumulate and to establish a secure title to his estates was in itself dependent on his political stature. A formidable warrior in his own right, he was quite prepared to use strong-arm tactics to advance his interests. Disregarding the protests of the duke of Lancaster and other interested parties, he took forcible possession of the Lathom inheritance in 1385. His military commands in Ireland and elsewhere drew into his service local soldiers of like temper. In 1394 he allegedly terrorised the city of Chester with 800 Lancashire men-at-arms and archers.[106] With his wealth and influence, he was well able to build up a party of local gentlemen who were willing to protect his interests and support his claims in the region. His kinsmen in Wirral, many of the lesser gentry of southwest Lancashire, several ambitious families from east Cheshire, all began to gravitate around the lord of Lathom. For his part, he was willing to maintain his supporters in their quarrels. Between 1407 and 1411 he backed John son of Peter Legh in his apparently dubious claims to the manor of Hale, while in 1412 he abetted Robert Fazacreley, another client, in his armed assault on the manor of Walton and disseisin of the occupant, John Walton.[107]

Inevitably Stanley's power was first constructed on a narrow factional base. As a prominent courtier and government official, Sir John Stanley was certainly in a strategic position to help his friends and confound his rivals. In the troubled politics of the age, however, he was also well placed to make his good offices indispensable to much larger sections of the local population. His role as broker between the government and the region is first apparent during the Cheshire rising of 1393, when he was dispatched from the king's side to bring his countrymen into line.[108] As controller of the wardrobe in the last years of Richard II's reign, he wielded considerable influence in the selection of local gentlemen and yeomen for the royal retinue. Significantly the few Lancashire men granted fees in the early days tended to be old cronies, like Sir Gilbert Halsall and Nicholas Orell.[109] In the critical weeks of August 1399 a great deal probably

---

[105] Roskell, *Lancashire Knights*, pp. 123–8; *Ches. R.R.*, II, pp. 668–9; *B.R.U.O.*, III, p. 1762.

[106] Burne, *Monks of Chester*, pp. 106–11.

[107] Lancashire R.O., DDIb, Hale Charter Roll; *V.C.H. Lancaster*, III, p. 25.

[108] Tuck, *Richard II and Nobility*, pp. 166–7.

[109] P.R.O., E 101/42/10. Halsall and Orell had served under Stanley in Ireland earlier in the decade: P.R.O., E 101/41/18.

depended on the actions of Sir John Stanley. His submission to Bolingbroke paved the way for other local families to come to terms with the new regime. His continued loyalty to the Lancastrian dynasty was of crucial importance in preventing a total conflagration in the region in 1403; in August he was appointed temporary governor of the palatinate of Chester, and was soon given full power to grant pardons in the prince's name to former rebels.[110] With stability returning to the realm, and with the stewardship of the king's household crowning his career in the royal service, Stanley was well able to indulge himself in a little *noblesse oblige*. He could even allow himself the luxury of a conscience. A short while before his death, he endowed masses for the souls of both Richard II and Henry IV.[111]

Entering into his inheritance in 1414, the new lord of Lathom was well suited to assume the mantle of 'good lordship'. A long apprenticeship under his father's guidance, and perhaps some formal training in law, nurtured in the second John Stanley a real flair for the exercise of power. His early attachment to the household of the prince of Wales brought him valuable connections, and from 1407 an annuity of £20. Perhaps on the strength of his relations with Henry V, he was elected as a knight of the shire for Lancashire in 1413 and again in 1414. The king certainly showed the young Stanley special favour. In 1414 he granted him the stewardship of Macclesfield and other local offices held by his father. In the following year Stanley led a company of men-at-arms and archers to France, and appears to have been knighted in the course of the Agincourt campaign.[112] Though he increasingly eschewed court life, he doubtless felt assured of the favour of the Lancastrian regime. With his interests in the capital under no apparent threat, he could concentrate his energies on his affairs in the Northwest.

While the first Stanley of Lathom had remained in a sense an intruder in local politics, his successor was born to a position of leadership in Cheshire and Lancashire society. As the most substantial lay landowner, Stanley could claim a natural precedence among the local gentry. Yet increasing effort was required to realise the full potentialities of his inheritance. After his return from the French wars, he applied himself singlemindedly and unflaggingly to the task of dynastic aggrandisement. From his mansions at Lathom and Liverpool, he brought the administration of his estates under tighter rein. He attempted to have his lordship at Lathom acknowledged as a barony, and pressed feudal rights over some

---

[110] *Ches. R.R.*, I, pp. 446, 502.
[111] Lancashire R.O., DDK/1/8.
[112] *Ches. R.R.*, I, p. 446; Roskell, *Lancashire Knights*, pp. 123–8; *Ches. R.R.*, II, p. 666.

local gentry. Elsewhere he similarly strove to make the most of his territorial endowment: the manor of Neston brought him within striking distance of the city of Chester; the manor of Bidston gradually led to a foreclosure on the barony of Dunham Massey; the barony of Weeton gave him a powerful presence north of the Ribble. At the same time, unlike his father, he took a direct interest in exercising the power inherent in local office. In Lancashire he served regularly as a justice of the peace and in various other commissions, and acquired additional power as steward of Blackburnshire.[113] In Cheshire, in addition to exercising in person the stewardship of Macclesfield, he served more or less continuously as a justice in the hundred.[114] His vigorous style is well exemplified by his role in the government of the Isle of Man. Unlike most other kings of Man, he visited the island regularly, presiding in regal splendour at meetings of the tynwald, organising the codification of Manx law, and on occasion suppressing rebellion.[115]

Needless to say, Stanley was able to build on the affinity of kinsmen, friends and clients assembled in his father's time. In southwest Lancashire, west Cheshire and Amounderness, many lesser landed families naturally gravitated around him. Nicholas Blundell of Crosby referred to Stanley as his 'sovereign master' in 1422,[116] and he was by no means the most slavish of the local gentlemen committing their fortunes to him at this stage. Further afield, the stewardships of Macclesfield and Blackburn provided important pockets of power and influence among the gentry of the eastern parts of the region, like the Savages, Leghs of Lyme and Radcliffes. Yet it must be stressed that Stanley had to devote considerable time to maintaining effective relations with his numerous allies and clients. The fragmentary evidence from private muniments and other sources reveal him continuously involving himself in the affairs of the local gentry, witnessing their property transactions, settling their disputes, serving them as a trustee, acting as a godfather of their children and so on.[117]

Stanley's emergence as the chief arbiter in the quarrels of the local gentry is particularly striking. Whereas prior to his time disputes tended to be referred to magnates of the realm or large panels of neighbours for adjudication, from the reign of Henry V onwards an increasing proportion of this work devolved on him. The Chester recognisance rolls attest his

---

[113] Somerville, *Duchy of Lancaster*, p. 500.

[114] *Ches. R.R.*, II, pp. 667 ff.

[115] *Legislation by Three of the Thirteen Stanleys, Kings of Man*, ed. W. MacKenzie (Manx Soc., III, 1860), esp. pp. 74–7, 82–98, 149–50.

[116] Lancashire R.O., DDM/48/18.

[117] E.g. he was godfather to John son of William Chauntrell, serjeant-at-law: Ormerod, *History of Cheshire*, II, p. 774.

almost continuous involvement in the settlement of feuds in all parts of
the shire. Soon after his first return from France in 1416 he arbitrated a
dispute between Sir John Savage and John Legh of Booths, and in the
following year acted as an umpire in at least four other Cheshire feuds.[118]
His award in the rather delicate proceedings between John Macclesfield,
the royal clerk, and John Kingsley, his concubine's brother, has survived
from this time: it ended on the strikingly modern note that Katherine
Kingsley should 'be free to governe hir as lagh, faith and conscience wold
withouten any interiptying of hom'.[119] In fact Stanley served as an arbiter
in seven of the sixteen arbitrations mentioned in the recognisance rolls
between 1416 and 1419, and acted as sole umpire in five of the seven
cases.[120] While reference to Lancashire arbitrations have to be culled
individually from local muniment collections, Stanley was clearly as active
north of the Mersey. On Good Friday, 1425, he made an award between
Sir John Ashton and Sir John Byron in their feud over Droylsden Moss.
Later in the 1420s he arbitrated in disputes between two mercantile
families from Liverpool, between the lord of Speke and his tenants, and
between Robert Fazacreley and John Walton.[121]

Manifestly Stanley was able to establish himself at the hub of regional
life, with men from both sides of the Mersey seeking his assistance in legal
matters. Presumably he acquired something of a reputation for making
expeditious and equitable settlements. His work in the Isle of Man and
his sensitive handling of the Kingsley case certainly suggest a real penchant
for jurisprudence. On the other hand, his popularity as an arbiter was also
a function of his political stature. Whatever the quality of his 'dooms',
he seems to have had the means to make his decisions authoritative and
binding. Like magnates in other parts of the realm, he was able to exert
considerable informal pressure on the administrative and legal system. He
could frame pleas and indictments to confound his rivals. His spurious
claim to the advowson of Kirkham in Amounderness was a cause of great
consternation to the abbot of Vale Royal in the reign of Henry V.[122]
He also maintained the quarrels of his clients, and even substantial
landowners, harassed by the litigation, had to surrender themselves to his
protection. Rather humiliatingly, Sir Lawrence Warren in 1422 felt
obliged to grant him the marriage of his heir and to enter a heavy bond

---

[118] *Ches. R.R.*, II, pp. 637, 447, 210, 431, 667, 760.
[119] Lancashire R.O., DDK/456/1.
[120] *Ches. R.R.*, II, pp. 210, 421, 447, 103, 667.
[121] Manchester Central Reference Library, Farrer MSS., 51/1/8; *Calendar of Ancient Deeds*,
IV, A10383; Bodleian Library, Oxford, MS. top. Cheshire B1, f. 240; *Norris Deeds*, nos.
63–5; 'The Chorley survey', ed. R. D. Radcliffe in *Lancashire and Cheshire Miscellanies*,
vol. III (L.C.R.S., 33, 1896), p. 36.  [122] *Vale Royal Ledger Book*, pp. 36–7.

not to make charges on his inheritance 'for to be mayntened and supported in the possession' of the barony of Stockport.[123] A few years later a hapless war veteran who had been ousted from his tenement in Bolton likewise had no doubt as to the real locus of power in the region. He petitioned the duke of Gloucester requesting him to send letters to Stanley, his son and the sheriff of Lancaster 'disirying hom to be favorable' to him 'with all hor power at comyn lawe or elles to ent the seide matter in a meene way so that [he] might have right in this partie for Goodes luf and in work of charities'.[124]

By the time of his death in 1437, the second Sir John Stanley had attained a position of undisputed leadership in the Northwest. He and his son naturally headed lists of local notables, as in 1434 when Lancashire knights and gentlemen had to take an oath to observe the laws against livery and maintenance.[125] Of course, his hegemony was far from total. Even in southwest Lancashire he could never wholly lord it over his neighbours. In 1425 Richard Molyneux of Sefton assembled hundreds of men in Liverpool in his feud with Stanley's heir.[126] Further afield, the lord of Lathom was even more dependent on the co-operation of such well-established lineages as the Harringtons, Radcliffes and Mascys, and such newly influential families as the Savages, Booths and Troutbecks. Yet it would be wrong to conclude that Stanley was no more than *primus inter pares*. His kingdom of Man and his vast territorial interests in the region placed him in a different league from other local knights. At the same time his standing in the realm at large set him apart from his colleagues in the region. Henry V sought his counsel and assistance; the duke of Gloucester was on good terms with him; the earl of Stafford feared to lose his friendship; Lord Talbot of Blackmere had a child raised in the Lathom household.[127] Long before the ennoblement of his successor in 1455, princes and noblemen were accepting him as their peer.

In the last analysis the house of Stanley owed its aggrandisement to the formidable combination of influence at court and power in the country. The twin pillars of Stanley rule were mutually supportive. Kings and magnates recognised that the lord of Lathom was the man who could deliver the goods in the Northwest and in their dealings with local men

---

[123] Bodleian Library, Oxford, MS. top. Cheshire B1, f. 199.

[124] Chetham Library, Manchester, Bailey Deeds, 32/18.

[125] *C.P.R. 1429–1436*, p. 379.

[126] R. Stewart-Brown, 'Two Liverpool medieval affrays', *L.C.H.S.*, 85 (1933), 85–7.

[127] K. H. Vickers, *Humphrey, Duke of Gloucester* (London, 1907), p. 437; Cambridge University Library, MS. Mm I/48, ff. 11–13; B. Ross, 'The accounts of the Talbot household at Blakemere in the county of Shropshire, 1394–1425', unpublished M.A. thesis, Australian National University, 1970, p. 49.

tended to work through him. In 1419 Henry V requested him and a number of other knights to raise a loan for the crown in Lancashire. Ten years later the royal council appointed him, along with the chamberlain of Chester and two exchequer officials, 'to treat with the people of Chester regarding a subsidy in aid of the war with France'. Similarly, the earl of Stafford was prepared to lean on the bishop of Lichfield to ensure that a valuable local benefice went to Stanley's candidate.[128] Conversely, Cheshire and Lancashire men naturally came to value his credit at court and in the capital, and looked to his 'good lordship' for the maintenance and advancement of their fortunes. With his informal influence at Westminster, he had the means to assist his friends and clients in the central law courts. As the trusted agent of the king and his councillors, he was doubtless able to moderate the demands made on the local communities. Above all, Stanley had the connections to ensure the flow of royal patronage to men of the region. Though he was no courtier himself, he experienced no difficulty in establishing young men of his acquaintance in the royal household. By the late 1420s Thomas Stanley was already far advanced on a distinguished career in the royal service which would emulate that of his grandfather. Appointed lieutenant of Ireland in 1430, he rose to become controller of the royal household in 1439. High in the favour of Henry VI and the curialist party, granted key offices in Cheshire, Lancashire and North Wales, and finally raised to the peerage in 1455, the third Stanley of Lathom was in a position to make his 'good lordship' indispensable to the ambitions of almost all local families.[129]

IV

The operations of royal patronage and the progress of careerism inevitably wrought major changes in Cheshire and Lancashire life. For the first time it brought large sections of regional society into the mainstream of national life. It allowed many local men to attain positions of wealth and power wholly unattainable in a provincial setting. At the same time it produced its own sort of dependancy. Increasingly, in order to maintain their fortunes through the vicissitudes of national politics, local families had to seek the favour of courtiers and government officials. It was on this sort

---

[128] *C.P.R. 1416–1422*, p. 252; *Ches. R.R.*, II, p. 670; Cambridge University Library, MS. Mm I/48, ff. 11–13. I owe this latter reference to Dr Paul Hosker.

[129] *C.P.R. 1429–1436*, p. 105; *C.P.R. 1436–1441*, p. 286. For Sir Thomas Stanley as the linchpin in 'an exclusive citadel of household power' in Cheshire, Lancashire and North Wales in the 1440s, see R. A. Griffiths, 'Patronage, politics and the principality of Wales, 1413–1461' in H. Hearder and H. R. Loyn (eds.), *British Government and Administration: Studies Presented to S. B. Chrimes* (Cardiff, 1974), esp. p. 86.

of need that the Stanleys capitalised so effectively, building on their role as brokers a remarkable regional hegemony. Yet, while the manner in which patronage and careerism effected local politics can be described with some assurance, their impact on provincial culture is difficult to ascertain. Obviously, such an assessment is fraught with problems. The study of culture in its social context is a methodological minefield, while the sources available for such an enquiry in the region are dauntingly meagre and present major difficulties of interpretation. Nevertheless it is possible to bring together important fragments of information which can be used to assess cultural developments, and in this section it is hoped to document both a material enrichment and a growing sophistication in local culture in the period around 1400. Furthermore, it is intended to claim that the character and timing of the finest cultural products not only accord well with the experience of local careerists, but also are incomprehensible in any other terms.

Buildings always appear the most unimpeachable witnesses to former glories. Unfortunately neither Cheshire nor Lancashire is at all well endowed with monuments from the middle ages. Chester and Lancaster can still boast castles, but their forms and functions have changed almost beyond recognition. Clitheroe, Halton and Beeston castles remain ghostly shells. Unlike other northern and marcher shires, no private castles survive to attest the pride and power of local magnates. Precious few of the numerous manor-houses which stud the landscape date back in their present form before the late fifteenth century. The region has little more to offer in terms of religious architecture. St Werburgh's abbey, Chester, has enjoyed a new lease of life as a cathedral; Furness, Whalley and Birkenhead survive in skeletal form; most other religious houses have left little more than occasional walls and buried foundations. While there are a few architectural gems, old parish churches are relatively thin on the ground, and their stature in no wise matches the vast size of their parishes. In truth, the most striking feature of the architectural heritage is its exiguous and modest nature. Of course, some allowances have to be made. More has been lost in the region than in many other parts of the country, and not solely through the ravages of industrialisation. Cheshire sandstone has weathered badly, and local timberwork, used so extensively in ecclesiastical as well as domestic buildings, has naturally proved even less durable. At the same time, no region was so completely transfigured in the 'great rebuilding' of Tudor and Stuart times. Obviously, documentary and archaeological evidence, where available, must be called into service to re-establish some of the old landmarks. While the relative architectural poverty of the region seems beyond contention, a consideration of the full range of sources might at least allow an evaluation of the period under discussion as an age of comparative vitality or stagnation.

Naturally enough, castles and monasteries rank as the most ambitious building-projects in the Northwest in the middle ages. For the most part the conception and construction of these imposing and expensive structures were the achievements of the economic expansion of the thirteenth century. Still, it must not be assumed that no work was done in the period around 1400. Chester castle underwent major improvements, a response in part to increased royal interest and in part to the renewed threat from Wales. Richard II visited the castle in 1386, 1398 and 1399, and ordered the building of a bath-house in the royal chambers.[130] Henry, prince of Wales, likewise spent a great deal of time there during the Glyndŵr rising. Lancaster castle appropriately found favour in the reign of Henry IV: its majestic gate-house has been dated to around 1400.[131] Despite mismanagement and internal dissension, St Werburgh's abbey continued to make additions to its fabric. During the 1390s the magnificent series of stalls with their exquisitely carved canopies and misericords were set in place in the choir. At the same time the abbot obtained permission to crenellate his manor-houses at Saighton, Sutton and Ince, the latter of which had a new banqueting hall and minstrels' gallery.[132] Planned as the largest Cistercian abbey in the realm and generously funded by the Black Prince in the 1360s, Vale Royal adapted itself to straitened circumstances in the late fourteenth century. With its magnificent *chevet* of thirteen chapels almost complete in 1360, a violent tempest destroyed the west end of the church, which was laboriously reconstructed, though on a smaller scale, during the period under discussion.[133] Unfortunately less is known about work on other religious houses at this time, though important archaeological work is in progress on Norton, where improvements to celebrate the promotion of the convent to the status of an abbey in 1391 might well be evidenced.[134] Yet, whatever conclusions are reached with regard to progress on these large-scale building projects in this period, their value as gauges of the prosperity and cultural vitality of the region is rather questionable. Local castles had largely outlived their original function, and survived for the most part as administrative centres,

[130] Davies, 'Richard II and principality of Chester', 272–3.

[131] N. Pevsner, *The Buildings of England. Lancashire*, part II. The Rural North (Harmondsworth, 1969), p. 17.

[132] Burne, *Monks of Chester*, pp. 105–6, 113–14.

[133] F. H. Thompson, 'Excavations at the Cistercian abbey of Vale Royal, Cheshire, 1958', *The Antiquaries Journal*, XLII (1962), 183–207.

[134] See J. P. Greene, 'The elevation of Norton Priory, Cheshire to the status of mitred abbey', *L.C.H.S.*, 128 (1978), esp. 108 ff.

stores and prisons, whose fate in any case depended on decisions taken at a national level. Similarly, the old monasticism was losing its appeal, and ceasing to attract the lavish royal and aristocratic patronage on which its ambitious building-programmes depended. With their incomes from land falling or stagnant, and with no opportunities to recoup their losses, local religious houses cannot be expected to furnish signs of affluence.

On the whole it seems more appropriate to focus attention on building-projects of a less grandiose nature. In so far as wealth was flowing into the region through careerism, it was lining the pockets of men whose aspirations did not run to the building of castles and the endowment of monasteries, but who did have the motivation and means to build themselves crenellated mansions and private chapels. Cheshire and Lancashire were already bejewelled with elegant mansions, many of them set apart in parkland. The testimonies recorded on behalf of Sir Robert Grosvenor in the heraldic dispute of 1386–7 include notices of many private houses and chapels in which his coat-of-arms was depicted, for example the *l'ostiel et chambres* of Sir Thomas Dutton at Dutton, the halls of William Praers and John Donne at Baddiley and Utkinton and the private chapels of the Vernons of Shipbrook and the Bolds of Bold.[135] Meanwhile the Lichfield registers reveal that local gentlefolk obtained the vast majority of licences for private oratories granted in the diocese in this period.[136] Unfortunately few of these buildings have survived to make any assessment of the wealth sunk into their construction, reconstruction or improvement in the decades around 1400. Doubtless most were timber-framed, the precursors of the celebrated piebald mansions of Tudor times. The more ambitious establishments, however, were in stone. In 1362 William Stanley drew up a contract with a mason to add five stone gables to Storeton hall for 10 marks, and his detailed specifications might perhaps be matched with archaeological remains on the site.[137] John Macclesfield constructed a palatial residence in Macclesfield, to which he was licensed to add battlements in 1398.[138] In the first decade of the fifteenth century, James Radcliffe and John Stanley likewise acquired licences to crenellate their mansions at Radcliffe and Liverpool, later known as Radcliffe tower and Liverpool tower.[139]

Parish churches also provide a useful barometer of changing fortunes in the Northwest, since it is possible to detect in their fabric phases of relative enrichment. It is significant that in his detailed studies of Cheshire

---

[135] Stewart-Brown, 'Scrope and Grosvenor controversy', 17–19.

[136] Lichfield R.O., B/A/1/6.     [137] B.L., Additional Charters, no. 66294.

[138] Cheshire R.O., DCH/R/4 (Unclassified).

[139] *C.P.R. 1401–1405*, p. 255; *V.C.H. Lancaster*, IV, p. 11.

churches F. H. Crossley was particularly impressed by the additions and improvements made in the reign of Richard II.[140] Several south Lancashire churches, like Warrington, Eccles and Ashton under Lyne, likewise survive to attest considerable material investment in the late fourteenth and early fifteenth centuries.[141] Interestingly enough, there is evidence to associate much of this work of rebuilding and beautification with the fruits of careerism. John Winwick, keeper of the privy seal, endowed a chantry in his native parish of Huyton; Sir William Butler established a family chapel in Warrington church; Sir Thomas Dutton instituted a chantry in the Austin friary at Warrington; Sir Hugh Calveley financed building work and the establishment of a college at Bunbury; John Kingsley founded a chantry at Nantwich; Thomas Langley, bishop of Durham, paid for the complete reconstruction of Middleton church; and William Troutbeck underwrote and had a hand in designing a new chapel in the church of St Mary on the Hill, Chester.[142] Others commemorated themselves and their families by having stone effigies, monumental brasses, and stained glass fitted in churches, or bequeathing vestments, books or sums of money to the fabric. Thus William Mainwaring had his memory perpetuated in an alabaster effigy in Acton church, while Thomas Holden bequested £10 for the purchase of glass and a bell for Whalley church.[143] Of course, not all the reconstruction and embellishment of local churches at this time is attributable to the vanity or philanthropy of particular individuals. The ambitious rebuilding of Nantwich church, with the installation of its finely carved stalls, is more probably a testimony of corporate pride.[144] Yet it can be no coincidence that the borough of Nantwich was also one of the fastest-developing urban centres in the region and the home town of a remarkable affinity of soldiers and administrators.

In a survey of the monuments to local careerism it is in any case inappropriate to adopt a rigidly regional perspective. To catalogue all their achievements, it would be necessary to embark on a far more protracted tour. Sir Robert Knolles, who left a mere pittance to his native parish of Malpas, helped to finance building-projects in Pontefract, Rochester,

[140] F. H. Crossley, 'On the importance of fourteenth-century planning in the construction of the churches of Cheshire', *J.C.A.S.*, 32 (1937), 5–52.

[141] *V.C.H. Lancaster*, III, pp. 308–9, IV, pp. 354, 347.

[142] Crooks, 'John de Winwick', 26–38; *V.C.H. Lancaster*, III, pp. 308–9; Cheshire R.O., DLT, Liber C, f. 167d; Bridge, 'Two Cheshire soldiers of fortune', 46–7; J. T. Driver, *Cheshire in the Later Middle Ages* (Chester, 1971), p. 136; *V.C.H. Lancaster*, V, p. 153; Ormerod, *History of Cheshire*, II, p. 41.

[143] Driver, *Cheshire in Later Middle Ages*, p. 76; *Register of Henry Chichele*, II, p. 580.

[144] Driver, *Cheshire in Later Middle Ages*, pp. 61, 69.

London and Rome which 'could have exhausted the treasuries, even of kings'.[145] Though Thomas Langley generously funded the rebuilding of Middleton church, he doubtless regarded his work on the Galilee chapel at Durham, or the St Cuthbert window at York, in which his service to four generations of Lancastrian kings and princes was commemorated, as his most precious monument.[146] Thomas Holden, his friend, bequeathed £10 to his native parish of Whalley, but left 155 marks towards the building of a chapel and library at St Mary's College, Oxford, £10 to the bridge of Catterick, £5 to glaze the windows of the cloister at Barking, and other sums to worthy projects in Durham, Yorkshire and Essex.[147] Indeed, in so far as successful careerists established themselves in other parts of the kingdom, their fortunes tended to contribute more to the architectural heritage of other counties than their own. Extant monumental brasses illustrate this point well. While no brasses survive in the Northwest from before 1450, more than a dozen brasses commemorating local men of this period can still be found in other regions. Thus Sir Hugh Holes, Matthew Ashton, Thomas Crewe, Matthew Swettenham and others are immortalised in parish churches as far afield as Watford in Hertfordshire, Shillington in Bedfordshire, Wixford in Warwickshire and Blakesley in Northamptonshire.[148] Meanwhile Robert Hallum, the humble don from Warrington, is commemorated in a splendid brass on the steps leading to the high altar in Constance cathedral.[149]

While buildings and their fixtures prove reasonably dogged and unequivocal witnesses to the achievements of earlier generations, most other forms of culture tend to be far more perishable, and rarely afford fixed points of reference. Since it was on cultural items like clothing, furnishings and ornamentation that ambitious individuals most typically spent their surplus wealth, their impermanence is to be particularly lamented. Obviously it is necessary to seek evidence from elsewhere. The statements by Froissart and other chroniclers regarding the enormous amount of rich apparel, jewellery and other luxury goods brought back as plunder from France, and the association in the writings of moralists and satirists between conspicuous consumption and social climbing, must be instructive in the study of a region so replete with soldiers and careerists. More specifically, the testimony of wills and inventories have considerable value. In 1415 Sir Thomas Dutton, a soldier in the French wars, in addition

---

[145] *St Albans Chronicle, 1406–1420*, p. 22.
[146] Storey, *Thomas Langley*, pp. 187, 220, 224–5.
[147] *Register of Henry Chichele*, II, pp. 579–84.
[148] R. le Strange, *A Complete Descriptive Guide to British Monumental Brasses* (London, 1972), pp. 65, 22, 129, 98.     [149] *B.R.U.O.*, II, p. 855.

to bequeathing his 'armoury' to his brother, left 'a bracelet of gold, adorned with pearls and other precious stones', a chain of gold and a gold ring set with a diamond to his parents.[150] John Macclesfield had his new mansion at Macclesfield well furbished with consumer durables. In 1416 he accused his mistress's brother of taking almost £200 worth of goods from the house, including several beds, large quantities of linen and household utensils, a 'tinder-box' and 'a vestment made of red satin of double Damasque with all the altar-apparel embroidered with harts and ostrich-feathers in Cyprus gold'.[151] Other successful careerists likewise surrounded themselves with treasured possessions. John Clitheroe had a robe lined with beaverskin, which he left to his brother, and a sapphire ring and a kerchief formerly belonging to Queen Joan, which he gave to his sister-in-law.[152] Robert Rainhill, the serious-minded vicar of Holy Cross, Canterbury, had a fine collection of books.[153] Thomas Holden owned at his death a crucifix enclosing a fragment of the true cross, a cup made wholly of gold and a gold brooch set with pearls, diamonds and a balas, but few of his precious possessions found a permanent home in his native parish of Whalley. Adorning his mansion at Clayhall in Essex during his life, the crucifix, cup and brooch were willed to no lesser figures than the archbishop of York, the bishop of Lincoln and the earl of Salisbury.[154]

At the same time local men almost certainly invested a great deal of wealth in cultural pursuits of an even more ephemeral nature. Feasting and hospitality, minstrels and merriment, hunting and other diversions, all were nourished on the proceeds of patronage and careerism. The increasing volume of wine imported through Chester, which rose dramatically in the 1390s and peaked in the early years of Henry V's reign, might well be indicative of an enrichment of these areas of cultural life.[155] Presumably the two county communities were maintained and invigorated by a convivial round of celebration and sport as well as by common chores and corporate obligations. The more ambitious knights and opulent careerists certainly attempted to affect aristocratic life-styles. Sir John Danyers called a tournament at Warrington; John Macclesfield feasted

---

[150] *Register of Henry Chichele*, II, pp. 88–9. For wills and inventories of other local soldiers see P.R.O., PROB 11/2A (Robert Winnington); Wigan R.O., Crosse Deeds, no. 132 (Matthew Kenyon); J.R.U.L., Jodrell Charters, no. 35 (Roger Jodrell).

[151] P.R.O., CHES 25/11, m. 12.

[152] *Register of Henry Chichele*, II, pp. 532–4.

[153] *Ibid.*, pp. lvi–lvii, 118–20.     [154] *Ibid.*, p. 581.

[155] Wilson, 'The port of Chester in later Middle Ages', pp. 114–16. There were, however, similar increases in other ports at this time: M. K. James, *Studies in the Medieval Wine Trade* (Oxford, 1971), pp. 30–4.

Richard II at his house in Macclesfield; the second Sir John Stanley owned manuscripts and employed minstrels at his mansion at Lathom. Further afield, Sir William Parr maintained a sizeable establishment at Kendal, and Thomas Langley lived in grand style in his town-house in London and his hunting-lodges in Durham.[156] Local soldiers-of-fortune who established themselves in lordships on the continent presumably committed themselves even more energetically to lives of conspicuous waste. Sir Robert Knolles was a generous warlord; Thomas Wettenhall entertained Sir Hugh Calveley and his retinue at his fortress in the Rouergue; Sir Richard Cradock kept distinguished company in Bordeaux; Sir John Radcliffe doubtless lived in some splendour as steward of Guyenne.[157]

At the same time increased wealth underwrote cultural activities of a more sober sort. Time and money were invested in religious observances, most of which have proved evanescent, at least in worldly terms. In their wills local men frequently authorised the spending of considerable sums on funeral expenses, while occasional references attest the popularity of pilgrimages. Adam Mottram left £2 for candles and torches to be placed around his corpse, and offered sums ranging from two shillings to three pence a head for each of various grades of clergymen attending his obsequies at Salisbury, while Richard Fitton made provision for someone to undertake a pilgrimage to St James at Compostella on his behalf.[158] Apparently first instituted in the late fourteenth century, the Chester cycle of mystery plays likewise attests to the enrichment of religious life in the region. If the new drama can be shown to owe debts to continental models or to the *via moderna* of scholastic theology,[159] this need occasion little surprise. Expatriate Cheshire men were involved in the shipment of a great gold shrine with a piece of the holy cross to Chester from Bordeaux some time before 1411,[160] while large numbers of local clerks studied at Oxford in this period. Indeed, as the lure of careerism became rooted in the region, and as its profits allowed modest capital accumulation, education became

---

[156] *B.P.R.*, III, p. 59; P.R.O., C1/69/281; Vickers, *Humphrey, Duke of Gloucester*, p. 437; Ross, 'Accounts of Talbot household', p. 49; *C.P.R. 1391–1396*, p. 711; Storey, *Thomas Langley*, pp. 93–5.

[157] Bridge, 'Two Cheshire soldiers of fortune', 68; Morgan, 'Cheshire and defence of Aquitaine', 154; Garton, *Nantwich*, p. 21; Vale, *Gascony*, p. 97. Radcliffe 'was welbelouet amonges the sawdiours' at Calais 'for he kept and helde a gud and open housold to who that wolde come, and welcome': *The Brut, or the Chronicle of England*, part II, ed. F. W. D. Brie (Early English Text Soc., original series 136, 1908), p. 573.

[158] *Register of Henry Chichele*, II, pp. 41–3; *Cheshire Sheaf*, third series, item 4275.

[159] E.g. see K. M. Ashley, 'Divine power in the Chester cycle and late medieval thought', *Journal of the History of Ideas*, 39 (1978), 387–405.

[160] J. Hemingway, *History of the City of Chester from its Foundation to the Present Time* (2 vols., Chester, 1831), I, pp. 138–9.

a major form of cultural investment. While little is known regarding the provision of elementary schooling in the region, it is clear that the dramatic upsurge in the number of local graduates in the last decades of the fourteenth century and the stature of local dons like Robert Hallum, Richard Ulverston and Andrew Holes must have owed a great deal to increased expenditure on education. Parents and patrons were willing to pay not only to have their sons and protégés equipped for advancement in the church. Large sums of money must also have been invested in providing young men with a training in arms, a legal education or the social graces necessary to make progress in aristocratic households or the royal court.

If the literature produced by local authors is any guide, there was a marked increase in literacy in the region in this period. Even though the odds were stacked heavily against the survival of verse in the remote dialect and archaic metre of the northwest Midlands, enough works have been preserved to document a veritable flowering of literary culture in Cheshire and south Lancashire, the heartland of the dialect area, in the late fourteenth century. Naturally enough, most interest has centred on *Sir Gawain and the Green Knight*, the masterpiece of alliterative revival. From its dialect, orthography and textual references, almost all authorities are convinced that it was composed by a local man and copied by a local scribe some time around 1400.[161] While the *Morte Arthure* appears to have been transmitted through other regional dialects, many other alliterative romances like *The Destruction of Troy*, *The Siege of Jerusalem*, *Sir Amadace* and *The Wars of Alexander* have been categorically assigned to the northwest Midlands.[162] The early satirical dialogues, *Wynnere and Wastoure* and *The Parlement of the Thre Ages*, likewise seem to have been produced by a man from Cheshire or its environs in the third quarter of the fourteenth century, while on religious themes the *Gawain*-poet or his colleague composed *Pearl*, *Purity* and *Patience* and other compatriots wrote the stanzaic *Life of Christ*, *The Three Dead Kings* and *St Erkenwald* in the decades around 1400.[163] Unfortunately, the authors of none of these

---

[161] A. C. Spearing, *The 'Gawain'-Poet. A Critical Study* (Cambridge, 1970), p. 2; A. McIntosh, 'A new approach to Middle English dialectology', *English Studies*, 44 (1953), 1–11.

[162] A. McIntosh, 'The textual transmission of the alliterative *Morte Arthure*' in N. Davis and C. L. Wrenn (eds.), *English and Medieval Studies presented to J. R. R. Tolkien* (London, 1962), pp. 231–40; J. B. Severs (ed.), *A Manual of the Writings in Middle English 1050–1500*, vol. I (New Haven, Connecticut, 1967), pp. 14, 169–70, 115–16, 160–2.

[163] A. E. Hartung (ed.), *A Manual of the Writings in Middle English 1000–1500*, vol. III (New Haven, Connecticut, 1972), p. 707; *Wynnere and Wastoure; The Parlement of the Thre Ages*, ed. M. Y. Offord (Early English Text Soc., original series 246, 1959); *Pearl*, ed. E. V. Gordon (Oxford, 1953); *Cleanness*, ed. J. J. Anderson (Manchester, 1977); *Patience*,

works can be identified. Richard Newton, who penned some doggerel lines in the 1390s and was the great-grandfather of a poet who has been hailed as an 'epigone' of the *Gawain*-poet, might well have been a member of their circle. The head of a freeholding family in the Macclesfield area, he seems to have served in the French wars and in Richard II's bodyguard.[164] At the same time, surprisingly little can be established firmly regarding the audience and readership of alliterative verse during the period under discussion. In view of the dialect and ethos of most of the work, and in view of the subsequent ownership of manuscripts by such families as the Booths of Dunham Massey, the Irelands of Hale and the Chethams of Nuthurst, it must be assumed that it had its greatest vogue among the local gentry and their dependants.[165] What is at least beyond dispute is that men from the region were maintaining a literary culture which in its vigour and artifice could rival Chaucer's London itself.

Of course, the development of a talented school of local poets in the late fourteenth century is in itself suggestive of a growing wealth and sophistication in regional life. More significant, the character of the literature itself bears eloquent testimony to the new prosperity and cultural influences engendered by careerism. Though their dialect and metre root them in the remote Northwest, and though the *Gawain*-poet brings his hero back to the 'wilderness of Wirral' and to the weird trysting-place on the eastern borders of Cheshire, none of the main works can be dismissed as provincial. Of course, many of the poems were reworkings of the Bible, Latin histories and French romances, and it is credible that their authors had access to such works in their own region. Local monasteries presumably had modest libraries: after all Ranulf Higden wrote his *Polychronicon* at St Werburgh's early in the fourteenth century, and his chronicle was continued at Whalley in Lancashire, while the stanzaic *Life of Christ* was very probably the product of a Franciscan friar based at Chester.[166] Yet, many of the major alliterative works incorporate

ed. J. J. Anderson (Manchester, 1969); *A Stanzaic Life of Christ*, ed. F. A. Foster (Early English Text Soc., original series 166, 1926), p. ix; A. McIntosh, 'Some notes on the text of the Middle English poem "*De Tribus Regibus Mortuis*"', *Review of English Studies*, new series 28 (1977), 385–6; *St Erkenwald*, pp. 8–12.

164 B.L., Additional MSS., no. 42134, f. 20; R. H. Robbins, 'The poems of Humphrey Newton, esquire, 1466–1536'. *Publications of the Modern Language Association of America*, 65 (1950), 294–81; Earwaker, *East Cheshire*, II, pp. 260–7; *B.P.R.*, III, p. 288; *Ches. R.R.*, I, p. 363.

165 See T. Turville-Petre, *The Alliterative Revival* (Cambridge, 1977), pp. 40–7, for a general discussion of readership. For identification of owners see *St Erkenwald*, p. 11; *Metrical Romances*; *The Gest Hystoriale of the Destruction of Troye*, ed. G. A. Panton and D. Donaldson (2 vols., Early English Text Soc., original series 39 and 56, 1869, 1874).

166 Taylor, *The 'Universal Chronicle' of Ranulf Higden*, pp. 1–2, 132–3; *A Stanzaic Life of Christ*, p. ix.

allusions, ideas and experiences which could only have been obtained further afield. The authors of the *Morte Arthure* and other alliterative romances show themselves to be well versed in chivalric lore, and seem to include eye-witness accounts of contemporary warfare. In addition to their delight in retailing the thrills of battles, the latest fashions in armour and military architecture, and the spoils of victory, several of the poems address themselves to the concerns of the more thoughtful soldiers by depicting the horrors and wastage of war.[167] Though their purposes are by no means clear, the authors of *Wynnere and Wastoure* and *The Parlement of the Thre Ages* likewise seem concerned to explore the threat posed to the traditional order by the greed, ambition and extravagance of soldiers and other careerists.[168] Well acquainted with topical issues and firmly eschewing a provincial perspective, the former was more likely a local man employed at Westminster than a country gentleman. Similarly, the author of *St Erkenwald*, whose Cheshire dialect and London interests appear superficially incongruous, would seem to have been a local careerist based in the capital. His affirmation of the redemptive powers of the church as against the limited value of human rationality reveal him as a man acquainted with contemporary theological issues and legal practice. It is appropriate that the sole surviving manuscript of *St Erkenwald* was owned by one of the Booths of Dunham Massey, the most remarkable dynasty of bishops and lawyers in fifteenth-century England.[169]

Above all, it is the work of the *Gawain*-poet, with its courtliness and effortless *savoir-faire*, with its total absorption of its French sources and its hints of Italian influences, which demand a far more courtly and cosmopolitan milieu than the Northwest alone provided.[170] Traditionally literary scholars have envisaged a major aristocratic court in the region, where this master of the alliterative school might have found his inspiration and patronage. Since few noblemen resided locally for any length of time, this scenario must be dismissed as implausible. At the same time, while it is likely enough that *Sir Gawain and the Green Knight* and *Pearl* assumed their final form in some local manor-house or monastery, there can be little doubt that the works were conceived, developed and probably first composed in a more metropolitan setting. Given the large numbers of local men in the royal service, the household of Richard II seems the most credible context. Sir Richard Cradock and Matthew

---

[167] Barnie, *War in Medieval English Society*, pp. 147–50.

[168] *Wynnere and Wastoure; The Parlement of the Thre Ages.* See discussion in T. H. Bestul. *Satire and Allegory in 'Wynnere and Wastoure'* (Lincoln, Nebraska, 1974).

[169] *St Erkenwald*, p. 11; Axon, 'Family of Bothe (Booth)', *passim*.

[170] In general see Spearing, '*Gawain*'-Poet, pp. 17–18, and Bennett, '*Sir Gawain and the Green Knight* and the literary achievement of the North-West Midlands'.

Swettenham were two Cheshire courtiers of some twenty years' standing. Cradock took charge of the book of verse presented to the king by Froissart, and might well have been a poet in his own right.[171] Swettenham held a corrody at Dieulacres abbey, on whose estates the 'Green Chapel' might well have been sited.[172] Sir John Stanley, Peter Legh of Lyme and John Macclesfield were also prominent in the royal service from the late 1380s. Stanley, a native of Wirral and Knight of the Garter, has special claims to be associated with *Sir Gawain and the Green Knight*, with its piquant allusion to Wirral and its possible status as a Garter poem.[173] Legh was a royal favourite, whose relationship with Richard II was the subject of some whimsical lines written in the vernacular by the Cheshire guardsmen.[174] Macclesfield, a royal clerk and controller of the wardrobe, owned manuscripts, and entertained the king in great style on one of his visits to Cheshire.[175] Finally, there were the hundreds of other Cheshire gentlemen and yeomen retained by the king in his final years. Among their number were Richard Newton, the amateur versifier of Prestbury parish, and at least seventeen members of the Mascy clan, a family sometimes linked with *Pearl* and *St Erkenwald*.[176]

If the household of Richard II is the most likely milieu for the work of the *Gawain*-poet, the late 1390s were certainly the most auspicious moment for the patronage of courtly poetry in the northwest Midlands dialect. Evidently the cultured and sensitive king found some at least of his Cheshire retainers congenial company. According to one chronicler, the latter addressed him familiarly as 'Dycun' and talked to him in their *materna lingua*, their regional dialect.[177] For the last two years of his reign the Cheshire men were continually at the king's side: overawing the proceedings of parliament at Westminster in September 1397 and at Shrewsbury in the following year; touring the 'principality' of Chester in the summer of 1398; celebrating Christmas with feasts and jousting at Lichfield; as fellow pilgrims to the shrine of St Thomas, and as guests of the archbishop of Canterbury early in 1399; as the guard of honour

[171] Froissart, *Chronicles*, II, p. 577.

[172] *C.C.R. 1381–1385*, p. 418. For the location of the 'Green Chapel' see R. W. V. Elliott, 'Staffordshire and Cheshire landscapes in *Sir Gawain and the Green Knight*', *North Staffordshire Journal of Field Studies*, 17 (1977), 20–49.

[173] See E. Wilson, '*Sir Gawain and the Green Knight* and the Stanley family of Stanley, Storeton and Hooton', *Review of English Studies*, new series 30 (1979), 308–16, for a review of possible connections with his lineage.

[174] B.L., Additional MSS., no. 35295, ff. 260r–v.

[175] Bruell, 'Edition of cartulary of John de Macclesfield', pp. 21–2; P.R.O., C1/69/281.

[176] Bennett, '*Sir Gawain and the Green Knight* and the literary achievement of the North-West Midlands', 67, 81.

[177] B.L., Additional MSS., no. 35295, f. 260r.

at the tournaments and feast for the Knights of the Garter at Windsor on St George's day; on campaign in Ireland in the early summer; and finally returning in haste to South Wales on hearing of the return of Bolingbroke.[178] At this point the Cheshire retinue was disbanded. While the seven 'masters of the watch' joined the king on his frantic dash across Wales to Conwy, the rest were left to follow the same tortuous track homewards to Cheshire. Significantly this is exactly the path envisioned by the *Gawain*-poet for his hero:

> Now rides this renk thurgh the ryalme of Logres,
>
> Til that he neghed ful negh into the North Wales,
> All the iles of Anglesay on lyft half he holdes,
> And fares over the fordes by the forlondes,
> Over at the Holy Hede, til he had eft bonk
> In the wyldrenesse of Wyrale[179] . . .

In July 1399 several hundred local courtiers, retainers and guardsmen made this itinerary in the most poignant circumstances. In all likelihood the *Gawain*-poet was one of their number, and on his return home sat down to re-work a poem first conceived, commissioned and composed at court. If this were the case, he wrote for a world which had been shattered, and the sudden collapse of the Ricardian regime perhaps accounts for this masterpiece's failure to make any impression on the literary consciousness of the time. Surviving by the fragile thread of a single manuscript, *Sir Gawain and the Green Knight* and *Pearl* remain to bear elegant testimony to the achievements of men from the Northwest in the decades around 1400.

[178] Tout, *Chapters*, IV, pp. 24, 29, 34–5, 53, 59–60.
[179] *Sir Gawain and the Green Knight*, lines 691 ff.

# Chapter 11

## CONCLUSION

Though aspiring to the universality of all great literature, *Sir Gawain and the Green Knight*, *Pearl* and other associated works eloquently attest the uniqueness of the Cheshire and Lancashire experience during the period under discussion. Their dialect, metrical form and range of allusion tie them firmly to a community of poets and patrons who hailed from the Northwest. In a similar fashion they are rooted in time. Few works and no texts can be dated before the last quarter of the fourteenth century, and both the form and content of the extant verse would argue for a 'golden age' roughly contemporaneous with the life of Chaucer. Obviously cultural movements cannot be rigidly compartmentalised. Despite the remarkable 'tightness' of their literary tradition, the *Gawain*-poet and his school cannot be seen in isolation from wider cultural influences, and their compositions can still be profitably read alongside their better-known contemporaries working in London and elsewhere. At the same time the alliterative style remained popular in the Northwest, despite the steady advance of Chaucerian models and metropolitan taste, throughout the fifteenth century and into Tudor times. Still, the literary evidence presents the social historian with the problems of national unity and regional variation, continuity and change in a peculiarly graphic form.

In this concluding chapter it is necessary to assess the 'typicality' of Cheshire and Lancashire society, and to offer some thoughts on points of comparison and contrast with patterns discernible elsewhere in late medieval England. Since there are few comparable studies of other localities, the conclusions will be necessarily tentative. Yet, in so far as a full understanding of late medieval society must await a conspectus of localised studies, such provisional statements are appropriate. In a similar fashion it is felt desirable to attempt a general description of the major structural changes taking place in the region in the late fourteenth and early fifteenth centuries. Again, it has been felt useful to proffer some thoughts, however provisional, on the main motors of development in the region in this period.

I

Of course, English society in the later middle ages cannot be divided into neat, well-defined provincial communities. While the better-connected and more mobile classes like the nobility, gentry, professional people and tradesmen often had loyalties and interests which can be regarded as 'national' in scope, their lesser countrymen operated within milieux far more narrowly delineated than even the smallest shire. Linguistic evidence is instructive in this regard. To a remarkable degree the literate sections of the population participated in a national written culture, whether Latin, French or the increasingly standardised English, while the vast majority of countryfolk maintained thousands of intensely localised dialects. The detailed study of Middle English dialects is proving most informative regarding the social geography of England in the early fifteenth century, but it reveals no iron curtains.[1] Still, it must not be concluded that regions have no more place in a study of English society than as convenient, but inherently arbitrary fields of investigation. Obviously the lines must always be tentative, and there will be overlapping spheres of influence, but a number of 'core' regions can perhaps be credibly established, which not only have an objective distinctiveness but also a subjective identity.

In all likelihood the degree to which English society can be dissected in this fashion is extremely variable. Manifestly, the extremities of the realm, such as Cornwall with its ethnic distinctiveness or the Scottish marches with their uncertain political loyalties, can be set apart with some degree of assurance. By contrast, it would be far more difficult to identify distinctive regions in the *champion* countryside of the Midlands and the Southeast. Doubtless the gravitational pull of court and capital served to break down provincial identities south and east of a line running between the Severn and the Wash, though it might still be possible to discern certain 'core' regions, like Norfolk with its imposing capital at Norwich, or some of the southern maritime counties. In between the heartlands and the peripheries of the kingdom, several other regions can certainly be distinguished, though with varying degrees of conviction. The West Country, the West Midlands, the North Midlands, Yorkshire, and the North, each have strong claims to be regarded as a separate region.[2] Yet the Northwest was perhaps exceptional in its physical integrity and isolation. Given the relative speed and directness of sea-communications, not even Northumberland and Cornwall were as remote from the centres

---

[1] E.g. see A. McIntosh, 'Word geography in the lexicography of medieval English', *Annals of the New York Academy of Sciences*, 211 (1973), 55–66.

[2] Note the discussion on regional boundaries in Hilton, *West Midlands*, pp. 7 ff.

of power and influence in the realm. While there was a significant amount of traffic and intercourse across the Dee into Wales, over the Pennines to Yorkshire, and over the much lower watershed into the Midlands, few English regions can have been less frequently visited in the later middle ages.

In addition to having a clear objective identity, apparent not only in its physical setting but also in many features of social life, the Northwest displayed a remarkable degree of provincial solidarity. The social links between the leading dynasties, professional groups and tradespeople across the Mersey boundary, the frequent association of the two counties in a wide range of contexts, and the pride apparent in many local poems and ballads, provide telling evidence in this regard. While more work is needed on the perception of regional identities in England, it is probable that men of the Northwest were more than averagely conscious of their own provenance. From being wholly marginal in the early fourteenth century, Cheshire and Lancashire were suddenly drawn into the mainstream of national life in the period under discussion. Even more important, through their connections with the royal household, through their success in arms and other forms of careerism, and through the adroit leadership of the house of Stanley, vague feelings of solidarity could be fanned into a rampant regional chauvinism.[3]

While regional identities are difficult to establish, county communities are readily identifiable in every shire in the realm. From Anglo-Saxon times the leading freeholders met regularly at the county court to hear royal proclamations, to act as jurymen and file suits, to conduct private business, and to assume corporate rights and responsibilities as communities of the shire. Perhaps it might be doubted that these county communities correspond to the politically sophisticated, socially cohesive gentry societies of later times, but the evidence from the Northwest seems instructive. In the decades around 1400 gentry families from all corners of Cheshire and Lancashire intermarried, reciprocated services as witnesses, trustees and arbiters, and shared administrative office. Despite the many divisions of interest among them, there can be no question of their sense of solidarity and their ability to act collectively on a wide variety of matters. Of course, being relatively remote, conservative communities set apart by their palatine privileges, neither can be regarded as wholly typical. There were many large, populous and disjointed counties, where the sense of community cannot have been so strong. Studies of the Leicestershire

---

[3] See the Cheshire and Lancashire ballads in *Bishop Percy's Folio Manuscript*, I, pp. 313–40, III, pp. 205–14, 233–59, 319–63. A similar regional chauvinism can perhaps be evidenced for the northern marcher communities from other ballads in this collection.

and Derbyshire gentry in the later middle ages have not found the degree of solidarity apparent in the Northwest,[4] though it should be noted that neither of the former counties has the range or richness of records which illuminate so well the social activities of the Cheshire and Lancashire gentry. At the same time, in other counties such as Warwickshire and Devon aristocratic leadership and clientage were more obviously important in galvanising and patterning shire life.[5] The rise of the Stanleys had similar consequences for the region under discussion from the reign of Henry VI onwards. Still, the demonstrable existence of well-developed county communities in the rather backward Northwest assuredly has significance in a wider understanding of English society, not only because it runs counter to the assumption that they were a post-medieval phenomenon, but also because it suggests that beneath the highly visible posturing and factionalism of noblemen and their retainers they continued to function and develop between the thirteenth and the sixteenth centuries.[6]

Turning to the lesser units of administrative geography, it is even more difficult to make general comparisons between the Northwest and the rest of the realm. On the whole it seems plausible to claim that the hundredal boundaries imposed a far clearer structure on local life than was perhaps typical elsewhere. In the palatinates of the Northwest the hundreds tended to assume some of the status and functions of counties elsewhere, and their jurisdictions less frequently suffered inroads from the immunities of wealthy urban centres and aristocratic and ecclesiastical franchise-holders. They were often well-defined and time-honoured territorial divisions, like Wirral and Blackburnshire, and more often than not congruent with the main units of ecclesiastical and feudal geography. In a countryside in which most landowners had very localised property-interests and few markets had more than narrowly circumscribed hinterlands, they seem to have been a primary focus of allegiance for the lesser gentry, yeomanry and

---

[4] G. G. Astill, 'The medieval gentry: A study in Leicestershire society, 1350–1399', unpublished Ph.D. thesis, University of Birmingham, 1977, ch. 3; S. M. Wright, 'A gentry society of the fifteenth century: Derbyshire, *c.* 1430–1509', unpublished Ph.D. thesis, University of Birmingham, 1978, esp. pp. 354–5. The author would like to express his gratitude to Dr Astill and Dr Wright for allowing him access to their theses prior to their publication.

[5] M. C. Carpenter, 'The Beauchamp affinity: A study of bastard feudalism at work', *E.H.R.*, xcv (1980), 514 ff; M. Cherry, 'The Courtenay earls of Devon: The formation and disintegration of a late medieval aristocratic affinity', *Southern History*, I (1979), esp. 76.

[6] Historians of Tudor and Stuart England still tend to regard the 'advent of the county community' as a post-medieval development: e.g. A. Everitt, 'Country, county and town: Patterns of regional evolution in England', *T.R.H.S.*, fifth series 29 (1979), 89.

other freeholders. With regard to the elemental communities of vill, manor and parish, social life was less firmly structured. Certainly all three institutions enforced collective obligations and nourished corporate identities. Still, the local population was rather more dispersed, single-township parishes were rarer, manorial discipline was on the whole lighter, and communal regulation of farming rather less important than elsewhere in *champion* England. Though there is no evidence to support the proposition, it might well be that at the lowest levels of society the bonds of kinship played a greater role in the region, compensating in some measure for the looser organisation of village life and the absence of tithing solidarities.

There would be general agreement that Cheshire and Lancashire ranked amongst the most sparsely settled counties in the realm. In national surveys, which can be relied on to provide an approximate guide to the distribution of population and wealth, Lancashire certainly tends to languish at the bottom of the table, marginally above only its bleak northern neighbours, Westmorland and Cumberland.[7] On the whole Cheshire, which was exempt from parliamentary taxation at this time, must have been more populous, and the assumption of comparable population densities on both sides of the Mersey can be shown to be false. J. C. Russell's figures for the population of England in 1377 must certainly be revised upwards to incorporate a more realistic estimate for Cheshire. At the same time a close scrutiny of the poll-tax returns for Lancashire casts grave doubts on his generally optimistic view of their comprehensiveness, suggesting an under-enumeration of at least twenty-five per cent. Presumably tax-evasion on this scale occurred in other parts of the realm as well, and there is some general corroboration for this conclusion from scholars working in other fields.[8] Of course, there is no good evidence in the Northwest on which to base analyses of the dynamics of population in the late medieval period. As in other parts of the realm, there are telling signs of a gradual redistribution of the population, with some deserted villages and some pockets of demographic expansion. Most important of all, there is evidence of substantial emigration from the region, and studies of the distribution of the population of pre-industrial England would do well to identify and assess the relative importance of such 'seed-plots'.

Cheshire and Lancashire exhibited a curiously compressed social

---

[7] Lancashire was the poorest of thirty-eight counties assessed in 1334 and 1515, when no figures for Cumberland and Westmorland were recorded. Per thousand acres, it raised only a tenth of the assessment of Holland in Lincolnshire. R. S. Schofield, 'The geographical distribution of wealth in England, 1334–1649', *Ec.H.R.*, second series XVIII (1965), esp. 504–6.

[8] Hatcher, *Plague, Population and English Economy*, pp. 13–14, 75–6.

structure. At its upper levels it had no resident peer or bishop, and only a handful of local abbots. Even including the holdings of the earl of Chester, the duke of Lancaster, the bishop of Lichfield and other absentee temporal and spiritual lords, the proportion of manors held by local knights, squires and gentlemen is seventy-six per cent. Though few other regional historians have indulged in the onerous and problematic task of 'counting manors', it seems that the Northwest was most peculiar in this regard. The preponderance of great ecclesiastical landlords in the Fenlands, Worcestershire and parts of Yorkshire can be readily noted. Even in Richmondshire, where there was an unusually large gentry community, the proportion of manors in their hands does not reach even fifty per cent.[9] In any case, this counting of manors under-estimates the proportion of land in local control. During the decades around 1400, there was a marked trend whereby royal, aristocratic and ecclesiastical holdings were leased or even sold outright to resident gentlemen. Doubtless this can be seen as part of the wider development whereby many absentee proprietors found it more attractive to cut their losses by endowing a local well-wisher than to attempt to extract a good return from an outlying manor. Interestingly enough it was on the basis of estates of this sort that the Stanleys built up their own territorial holdings in the later fifteenth century. Still, it must not be thought that the gentlemen of the region were at all affluent. The Lancashire gentry, in particular, had a reputation for the meagreness of their patrimonies, and certainly their average income from land was substantially smaller than the sorts of figures cited in studies of other regions.[10]

At the lower end of the social scale it is improbable that men on the land were quite so depressed as their fellows in other parts of the country. As regards status at least, few local peasants laboured under harsh seignorial regimes. Apart from Chester with its sizeable population of clergy and tradesmen, the relatively modest size of the market-towns and monasteries would not have served to encourage the development of large-scale demesne-cultivation with its associated social arrangements. At the same time the availability of land for assarting right up until the eve of the Black Death provided local peasants with a degree of bargaining-power lacking in more densely settled regions. Heavy labour-services had disappeared without trace by the period under discussion, and other servile dues are documented only spasmodically. While villeinage was in decay right across the realm in the late fourteenth century, the trend towards

---

[9] Pollard, 'Richmondshire community of gentry', 43–7.

[10] See the jibe that one Essex gentleman could buy up the whole of Lancashire in *Paston Letters and Papers of the Fifteenth Century*, ed. N. Davis (2 vols., Oxford, 1971, 1976), I, p. 654.

leasehold was unusually well advanced in the Northwest. Similarly, while the ratio of land to man was improving in all quarters, local farmers do seem to have been uncommonly successful in increasing the size of their tenancies. Judging from the fragmentary evidence of rent-rolls, the proportions of large and medium-sized holdings were greater than was typical in many other regions.[11] Of course, it is impossible to be certain about the fate of the poorer class of sub-lessors which this sort of evidence conceals, but it is perhaps significant that the Lancashire poll-tax returns do not reveal the large numbers of agricultural servants attested in the West Midlands.[12] On the other hand, there were certainly many substantial yeoman-farmers who could afford to distance themselves from manual work by sub-letting land and hiring labourers, to invest in education and other forms of advancement, and to edge their way into the gentry class.

In common with their fellows in other parts of the country, freeholders and even tenants in villeinage were able to diversify their incomes through handicrafts and trade. Admittedly the Northwest remained one of the least economically developed regions, and could boast only one major urban centre and no sizeable non-agrarian communities, such as miners, in the countryside. Judging from the poll-tax returns, the numbers of traders and craftsmen in both small towns and ordinary villages in the West Midlands were substantially greater than their counterparts in Cheshire and Lancashire.[13] Yet the picture cannot have been so bleak for local men seeking openings in manufacturing and commerce. There were a few small towns which seem to have grown in strength in the fifteenth century, and some significant clusterings of metalworkers and textile-workers which betoken the later industrialisation of the eastern parts of the region. At the same time there is clear evidence that tradespeople from these very areas were participating in nationwide commercial networks. From the late fourteenth century onwards a whole stream of local merchants and craftsmen seem to have settled in London. Although their contribution to the population of the metropolis was never as large as several other regions, men from the Northwest were disproportionately represented among both the entrants to two major guilds, and on the aldermanic council itself in the late fifteenth century.[14]

---

[11] Cf. Hilton, *English Peasantry in Later Middle Ages*, pp. 39–40; Harvey, *Westminster Abbey and its Estates*, pp. 288–90; Hatcher, *Rural Economy and Society in Cornwall*, p. 139; Dewindt, *Land and People in Holywell-cum-Needingworth*, pp. 112–13.

[12] Cf. Hilton, *English Peasantry in Later Middle Ages*, pp. 31 ff.

[13] *Ibid.*, pp. 79–81.

[14] On J. C. Russell's estimation, the population of Cheshire and Lancashire was less than 3% of England as a whole. Yet, natives of the region represented 9% of the apprentices admitted

# Conclusion

With regard to the church, there is the analogous pattern of a meagre Cheshire and Lancashire establishment alongside evidence of large-scale local participation in clerical careerism in the realm at large. Certainly few regions were so poorly endowed with illustrious monastic houses and minster churches, and nowhere were beneficed clergymen so thin on the ground. Yet it is unlikely that any county contributed proportionately more to the manning of the English church in the hundred years before the Reformation than Lancashire. Local traditions of clerical careerism seem to have first flowered in the 1330s, with the establishment of a number of Lancastrian clerks in the royal administration. Like the better known coterie of royal clerks from Humberside,[15] the Lancashire men in their turn trained and secured placements at Westminster for younger relatives and friends, and in this fashion opportunities were diffused through networks of kinship and local association. Although the Northwest was more poorly endowed with schools than most other regions,[16] young men seem to have had a reasonable degree of access to educational facilities elsewhere. Since many of them had younger kinsmen who achieved high academic honours, the clerks at Westminster must be presumed to have been great encouragers of local learning. On the whole this second generation of clerical careerists sought careers in the church, and there was a veritable invasion of the university of Oxford by clerks from the region in the last quarter of the fourteenth century. With the appointment of Langley and Hallum as bishops in the reign of Henry IV, the fortunes of their more able and ambitious compatriots were assured. Whatever is found to be the case with regard to the clerical population as a whole,[17] for graduates from the Northwest the period under discussion was less a 'crisis of patronage' and more an era of wholly unprecedented opportunity.

Of course, the Northwest was most famed for its soldiers. The scale of its contribution to the national war-effort has often been noted, and can only have been matched by the turbulent marcher communities of the North. The strong traditions of soldiering, coupled with the relative

in the skinners' and tailors' companies in the late fifteenth century, and 6% of the aldermen whose birthplaces were identified by S. L. Thrupp: Bennett, 'Social mobility', esp. 87; Thrupp, *Merchant Class*, appendices C and A.

[15] Grassi, 'Royal clerks from archdiocese of York', 12ff.

[16] Cf. the range and richness of educational endowments in York: J. H. Moran, *Education and Learning in the City of York, 1300–1560* (York, Borthwick Papers 55, 1979).

[17] Cf. G. F. Lytle, 'Patronage patterns and Oxford colleges c. 1300–c. 1530' in L. Stone (ed.), *The University in Society*, vol. I. Oxford and Cambridge from the Fourteenth to the Early Nineteenth Century (Oxford, 1975), pp. 111–49, but note the reservations in T. H. Aston, 'Oxford's medieval alumni', *Past and Present*, 74 (1977), 31–2.

poverty of its urban sector and its ecclesiastical establishment, doubtless distinguished the region from areas where civilian life was more deeply rooted. Predictably enough, the region seems to have been unusually prone to violence, and contemporaries certainly saw a correlation between martial traditions and lawlessness. Yet military experience could be put to more constructive ends. Unlike the fighting men of the North, whose energies were largely confined to border warfare, the chivalry and yeomen of the Northwest were given full rein in the more glorious and lucrative hunting-grounds of the Hundred Years War. While historians debate the impact of a few prodigiously profitable military careers on a national economy crippled by heavy taxation, there is the interesting prospect of a region which had more than its share of successful soldiers-of-fortune, but seems to have borne less than its share of the fiscal burden. Not surprisingly there is evidence of a strong commitment to the profession of arms in the region, but it must not be thought that the gentry and yeomanry were caught up in a circular process of living, but ultimately perishing by the sword. From the first a proportion at least of the capital amassed and the connections forged on campaign were deployed in safer strategies of social advancement, and though none of the crucial investments can be fully documented the rather sudden prominence in many trades and professions of men from the Northwest, many of whom were demonstrably the kinsmen of notable soldiers, must be instructive.

From the early fourteenth century the strong tenurial links between Cheshire and Lancashire and members of the royal family had begun to give distinctive shape to the political destiny of the two counties in the later middle ages. The burgeoning reputation of the Northwest as a recruiting-ground during the course of the Hundred Years War was not lost on the royal earls of Chester and dukes of Lancaster, who themselves had played a major role in fostering it. By the reign of Richard II the two royal palatinates had acquired considerable significance in national politics, most notably in the crises of 1386–7 and 1397–9. The Lancastrian kings likewise relied heavily on the military power of the region both to maintain their rule at home and extend it abroad. Naturally enough, Richard II and his successors were willing to nourish this relationship with generous patronage. There can have been few parts of the realm, even including London, that were so favourably treated at this time. In addition to a high proportion of royal revenues in the region being regularly assigned for the payment of local annuities, many other sources of profit were opened up to men from the Northwest. Successful soldiering led on naturally to governmental work, usually in militarily sensitive areas but occasionally at court. Judging from the regular appointment of the

Stanleys of Lathom as controllers of the household, successive regimes felt it desirable to have at hand Cheshire and Lancashire retainers who in times of need could draw in a larger number of their compatriots. Traditions of clerical careerism were also bringing into positions of prominence other local men, and at times the region was extremely well represented among the ruling élite. Increasingly, through the acquisition of experience and connections, and through further investment in education, local careers became less dependent on factional connection. Though perhaps no rival for East Anglia, Yorkshire or the West Country, the region made a far from negligible contribution to the legal profession in the fifteenth century. Still, for the majority of the local population access to royal patronage, all important in a region in which alternative sources of wealth and power were so weak, remained dependent on personal connection. Few other magnates had the opportunities for brokerage between crown and community that were afforded the house of Stanley in the Northwest, and certainly no other lineage was as successful in exploiting them.

In its geographical position, its class structure and its ties with its royal lords, the Northwest cannot be regarded as a 'typical' region. Still, it is inappropriate to dismiss its experiences as being wholly exceptional. After all, Cheshire and Lancashire had a great deal in common with other English counties, each of which in any case had their own claims to singularity. Indeed most of the distinguishing characteristics of the region have no greater status than as variations on national themes. In no field is this pattern of regional diversity and national unity more intricate than in the realm of culture. Obviously the men of the Northwest shared many of the fundamental assumptions and aspirations, for the most part Christian and chivalric, of their fellows in other parts of England. Visitors to the region, even if sensible of slight differences in architectural style, would have found nothing alien in the building of church towers, the endowment of chantries and the crenellation of mansions. *Literati* from London leafing through manuscripts of alliterative romances and saints' lives would have perhaps found the language rebarbative and the metre quaint, but in most cases they would have recognised the poets' themes and sources. On the other hand, even the most cursory survey of provincial culture would indicate that its distinctiveness was not merely idiosyncratic or superficial. Although there is far too little concrete evidence to be dogmatic, it is possible to infer distinctive patterns of investment, preoccupations and values to set alongside the distinctive experiences of those small sections of the local population involved in the production of 'high culture'.

On the whole cultural patronage in the Northwest was meagre and conservative as befitted a basically poor and remote part of the realm. Most striking is the absence of any major aristocratic court or ecclesiastical establishment to underwrite large-scale building-programmes or offer lavish patronage of the arts, but probably more significant, in view of the new cultural directions of the later middle ages, is the modest size of the urban sector and the extremely small number of educated clergymen and literate laymen actually resident in the region. Doubtless Cheshire and Lancashire gentlemen, like Sir Bertilak in *Sir Gawain and the Green Knight*, prided themselves on their hospitality and hunting, but there was precious little to appeal to more serious-minded visitors. Local men rarely aspired beyond vigorous vernacular redactions of Latin histories and French romances, while their religious tastes seem largely innocent of the new mystical and devotional interests so prevalent among the laity in eastern England, let alone Lollardy. While there is clear evidence of a relative enrichment and a growing sophistication of certain elements of provincial culture in the late fourteenth century, their dependence on the profits and experience of careerism is all too evident. The finest works of the alliterative revival, for example, were assuredly the achievement of soldiers and clerks who had sought their fortunes and found inspiration in more courtly and cosmopolitan milieux. Even in the least 'provincial' of the poems, however, there remains a distinctive ethos to set alongside the distinctive dialect and metre. Despite some underlying similarities in style and approach among the so-called 'Ricardian' poets,[18] the authors of *Sir Gawain and the Green Knight*, *Pearl* and *St Erkenwald* share neither the ironic detachment of Chaucer nor the emotional engagement of Langland. As the talented members of a first generation of provincials entering fully into their national inheritance, the masters of alliterative verse appear to have embraced more wholeheartedly and elaborated more fondly the time honoured values of the old order than the worldly-wise narrator of *The Canterbury Tales* or the zealous preacher of *Piers Ploughman*. By no means unaware and uncritical, the men from the Northwest seem to have continued to find social significance and spiritual comfort in the conventions of chivalry and the institutions of the established church.

II

Obviously Cheshire and Lancashire society underwent no radical transformation in the period under discussion, but alongside impressive signs of continuity must be set clear indicators of change. At one end of the social spectrum there can be no doubt that greater landlords lost ground

[18] J. A. Burrow, *Ricardian Poetry. Chaucer, Gower, Langland and the 'Gawain' Poet* (London, 1971).

in the Northwest, as elsewhere, in the late fourteenth century. The earls of Chester and the dukes of Lancaster relinquished control of many of their interests; other noblemen completely divested themselves of their holdings; and many ecclesiastical proprietors were in grave difficulties. At the opposite end of the tenurial hierarchy, the men working on the land assuredly inched their way towards better conditions. While levels of rent do appear to have remained stable in many places, it must be remembered that this was an era of generally higher wages and expanding opportunities in all fields of endeavour. In view of the rapid turnover in tenants on some manors, it can be assumed that reasonably priced customary holdings were becoming available to many husbandmen who had previously had to be content with expensive sub-tenancies. In their intermediary position, the gentry families of the Northwest seem also to have been able to gain, through the acquisition or leasing of royal and aristocratic estates and through participation in various forms of careerism, much of what they had lost to their own tenantry. In the meantime, all classes of Cheshire and Lancashire society, even the highest, were continually absorbing new blood. Of the thirty well-documented patrimonies which included the advowsons of churches, at least nine passed to other lineages between 1375 and 1425, far more than in any other similar period in the later middle ages.[19]

The character of Cheshire and Lancashire society changed in a number of less tangible ways. The men of the Northwest grew in political maturity. Out of the turbulent marcher communities whose feudings earlier lords of Chester and Lancaster had done more to inflame than tame, there began to emerge two county societies displaying a precocious sophistication in the management of their affairs and representation of their interests. Increasingly the region was being drawn into the mainstream of national life. In part through the policies of its royal lords and in part through its own traditions of careerism, these two palatinates assumed an importance in the kingdom out of all proportion to their size in the decades around 1400. In the realm of culture as well, this period takes on the lustre of a 'golden age' for the region. The achievement of the masters of the alliterative revival, with their skilful integration of provincial dialect, traditional metre, and courtly sensibility, is impressive in quantitative and qualitative terms. Unfortunately the world of the *Gawain*-poet was all too transient, and in the early fifteenth century a number of other developments tarnish the picture. The rise of the Stanleys was obviously not an unmixed

---

[19] The nine which changed hands were all in Cheshire, namely Davenham, Thornton, Wilmslow, Barrow, Aldford, Alderley, Pulford, Mobberley and Stockport: Ormerod, *History of Cheshire, passim.*

blessing: their power and influence inevitably served to undermine the vigorous independence of the county communities, and to restructure relations between the local gentry and the court and capital. The failure of the alliterative revival to sustain its vigour and refinement certainly attests an impoverishment of certain sections of provincial culture from the 1420s onwards.

It is far from easy to identify the motors of change in the Northwest in this period.[20] Demographic factors are perhaps of fundamental importance in accounting for the apparent dynamism of regional society during this time. At the beginning of the fourteenth century, when many other parts of the realm were already pressing at the margins of subsistence, the region was still very much a 'frontier' society: there was still new land to be brought under the plough, forests to be cleared, and possibilities of expansion into the Celtic fringe. In all likelihood local population was still on the increase at the time when the Black Death swept across the countryside. Thus, while mortality-rates were doubtless no less severe than elsewhere, it is a fair supposition that the region was better equipped demographically to recoup its losses in the following generations. In the period under discussion large numbers of Cheshire and Lancashire men certainly seem to have taken advantage of the many openings left in a realm so bereft of souls. Yet, if the Northwest was an important reservoir of man-power at this time, it was not a bottomless well. The wholesale diversion of talent and labour to soldiering and adventurism ultimately took its toll on the region. If the dynamism of local society in the late fourteenth century is attributable to its demographic vigour, the recurrence of plague in the early fifteenth century, coming on top of several generations of population loss through soldiering, celibacy and emigration, goes a long way towards explaining the diminishing vitality of the region in the later period.

Of course, demographic forces operated on and through the particular social formations of the Northwest. Moulded in an age of relatively low population densities, the structure of economic and social life in the region likewise contributed to its dynamism. Labour-intensive cereal production for the market was never the dominant mode in the vast majority of the local villages, and manorial regimes were far less well entrenched than in many other regions. With new land still to be cultivated, there were inevitably fewer constraints on peasant mobility. Even on the eve of the Black Death the maintenance of large-scale demesne-cultivation was

---

[20] In general, see the debate in *Past and Present* inaugurated by R. Brenner, 'Agrarian class structure and economic development in pre-industrial Europe', *Past and Present*, 70 (1976), 30–75.

hamstrung by the recalcitrance of the labour force, and such difficulties were compounded by the Black Death. Generally offering more advantageous terms to tenants, some Cheshire and Lancashire gentlemen were able to benefit from the retreat of royal and aristocratic influence in the region. Prolific and impoverished, most sought to compensate for the relative modesty of their patrimonies by careerism. Local traditions of primogeniture were apparently harsh, and younger sons were set adrift with little to make their own way in the world.[21] The knights and gentlemen of the Northwest certainly proved more enthusiastic men-at-arms than their better-heeled counterparts elsewhere, just as the yeomen and herdsmen of the Cheshire forests and Lancashire hills proved doughtier bowmen than the peasants of *champion* England. Well before the Black Death obligations for defence on the borders of the realm had blossomed into strong traditions of careerism in the region, and not merely in the field of soldiering. If the knights and bowmen of the Northwest played a major part in the victories of Crécy and Poitiers, it must not be forgotten that the minister who negotiated the treaty of Brétigny was John Winwick, whose achievements in the royal service were to inspire and materially support the ambitions of later generations of local clerks.

Yet the main changes in Cheshire and Lancashire society in this period cannot be explained solely in terms of indigenous factors. Demographic movements, economic conditions, class relations and even traditions of careerism, mean little in isolation, and have to be seen in terms of their relationship with a far wider society. If the Northwest was well placed to recoup some of its losses fairly rapidly after the Black Death, this recovery assumes importance only in terms of the demographic torpor setting in elsewhere in the kingdom. The economic marginality of the region and the restless ambition of its people again acquire consequence only in terms of the opportunities becoming available elsewhere. With governmental, military and ecclesiastical institutions largely intact, but with the national population severely depleted, with the royal earls of Chester and Lancaster providing impetus and direction to traditions of soldiering and careerism, local men were well placed to prosper. At the same time, with the reinvestment of the profits of war and the proceeds of office, and with the articulation of political connection, new generations of local men were able to set themselves up in trade, acquire an education at the universities and inns of court, and benefit from the growing demand for men with professional qualifications in church and state. The decades

---

[21] Note the comment by the earl of Clarendon in the seventeenth century on his Cheshire ancestry: E. Hyde, *The History of the Rebellion and Civil Wars in England, and His Life Written by Himself* (Oxford, 1843), p. 915.

around 1400, when the political fortunes of both county communities reached their zenith, marked the consolidation of regional interests in all the main trades and professions. Significantly it was around this time, when large numbers of local men were transposed into more courtly and cosmopolitan settings, that local literary traditions reached their consummate expression. Bridging both court and country, drawing its life from both metropolitan and provincial influences, the world of the *Gawain*-poet was inevitably fragile. With their concern to stabilise and maintain the fitful flow of royal patronage, the Cheshire and Lancashire gentry were willing to sacrifice direct relations with court and capital and to surrender their interests to the skilled brokerage of the Stanleys. With the passing of time, the feeling of distance and a growing sense of professionalism, expatriate careerists in their turn lost their regional identity. The later history of literary patronage seems symptomatic of the breaking apart of this vibrant world. While John Stanley of Battersea, the urbane usher of the household of Henry VI, commissioned a handsome manuscript full of the latest Chaucerian verse, and while the gifted sons of Hugh Bostock and Hugh Holes indulged themselves in Petrarchan elegancies, their country cousins reverted to the crude, regional chauvinism typical of the later works of the alliterative revival.[22]

---

[22] For the manuscript owned by John Stanley see *Bodleian Library, MS. Fairfax 16*, ed. J. Norton-Smith (London, 1979).

# BIBLIOGRAPHY

CLASSES OF DOCUMENTS USED

I. *Public Record Office*

*Palatinate of Chester*
CHES 2  Enrolments
CHES 3  Inquisitions Post Mortem
CHES 17 Eyre Rolls
CHES 19 Sheriffs' Tourn Rolls
CHES 24 Gaol Files, Writs etc.
CHES 25 Indictment Rolls
CHES 29 Plea Rolls
CHES 31 Fines and Recoveries

*Duchy of Lancaster*
DL 29   Ministers' Accounts
DL 30   Court Rolls
DL 42   Miscellaneous Books

*Palatinate of Lancaster*
PL 15   Plea Rolls

*Exchequer*
E 101   King's Remembrancer, Accounts Various
E 154   King's Remembrancer, Inventories of Goods and Chattels
E 163   King's Remembrancer, Exchequer Miscellanea
E 179   King's Remembrancer, Subsidy Rolls
E 359   Lord Treasurer's Remembrancer, Enrolled Accounts of Subsidies, Aids etc.

*Probate Records*
PROB 11 Prerogative Court of Canterbury Wills

*Special Collections*
SC 2    Court Rolls
SC 6    Ministers' and Receivers' Accounts
SC 11   Rentals and Surveys

# Bibliography

II. *Cheshire Record Office*
DAL    Aldersey of Aldersey Deeds
DAR    Arderne of Alvanley and Harden Deeds
DBA    Barnston of Churton Deeds
DCH    Cholmondeley of Cholmondeley Deeds
DCR    Crewe of Crewe Collection
DDA    Davenport of Bramhall Deeds
DLT    Leicester-Warren of Tabley Collection
DMW    Massey of Whitepool Deeds
DVE    Vernon Collection
DBW    Wilbraham of Nantwich Deeds
DDX    Miscellaneous Deposits

III. *Lancashire Record Office*
DDIn    Blundell of Ince Blundell Deeds
DDBl    Blundell of Little Crosby Deeds
DDCl    Clifton of Lytham Deeds
DDSh    Crosse of Shaw Hill Deeds
DDHo    De Hoghton of Hoghton Deeds
DDK    Derby Muniments
DDTr    De Trafford of Trafford Deeds
DDF    Farington of Worden Deeds
DDFi    Finch of Mawdesley Deeds
DDFo    Formby of Formby Deeds
DDHe    Hesketh of Rufford Deeds
DDHp    Hopwood of Hopwood Deeds
DDHu    Hulton of Hulton Deeds
DDLi    Lilford of Bank Hall Deeds
DDM    Molyneux of Sefton Deeds
DDPt    Petre of Dunkenhalgh Deeds
DDSc    Scarisbrick of Scarisbrick Deeds
DDCr    Stanley of Crosse Hall Deeds
DDTo    Towneley of Towneley Deeds

IV. *Bodleian Library, Oxford*
Miscellaneous Latin Manuscripts
Topographical Manuscripts

V. *British Library*
Additional Charters
Additional Manuscripts
Cotton Manuscripts
Harleian Manuscripts

VI. *Chester Record Office*
Earwaker Manuscripts

# Bibliography

Mayors Books
Pentice Rolls
Portmote Rolls

VII. *Chetham Library, Manchester*
Bailey Deeds
Raines Manuscripts
Tarbock Cartulary

VIII. *Derbyshire Record Office*
Vernon Deeds

IX. *Eaton Hall, Chester*
Eaton Charters

X. *John Rylands University Library, Manchester*
Arley Charters
Bromley–Davenport Muniments
Clowes Deeds
Cornwall–Legh Manuscripts
Haigh Muniments
Jodrell Charters
Langford-Brooke Muniments
Legh of Lyme Muniments
Mainwaring Manuscripts
Rylands Charters
Tatton Manuscripts

XI. *Keele University Library*
Legh of Booths Charters

XII. *Lichfield Joint Record Office*
Register of Bishop Stretton
Register of Bishop Scrope

XIII. *Liverpool Record Office*
Plumbe Tempest Deeds

XIV. *Manchester Cathedral*
Manchester Cathedral Records

XV. *Manchester Central Reference Library*
Farrer Manuscripts

XVI. *Manchester Town Hall*
Manchester Corporation Manuscripts

XVII.  *Shropshire Record Office*
Bridgewater Estates Records

XVIII.  *Staffordshire Record Office*
Stafford Manuscripts

XIX.  *Warrington Municipal Library*
Bold Deeds

XX.  *Westminster Abbey*
Westminster Abbey Manuscripts

XXI.  *Wigan Record Office*
Crosse Deeds
Standish Deeds


PRINTED PRIMARY SOURCES

I.  *Chronicles and Miscellaneous Texts*

'*Annales Ricardi Secundi et Henrici Quarti*' in *Chronica Monasterii Sancti Albani*, vol.
    3, ed. H. T. Riley (R.S., 1866), pp. 129–420
*Bishop Percy's Folio Manuscript, Ballads and Romances*, ed. J .W. Hales and F. J. Furnivall
    (3 vols., London, 1868)
*Bodleian Library, MS. Fairfax 16*, ed. J. Norton-Smith (London, 1979)
*The Brut, or the Chronicle of England*, part II, ed. F. W. D. Brie (Early English Text
    Soc., original series 136, 1908)
Camden, W., *Britannia*, ed. E. Gibson (London, 1695)
*Chronicon Adae Usk*, ed. E. M. Thompson (London, 1904)
*Chronicon Henrici Knighton*, ed. J. R. Lumby (2 vols., R.S., 1889, 1895)
*Cleanness*, ed. J. J. Anderson (Manchester, 1977)
'*De Altaribus, Monumentis, et Locis Sepulcrorum, in Ecclesia Monasterii Sancti Albani,
    Quaedam Annotationes*' in *Chronica Monasterii Sancti Albani*, vol. 5, ed. H. T. Riley
    (R.S., 1870), pp. 431–50
Drayton, M., *Polyolbion* (London, 1612)
*Facsimile of the Ancient Map of Great Britain in the Bodleian Library, Oxford. A.D. 1325–50*
    (Ordnance Survey, 1935)
Froissart, J., *Chronicles of England, France and Spain*, ed. T. Johnes (2 vols., London,
    1842)
*The Gest Hystoriale of the Destruction of Troye*, ed. G. A. Panton and D. Donaldson
    (2 vols., Early English Text Soc., original series 39 and 56, 1869, 1874)
Higden, R., *Polychronicon*, ed. C. Babington and J. R. Lumby (9 vols., R.S., 1865–86)
*Historia Vitae et Regni Ricardi Secundi*, ed. G. B. Stow (Philadelphia, 1977)
Holinshed, R., *Chronicles*, ed. H. Ellis (6 vols., London, 1807–8)
Hyde, E., Earl of Clarendon, *The History of the Rebellion and Civil War in England,
    and His Life Written by Himself* (Oxford, 1843)
King, D., *The Vale Royal of England, or the County Palatine of Chester* (London, 1656)
*Mum and the Sothsegger*, ed. M. Day and R. Steele (Early English Text Soc., original
    series 199, 1936)

# Bibliography

*Palatine Anthology. A Collection of Ancient Poems and Ballads relating to Lancashire and Cheshire*, ed. J. O. Halliwell (London, 1850)

*The Parlement of the Thre Ages*, ed. M. Y. Offord (Early English Text Soc., original series 246, 1959)

*Paston Letters and Papers of the Fifteenth Century*, ed. N. Davis (2 vols., Oxford, 1971, 1976)

*Patience*, ed. J. J. Anderson (Manchester, 1969)

*Pearl*, ed. E. V. Gordon (Oxford, 1953)

*The Poems of John Audelay*, ed. E. K. Whiting (Early English Text Soc., 184, 1931)

*The St Albans Chronicle, 1406–1420*, ed. V. H. Galbraith (Oxford, 1937)

*St Erkenwald*, ed. R. Morse (Cambridge, 1975)

*Sir Gawain and the Green Knight*, ed. J. R. R. Tolkien and E. V. Gordon, 2nd edn (Oxford, 1967)

*Six Town Chronicles of England*, ed. R. Flenley (Oxford, 1911)

*A Stanzaic Life of Christ*, ed. F. A. Foster (Early English Text Soc., 166, 1926)

*Three Early English Metrical Romances*, ed. J. Robson (Camden Soc., first series 18, 1842)

*Wynnere and Wastoure*, ed. I. Gollancz (London, 1920)


## II. Published and Calendared Documents

*Actes de la Chancellerie d'Henri VI concernant La Normandie sous la Domination Anglaise*, ed. P. le Cacheux (2 vols., Rouen, 1907–8)

*Anglo-Norman Letters and Petitions*, ed. M. D. Legge (Anglo-Norman Text Soc., III, 1941)

'The Book of the Abbot of Combermere, 1289–1529', ed. J. Hall in *Lancashire and Cheshire Miscellanies*, vol. II (L.C.R.S., 31, 1896)

'Calendar of the Chancery Rolls of the County Palatine of Lancaster', part I in *32nd D.K.R.* (H.M.S.O., 1871 for 1870), appendix 1.4, pp. 331–65, part II in *33rd D.K.R.* (H.M.S.O., 1872 for 1871), appendix 1.1, pp. 1–42

*Calendar of Charter Rolls* (6 vols., H.M.S.O., 1903–27)

*Calendar of Close Rolls*, Edward III to Henry VI (33 vols., H.M.S.O., 1896–1947)

*Calendar of Crosse Deeds and Documents*, ed. R. D. Radcliffe (privately printed, 1895)

'Calendar of Deeds, Inquisitions and Writs of Dowe, enrolled on the Plea Rolls of the Palatinate of Chester', part I in *28th D.K.R.* (H.M.S.O., 1867 for 1866), part II in *29th D.K.R.* (H.M.S.O., 1868 for 1867)

*Calendar of Fine Rolls* (H.M.S.O., in progress)

'Calendar of French Rolls', part I in *44th D.K.R.* (H.M.S.O., 1883 for 1882), appendix 3, pp. 543–638, part II in *48th D.K.R.* (H.M.S.O., 1887 for 1886), appendix 2, pp. 217–450

*Calendar of the Gormanston Register*, ed. J. Mills and M. J. McEnery (Royal Soc. of Antiquaries of Ireland, 1916)

*Calendar of Inquisitions Miscellaneous* (H.M.S.O., in progress)

*Calendar of Inquisitions Post Mortem* (H.M.S.O., in progress)

*Calendar of Letters from the Mayor and Corporation of the City of London*, ed. R. R. Sharpe (London, 1885)

'Calendar of Norman Rolls', part I in *41st D.K.R.* (H.M.S.O., 1880 for 1879), appendix 1.2, pp. 671–810, part II in *42nd D.K.R.* (H.M.S.O., 1881 for 1880), appendix 3, pp. 313–472

*Calendar of Ormond Deeds*, part II. 1350–1413, ed. E. Curtis (Irish Manuscripts Commission, 1934)

*Calendar of Papal Registers. Papal Letters* (H.M.S.O., in progress)

*Calendar of Papal Registers. Petitions*, vol. I. 1342–1419 (H.M.S.O., 1896)

*Calendar of Patent Rolls*, Edward III to Henry VI (34 vols., H.M.S.O., 1891–1910)

*Calendar of Plea and Memoranda Rolls of the City of London, 1361–1381*, ed. A. H. Thomas (Cambridge, 1929)

'Calendar of Privy Seals and Warrants of the Palatinate of Lancaster' in *43rd D.K.R.* (H.M.S.O., 1882 for 1881), appendix 1.3, pp. 363–70

'Calendar of Recognizance Rolls of the Palatinate of Chester', part I in *36th D.K.R.* (H.M.S.O., 1875 for 1874), appendix 2, separate pagination, part II in *37th D.K.R.* (H.M.S.O., 1876 for 1875)

*Calendar of Signet Letters of Henry IV and Henry V (1399–1422)*, ed. J. L. Kirby (H.M.S.O., 1978)

*Calendar of Standish Deeds*, ed. T. C. Porteus (Wigan, 1933)

*The Cartulary of Burscough Priory*, ed. A. N. Webb (C.S., third series, 18, 1970)

*Catalogue of Ancient Deeds* (H.M.S.O., in progress)

*The Chartulary of Cockersand Abbey*, ed. W. Farrer (7 vols., C.S., new series 38, 39, 40, 43, 56, 57, 64, 1898–1909)

*The Chartulary of St Werburgh's Abbey, Chester*, ed. J. Tait (2 vols., C.S., new series 79, 82, 1920, 1923)

*Cheshire Chamberlains' Accounts, 1301–1360*, ed. R. Stewart-Brown (L.C.R.S., 59, 1910)

*Cheshire and Lancashire Wills*, ed. W. F. Irvine (L.C.R.S., 30, 1896)

*The Cheshire Sheaf* (Chester, in progress)

*Chester Customs Accounts, 1301–1566*, ed. K. P. Wilson (L.C.R.S., 111, 1969)

*Chester Freeman Rolls*, part I, ed. J. H. E. Bennett (L.C.R.S., 51, 1906)

'The Chetwynd Chartulary', ed. G. Wrottesley in *Collections for a History of Staffordshire*, vol. XII (William Salt Archaeological Soc., 1891)

'The Chorley Survey', ed. R. D. Radcliffe in *Lancashire and Cheshire Miscellanies*, vol. III (L.C.R.S., 33, 1896)

*The Coucher Book of Furness Abbey*, part I, ed. J. C. Atkinson (2 vols., C.S., new series 9, 11, 1886–7)

*The Coucher Book of Furness Abbey*, part II, ed. J. Brownbill (3 vols., C.S., new series 74, 76, 78, 1915–19)

*The Coucher Book or Chartulary of Whalley Abbey*, ed. W. A. Hulton (4 vols., C.S., old series 10, 11, 16, 20, 1847–9)

*The Court Rolls of the Honour of Clitheroe*, ed. W. Farrer (3 vols., Manchester, 1897, and Edinburgh, 1912–13)

*De Hoghton Deeds and Papers*, ed. J. H. Lumby (L.C.R.S., 88, 1936)

*The Diplomatic Correspondence of Richard II*, ed. E. Perroy (Camden Soc., third series 48, 1933)

*Documents relating to Penwortham Priory*, ed. W. A. Hulton (C.S., old series 30, 1853)

*The Early Yorkshire Woollen Trade*, ed. J. Lister (Yorkshire Archaeological Soc., record series 64, 1924)

# Bibliography

*English Historical Documents*, vol. IV. 1327–1485, ed. A. R. Myers (London, 1969)

'The Exchequer Lay Subsidy Roll, 1332', ed. J. P. Rylands in *Lancashire and Cheshire Miscellanies*, vol. II (L.C.R.S., 31, 1896), separate pagination

*Expeditions to Prussia and the Holy Land made by Henry, Earl of Derby, 1390–1 and 1392–3*, ed. L. T. Smith (Camden Soc., second series 52, 1894)

*Feudal Aids* (6 vols., London, 1899–1920)

'Homage Roll of the Manor of Warrington', ed. W. Beamont in *Lancashire and Cheshire Miscellanies*, vol. I (L.C.R.S., 12, 1885)

*Issues of the Exchequer. Henry III to Henry VI*, ed. F. Devon (London, 1837)

*John of Gaunt's Register, 1371–1375*, ed. S. Armitage-Smith (2 vols., Camden Soc., third series 20 and 21, 1911)

*John of Gaunt's Register, 1379–1383*, ed. E. C. Lodge and R. Somerville (2 vols., Camden Soc., third series 56 and 57, 1937)

*Lancashire Final Concords*, part III. 1377–1509, ed. W. Farrer (L.C.R.S., 50, 1905)

*Lancashire Inquests, Extents and Feudal Aids*, part III. 1313–1355, ed. W. Farrer (L.C.R.S., 70, 1915)

*Lancashire Inquisitions Post Mortem*, ed. W. Langton (2 vols., C.S., old series 95, 99, 1875–6)

*Lancashire Palatine Plea Rolls*, ed. J. Parker (C.S., new series 87, 1928)

*The Ledger Book of Vale Royal Abbey*, ed. J. Brownbill (L.C.R.S., 68, 1914)

*Legislation by Three of the Thirteen Stanleys, Kings of Man*, ed. W. MacKenzie (Manx Soc., III, 1860)

*A Middlewich Chartulary*, part I, ed. J. Varley (C.S., new series 105, 1941)

*A Middlewich Chartulary*, part II, ed. J. Varley and J. Tait (C.S., new series 108, 1944)

*Monumenta de Insula Manniae*, ed. J. R. Oliver (3 vols., Manx Soc., IV, VII and IX, 1860–2)

*Moore MSS.*, ed. J. Brownbill (L.C.R.S., 67, 1913)

*Norris Deeds*, ed. J. H. Lumby (L.C.R.S., 93, 1939)

*Original Letters Illustrative of English History*, second series, ed. H. Ellis (2 vols., 1827)

*Preston Guild Rolls, 1397–1682*, ed. W. A. Abram (L.C.R.S., 9, 1884)

*Proceedings before the Justices of the Peace in the Fourteenth and Fifteenth Centuries*, ed. B. H. Putnam (London, 1938)

*Register of Edward the Black Prince* (4 vols., H.M.S.O., 1930–3)

*The Register of Henry Chichele, Archbishop of Canterbury, 1414–1443*, ed. E. F. Jacob (4 vols., Canterbury and York Soc., 1937–47)

'The Register of Robert Stretton, Bishop of Lichfield', ed. R. A. Wilson, part I in *Collections for a History of Staffordshire*, new series vol. VIII, part II in *Collections for a History of Staffordshire*, new series vol. X (William Salt Archaeological Society, 1905, 1907)

*The Register of Simon de Langham, Archbishop of Canterbury, 1366–1368*, ed. A. C. Wood (Canterbury and York Soc., 1956)

*The Register of Thomas Langley, Bishop of Durham, 1406–1437*, ed. R. L. Storey (6 vols., Surtees Soc., 164, 166, 169, 170, 177, 182, 1956–70)

*The Register of the Trinity Guild, Coventry*, ed. M. D. Harris (Dugdale Soc., XIII, 1935)

*Reports of the Deputy Keeper of Public Records* (H.M.S.O., in progress)

*Reports of the Royal Commission on Historical Manuscripts* (H.M.S.O., in progress)

*Rotuli Parliamentorum*, ed. J. Strachey (6 vols., London, 1783–1832)

# Bibliography

*Rotulorum Patentium et Clausorum Cancellariae Hiberniae Calendarium* (Irish Record Commission, 1828)

*Royal Historical Letters during the Reign of Henry the Fourth*, ed. F. C. Hingeston (2 vols., R.S., 1860, 1865)

*Select Cases in the Court of King's Bench*, vol. VII, ed. G. O. Sayles (Selden Soc., 1971)

*The Shropshire Peace Roll, 1400–1414*, ed. E. G. Kimball (Shrewsbury, 1959)

*Talbot Deeds, 1200–1682*, ed. E. Barker (L.C.R.S., 103, 1953)

*Testamenta Eboracensia. A Selection of Wills from the Registry of York*, vol. II, ed. J. Raine (Surtees Soc., 30, 1855)

*Two FitzAlan Surveys*, ed. M. Clough (Sussex Record Soc., 67, 1969)

'Unpublished Documents in the Manx Museum', *Journal of the Manx Museum*, 5 (1941)

*The Visitation of the County of Dorset*, ed. J. P. Rylands (Harleian Soc. Visitations, 20, 1885)

*The Visitation of the County of Gloucester*, ed. J. Maclean and W. C. Heane (Harleian Soc. Visitations, 21, 1885)

*The Visitations of the County of Nottingham*, ed. G. W. Marshall (Harleian Soc. Visitations, 4, 1871)

*The Visitations of the County of Oxford*, ed. W. H. Turner (Harleian Soc. Visitations, 5, 1871)

*The Visitation of the County of Warwick*, ed. J. Fetherston (Harleian Soc. Visitations, 12, 1877)

### SECONDARY WORKS

Allmand, C. T., 'The Lancastrian land settlement in Normandy, 1417–50', *Ec.H.R.*, second series XXI (1968), 461–79

    *Society at War. The Experience of England and France during the Hundred Years War* (Edinburgh, 1973)

Armitage-Smith, S., *John of Gaunt* (London, 1904)

Ashley, K. M., 'Divine power in the Chester cycle and late medieval thought', *Journal of the History of Ideas*, 39 (1978), 387–405

Astill, G. G., 'The medieval gentry: A study in Leicestershire society 1350–1399', unpublished Ph.D. thesis, University of Birmingham, 1977

Aston, T. H., 'Oxford's medieval alumni', *Past and Present*, 74 (1977), 3–40

Ault, W. O., *Private Jurisdiction in England* (New Haven, Conn., 1923)

    *Open-Field Farming in Medieval England. A Study of British By-Laws* (London, 1972)

Axon, E., 'The family of Bothe (Booth) and the Church in the fifteenth and sixteenth centuries', *L.C.A.S.*, 53 (1938), 32–82

Baker, A. R. H. and Butlin, R. A. (eds.), *Studies of Field Systems in the British Isles* (Cambridge, 1973)

Baker, D. (ed.), *Sanctity and Secularity. The Church and the World* (Studies in Church History 10, 1973)

Barber, M., 'John Norbury (*c.* 1350–1414). An esquire of Henry IV', *E.H.R.*, LXVIII (1953), 66–76

Barnie, J., *War in Medieval English Society. Social Values in the Hundred Years War* (Ithaca, N.Y., 1974)

# Bibliography

Barraclough, G., 'The earldom and county palatine of Chester', *L.C.H.S.*, 103 (1952 for 1951), 23–57

Barron, C. M., 'The tyranny of Richard II', *B.I.H.R.*, 41 (1968), 1–18

Bateson, M., 'The creation of boroughs: Charters of Deganwy, Dunster, Higham Ferrers, Bolton, Warton and Roby', *E.H.R.*, XVII (1902), 284–96

Beamont, W., 'History of Warrington Friary' in *Chetham Miscellanies*, old series vol. IV (C.S., old series 83, 1872)

    *Annals of Warrington* (2 vols., C.S., old series 86, 87, 1872–3)

    *History of the Castle of Halton and the Abbey of Norton* (Warrington, 1873)

    *An Account of the Rolls of the Honour of Halton* (Warrington, 1879)

Bean, J. M. W., 'Plague, population and economic decline in England in the later Middle Ages', *Ec.H.R.*, second series XV (1963), 423–37

    *The Decline of English Feudalism, 1215–1540* (Manchester, 1968)

Bellamy, J. G., 'The northern rebellions in the later years of Richard II', *B.J.R.L.*, 47 (1965), 254–74

Bennett, J. H. E., 'The grey friars of Chester', *J.C.A.S.*, 24 (1921), 5–85

    'The white friars of Chester', *J.C.A.S.*, 31 (1935), 5–54

    'The black friars of Chester', *J.C.A.S.*, 39 (1952), 29–58

Bennett, J. W., 'Andrew Holes. A neglected harbinger of the English Renaissance', *Speculum*, XIX (1944), 314–35

Bennett, M. J., 'A county community: Social cohesion amongst the Cheshire gentry, 1400–1425', *Northern History*, 8 (1973), 24–44

    'The Lancashire and Cheshire clergy, 1379', *L.C.H.S.*, 124 (1973), 1–30

    'Sources and problems in the study of social mobility: Cheshire in the later Middle Ages', *L.C.H.S.*, 128 (1979 for 1978), 59–95

    '*Sir Gawain and the Green Knight* and the literary achievement of the North-West Midlands: The historical background', *Journal of Medieval History*, 5 (1979), 63–88

    'Spiritual kinship and the baptismal name in traditional European society' in L. O. Frappell (ed.), *Principalities, Powers and Estates. Studies in Medieval and Early Modern Government and Society* (Adelaide, 1979), 1–13

    '"Good Lords" and "King-Makers": The Stanleys of Lathom in English politics, 1385–1485', *History Today*, 31 (1981), 12–17

Bestul, T. H., *Satire and Allegory in 'Wynnere and Wastoure'* (Lincoln, Nebraska, 1974)

Booth, P. H. W., 'Taxation and public order: Cheshire in 1353', *Northern History*, 12 (1976), 16–31

    '"Farming for profit" in the fourteenth century: The Cheshire estates of the earldom of Chester', *J.C.A.S.*, 62 (1980 for 1979), 73–90

    *The Financial Administration of the Lordship and County of Chester, 1272–1377* (C.S., forthcoming)

Booth, P. H. W. and Dodd, J. P., 'The manor and fields of Frodsham, 1315–74', *L.C.H.S.*, 128 (1979 for 1978), 27–57

Bossy, J., 'Blood and baptism: Kinship, community and Christianity in western Europe from the fourteenth to the seventeenth centuries' in D. Baker (ed.), *Sanctity and Secularity. The Church and the World* (Studies in Church History 10, 1973), pp. 129–43 du Boulay, F. R. H., *The Lordship of Canterbury. An Essay on Medieval Society* (London, 1966)

*An Age of Ambition. English Society in the Late Middle Ages* (London, 1970)

du Boulay, F. R. H. and Barron, C. M. (eds.), *The Reign of Richard II. Essays in Honour of May McKisack* (London, 1971)

Bowman, W. M., *England in Ashton under Lyne* (Altrincham, 1960)

Breese, E., *Kalendars of Gwynedd* (London, 1873)

Brenner, R., 'Agrarian class structure and economic development in pre-industrial Europe', *Past and Present*, 70 (1976), 30–75

Bridbury, A. R., *Economic Growth: England in the Later Middle Ages* (London, 1962)

Bridge, J. C., 'Two Cheshire soldiers of fortune: Sir Hugh Calveley and Sir Robert Knolles', *J.C.A.S.*, 14 (1908), 112–231

Bridgeman, G. T. O., *The History of the Church and Manor of Wigan* (4 vols., C.S., new series 15, 16, 17, 18, 1888–90)

Brown, A. L., 'The reign of Henry IV. The establishment of the Lancastrian regime' in S. B. Chrimes, C. D. Ross and R. A. Griffiths (eds.), *Fifteenth-Century England. Studies in Politics and Society* (Manchester, 1972), pp. 1–28

Brownbill, J., 'The Troutbeck family', *J.C.A.S.*, 28, part 2 (1929), 149–57

Bruell, J. L. C., 'An edition of the cartulary of John de Macclesfield', unpublished M.A. thesis, University of London, 1969

Burne, R. V. H., *The Monks of Chester* (London, 1962)

Burrow, J. A., *Ricardian Poetry. Chaucer, Gower, Langland and the 'Gawain' Poet* (London, 1971)

Butcher, A. F., 'The origins of Romney freemen, 1433–1523', *Ec.H.R.*, second series XXVII (1974), 16–27

Cam, H. M., *Liberties and Communities in Medieval England* (Cambridge, 1944)

Carpenter, M. C., 'The Beauchamp affinity: A study of bastard feudalism at work', *E.H.R.*, XCV (1980), 514–32

Chambers, E. K., *English Literature at the Close of the Middle Ages* (Oxford, 1945)

Cherry, M., 'The Courtenay earls of Devon: The formation and disintegration of a late medieval aristocratic affinity', *Southern History*, 1 (1979), 79–97

Chrimes, S. B., Ross, C. D. and Griffiths, R. A. (eds.), *Fifteenth-Century England. Studies in Politics and Society* (Manchester, 1972)

Clarke, M. V., *Fourteenth-Century Studies* (Oxford, 1937)

Clarke, M. V. and Galbraith, V. H., 'The deposition of Richard II', *B.J.R.L.*, 14 (1930), 125–81

Clemensha, H. W., *A History of Preston in Amounderness* (Manchester, 1912)

Copinger, W. A., *History and Records of the Smith-Carrington Family* (London, 1907)

Cornwall, J., 'The early Tudor gentry', *Ec.H.R.*, second series XVII (1964–5), 456–71

Crooks, F., 'John de Winwick and his chantry in Huyton Church', *L.C̄.H̄.S̄.*, 77 (1926 for 1925), 26–38

Crossley, F. H., 'On the importance of fourteenth-century planning in the construction of the churches of Cheshire', *J.C.A.S.*, 32 (1937), 5–52

Croston, J., *County Families of Lancashire and Cheshire* (London, 1887)

Crump, W. B., 'Saltways from the Cheshire Wiches', *L.C.A.S.*, 54 (1940), 84–142

Curry, A. E., 'Cheshire and the royal demesne, 1399–1422', *L.C.H.S.*, 128 (1979 for 1978), 113–38

Curtis, E., *Richard II in Ireland* (Oxford, 1927)

Darby, H. C. (ed.), *An Historical Geography of England before A.D. 1800* (Cambridge, 1936)

*The Medieval Fenland* (Cambridge, 1940)

Darby, H. C. and Maxwell, I. S. (eds.) *The Domesday Geography of Northern England* (Cambridge, 1962)

Davies, C. S. (ed.), *A History of Macclesfield* (Manchester, 1961)

Davies, R. R., 'Richard II and the principality of Chester, 1397–9' in F. R. H. du Boulay and C. M. Barron (eds.), *The Reign of Richard II. Essays in Honour of May McKisack* (London, 1971), pp. 256–79

'Colonial Wales', *Past and Present*, 65 (1974), 6–23

Davis, N. and Wrenn, C. L. (eds.), *English and Medieval Studies presented to J. R. R. Tolkien* (London, 1962)

Dewindt, E. B., *Land and People in Holywell-cum-Needingworth. Structures of Tenure and Patterns of Social Organisation in an East Midlands Village 1272–1457* (Toronto, 1972)

Dickins, B., 'Premonstratensian itineraries from a Titchfield Abbey MS. at Welbeck', *Proceedings of the Leeds Philosophical and Literary Society. Literary and Historical Section*, 4 (1936), 349–61

Dobson, R. B., *The Peasants' Revolt of 1381* (London, 1970)

*Durham Priory, 1400–1450* (Cambridge, 1973)

'The residentiary canons of York in the fifteenth century', *Journal of Ecclesiastical History*, 30 (1979), 145–73

Dodgson, J. McN., 'The English arrival in Cheshire', *L.C.H.S.*, 119 (1968 for 1967), 1–37

'Place-names and street-names at Chester', *J.C.A.S.*, 55 (1968), 29–61

*The Place-Names of Cheshire* (4 vols., English Place-Name Soc., 1970–2)

Douglas, D. C., *The Social Structure of Medieval East Anglia* (Oxford Studies in Social and Legal History IX, 1927)

Driver, J. T., *Cheshire in the Later Middle Ages* (Chester, 1971)

Earwaker, J. P., *East Cheshire* (2 vols., London, 1877, 1880)

(ed.), *Local Gleanings relating to Lancashire and Cheshire*, vol. I (Manchester, 1880)

Edwards, J. G., Galbraith, V. H. and Jacob, E. F. (eds.), *Historical Essays in Honour of James Tait* (Manchester, 1933)

Ekwall, E., *The Place-Names of Lancashire* (C.S., new series 81, 1922)

Elliott, G., 'Field systems of Northwest England' in A. R. H. Baker and R. A. Butlin (eds.), *Studies of Field Systems in the British Isles* (Cambridge, 1973)

Elliott, R. W. V., 'Staffordshire and Cheshire landscapes in *Sir Gawain and the Green Knight*', *North Staffordshire Journal of Field Studies*, 17 (1979 for 1977), 20–49

Emden, A. B., *A Biographical Register of the University of Oxford to A.D. 1500* (3 vols., Oxford, 1957–9)

*A Biographical Register of the University of Cambridge to 1500* (Cambridge, 1963)

Everitt, A., 'The county community' in E. W. Ives (ed.), *The English Revolution 1600–1660* (London, 1968), pp. 48–63

'Country, county and town: Patterns of regional evolution in England', *T.R.H.S.*, fifth series 29 (1979), 79–108

Finberg, H. P. R., *Tavistock Abbey. A Study in the Social and Economic History of Devon* (Cambridge, 1951)

# Bibliography

Fishwick, H., *The History of the Parish of Rochdale* (Rochdale, 1889)

Fletcher, W. G. D., 'The poll-tax for the town and liberties of Shrewsbury, 1380', *Transactions of the Shropshire Archaeological and Natural History Society*, second series II (1890), 17–28

Foss, E., *The Judges of England* (9 vols., London, 1848–64)

Fowler, K., *The King's Lieutenant. Henry of Grosmont, First Duke of Lancaster, 1310–1361* (London, 1969)

France, R. S., 'A history of plague in Lancashire', *L.C.H.S.*, 90 (1939 for 1938), 1–175

Frappell, L. O. (ed.), *Principalities, Powers and Estates. Studies in Medieval and Early Modern Government and Society* (Adelaide, 1979)

Freeman, T. W., Rodgers, H. B. and Kinvig, R. H., *Lancashire, Cheshire and the Isle of Man* (London, 1966)

Garton, E., *Nantwich, Saxon to Puritan* (Nantwich, 1972)

Gillespie, J. L., 'Richard II's Cheshire archers', *L.C.H.S.*, 125 (1975), 1–39

Goodman, A., *The Loyal Conspiracy. The Lords Appellant under Richard II* (London, 1971)

Grassi, J. L., 'Royal clerks from the archdiocese of York in the fourteenth century', *Northern History*, 5 (1970), 12–33

Gray, H. L., 'Incomes from land in England in 1436', *E.H.R.*, XLIX (1934), 607–39

Greene, J. P., 'The elevation of Norton Priory, Cheshire to the status of mitred abbey', *L.C.H.S.*, 128 (1979 for 1978), 97–112

Griffiths, R. A., *The Principality of Wales in the Later Middle Ages. The Structure and Personnel of Government. I. South Wales, 1277–1536* (Cardiff, 1972)

'Patronage, politics and the principality of Wales, 1413–61' in H. Hearder and H. R. Loyn (eds.), *British Government and Administration: Studies Presented to S. B. Chrimes* (Cardiff, 1974), pp. 68–86

(ed.), *Boroughs of Mediaeval Wales* (Cardiff, 1978)

'Public and private bureaucracies in England and Wales in the fifteenth century', *T.R.H.S.*, fifth series 30 (1980), 109–30

Hall, J., *A History of the Town and Parish of Nantwich* (Nantwich, 1883)

Hampson, C. P., *The Book of the Radclyffes* (Edinburgh, 1940)

Harding, A., *A Social History of English Law* (Harmondsworth, 1966)

Harland, J., *Manchester Collectanea*, vol. II (C.S., old series 72, 1867)

Hartung, A. E. (ed.), *A Manual of the Writings in Middle English, 1000–1500*, vol. III (New Haven, Conn., 1972)

Harvey, B., *Westminster Abbey and its Estates in the Middle Ages* (Oxford, 1977)

Harvey, J. H., 'Richard II and York' in F. R. H. du Boulay and C. M. Barron (eds.), *The Reign of Richard II. Essays in Honour of May McKisack* (London, 1971), pp. 202–17

Hatcher, J., *Rural Economy and Society in the Duchy of Cornwall 1300–1500* (Cambridge, 1970)

*Plague, Population and the English Economy 1348–1530* (London, 1977)

Hearder, H. and Loyn, H. R. (eds.), *British Government and Administration: Studies Presented to S. B. Chrimes* (Cardiff, 1974)

Heath, P., *The English Parish Clergy on the Eve of the Reformation* (London, 1969)

'The medieval archdeaconry and the Tudor bishopric of Chester', *Journal of Ecclesiastical History*, 20 (1969), 243–52

# Bibliography

Heginbotham, H., *Stockport Ancient and Modern* (2 vols., London, 1882, 1892)

Hemingway, J., *History of the City of Chester from its Foundation to the Present Time* (2 vols., Chester, 1831)

Hewitt, H. J., *Medieval Cheshire. An Economic and Social History* (C.S., new series 88, 1929)

    *The Black Prince's Expedition of 1355–1357* (Manchester, 1958)

    *The Organization of War under Edward III, 1338–1362* (Manchester, 1966)

    *Cheshire under the Three Edwards* (Chester, 1967)

Hilton, R. H., *The Economic Development of Some Leicestershire Estates* (Oxford, 1947)

    'Peasant movements in England before 1381', *Ec.H.R.*, second series II (1949), 117–36

    *A Medieval Society. The West Midlands at the End of the Thirteenth Century* (London, 1966)

    *The Decline of Serfdom in Medieval England* (Economic History Society: Studies in Economic History, London, 1969)

    *Bond Men Made Free. Medieval Peasant Movements and the English Rising of 1381* (London, 1973)

    *The English Peasantry in the Later Middle Ages* (Oxford, 1975)

Hodge, C. E., 'The Abbey of St Albans under John of Wheathamstede', unpublished Ph.D. thesis, University of Manchester, 1933

Hodgkiss, F. D., 'Robert Hallum', unpublished M.A. thesis, University of Manchester, 1931

Hollaender, A. E. J. and Kellaway, W. (eds.), *Studies in London History presented to Philip Edmund Jones* (London, 1969)

Holland, B., *The Lancashire Hollands* (London, 1917)

Holmes, G. A., *The Estates of the Higher Nobility in Fourteenth Century England* (Cambridge, 1957)

Homans, G. C., *English Villagers of the Thirteenth Century* (Cambridge, Mass., 1941)

Hoskins, W. G., *The Midland Peasant. The Economic and Social History of a Leicestershire Village* (London, 1957)

Husain, B. M. C., 'Delamere Forest in later medieval times', *L.C.H.S.*, 107 (1956 for 1955), 23–39

Imray, J. M., '"*Les Bones Gentes de la Mercerye de Londres*". A study of the membership of the medieval mercers' company' in A. E. J. Hollaender and W. Kellaway (eds.), *Studies in London History presented to Philip Edmund Jones* (London, 1969), pp. 153–78

Irvine, W. F., 'The early Stanleys', *L.C.H.S.*, 105 (1954 for 1953), 45–68

Ives, E. W., 'The reputation of the common lawyers in English society, 1450–1550', *University of Birmingham Historical Journal*, VII (1959–60), 130–61

    'The common lawyers in pre-Reformation England', *T.R.H.S.*, fifth series 18 (1968), 145–73

    *The English Revolution, 1600–1660* (London, 1968)

James, M. K., *Studies in the Medieval Wine Trade* (Oxford, 1971)

Jewell, H. M., *English Local Administration in the Middle Ages* (Newton Abbot, 1972)

Jolliffe, J. E. A., 'Northumbrian institutions', *E.H.R.*, XLI (1926), 1–42

    *Pre-Feudal England. The Jutes* (Oxford, 1933)

Jones, D., *The Church in Chester 1300–1540* (C.S., third series 7, 1957)

# Bibliography

Jones, M., *Ducal Brittany, 1364–1399* (Oxford, 1970)

Jones, R. H., *The Royal Policy of Richard II* (Oxford, 1968)

Jones-Pierce, T., 'Some tendencies in the agricultural history of Caernarvonshire in the later Middle Ages', *Transactions of the Caernarvonshire Historical Society*, I (1939), 18–36

Kingsford, C. L., *The Grey Friars of London* (British Soc. of Franciscan Studies VI, 1915)

Kirby, J. L., *Henry IV of England* (London, 1970)

Kirby, T. F., *Winchester Scholars* (London, 1888)

Kosminsky, E. A., *Studies in the Agrarian History of England in the Thirteenth Century* (Oxford, 1956)

Krause, J., 'The medieval household: Large or small?', *Ec.H.R.*, second series IX (1956–7), 420–32

Kristensson, G., *A Survey of Middle English Dialects 1290–1350. The Six Northern Counties and Lincolnshire* (Lund, 1967)

Laslett, P., *The World We Have Lost* (London, 1965)

Leach, A. F., *A History of Winchester College* (London, 1899)

Le Neve, J., *Fasti Ecclesiae Anglicanae*, vol. III. Salisbury Diocese, ed. J. M. Horn (London, 1962)

*Fasti Ecclesiae Anglicanae*, vol. XI. The Welsh Dioceses, ed. B. Jones (London, 1962)

Le Strange, R., *A Complete Descriptive Guide to British Monumental Brasses* (London, 1972)

Lewis, N. B., 'The last medieval summons of the English feudal levy, 13 June 1385', *E.H.R.*, LXIII (1958), 1–26

'Indentures of retinue with John of Gaunt, Duke of Lancaster, enrolled in chancery, 1367–1399' in *Camden Miscellany*, vol. XXII (Camden Soc., fourth series 1, 1964), 77–112

Little, A. G., 'The Black Death in Lancashire', *E.H.R.*, V (1890), 524–30

Longford, W. W., 'Some notes on the family of Osbaldeston', *L.C.H.S.*, 87 (1936 for 1935), 59–85

Lunn, J., *History of the Tyldesleys of Lancashire* (Altrincham, 1966)

Lydon, J. F., 'Richard II's expeditions to Ireland', *Journal of the Royal Society of Antiquaries of Ireland*, XCIII (1963), 135–49

Lytle, G. F., 'Patronage patterns and Oxford Colleges c. 1300–c. 1530' in L. Stone (ed.), *The University in Society*, vol. I. Oxford and Cambridge from the Fourteenth to the Early Nineteenth Century (Oxford, 1975), pp. 111–49

Maddicott, J. R., 'The county community and the making of public opinion in fourteenth-century England', *T.R.H.S.*, fifth series 28 (1978), 27–43

Maitland, F. W., *Domesday Book and Beyond* (Cambridge, 1897)

Mathew, G., *The Court of Richard II* (London, 1968)

Miller, E., *The Abbey and Bishopric of Ely. The Social History of an Ecclesiastical Estate from the Tenth to the Early Fourteenth Century* (Cambridge, 1951)

Moran, J. H., *Education and Learning in the City of York, 1300–1560* (York, Borthwick Papers 55, 1979)

Morgan, P. J., 'Cheshire and the defence of the principality of Aquitaine', *L.C.H.S.*, 128 (1979 for 1978), 139–60

Morris, J. E., *The Welsh Wars of Edward I* (Oxford, 1901)

# Bibliography

Morris, R. H., *Chester in the Plantagenet and Tudor Reigns* (Chester, 1894)

Myers, A. R., 'An official progress through Lancashire and Cheshire in 1476', *L.C.H.S.*, 115 (1964 for 1963), 1–29

Myres, J. N. L., 'The campaign of Radcot Bridge in December 1387', *E.H.R.*, XLII (1927), 20–33

McFarlane, K. B., 'England and the Hundred Years War', *Past and Present*, 22 (1962), 3–13

    *Lancastrian Kings and Lollard Knights* (Oxford, 1972)

    *The Nobility of Later Medieval England* Oxford, 1973)

McIntosh, A., 'A new approach to Middle English dialectology', *English Studies*, 44 (1953), 1–11

    'The textual transmission of the alliterative *Morte Arthure*' in N. Davis and C. L. Wrenn (eds.), *English and Medieval Studies presented to J. R. R. Tolkien* (London, 1962), pp. 231–40

    'Word geography in the lexicography of medieval English', *Annals of the New York Academy of Sciences*, 211 (1973), 55–66

    'Some notes on the text of the Middle English poem "*De Tribus Regibus Mortuis*"', *Review of English Studies*, new series 28 (1977), 385–92

McNiven, P., 'Rebellion and disaffection in the North of England, 1403–1408', unpublished M.A. thesis, University of Manchester, 1967

    'The Cheshire rising of 1400', *B.J.R.L.*, 52 (1970), 375–96

    'The men of Cheshire and the rebellion of 1403', *L.C.H.S.*, 129 (1980 for 1979), 1–29

McRobbie, K., 'The concept of advancement in the fourteenth century in the *Chroniques* of Jean Froissart', *Canadian Journal of History*, 6 (1971), 1–19

Nicholson, R. A., *Edward III and the Scots* (Oxford, 1965)

Nicolas, N. H., *The Scrope and Grosvenor Controversy* (2 vols., London, 1832)

    *History of the Battle of Agincourt and the Expedition of Henry the Fifth into France* (London, 1832)

Oakden, J. P., *Alliterative Poetry in Middle English* (2 vols., Manchester, 1930 and 1935)

Orme, N., *English Schools in the Middle Ages* (London, 1973)

Ormerod, G., *The History of the County Palatine and City of Chester*, ed. T. Helsby, 2nd edn (3 vols., London, 1882)

Otway-Ruthwen, A. J., *A History of Medieval Ireland* (London, 1968)

Pantin, W. A., *The English Church in the Fourteenth Century* (Cambridge, 1955)

Pelham, R. A., 'Fourteenth-century England' in H. C. Darby (ed.), *An Historical Geography of England before A.D. 1800* (Cambridge, 1936), pp. 230–65

Pevsner, N., *The Buildings of England. Lancashire*, part II. The Rural North (Harmondsworth, 1969)

Pilkington, J., *History of the Pilkington Family, 1066–1600* (Liverpool, 1894)

Pollard, A. J., 'The Richmondshire community of gentry during the Wars of the Roses' in C. Ross (ed.), *Patronage, Pedigree and Power in Later Medieval England* (Gloucester, 1979), pp. 37–59

Postan, M. M., 'Some social consequences of the Hundred Years War', *Ec.H.R.*, XII (1942), 1–12

    'The costs of the Hundred Years War', *Past and Present*, 27 (1964), 34–53

# Bibliography

(ed.) *The Cambridge Economic History of Europe*, vol. I. The Agrarian Life of the Middle Ages, 2nd edn (Cambridge, 1966)

Prince, A. E., 'The indenture system under Edward III' in J. G. Edwards, V. H. Galbraith and E. F. Jacob (eds.), *Historical Essays in Honour of James Tait* (Manchester, 1933), pp. 283–97

Pugh, T. B., 'The magnates, knights and gentry' in S. B. Chrimes, C. D. Ross and R. A. Griffiths (eds.), *Fifteenth-Century England. Studies in Politics and Society* (Manchester, 1972), pp. 86–128

Raftis, J. A., *The Estates of Ramsey Abbey. A Study in Economic Growth and Organisation* (Toronto, 1957)

*Tenure and Mobility. Studies in the Social History of the Medieval English Village* (Toronto, 1964)

Renouard, Y., *Bordeaux sous les Rois d'Angleterre* (Bordeaux, 1965)

Richardson, H. G., 'John of Gaunt and the parliamentary representation of Lancashire', *B.J.R.L.*, 22 (1938), 175–222

Robbins, R. H., 'The poems of Humphrey Newton, esquire, 1466–1536', *Publications of the Modern Language Association of America*, 65 (1950), 249–81

Rogers, J. T., *A History of Agriculture and Prices in England*, vol. I (Oxford, 1866)

Roskell, J. S., *The Knights of the Shire for the County Palatine of Lancaster 1377–1460* (C.S., new series 96, 1937)

'Sir James Strangeways of West Harlsey and Whorlton. Speaker in the Parliament of 1461', *Yorkshire Archaeological Journal*, 39 (1956–8), 455–82

Ross, B., 'The accounts of the Talbot household at Blakemere in the county of Shropshire, 1394–1425', unpublished M.A. thesis, Australian National University, 1970

Ross, C. (ed.), *Patronage, Pedigree and Power in Later Medieval England* (Gloucester, 1979)

Russell, J. C., *British Medieval Population* (Albuquerque, 1948)

Russell, P. E., *The English Intervention in Spain and Portugal in the Time of Edward III and Richard II* (Oxford, 1955)

Saul, N., *Knights and Esquires. The Gloucestershire Gentry in the Fourteenth Century* (Oxford, 1981)

Schofield, R. S., 'The geographical distribution of wealth in England, 1334–1649', *Ec.H.R.*, second series XVIII (1965), 483–510

Severs, J. B. (ed.), *A Manual of Writings in Middle English 1050–1500*, vol. I (New Haven, Conn., 1967)

Sharp, M., 'Contributions to the history of the earldom and county of Chester, 1237–1399', unpublished Ph.D. thesis, University of Manchester, 1925

Shaw, R. C., *The Records of a Lancashire Family* (Preston, 1940)

'Two fifteenth-century kinsmen. John Shaw of Dukinfield, mercer, and William Shaw of Heath Charnock, surgeon', *L.C.H.S.*, 110 (1959 for 1958), 15–30

Sherborne, J. W., 'Indentured retinues and English expeditions to France, 1369–1380', *E.H.R.*, LXXIX (1964), 718–46

Shrewsbury, J. F. D., *A History of Bubonic Plague in the British Isles* (Cambridge, 1970)

Singleton, F. J., 'The influence of geographical factors on the development of the common fields of Lancashire', *L.C.H.S.*, 115 (1964 for 1963), 31–40

Smith, E. H., 'Lancashire long measure', *L.C.H.S.*, 110 (1959 for 1958), 1–14

# Bibliography

Smith, R. B., *Blackburnshire. A Study in Early Lancashire History* (University of Leicester, Department of English Local History, Occasional Papers no. 15, 1961)

Somerville, R., 'The duchy and county palatine of Lancaster', *L.C.H.S.*, 103 (1952 for 1951), 59–67

*History of the Duchy of Lancaster*, part I. 1265–1603 (London, 1953)

Spearing, A. C., *The 'Gawain'-Poet. A Critical Study* (Cambridge, 1970)

Stephens, W. B. (ed.), *History of Congleton* (Manchester, 1970)

Stewart-Brown, R., *The Wapentake of Wirral* (Liverpool, 1907)

'The disafforestation of Wirral', *L.C.H.S.*, 59 (1908 for 1907), 165–80

'The royal manor and park of Shotwick', *L.C.H.S.*, 64 (1913 for 1912), 82–142

*Birkenhead Priory and the Mersey Ferry* (Liverpool, 1925)

'Two Liverpool medieval affrays', *L.C.H.S.*, 85 (1935 for 1933), 71–87

*The Serjeants of the Peace in Medieval England and Wales* (Manchester, 1936)

'The Scrope and Grosvenor controversy, 1385–91', *L.C.H.S.*, 89 (1938 for 1937), 1–22

Stone, L. (ed.), *The University in Society*, vol. I. Oxford and Cambridge from the Fourteenth to the Early Nineteenth Century (Oxford, 1975)

Storey, R. L., *Thomas Langley and the Bishopric of Durham* (London, 1961)

*The End of the House of Lancaster* (London, 1966)

Syers, R., *The History of Everton* (Liverpool, 1830)

Sylvester, D., 'The open fields of Cheshire', *L.C.H.S.*, 108 (1957 for 1956)

'The manor and the Cheshire landscape', *L.C.A.S.*, 70 (1961 for 1960), 1–15

*The Rural Landscape of the Welsh Borderland. A Study in Historical Geography* (London, 1969)

Tait, J., *Medieval Manchester and the Beginnings of Lancashire* (Manchester, 1904)

Taylor, J., *The 'Universal Chronicle' of Ranulf Higden* (Oxford, 1966)

Terrett, I. B., 'Cheshire' in H. C. Darby and I. S. Maxwell (eds.), *The Domesday Geography of Northern England* (Cambridge, 1962), pp. 330–91

'Lancashire' in H. C. Darby and I. S. Maxwell (eds.), *The Domesday Geography of Northern England* (Cambridge, 1962), pp. 392–418

Thompson, A. H., *The English Clergy and their Organisation in the Later Middle Ages* (Oxford, 1947)

Thompson, F. H., 'Excavations at the Cistercian abbey of Vale Royal, Cheshire, 1958', *The Antiquaries Journal*, XLII (1962), 183–207

Thrupp, S. L., *The Merchant Class of Medieval London* (Chicago, 1948)

'The problem of replacement-rates in late medieval England', *Ec.H.R.*, second series XVIII (1965), 101–19

Titow, J. Z., *English Rural Society, 1200–1350* (London, 1969)

Topham, J., 'Subsidy roll of 51 Edward III', *Archaeologia* VII (1785), 337–47

Tout, T. F., 'The English civil service in the fourteenth century', *B.J.R.L.*, 3 (1916), 185–214

*Chapters in the Administrative History of Medieval England* (6 vols., Manchester, 1923–35)

Tuck, J. A., 'Richard II's system of patronage' in F. R. H. du Boulay and C. M. Barron (eds.), *The Reign of Richard II. Essays in Honour of May McKisack* (London, 1971), pp. 1–20

*Richard II and the English Nobility* (London, 1973)

Tupling, G. H., *The Economic History of Rossendale* (C.S., new series 86, 1927)

'Markets and fairs in medieval Lancashire' in J. G. Edwards, V. H. Galbraith and E. F. Jacob (eds.), *Historical Essays in Honour of James Tait* (Manchester, 1933), pp. 345–56

'The royal and seignorial bailiffs of Lancashire in the thirteenth and fourteenth centuries' in *Chetham Miscellanies*, new series VIII (C.S., new series 109, 1945), separate pagination

(ed.), *South Lancashire in the Reign of Edward II* (C.S., third series 1, 1949)

'The pre-Reformation parishes and chapelries of Lancashire', *L.C.A.S.*, 67 (1957), 1–16

Turville-Petre, T., *The Alliterative Revival* (Cambridge, 1977)

Vale, M. G. A., *English Gascony 1399–1453* (Oxford, 1970)

Vickers, K. H., *Humphrey, Duke of Gloucester* (London, 1907)

*The Victoria History of the Counties of England* (London, in progress)

Wainwright, F. T., 'The Anglian settlement of Lancashire', *L.C.H.S.*, 93 (1942 for 1941), 1–44

'North-West Mercia, 871–924', *L.C.H.S.*, 94 (1943 for 1942), 3–55

'The Scandinavians in Lancashire', *L.C.A.S.*, 58 (1946), 71–116

Walker, F., *The Historical Geography of South-West Lancashire* (C.S., new series 103, 1939)

Whitaker, T. D., *An History of the Original Parish of Whalley and Honour of Clitheroe*, ed. J. G. Nichols and P. A. Lyons, 4th edn (2 vols., 1872, 1876)

Wilkinson, B., *The Chancery under Edward III* (Manchester, 1929)

Williams-Jones, K., 'Caernarvon' in R. A. Griffiths (ed.), *Boroughs of Mediaeval Wales* (Cardiff, 1978)

Wilson, E., '*Sir Gawain and the Green Knight* and the Stanley family of Stanley, Storeton and Hooton', *Review of English Studies*, new series 30 (1979), 308–16

Wilson, K. P., 'The port of Chester in the later Middle Ages', unpublished Ph.D. thesis, University of Liverpool, 1965

Wilson, R. M., *The Lost Literature of Medieval England* (London, 1952)

Wolffe, B. P., *The Royal Demesne in English History* (London, 1971)

Woodward, D. M., 'The Chester leather industry, 1558–1625', *L.C.H.S.*, 119 (1968 for 1967), 65–111

Wright, S. M., 'A gentry society of the fifteenth century: Derbyshire, *c*. 1430–1509', unpublished Ph.D. thesis, University of Birmingham, 1978

Wylie, J. H. and Waugh, W. T., *The Reign of Henry V* (3 vols., Cambridge, 1914–29)

Youd, G., 'The common fields of Lancashire', *L.C.H.S.*, 113 (1963 for 1961), 1–41

Youings, J., *The Dissolution of the Monasteries* (London, 1971)

Ziegler, P., *The Black Death* (London, 1969)

# INDEX

# Index

# Index

Churton Heath (Ches.), 62

Clapham, 133

Clarence, dukes of, *see* Lionel of Antwerp
and Thomas of Lancaster

Clayhall (Essex), 229

Clayton le Dale (Lancs.), 63

Clifford, Sir Thomas (of Cumb.), 72n

Clifton, Sir Nicholas, 169

Clifton, Thomas, 23n, 24

Clitheroe (Lancs.), 44, 69, 71, 72, 73, 74,
97, 99, 112, 138n, 224

Clitheroe, Ellis, 127

Clitheroe, John, bishop of Bangor, 127,
146, 147, 152, 229

Clitheroe, John, apprentice, 127

Clitheroe, Richard, 127

Cliviger (Lancs.), 106

Clopton, John (of Warw.), 188

Clotton (Ches.), 116

Cocker, Richard, 43

Cognac (France), 17n

Colfox, Sir Nicholas, 165n, 175, 182, 188

Coly, Hugh, 179n

Coly, John, 123

Combermere, abbey of, 77, 78, 81, 83

Como, battle of, 173

Compostella (Spain), 230

Congleton (Ches.), 62, 112, 116, 122, 124

Constance (West Germany), 145, 157, 228

Conwy (Wales), 124, 176, 180, 211, 235

Cooper, Richard, chaplain, 138

Cooper, William, 185

Corbie, battle of, 183

Cornwall, 166, 204, 237

Cotentin (France), 172

Cotswolds, 89, 188, 189

Cotton (Ches.), 41

Cotton, family of, 89

Cotton, Hugh, 22n

Cotton, John, 104

Cotton, Richard, 94

Cotton, Thomas, 22n, 41

Courtenay, William, bishop of London,
archbishop of Canterbury, 144, 145,
156, 157

Coutances (France), 172

Coventry, 12, 14, 106, 121, 123, 130

Cradock, family of, 187

Cradock, Sir David, 17, 130, 167, 175, 182,
187, 200

Cradock, Sir Richard, 180, 181, 213, 230,
233, 234

Cradock, Roger, bishop of Llandaff, 141,
146, 147, 205

Crécy, battle of, 173, 178, 182, 186, 249

Crewe, David, 22n, 24, 31

Crewe, Thomas, 165n, 188, 189, 200, 203,
206, 228

Crosby (Lancs.), 220

Crosby, Sir John, 125, 129

Crosse, family of, 13

Croston (Lancs.), 172

Croughton (Ches.), 62

Cuerdale (Lancs.), 63, 81, 168n

Cuerdley (Lancs.), 92

Cumberland, Cumbria, 121, 240, 240n

Dacre (of Gilsland, Cumb.), family of, 75,
202

Dane river, 62

Danyers, family of, 16

Danyers, Sir John, 16, 166, 229

Danyers, John (of Grimsditch), 43

Danyers, Sir Thomas, fl. 1346, 17, 178, 182,
186

Danyers, Sir Thomas, fl. 1380, 167

Danyers, Thomas, fl. 1412, 22n, 28

Danyers, William, 44n, 208

Darnhall (Ches.), 50, 78, 92, 96

Davenham (Ches.), 83, 136, 247n

Davenport, family of, 26, 82

Davenport (of Calveley), family of, 27

Davenport, Adam, clerk, 144

Davenport, Hugh, 22n, 24, 26, 27

Davenport, John, 87

Davenport, Nicholas, 22n

Davenport, Ralph, 22n, 29, 35, 36, 38, 209

Davenport, Robert, 22n, 24, 36, 38

Davenport, Thomas, 199

Dee river, 45, 62, 71, 78, 238 mills on, 148,
149

Delamere forest, 35, 71, 72n

De La Warre (of Swineshead, Lincs.),
family of, 74, 75, 76

Delves, Sir John, fl. 1360, 175, 205

Delves, Sir John, fl. 1412, 23n

Denton, near Widnes (Lancs.), 93

*De Officio Militari*, 143

Derby, earl of, *see* Henry of Bolingbroke

Derby, Roger, 13

Derbyshire, 7, 55, 80, 239

Despenser, family of, 202

Despenser, Henry, bishop of Norwich, 167,
181

Despenser, Sir Hugh, 72n

*Destruction of Troy*, 231

De Vere, Robert, earl of Oxford, d. 1392,
200, 208, 209, 216

273

# Index

# Index

# Index